# COUNSELING DIVERSE POPULATIONS

**Donald R. Atkinson**
University of California–Santa Barbara

**Gail Hackett**
Arizona State University

**WCB** Brown &
Benchmark
PUBLISHERS
Madison, Wisconsin • Dubuque, Iowa

**Book Team**

Editor *Michael Lange*
Developmental Editor *Sheralee Connors*
Production Editor *Diane Clemens*
Photo Editor *Rose Deluhery*
Visuals/Design Developmental Consultant *Marilyn A. Phelps*
Visuals/Design Freelance Specialist *Mary L. Christianson*
Marketing Manager *Steven Yetter*
Advertising Coordinator *Mike Matera*

**WCB Brown & Benchmark**

A Division of Wm. C. Brown Communications, Inc.

Executive Vice President/General Manager *Thomas E. Doran*
Vice President/Editor in Chief *Edgar J. Laube*
Vice President/Marketing and Sales Systems *Eric Ziegler*
Director of Production *Vickie Putman Caughron*
Director of Custom and Electronic Publishing *Chris Rogers*

**Wm. C. Brown Communications, Inc.**

President and Chief Executive Officer *G. Franklin Lewis*
Corporate Senior Vice President and Chief Financial Officer *Robert Chesterman*
Corporate Senior Vice President and President of Manufacturing *Roger Meyer*

Cover design by Joslin Design

Interior design by Elaine G. Allen and Joslin Design

Part Opener photo credits: 1 and 4 © Jean-Claude Lejeune;
2 and 5 © Michael Siluk; 3 and 6 © Joel Gordon

A Times Mirror Company

Library of Congress Catalog Card Number: 94–70182

ISBN 0–697–21129–0

Printed in the United States of America by Wm. C. Brown Communications, Inc.,
2460 Kerper Boulevard, Dubuque, IA 52001

10  9  8  7  6  5  4  3  2  1

This book is dedicated to those individuals who, because of their physical ability, age, gender, or sexual orientation, have been singled out for differential and inferior treatment.

We'd also like to dedicate this book to Ryan and Audrey and to the memory of Jimmie Atkinson.

D. A. and G. H.

# CONTENTS

## PART 2
## The Client with a Disability    119

## PART 3
## The Elderly Client    187

# PREFACE

For many years the mental health professions ignored membership-group as a variable of interest in the psychotherapeutic process. Diagnostic and treatment models were developed and promulgated with little attention to racial/ethnic, cultural, gender, sexual orientation, and other demographic differences. The human rights movements of the past 30 years, however, have drawn attention to the various minority groups in American society and to the unique experiences of their members. Despite this increased attention, awareness of and sensitivity to mental health needs that are a function of the client's membership-group are uneven, both across groups and across mental health practitioners. For the most part, mental health practitioners continue to apply diagnostic and treatment models to clients without making adjustments based on their unique needs and experiences.

The purpose of this book is to call the attention of mental health practitioners to the unique experiences and needs of four groups within the American society that, along with ethnic and selected other groups, share the common experience of oppression. These four groups are persons with disabilities, elders, women, and gay people. Each of these four groups has a common physical and/or behavioral feature that identifies individuals as members of the group and that has served to single them out for differential and inferior treatment. Each of these groups has in the past experienced (and continues to experience) discrimination as a result of their physical and/or behavioral uniqueness. Discrimination for all four groups has ranged from negative stereotypes to physical violence.

It is our thesis that mental health practitioners need to be aware of the unique experiences of these groups in order to effectively intervene on their behalf. This book is an attempt to acquaint mental health professionals with those unique experiences. The first chapter describes how traditional psychotherapeutic approaches have ignored these experiences and have, in effect, failed to meet the needs of persons with disabilities, elders, women, and gay people. The first chapter also provides a rationale for identifying the four groups as minorities as well as a brief profile of each group. In Chapter 2 we review the treatment of each group across history. Current discrimination experienced by persons with disabilities, elders, women, and gay people, is presented in Chapter 3.

Chapters 4–15 consist of readings concerning the four groups covered by this book. The readings were selected because they provide insight into the experiences of the group and offer suggestions for meeting the mental health needs of the group. All of the articles were selected because they are sensitive to human rights issues as they relate to psychotherapy. The last chapter (Chapter 16) examines the implications of diversity issues for counseling practice, counselor training, and counseling research.

This book is intended as a text for undergraduate and graduate courses in counseling psychology, clinical psychology, social work, and other mental health professions where human rights issues are discussed. The book might be used as a primary text in courses where diversity or human rights issues are the primary focus or as a supplemental text in counseling theory and technique courses. When used in conjunction with another Brown and Benchmark publication, *Counseling American Minorities: A Cross-Cultural Perspective,* the book provides an excellent introduction to a broad range of diversity issues.

An earlier version of this book was published under the title *Counseling Non-Ethnic American Minorities.* However, the readings in the current book are all new and the chapters we wrote (Chapters 1, 2, 3, and 16) have been extensively revised. Every effort has been made to make the current book relevant to the issues faced by these four groups in contemporary society. We hope the book will help mental health professionals look beyond the current *Diagnostic and Statistical Manual of Mental Disorders* when diagnosing clients and beyond conventional psychotherapeutic strategies when treating clients. It is our belief that experiences, behaviors, attitudes, values, and needs based on membership in the groups discussed in this book must be taken into account as part of diagnosis and treatment.

D. R. A.
G. H.

# PART 1

## Counseling and Diverse Populations

# 1

# Introduction

## Traditional Approaches to Counseling and Psychotherapy

Most, if not all, mental health professions that practice counseling and psychotherapy can trace their roots to Freud and psychoanalysis; Shilling (1984) refers to Freud as "grandfather to all of us . . . who are psychologists and/or counselors" (p. 17). Many of the concepts and constructs developed by Freud are still perceived as necessary and sufficient conditions for psychotherapy. Indeed, Corey (1991) suggests that Freud's theory "is a benchmark against which many other theories are measured" (p. 96). While many of Freud's contributions to the mental health professions have been widely applauded, some of his ideas have been criticized as ineffective or even counterproductive.

Two of the unfortunate legacies that Freud left to mental health professionals are the overemphasis on individual psychopathology and the exclusive reliance on one-to-one psychotherapy. Freud believed an individual's behavior was the result of instinctual, biological drives, thus originating within the individual. While neo-Freudians and subsequent theorists have moved away from the heavy stress Freud placed on sexual instinct and aggression as determinants of behavior, they continue to emphasize an internal model of psychopathology, one that views the etiology of the client's problem (and the resources to resolve it) as residing within the client. Thus, for example, advocates of person-centered therapy believe that psychological maladjustment occurs when "the *organism denies* to awareness, or *distorts* in awareness, significant experiences" (italics added, Meador & Rogers, 1984, p. 159). Gestalt therapists believe that individuals are responsible for their own behavior, that "*People are responsible* for what they choose to do" (italics added, Simkin & Ontef, 1984, p. 291). Even behavior therapists, who eschew needs, drives, motives, traits, and conflicts as underlying causes of behavior, believe that "A crucial factor in therapy is the *client's motivation,* and *willingness to cooperate* in the arduous and challenging task of making significant changes in real-life behavior" (italics added, Wilson, 1984, p. 253).

If the primary mechanisms that shape and maintain affect, behavior, and cognition reside within the individual, then it follows that psychotherapy should focus attention on the individual. Freud's use of the psychoanalytic situation, a one-to-one therapeutic environment in which the analyst facilitates critical self-examination, had a significant and enduring impact on counseling and psychotherapy. This emphasis on individual psychopathology and psychotherapy is evident in the goals therapists have for counseling. Although the client may be encouraged to state therapeutic goals as part of the counseling process, therapists conventionally pursue metagoals of changing the client's affect, behavior, and/or cognitions. The therapist works on these metagoals by encouraging catharsis, interpreting feelings, challenging negative self-perceptions, assigning homework, and a myriad of other counseling strategies. Regardless of the counselor's metagoal and the strategies employed to reach it, an underlying assumption of nearly all conventional counseling approaches is that some aspect of the client must change in order to resolve the problem. With the exception of embryonic group and family counseling efforts, counseling and psychotherapy prior to the 1950s involved a one therapist, one client model.

Family therapists were among the first to recognize the limitations of focusing therapy on the individual outside the context of the family. According to Nichols (1984), Freud actively discouraged psychotherapists from involving other family members when they were treating a patient; involving other family members in therapy was discouraged because it would undermine the transference process, considered essential for treatment success. As a result, early attempts at interviewing with families were little more than individual psychotherapy for each family member. It was not until the early 1950s that researchers examining communication patterns in the families of schizophrenics developed a system theory approach to therapy and with it the concept that it is more effective to treat a family system conjointly than a single family member individually (Nichols, 1984).

The social conditions of the 1960s set the stage for a second, more disparate, group of mental health professionals to criticize the shortcomings of individual psychopathology and psychotherapy. Civil rights, anti-war, feminist, and other human rights movements directly and indirectly motivated many disfranchised groups to seek (and in some cases demand) mental health services. Counselors and other mental health professionals soon discovered that their training did not prepare them to work with such issues as discrimination, alienation, and basic survival (Aubrey & Lewis, 1983). The result of pressure by disfranchised groups for counseling services has been referred to as a "fundamental if not revolutionary change" (Larson, 1982, p. 843) in counseling.

By the late 1960s, radical psychiatrists, social change psychologists, feminist counselors, and others were suggesting that psychological problems experienced by many clients were the result of oppressive environments, not individual psychopathology. Concurrently, a number of authors began criticizing the mental health professions for their neutral stance with respect to social issues. Seymour Halleck (1971) indicted psychotherapists for helping to maintain the status quo in social institutions that are oppressive. According to Halleck, psychotherapists, whether they intend to or not, commit a political act every time they reinforce the positions of persons who hold power. Intrapsychic views of client problems were criticized for being shortsighted and for promoting institutional oppression through passive acceptance. This position is articulated in its extreme by Claude Steiner (1975) in his Manifesto for psychiatrists.

> Extended individual psychotherapy is an elitist, outmoded, as well as nonproductive, form of psychiatric help. It concentrates the talents of a few on a few. It silently colludes with the notion that people's difficulties have their source within them while implying that everything is well with the world. It promotes oppression by shrouding its consequences with shame and secrecy. . . . People's troubles have their source not within them but in their alienated relationships, in their exploitation in polluted environments, in war, and in the profit motive. (Steiner, 1975, pp. 3–4)

Despite the criticisms of psychology that arose in the late 1960s and early 1970s, the field has continued to rely almost exclusively on an intrapsychic model of psychopathology and an individual model of psychotherapy. More recently Sarason (1981) chastised American psychology as "quintessentially a psychology of the individual organism, a characteristic that however it may have been and is productive has severely and adversely affected psychology's contribution to human welfare" (p. 827). In examining the social issues and counseling needs of the 1980s and 1990s, Aubrey and Lewis (1983) expressed concern that "counselors still tend to overlook the impact of environmental factors on individual functioning, to distrust the efficacy of preventative interventions, and to narrow the score of their attention to the individual psyche" (p. 10). We share these authors' concern that counselors have drifted back toward exclusive reliance on an intrapsychic model of psychopathology and a one-to-one model of psychotherapy.

We believe that for some of the issues clients bring to counseling, particularly for clients from groups that are victims of oppression, counselors need to consider alternatives to the individual psychopathology and psychotherapy models. This book examines the experiences of four oppressed groups with the goal of sensitizing counselors to the external sources of the psychological problems and to the nontraditional interventions designed to assist them with these problems.

## Defining Oppressed Groups as Minorities

The term minority has been widely used in the United States since the 1950s with reference to racial and ethnic groups and more recently with respect to nonethnic groups. Based on Wirth's (1945) definition that minorities are groups who "because of physical or cultural characteristics, are singled out from the others in the society in which they live for differential and unequal treatment" (p. 347), the term has been generalized to any group oppressed by those in power. The concept of minorities being groups that are singled out for differential and unequal treatment allows us to expand the list of minorities beyond ethnic groups who are a numerical minority in the society. As applied to Blacks in South Africa and women in the United States, the term applies to groups that are actually a numerical majority of the population. Gay men and lesbian women, young children, and elders, to the extent they are oppressed by the social system in which they live, also can be identified as minorities.

Dworkin and Dworkin (1976) have proposed that "a minority group is a group characterized by four qualities: identifiability, differential power, differential and pejorative treatment, and group awareness" (p. 17). Biological (skin color, eye shape and color, facial structure) and cultural (religion, dress, behavior) variables serve to identify a minority group as does the position of inferior power relative to a power group (a group that uses power to influence and control others). When such differential power exists between two groups, it is probably inevitable that the dominant group exercise their power, resulting in differential and discriminatory treatment of the minority group. One effect of experiencing differential and discriminatory treatment is to make the minority group more aware of its common bond.

A definition offered by Kinloch (1979) also addresses the issue of power. Kinloch (1979) defines a minority as "any group that is defined by a power elite as different and/or inferior on the basis of certain perceived characteristics and is consequently treated in a negative fashion" (p. 7). Further, he identifies four types of minorities, those who are identified as different or inferior based on physiological criteria (e.g., non-White racial minorities, women, elders), cultural criteria (non-Anglo-Saxon ethnic groups), economic criteria (the poor and/or lower class), and behavioral criteria (e.g., gay men and women, persons with mental disabilities, persons with physical disabilities).

Similarly Larson (1982) identifies minorities as groups of people who are stigmatized by the majority group in some way. He refers to Goffman's (1963) classification system for identifying conditions subject to stigma. The system consists of three categories:

> (a) physical—for example, visible manifestations of disability; (b) blemishes of character—for example, conditions that are viewed as voluntary deviant choices such as political dissidents, alternate sexual orientations, criminals, some categories of mental illness, such as addictions; and (c) tribal—for example, racial, ethnic, linguistic, or religious groups. (Larson, 1982, p. 845)

Not only are minority groups singled out for stigmatization and discrimination, they are placed in double jeopardy by a society that blames them for the social conditions they experience as a result of discrimination. This phenomenon, known as victim-blaming, "is the tendency when examining a social problem to attribute that problem to the characteristics of the people who are its victims" (Levin & Levin, 1980, p. 36). Early forms of victim-blaming cited assumed biological inferiorities as causes of the groups' social problems (e.g., Mexican-American assumed intellectual inferiority cited as a reason for Mexican-American underachievement in school). More recently, cultural deviance has been cited as a cause of social problems (e.g., breakdown of the traditional two-parent family among Blacks cited as a reason for a myriad of problems experienced by Blacks). Thus, victim-blaming overlooks the societal and institutional causes of social problems experienced by minorities and instead blames the problem on assumed biological or cultural inferiority.

A further negative effect of victim-blaming is to misdirect the resources expended to resolve the social problems faced by a minority. Ryan (1971) has suggested that once we identify a social problem, we study the group affected by it to determine how they are different from the rest of us. We next define those differences as the source of the problem and develop a bureaucratic program to correct the differences, not the social cause of the problem. Further, we often withhold resources from minorities needed to resolve the social sources of their problems because we assume they are incapable of resolving their own difficulties. The National Council on Aging has suggested that "The social and economic opportunities available to any group in this society depend not only on their own resources, capabilities and aspirations but, as importantly, on the resources, capabilities and aspirations that the public at large attribute to them" (Harris, 1975, p. i).

This book focuses on two groups who are perceived as different and treated in a negative fashion because of physical characteristics (women and elders), one group because of behavioral characteristics (gay people), and one group because of either physical or behavioral characteristics (people with disabilities). As we shall see in Chapters 2 and 3, these four groups have experienced discrimination and victim-blaming much like ethnic minorities have.

Our readings relating to these four groups focus by necessity on the distinctiveness of each group and may serve to reinforce the view that they are mutually exclusive populations. Nothing could be further from the truth. For example, the greater survival rate of Americans with life-long disabilities and the growing number of elders with later-life disabilities (Ansello, 1991) means that there is considerable overlap between these two groups. Further, the fact that there are only 67 elderly men for every 100 elderly women in the United States suggests that there are a large number of elderly women with disabilities. Since some of those elderly women with disabilities are also lesbians, the overlap of all four groups on which we have chosen to focus becomes obvious. The fact that the four groups are not mutually exclusive is significant because it suggests that many individuals in our society are subject to multiple layers of discrimination.

Brief profiles of these four groups, who were selected for the current discussion because they include substantial numbers of people who seek counseling services, are provided in the following section.

# Profiles of Selected Minorities

## *Persons with Disabilities*

Any discussion of persons with disabilities by necessity must begin with a discussion of the terms *handicap, handicapped, disability,* and *disabled.* Those who have followed the literature on people with disabilities have witnessed an evolution in terminology (not unlike the evolution in terminology used to designate members of racial/ethnic minority groups) applied to this population. Professional articles and federal laws in the 1970s followed the convention of referring to people with disabilities as "handicapped people" or "people with handicaps." During the 1970s the terms "handicapped person" and "disabled person" were often used interchangeably. By the 1980s, however, advocates for people with disabilities began to make distinctions between handicap and disability. The term disability began to be used with reference to some physical or mental diagnosis, one which may or may not limit the individual's major life activities. The term handicap began to be used to indicate the restricting consequences of the diagnosed disability. Thus, a handicap is more situationally defined than is a disability.

> The disability may be considered as the persons' observable, measurable characteristic that is judged to be deviant or discrepant from some acceptable norm. In contrast, the handicap may be considered as the barriers, demands, and general environmental press placed on the person by various aspects of his or her environment, including other persons. (Fagan & Wallace, 1979, p. 216)

Thus, an individual may have a disability (e.g., hearing loss) but may not define it as a handicap. Significant others in his/her environment, however, may perceive the disability as a handicap. As a result of this distinction, many professionals in the 1980s dropped the term "handicapped person" in favor of "disabled person."

More recently, "person with a disability" has become the more accepted terminology. According to Grealish and Salomone (1986), "disabled person" implies that the person is disabled in a total sense (physically, emotionally, intellectually). Although more cumbersome, "person with a disability" puts the emphasis on the whole person and recognizes that the disability is just one aspect of their personhood. In fact, some advocates for persons with disabilities prefer to use the expression "differently able" since it more accurately reflects the fact that we all have varying levels of mental and physical ability given the environmental conditions in which we happen to be (in the case of a blind and a sighted person in an unlighted room, being sightless may actually be an asset). However, some persons with disabilities object to this terminology since it tends to deny their disability and their status as an oppressed person. At this point most professionals and advocates for people with disabilities have accepted the term "person with a disability."

In addition to some confusion about appropriate terminology, there is also some ambiguity regarding what constitutes a disability. According to Kuehn (1991), "disability resists precise definition and measurement" (p. 8). One approach is to identify specific mental or physical conditions that are diagnosable. Thus, the Education for All Handicapped Act (PL 94–142) includes the following categories of disabilities for children: (a) hearing impaired, (b) deaf-blind, (c) visually impaired, (d) speech impaired, (e) mentally retarded, (f) learning disabled, (g) emotionally disturbed, (h) orthopedically impaired, (i) other health impaired, and (j) multi-handicapped (Fagan & Wallace, 1979). Disabling conditions in the "other health impaired" category range from asthma to lead poisoning and include many chronic or acute health problems. The recently passed Americans with Disabilities Act (ADA) includes a broad definition of disability encompassing such chronic diseases as AIDS and diabetes.

Another approach to defining disability is to identify the life activity affected. Thus, the Rehabilitation Act of 1973 defines an "individual with severe handicaps" as a person:

1. who has a severe physical or mental disability which seriously limits one or more functional capacities (such as mobility, communication, self-care, self-direction, interpersonal skills, work tolerance or work skills) in terms of employability;

2. whose vocational rehabilitation can be expected to require multiple vocational rehabilitation services over an extended period of time; and

3. who has one or more physical or mental disabilities resulting from a list of disorders/diseases or a combination of disabilities determined on the basis of an evaluation of rehabilitation potential to cause comparable substantial functional limitation. (Perlman & Kirk, 1991)

The effect on employment is an inherent part of any government definition of disability. The U.S. Bureau of the Census has based their definition of a person with a *work disability* on the concept that "a person has a disability if he or she has a limitation in the ability to perform one or more of the life activities expected of an individual within a social environment" (U.S. Bureau of the Census, 1989, p. 1). The Bureau defines a person with a work disability as someone for whom one or more of the following conditions are met:

1. Identified by a question that asks "does anyone in this household have a health problem or disability which prevents them from working or which limits the kind or amount of work they can do?"

2. Identified by a question that asks "Is there anyone in this household who ever retired or left a job for health reasons?"

3. Did not work in the survey week because of a long term physical or mental illness or disability which prevents the performance of any kind of work (based on the "main activity last week" question on the basic CPS [Current Population Survey] questionnaire).

4. Did not work at all in previous year because ill or disabled (based on the "reason did not work last year" question on the March CPS supplement).

5. Under 65 years of age and covered by Medicare.

6. Under 65 years of age and a recipient of Supplemental Security Income (SSI). (U.S. Bureau of the Census, 1989, p. 1)

The person is considered to have a "severe" work disability if one or more of the final four conditions are met.

Even when there is agreement about the categories of disabilities, there may be disagreement about whether an individual satisfies the criteria for the category. According to Bowe (1985), two trained observers may differ as to whether a person has a disability or not. Questions used by the Census Bureau to identify persons with a work disability "may screen out some legitimately disabled persons; less often, they may screen in some individuals who may not be disabled" (Bowe, 1985, p. 2).

Perhaps because there is not a clear consensus on what constitutes a disability, even among U.S. governmental agencies, there are no clear-cut national estimates of the number of people with disabilities. One source of data is the U.S. Bureau of the Census, which has prepared special reports in 1983 and 1989 on people with work disabilities. According to their 1989 report, almost 13.4 million noninstitutionalized people (6.7 million men and 6.7 million women) ages 16 to 64 had a work disability in 1988. Of those, 7.5 million (3.8 million men and 3.7 million women) had a severe work disability (U.S. Bureau of the Census, 1989).

The 1989 Census Bureau report suggests a strong relationship between work disability and age, education, and race. With respect to age there is a strong direct relationship; 3.8 percent of the age group 16–24 have work disabilities, 5.6 percent of the age group 25–34, 7.1 percent of the age group 35–44, 10.3 percent of the age group 45–54, and 22.3 percent of the age group 55–64. On the other hand, there is a strong inverse relationship between work disability and education. "Persons who have completed less than 8 years of school have a disability rate that is more than three times as high as the rate for high school graduates and eight times the rate for college graduates" (U.S. Bureau of the Census, 1989, p. 5). At the educational extremes, 29.7 percent of those with less than an eighth-grade education have a work disability, while only 3.8 percent of persons who are college graduates have a work disability. With respect to race, Black persons are much more likely (13.7 percent) than Whites (7.9 percent) or persons of Hispanic origin (8.2 percent) to have a work disability.

The U.S. Bureau of the Census (1983a) reported that over 6 million noninstitutionalized persons age 16 and over had a public transportation handicap in 1982. A person with a public transportation handicap is someone who, due to a mental or physical condition lasting over six months, cannot use buses, trains, subways, or other forms of public transportation.

These data on people with work and/or transportation disabilities are necessarily restrictive because they exclude persons under 16 and over 65 as well as those who have disabilities but who manage to work full-time and/or use public transportation. According to Tomes (1992), "14 percent of 231 million noninstitutionalized U.S. residents [in the mid-1980s] were limited in ability to perform some normal activity" (p. 13). Bowe (1980) estimated the total for all people with disabilities in 1979 to be 36 million or approximately 15 percent of the U.S. population. A sizable portion of the number of persons with disabilities are elderly, since the incidence of disability increases in old age. Van Hasselt, Strain, and Hersen (1988) cite evidence that as much as 46 percent of the persons 65 years of age and older have a serious and disabling health impairment. Thus, as the number and percentage of the U.S. population that are elderly increases (discussed in the next section), the number and percentage of people with disabilities will increase. It should be noted, however, that Van Hasselt et al. (1988) also found evidence that as much as 10 percent of the children under 21 years of age in the United States have disabilities.

Citing World Health Organization data, Driedger (1989) estimates that 10 percent of the world's population or over 500 million people worldwide are persons with disabilities. Approximately 80 percent of these people live in the developing countries in Africa, Asia, the Middle East, Latin America, and the Caribbean. Regardless of the exact numbers and percentages, it is evident that people with disabilities make up a significant proportion of the population both in the U.S. and worldwide.

## *Elders*

The determination of who is elderly and who is not is arbitrary at best. Even defining the term "aging" is problematic. According to Griffiths and Meechan (1990), the definition most widely accepted by biologists is that aging involves a "progressive failure of the body's various homeostatic adaptive responses" (Vander, Sherman & Luciano, 1985).

> This definition has the advantage that it allows us to distinguish the aging process from degenerative changes that result from diseases. Although diseases such as cancer and atherosclerosis can interact and compound the aging process, they do not always accompany aging and therefore must be thought of as distinct processes. (Griffiths & Meechan, 1990, p. 45)

Biologists, physicians, and chemists who have studied the physiological aging process (senescence) have long recognized that it occurs at varying rates among individuals (Strehler, 1962). Various measures of physical aging have been employed; for example, hair color and loss, skin tone and texture, and muscle tone and flexibility have been examined as evidence of senescence. But since individuals evidence changes in these physical attributes at widely varying chronological ages, physical standards of aging are averages for the population as a whole and are seldom useful in assessing the individual's status with respect to his/her own aging process.

The Social Security Act of 1935 had a major impact on our perceptions about who is elderly and who is not when it identified 65 as the magic age for determining who will receive full social security benefits. According to Achenbaum (1978), however, "The Committee on Economic Security determined that at least six other birthdays (60, 62, 68, 70, 72, and 75) were used as an eligibility criterion in public and private schemes operating in the 1930s" (p. 149). Legislators selected age 65 for social security purposes in the final analysis on the basis of cost estimates, actuarial data, and the spirit of compromise rather than on scientific information about the aging process. Recent discussions in Congress aimed at raising the age for full social security benefits also reflect economic and demographic pressures, not scientifically-based knowledge about aging.

Recent proposals to increase the age of qualification for full social security benefits are the result of people living longer than ever before and a shrinking number of people paying into social security.

> For the first time in history, most people can expect to live into the "long late afternoon of life." Whereas American life expectancy in 1900 was about forty-nine, today's children will live an average of about seventy-five years (seventy-one for men, seventy-eight for women). This increase represents two-thirds of all the gains in life expectancy achieved since the emergence of the human species! (Cole, 1991, p. 25)

Due to an increasing life expectancy, the number of elderly people living in the United States has been increasing steadily since 1830, the first year for which census data are available. In 1830 there were 421,000 White persons (non-Whites were not counted in the early reports) over 60 years of age. In 1870 the Census Bureau reported over 1,153,000 citizens were age 65 or older. By 1900 that figure had more than doubled to just over 3 million. By 1940 the number of elderly had increased to 9 million and by 1970 had soared to over 20 million (Achenbaum, 1978). As of the 1990 census report, there were almost 31.2 million Americans age 65 and over; of these 13.1 million were age 75 and over and 3 million were age 85 and over (U.S. Bureau of the Census, 1992a). By the year 2000, it is projected that the figure for persons 65 and over will increase to 35 million and by 2025 to almost 59 million (U.S. Bureau of the Census, 1983b). Not only are elders increasing in absolute numbers but they are increasing in proportion to the rest of the population. In 1900 elders comprised about four percent of the U.S. population but in 1990 they represent more than 12 percent. While the total U.S. population grew 13.5 percent from 1970 to 1982, the 65 and over age group grew 34.3 percent.

At the same time that life expectancy has been increasing the birth rate has been declining steadily (since 1790 with the exception of the post World War II "baby boom"), causing the proportion of elderly in the American population, as well as their absolute number, to increase dramatically. The proportion of the population age 65 or older was 4.0 percent in 1900, 9.9 percent in 1970, and 12.6 percent in 1990 (U.S. Bureau of the Census, 1992a). The elderly population is expected to comprise 17 percent of the population by 2020 (Gerber, Wolff, Klores & Brown, 1989) and 19.5 percent of the population in 2025 (Achenbaum, 1978; U.S. Bureau of the Census, 1983b).

As might be expected, the differing life expectancies for men and women affect their representation in the elderly population. According to Hess (1980), the sex ratios of older men and women were approximately equal in 1930 but have changed dramatically since then. The trend in recent years is for women to live longer than men. The life expectancy of a woman in 1981 was 78 years but for a man was less than 71 years. As a result, a disproportionate share of the elderly population is made up of women. There were 67 elderly men for every 100 elderly women in 1982. When only those elderly over age 85 are considered, the ratio is even lower—42 men per 100 women (U.S. Bureau of the Census, 1983b).

Contrary to earlier generations, most of today's elderly retire before age 65. About 50 percent of the men age 65 and older were retired in 1950; by the mid-1980s this figure had dropped to 15 percent (comparable figures on women were not provided by Gerber, Wolff, Klores & Brown, 1989, the source of these data). This pattern is expected to reverse itself, however, due to increases in the qualifying age for Social Security benefits, less generous pension plans in the future, and the demand for elder workers. For those elderly who do retire early, the extra time has provided an opportunity to do volunteer work. According to Gerber et al. (1989), 44 percent of the population between the ages of 50 and 74 do volunteer work.

A common misperception is that the majority (or at least a large percentage) of elders live in nursing homes; in reality, only 5 percent live in nursing homes. Almost 90 percent of all older couples (and 75 percent of all elderly persons) own and live in their own home. Of these older people who own their own home, almost 75 percent have paid off their mortgages. For most elderly householders, their home is their major asset. However, the property values of the homes owned by elders are lower than those owned by younger homeowners. In many cases the homes of elderly persons are at least 40 years old and in need of structural repairs (Hess, 1991).

Contrary to another common misperception, most noninstitutionalized elderly do not live with a relative. The majority (64%) of persons ages 65 to 74 were married and living with their spouse in 1991, while 25 percent lived alone and 10 percent lived with relatives. However, the living arrangements of the elderly are, to some extent, a function of age, ethnicity, and sex. For persons 75 and over, the percent living with their spouses decreases (39%), the percent living alone increases (41%), and the percent living with other relatives increases (17%). Black elderly age 75 and older are less likely to live alone (36% versus 42%), less likely to live with a spouse (28% versus 41%), and more likely to live with other relatives (33% versus 15%) than their White counterpart (U.S. Bureau of the Census, 1992b).

With women outliving men, it is not surprising that elderly women are more likely than elderly men to be living alone. Of 14.3 million persons aged 65 and older living alone in 1991, over 75 percent were women. One-third of the women ages 65 to 74 lived alone in 1991 compared to 13 percent of the men. More than half the women age 75 and older lived alone compared to 21 percent of the men. While 3 out of 4 elderly men were married and living with their wives only 2 out of every 5 elderly women were married and living with their husbands in 1991 (U.S. Bureau of the Census, 1992b).

According to Margolis (1990), about 1.5 million older Americans were housed in 16,000 nursing homes in 1989. Of those who live in nursing homes, almost all (93%) are White and the majority (75%) are women (Hess, 1991). While it is a myth that most elderly people live in nursing homes, the percentage that do increases steadily with age. Of those aged 65 to 74 in 1982, only 1.5 percent lived in nursing homes. For persons aged 75 to 84, however, 6 percent lived in nursing homes in 1982, and this figure increased to 23 percent for those persons 85 and older. Because of this relationship between age and nursing home care, between one-third and two-fifths of persons 65 or older will spend some time in a nursing home during their lifetime. Due to the increasing numbers of elderly, however, it is anticipated that those requiring long-term nursing care will rise from about 7 million today to 17 million by 2040 (Hess, 1991).

It is estimated that 5 million elderly who are ill or have severe disabilities live in the community, a figure that is almost four times the number living in nursing homes. Most of these elderly are women who are being cared for by a relative, usually a daughter; only 22 percent of the careproviders are husbands or sons. As we point out in Chapter 3, caring for an elderly person with a severe disability places incredible stress on the care provider and not infrequently leads to elder abuse. The strain on care providers may become worse in the near future as the number of offsprings available to provide the care decreases (due to smaller families) and the financial pressures on women in their middle years to work increases (Hess, 1991).

There is some evidence that "in terms of capacities, needs, and resources, we may be moving toward a two tiered old age" (Hess, 1980). Neugarten (1974) has identified these two tiers as the young-old and the old-old. The young-old are characterized by relatively good health and financial condition while the old-old experience declining financial, physical, social, and psychological resources. To some extent this division between the young-old and the old-old is an artifact due to the varying economic, medical, and social opportunities available to different age cohorts, but the dichotomy is useful in other respects. Some of the comprehensive data on age discrimination cited in Chapter 3, for example, will necessarily overstate the privations of the young-old while understating those of the old-old.

## Women

Ostensibly the easiest of the four groups under discussion to define and identify, the issues related to women's status as an oppressed group are actually quite complex. Social scientists have had great difficulty clarifying the issues, much less reaching agreement; conflicting definitions of terms plague the field (Henley, 1985). We will employ descriptors in keeping with the consensus of opinion in the literature on the psychology of women, with the caveat that the usage of other writers may differ considerably.

## Definitions

Ask anyone to describe the crucial differences between men and women, and you will get a hodgepodge of physical, mental, behavioral, and characterological distinctions. Yet contained within commonplace descriptions of sex differences are innumerable unfounded assumptions. There are some very real physical and genetic differences (e.g., average height, weight, muscle mass) between the sexes, but there are not the widespread intellectual, personality, and behavioral differences assumed by so many. In fact, there are *very few* sex differences that have been supported in the research literature; there are many more similarities than differences between boys and girls, men and women (Matlin, 1987). Why, then, are assumptions of significant sex differences so prevalent? The answer rests in society's gender-based norms and expectations (Gilbert, 1992).

Fundamental to this discussion of women and women's status in society is the crucial distinction between *sex* and *gender* (Unger, 1979). *Sex* refers to the biological condition of maleness or femaleness, the possession of the XY chromosomal configuration for men and boys, and the XX pattern for women and girls, along with the corresponding anatomical, hormonal, and physiological structures. In sociological parlance, sex is an *ascribed* status; we are assigned to a sex at birth (Richardson, 1981). *Gender,* on the other hand, is an *achieved* status, that is, one we learn. Gender refers to the psychological, social, and cultural aspects of being female or male within a particular social context (Richardson, 1981). Gender, therefore, is a social label describing the aspects of male and female behavior that are a result of socialization to the culturally-prescribed norms for women and men. Gender *identity* is one's self-defined sex, male or female, which usually, but not always (in the case of transsexuals), corresponds with one's ascribed sex.

Far from semantic nitpicking, these distinctions reflect a crucial point: Most differences assumed to exist between the sexes have been found to be socially-based rather than innate. Our language affects how we see the world, and the continuing use of the term *sex differences* to characterize observed differences in personality, cognitive functioning, interpersonal behavior, and vocational behavior only serves to reinforce outdated notions of the biological source of such observed differences (Unger, 1979). Historically, observed or assumed sex differences have been employed to support arguments for the inferiority of women. Employing the term *gender* emphasizes the social construction of behavior and the existence of environmental causes for behavioral differences between women and men. To briefly illustrate: There do not seem to be any overall differences between men and women in the capacity to act assertively, yet in certain situations women *do* act less assertively than men, because they have learned what is expected of them as women (Gilbert, 1992).

## Gender-Role Socialization

Immediately upon sex assignment at birth, the process of differential socialization begins. Our society holds certain beliefs about personality differences between, and appropriate behavior for, boys and girls. These gender-role stereotypes (sometimes inaccurately referred to as sex-role stereotypes), or widely held but simplistic beliefs about the roles of women and men, influence how we act, what we see, how we interpret behavior, and how we respond to others. Studies have documented the content of the gender-role stereotypes commonly held within the mainstream American culture. Women are characteristically seen as expressive, that is, compassionate, tactful, emotional, nurturing, and dependent; men are seen as instrumental, for example, objective, aggressive, independent, dominant, and competitive (Bem, 1974; Spence & Helmreich, 1978). Parents, family, the educational system, the media—all significant sources of influence on a growing child—communicate these expectations. As a result of gender-role socialization we learn what behaviors and attitudes to exhibit according to our label, male or female. When men act in a culturally-approved, gender-appropriate way, they are viewed as *masculine;* women are viewed as *feminine* when they act in ways considered appropriate for women in their culture.

The importance of understanding the social construction of gender lies in the consequent exposure of the political ideology underlying gender roles, and the costs of adherence to this political ideology that result for both women and men. Margaret Mead's classic anthropological study (1935/1971) convincingly demonstrated the cultural relativity of gender roles and the place of social conditioning rather than biology in the development of gender differences in personality. She investigated three tribes in New Guinea, finding one in which both men and women displayed what our culture would consider "feminine" traits; another in which both sexes displayed the instrumental traits we usually describe as "masculine"; and a third in which adult males demonstrated expressive ("feminine") characteristics while normal adult females displayed the aggressive, instrumental behaviors we label as "masculine."

Despite Mead's research and other anthropological studies refuting the universality of the content of gender-role expectations, and thus their biological immutability, within a given culture people tend to assume that what they are used to is "normal" and therefore good, desirable, and natural. It has been argued that our culture (along with many others) is patriarchal, or male-dominated. The ideology underlying patriarchy is sexism, a political ideology resting squarely on the assumed inequality of women and men. As a consequence, our assumption that this culture's gender-role expectations for women are "normal," and our failure to question these stereotypical expectations, produces a situation where society is training over half of its population to behave and think in ways detrimental to the achievement of gender equality. Further, as we shall see in Chapter 3, many of the gender-appropriate feminine characteristics, traits, and behaviors adhered to in our society are devalued and some are inherently harmful to the mental and physical health and well-being of women (Schaffer, 1981). Men, too, pay a price for strict adherence to the cultural masculine gender role (O'Neil, 1980).

## Women as a Minority

Gender stereotyping, the result of sexist ideology, functions to maintain the status quo. The dominant group, men, are trained to behave in culturally-defined masculine ways that serve to preserve the dominance of men as a group. It takes informed and concerted efforts on the part of men to circumvent their conditioning and societal pressures, even when they consciously ascribe to gender equality (O'Neil, 1980). Women, too, are socialized to think and behave in ways that serve to preserve their relatively inferior status. The consequence is social and economic inequality, resulting in women's disadvantaged status in society. It is this inequitable situation, both a determinant and a result of longstanding and continuing sex discrimination, that defines women as a "minority" or oppressed group (Hacker, 1975).

The minority status of women, then, is due to their economic, legal, political, and social disadvantages rather than their numerical minority, as is the case with other minority groups. However, we must remember as we are discussing women's status throughout this book, that gender combines with other minority statuses to produce multiple, often nonadditive, sources of oppression. For example, because of the gender differences in mortality rates, the ratio of women to men increases greatly with age (Collier, 1982); thus, most women experience at least a dual oppression as they grow older. Older women suffer differentially from problems of loneliness, isolation, and lack of potential partners (Collier, 1982). Different standards of physical attractiveness for the sexes produce a situation where women generally encounter a type of age discrimination that is much more profound than that encountered by men (Collier, 1982). Women of color experience the "double jeopardy" of sexism and racism; lesbian women encounter homophobia as well as sexism; and disabled women face similar double discrimination. We could continue indefinitely with the possibilities for multiplication of sources of discrimination and bias.

How can such a situation still exist in a country founded on the concepts of freedom and human equality? Are we exaggerating the scope of the problem? The answer is complicated, but is intimately tied to the ideology of sexism, the oppression that is common to all women. As Amundsen (1971) states:

> Sexism, then, is an "ideology" in the sense that its beliefs and postulates are well-integrated, it functions to direct and guide social and political activity, and it rests on assumptions that are not reliably tested, but that to some degree are accepted on faith. (p. 108)

Feminism, defined simply as the advocacy of equality between men and women, has been a potent force in exposing unexamined sexist beliefs and behaviors.

Conversely, popular wisdom has it that we are now in a postfeminist era, where women have finally achieved equality and where sexism no longer holds sway. Compelling evidence to the contrary exists, despite the real gains made by women on a variety of fronts. Faludi (1991), in particular, argued persuasively that we are now in a period of profound backlash against women's quest for equality. "The antifeminist backlash has been set off not by women's achievement of full equality but by the increased possibility that they might win it. It is a preemptive strike that stops women long before they reach the finish line" (Faludi, 1991, p. xx).

The history of sexism is long, and, though its specific manifestations have changed over time, its potency as an ideology remains with us today. What is "normal" is seen as right and correct, and largely goes unquestioned. As John Stuart Mill, an early advocate of women's rights, so aptly stated, "So true is it that unnatural generally means only uncustomary and that everything which is usual appears natural. The subjection of women to men being a universal custom, any departure from it quite naturally appears unnatural" (1869/1970, p. 14). Women are surely in a better position than they were when Mill wrote these words, but equality in education, the workforce, politics, and in the family is far from being achieved. In Chapter 2 we will examine the status of women from a historical perspective, tracing the origin and development of sexism over time. As we will see, women's equality with men has not been one of linear, forward-moving progress, but rather one of fits and starts, progression and regression. In Chapter 3 we will discuss the legacy of sexism and its current manifestations in society, psychology, and the practice of counseling.

## *Gay Men and Lesbian Women*

### Descriptors

As is the case with labels employed for and by racial/ethnic minority groups, the nomenclature used when referring to gay people reveals strongly held assumptions about the group. *Homosexual* is the term often applied to individuals whose sexual preferences are predominantly for those of the same sex. Yet the term "homosexuality" places primary emphasis on sexual preference, which is but one aspect of the life experience of the people so labeled (Clark, 1977).

An alternative term, *gay,* like the labels preferred by other minorities (e.g., African-American, Chicano), emphasizes the positive and was developed within the homosexual community itself:

> Gay is a descriptive label we assign ourselves as a way of reminding ourselves and others that awareness of our sexuality facilitates a capacity rather than creating a restriction. It means that we are capable of fully loving a person of the same gender by involving ourselves emotionally, sexually, spiritually, and intellectually. (Clark, 1977, p. 73)

Thus, the term *gay* affirms all aspects of this orientation. Clark (1977) also explains that the designation "homosexual" is a clinical term with many negative associations, a term often used to separate gay people from the rest of society. The label "gay," on the other hand, goes beyond a rigid classification of people into one group or the other:

> . . . It may even imply a frequent or nearly constant preference or attraction for people of the same gender, meaning I (as a Gay man) might notice more men than women on the street or might notice men before women. But the label does not limit us. We who are Gay can still love someone of the other gender. Homosexual and heterosexual when used as nouns are naive and destructive nonsense in the form of labels that limit. (Clark, 1977, p. 73)

In this book we will generally use *gay,* although the term *homosexual* will be employed when referring strictly to sexual behavior or when it is most descriptive of the issue under discussion. As much as possible we will refer to gay women as lesbian women in order to make visible a group of people who are often relegated to invisibility (Faderman, 1991; Martin & Lyon, 1972). Lesbian is an adjective that has been embraced by gay women because of the tendency of society to assume that gay people are exclusively male (Moses & Hawkins, 1982). Finally, we will avoid the use of the term "straight" to describe heterosexuals; if one is not "straight" the implication is that the other is somehow crooked, deviant, or criminal (Woodman & Lenna, 1980). Gays often use the word "non-gay" rather than either heterosexual or straight.

## Sexual Orientation

Homosexuality has traditionally been viewed as a rare and deviant form of behavior, in contrast to the societal norm of heterosexuality; the two are often seen as mutually exclusive categories. Yet in the landmark Kinsey Studies, researchers found that over 60 percent of male respondents had engaged in same-sex sexual behavior before the age of 16, and 30 percent had homosexual experiences in their early twenties (Kinsey, Pomeroy & Martin, 1948). Findings for women were not as dramatic, but were consistent with the data regarding men; homosexuality is far from rare, and homosexuality-heterosexuality is not, in the general population, a clear dichotomous classification (Kinsey, et al., 1948; Kinsey, Pomeroy, Martin & Gebhard, 1953).

The Kinsey reports (Kinsey et al., 1948; 1953) and subsequent research (Churchill, 1971; Kingdon, 1979) demonstrated that, conservatively, about 10 percent of the population are predominantly homosexual, and this figure appears to be fairly stable throughout history and across cultures. Thus, although gay people are clearly a minority due to their oppressed status (which will be documented in Chapter 2) and their numbers, they are a significant minority. Recently a "national survey" questioning this 10 percent figure has received considerable media attention (Cole, Gorman, Barrett & Thompson, 1993). As of this writing, the actual research has not been made widely available, nor has the survey methodology been formally examined for scientific adequacy. However, the survey asked questions dealing only with sexual behavior within a relatively narrow age span, raising doubts about the accuracy of the statistics.

Kinsey and his associates (1948; 1953) argued that sexual preference should be viewed along a continuum. They developed a seven-point scale to measure the degree to which respondents in their studies were "homosexual" or "heterosexual" in their sexual behaviors. The zero point on the Kinsey Scale means that a man or woman has never had *any* overt homosexual experience, while a six on the scale indicates no overt heterosexual experience. Moving up the scale from zero, a one means that an individual has some minimal amount of homosexual experience, but that this is overshadowed by heterosexual experiences; a person scoring two on the Kinsey Scale has had significantly more homosexual experience, but is still predominantly heterosexual; a Kinsey 3 indicates a person with about equal experience of both a homosexual and heterosexual nature; a 4 describes a person who has had a great deal of heterosexual experience, but is predominantly homosexual; the 5th point indicates some minimal heterosexual experience in a very dominantly homosexual individual; and as discussed before, a Kinsey 6 is an exclusive homosexual.

In the Kinsey research surprisingly few people fell on either end of the continuum, that is, "exclusively" heterosexual or homosexual. About half of all American men fell somewhere *between* the two end points. Women's responses were also distributed across the continuum, but, as mentioned previously, fewer women than men indicated that their behavior was exclusively homosexual. Individuals falling at the midpoint of the Kinsey Scale sometimes describe themselves as "bisexual," but often have a preference for one sex or the other, in spite of their ability to relate to both (Moses & Hawkins, 1982).

Thus we see one way in which the issue of sexual orientation is more complex than it appears at first glance, but Kinsey and his colleagues only addressed sexual *behavior*. Sexual preference is only one aspect of sexual orientation; affectional/emotional factors are, for many, far more important than the sexual attraction to a partner. Moses and Hawkins (1982) identify two of the major components of sexual orientation: "(1) the physical, which includes gender preference for sexual partners and sexual relationships, and (2) the affectional, which includes gender preference for primary emotional relationships" (p. 36). One's exploration of partners in fantasy and one's personal history must also be taken into account. A person may have had various types of sexual, affectional, or fantasy experiences in the past, but have different types of experiences currently. If all components of an individual's sexual orientation are congruent, labeling is fairly easy. However, factors influencing sexual orientation may be inconsistent, defying simple categories.

Due to their unique status, gay people encounter barriers not experienced by other minority group members. First, gay people represent a statistically significant minority group in this country (i.e., well over 20 million individuals) and suffer from various forms of intolerance and oppression including lack of legal protection, harassment, loss of their jobs, and violence, all of which usually serve to identify a minority group. Yet many still deny that gays are a true minority (Woodman & Lenna, 1980). Some of the arguments against affording minority status to gay people hinge on religious beliefs, others on the view that sexual orientation is a choice rather than a natural orientation (despite evidence to the contrary), and some of the arguments are reflective of ignorance and/or bias (Dworkin & Gutierrez, 1992a; Fassinger, 1991). Interestingly, virulently anti-gay statements routinely appear in the media, and these are accepted in due course in a way that would be considered unconscionable if such statements were directed at any other minority group.

Secondly, lesbian women and gay men grow up learning the same negative attitudes and hostility toward homosexuality that nongays do. *Homophobia* is the term used to describe ". . . the irrational fear of anyone gay or lesbian, or of anyone perceived to be gay or lesbian" (Dworkin & Gutierrez, 1992b, p. xx). Although this definition is commonly used, some believe that the emphasis on fear alone (homo*phobia*) does not adequately impart the severity of responses, including violence, toward gays in this society. Other terms have been proposed as more adequate descriptors antigay prejudice, for example, gay and lesbian hatred and heterosexism (Blumenfeld, 1992). *Heterosexism* refers not only to the belief that heterosexuality is the only acceptable sexual orientation, but also to the accompanying fear, disgust, and hatred of gay people that results in discrimination (Blumenfeld, 1992). We will retain the term *homophobia,* but employ it in the expanded sense to indicate not only the fear of, but also the prejudice and hatred toward, gay men and lesbian women.

Homophobic reactions are prevalent not only in society at large, but also characterize the responses of friends and family of gay people, as well as gays themselves (Dworkin & Gutierrez, 1992a; Weinberg, 1972). Gay people experience a unique situation among minority groups in that they are reared in heterosexual families that rarely provide the type of support needed in coping with a socially oppressed self-identity. Families of gays are therefore often an additional source of oppression (Beane, 1981). *Internalized* homophobia is also a major obstacle for lesbian women and gay men wrestling with their sexual orientation, further complicating an already complex process of self-definition. Heterosexuality is expected of everyone. When people begin to realize that they are not heterosexually-oriented, they struggle with a highly charged and stigmatized self-label.

> "Coming out" or "coming out of the closet" is argot for acknowledging to self, being open about or asserting one's gay identity. Being "in the closet" is to conceal that identity. Among gays, the idea of coming out is more than just asserting a gay identity—it is a process by which an individual moves from the realization of homoerotic feelings to the acceptance of the sexual-affectional preference for people of the same sex. The next crucial step is to integrate those feelings positively into one's total self so that they can be asserted and to find affirmation in interactions with others. To use client's phraseology, the process involves a "coming out to self" and a "coming out to others." (Woodman & Lenna, 1980, p. 13)

Internalized homophobia and the coming out process are often major issues for gay men and lesbian women seeking counseling.

## Gender Identity versus Sexual Orientation

As discussed in the previous section, the term *gender identity* refers to one's self-identity as a male or female (Richardson, 1981). Sexual orientation should not be mistaken for gender identity. Gay men are men and lesbian women are women. The stereotype of the gay man as feminine equates sexual orientation with *gender-role,* not gender identity, and though the stereotypes do fit some gay men, they do not fit many others. Most gay men exhibit the same range of masculine gender-role behavior as heterosexual men. Likewise, lesbian women may act in feminine or masculine ways, just as nongay women do; their gender identity as women is not dependent on their sexual orientation (Richardson, 1981).

Neither should sexual orientation be confused with transexuality or transvestitism. Transsexuals are individuals whose gender identity is different from their sex assignment, for example, a man who feels he is a woman "trapped" in a man's body (Richardson, 1981). Some individuals who encounter such gender incongruence seek sex-reassignment surgery in order to resolve their dilemma, but transexuality is fundamentally different from sexual orientation.

Finally, transvestites are people who enjoy dressing in clothing considered socially-inappropriate for their sex. Because of the more stringent sanctions for gender-inappropriate behavior for men in our society, cross-dressing appears to be much more of an issue for men than women. Despite the stereotypes, cross-dressing is unusual among gay men (Moses & Hawkins, 1982). Many men whose sexual orientation is predominantly or exclusively heterosexual cross-dress; gender identity and sexual orientation are often not an issue for transvestites (Moses & Hawkins, 1982).

In Chapter 2 we will briefly describe the history of oppression of gay people. In Chapter 3 we will explore current societal attitudes, along with the responses of the mental health establishment. Counseling issues related to the concepts introduced in this chapter will be expanded upon in later chapters.

# References

Achenbaum, W. A. (1978). *Old age in the new land: The American experience since 1790.* Baltimore: The Johns Hopkins University Press.

Amundsen, K. (1971). *The silenced majority.* Englewood Cliffs, NJ: Prentice Hall.

Ansello, E. F. (1991). The intersecting of aging and disabilities. In B. B. Hess & E. W. Markson (Eds.), *Growing old in America* (4th Edition, pp. 207–218). New Brunswick, NJ: Transaction Books.

Aubrey, R. F., & Lewis, J. (1983). Social issues and the counseling profession in the 1980s and 1990s. *Counseling and Human Development, 15*(10), 1–15.

Beane, J. (1981). "I'd rather be dead than gay": Counseling gay men who are coming out. *Personnel and Guidance Journal, 60,* 222–226.

Bem, S. L. (1974). The measurement of psychological androgyny. *Journal of Consulting and Clinical Psychology, 42,* 155–162.

Blumenfeld, W. J. (Ed.). (1992). *Homophobia: How we all pay the price.* Boston: Beacon Press.

Bowe, F. (1980). *Rehabilitating America.* New York: Harper & Row.

Bowe, F. (1985). *Disabled adults in America: A statistical report drawn from census bureau data.* Washington, DC: U.S. Government Printing Office.

Churchill, W. (1971). *Homosexual behavior among males: A cross-cultural and cross-species investigation.* Englewood Cliffs, NJ: Prentice Hall.

Clark, D. (1977). *Loving someone gay.* Millbrae, CA: Celestial Arts.

Cole, T. (1991). The specter of old age: History, politics, and culture in an aging America. In B. B. Hess & E. W. Markson (Eds.), *Growing old in America* (4th Edition, pp. 23–37). New Brunswick, NJ: Transaction Books.

Cole, W., Gorman, C., Barrett, L. I., & Thompson, D. (1993, April 26). The shrinking ten percent. *Time, 27*–29.

Collier, H. V. (1982). *Counseling women.* New York: Free Press.

Corey, G. (1991). *Theory and practice of counseling and psychotherapy.* Pacific Grove, CA: Brooks/Cole Publishing Company.

Driedger, D. (1989). *The last civil rights movement.* London: Hurst & Company.

Dworkin, A. G., & Dworkin, R. J. (1976). *The minority report.* New York: Praeger.

Dworkin, S. H., & Gutierrez, F. J. (Eds.). (1992a). *Counseling gay men and lesbians: Journey to the end of the rainbow.* Alexandria, VA: American Association of Counseling and Development.

Dworkin, S. H., & Gutierrez, F. J. (1992b). Introduction: Opening the closet door (pp. xvii–xxvii). In S. H. Dworkin & F. J. Gutierrez. (Eds.), *Counseling gay men and lesbians: Journey to the end of the rainbow.* Alexandria, VA: American Association of Counseling and Development.

Faderman, L. (1991). *Odd girls and twilight lovers.* New York: Penguin.

Fagan, T., & Wallace, A. (1979). Who are the handicapped? *Personnel and Guidance Journal, 58,* 215–220.

Faludi, S. (1991). *Backlash: The undeclared war against American women.* New York: Crown.

Fassinger, R. (1991). The hidden minority: Issues and challenges in working with lesbian women and gay men. *The Counseling Psychologist, 19,* 157–176.

Gerber, J., Wolff, J., Klores, W., & Brown, G. (1989). *Lifetrends: The future of baby boomers and other aging Americans.* New York: Macmillian Publishing Co.

Gilbert, L. A. (1992). Gender and counseling psychology: Current knowledge and directions for research and social action. In S. D. Brown & R. W. Lent (Eds.), *Handbook of Counseling Psychology,* (2nd Ed.) (pp. 383–416). New York: Wiley.

Goffman, D. (1963). *Stigma: Notes on the management of spoiled identity.* Englewood Cliffs, NJ: Prentice Hall.

Grealish, C. A., & Salomone, P. R. (1986). Devaluing those with disability: Take responsibility, take action. *The Vocational Guidance Quarterly, 34,* 147–150.

Griffiths, T. D., & Meechan, P. J. (1990). Biology of aging. In Kenneth F. Ferraro (Ed.), *Gerontology: Perspectives and Issues* (pp. 45–57). New York: Springer Publishing Company.

Hacker, H. M. (1975). Women as a minority group. In R. K. Unger & F. L. Denmark (Eds.), *Woman: Dependent or independent variable* (pp. 85–115). New York: Psychological Dimensions.

Halleck, S. L. (1971). Therapy is the handmaiden of the status quo. *Psychology Today, 4,* 30–34, 98–100.

Harris, L., and Associates (1975). *The myth and reality of aging in America.* Washington, DC: The National Council on Aging.

Henley, N. M. (1985). Psychology and gender. *Sign, 11,* 101–119.

Hess, B. B. (1980). *Growing old in America.* New Brunswick, NJ: Transaction Books.

Hess, B. B. (1991). Growing old in the 1990s. In B. B. Hess & E. W. Markson (Eds.), *Growing old in America* (4th Edition, pp. 5–22). New Brunswick, NJ: Transaction Books.

Kingdon, M. A. (1979). Lesbians. *The Counseling Psychologist, 8,* 44–45.

Kinloch, G. C. (1979). *The sociology of minority group relations.* Englewood Cliffs, NJ: Prentice Hall.

Kinsey, A. C., Pomeroy, W. B., & Martin, C. E. (1948). *Sexual behavior in the human male.* Philadelphia: Saunders.

Kinsey, A. C., Pomeroy, W. B., Martin, C. E., & Gebhard, P. H. (1953). *Sexual behavior in the human female.* Philadelphia: Saunders.

Kuehn, M. D. (1991). Agenda for professional practice in the 1990s. *Journal of Applied Rehabilitation Counseling, 22,* 6–15.

Larson, P. C. (1982). Counseling special populations. *Professional Psychology, 13,* 843–858.

Levin, J., & Levin, W. C. (1980). *Ageism: Prejudice and discrimination against the elderly.* Belmont, CA: Wadsworth.

Margolis, R. J. (1990). *Risking old age in America.* Boulder, CO: Westview Press.

Martin, D., & Lyon, P. (1972). *Lesbian woman.* San Francisco: New Glide.

Matlin, M. W. (1987). *The psychology of women.* New York: CBS College Publishing.

Mead, M. (1935). *Sex and temperament in three primitive societies.* New York: Dell.

Meador, B. D., & Rogers, C. R. (1984). Person-centered therapy. In R. J. Corsini (Ed.), *Current psychotherapies.* Itasca, IL: F. E. Peacock.

Mill, J. S. (1869). *The subjection of women.* Cambridge, MA: M.I.T. Press.

Moses, A. E., & Hawkins, R. O. (1982). *Counseling lesbian women and gay men.* St. Louis: Mosby.

Neugarten, B. L. (1974). Age groups in American society and the rise of the young-old. *Annals of the American Academy, 415,* 187–198.

Nichols, M. P. (1984). *Family therapy: Concepts and methods.* New York: Gardner Press.

O'Neil, J. M. (1980). Male sex role conflicts, sexism, and masculinity: Psychological implications for men, women, and the counseling psychologist. *The Counseling Psychologist, 9,* 61–80.

Perlman, L. G., & Kirk, F. S. (1991). Key disability and rehabilitation legislation. *Journal of Applied Rehabilitation Counseling, 22,* 21–27.

Richardson, L. W. (1981). *The dynamics of sex and gender: A sociological perspective* (2nd Ed). Boston: Houghton-Mifflin.

Ryan, W. (1971). *Blaming the victim.* New York: Vintage.

Sarason, S. B. (1981). An asocial psychology and a misdirected clinical psychology. *American Psychologist, 36,* 827–836.

Schaffer, K. F. (1981). *Sex roles and human behavior.* Cambridge, MA: Winthrop.

Shilling, L. E. (1984). *Perspectives on counseling theories.* Englewood Cliffs, NJ: Prentice-Hall.

Simkin, J. S., & Yontef, G. M. (1984). Gestalt therapy. In R. J. Corsini (Ed.), *Current psychotherapies.* Itasca, IL: F. E. Peacock.

Spence, J. T., & Helmreich, R. L. (1978). *Masculinity and femininity: Their psychological dimensions, correlates, and antecedents.* Austin: University of Texas Press.

Steiner, C. (1975). Manifesto. In C. Steiner et al. (Eds.), *Readings in radical psychiatry.* New York: Grove.

Strehler, B. L. (1962). *Time, cells and aging.* New York: Academic.

Tomes, H. (March, 1992). Disabilities are major public interest issue. *APA Monitor.*

Unger, R. K. (1979). Toward a redefinition of sex and gender. *American Psychologist, 34,* 1085–1094.

United States Bureau of the Census. (1983a). *Labor force status and other characteristics of persons with a work disability: 1982* (Current Populations Reports, Series P-23, No. 127). Washington, DC: U.S. Government Printing Office.

United States Bureau of the Census. (1983b). *Population Profile of the United States: 1982* (Current Population Reports, Series P-23, No. 130). Washington, DC: U.S. Government Printing Office.

United States Bureau of the Census. (1989). *Labor force status and other characteristics of persons with a work disability: 1981 to 1988* (Current Population Reports, Series P-23, No. 160). Washington, DC: U.S. Government Printing Office.

United States Bureau of the Census. (1992a). *1990 census of population and housing, summary population and housing characteristics: United States* (1990 CPH-1-1). Washington, DC: U.S. Government Printing Office.

United States Bureau of the Census. (1992b). *Marital status and living arrangements: March, 1991* (Current Population Reports, Series P-20, No. 461). Washington, DC: U.S. Government Printing Office.

Vander, A. J., Sherman, J., & Luciano, D. (1985). Homeostatic mechanisms. In *Human physiology: The mechanisms of body function* (pp. 147–171). New York: McGraw-Hill.

Van Hasselt, V. B., Strain, P. S., & Hersen, M. (1988). *Handbook of developmental and physical disabilities.* New York: Pergamon Press.

Weinberg, G. H. (1972). *Society and the healthy homosexual.* New York: St. Martin's.

Wilson, G. T. (1984). Behavior therapy. In R. J. Corsini (Ed.), *Current psychotherapies.* Itasca, IL: F. E. Peacock.

Wirth, L. (1945). The problem of minority groups. In R. Linton (Ed.), *The science of man in the world crisis.* New York: Columbia University Press.

Woodman, N. J., & Lenna, H. R. (1980). *Counseling with gay men and women.* San Francisco: Jossey-Bass.

# 2

# Treatment of Diversity: A Historical Overview

In order to understand the experiences of persons with disabilities, elders, gay people, and women today, it is helpful to understand how members of these groups have been treated historically. In this chapter we trace the treatment of these four groups by both society in general and psychology in particular from prehistoric times to the present. Since attitudes toward these groups in the United States have been shaped primarily by European views, the histories we describe, by necessity, reflect a western bias. For all four groups there is evidence of discrimination since the beginning of human existence, although the nature and degree of this discrimination has varied both within and between the four groups as well as across time.

## Treatment of Persons with Disabilities

### Society's Treatment of Persons with Disabilities

Hohenshil and Humes (1979) summarized the treatment of persons with disabilities since prehistoric times as follows:

> Throughout the course of recorded human history, those persons who were different have often been destroyed, tortured, exorcised, sterilized, ignored, exiled, exploited, and even considered divine. Their problems have been crudely explained in terms of superstition and varying levels of scientific understanding. In the earliest primitive societies, physical abnormalities were not common beyond infancy because many tribes permitted the killing of such newborn children. . . . In more recent societies the handicapped have been pitied and cared for and finally, they have been gradually accepted, educated, and often employed, with the same rights as those who are not handicapped. (p. 221)

As Hohenshil and Humes (1979) suggest, three views of persons with disabilities have been widely held from prehistoric through contemporary times in Western culture. Each is still present to some extent in modern society in the United States.

## Burdensome View

The first view, that persons with disabilities are a burden on the community, originated with our first human ancestors. Early humans were almost certainly nomads, foraging for fruits, nuts, and plants and following game for food. Communities of humans presumably formed to enhance self-protection and food-gathering efficiency. Under these conditions individuals who could not ambulate well enough to keep up with the group or who could not contribute to the food gathering activities were rejected, destroyed, or left to survive on their own (Obermann, 1965). In addition to the ability to ambulate, visual acuity, hearing ability, and other physical capabilities were presumably needed to contribute to group welfare. Limited mental ability was probably not viewed by the group as a burden, but no doubt contributed to each individual's ability to survive in an environment in which humans were both predators and prey.

As agricultural societies developed, permanent villages began to appear. Although ambulation and other physical and mental abilities were still needed for farming activities, individuals no longer needed to keep up with the nomadic movements of the group. Persons with mild disabilities often were able to contribute to the welfare of the community and to maintain themselves to a degree not possible in earlier stages of human development. Some people with disabilities could plant fields, use hand tools, make pottery, and contribute to the commonweal in other ways. Severe physical disabilities were still viewed as "deformities," however, and the belief that disabilities were somehow supernaturally inspired, a belief dating back to prehistoric times, still persisted (Bowe, 1978).

> Lacking the technical means to find and demonstrate germs or histopathology, ancient doctors had to explain disease and physiological disorders in terms of evil spirits and cures had to be offered in terms of exorcism and magic. If the gods were smiling upon the well and the whole and the strong, the sick and the disabled and the weak must be the special property of demons. Thus the disadvantaged individual not only felt the frustrations resulting from lack of capability, he (sic) suffered social ostracism and personal feelings of unworthiness as well. (Obermann, 1965, p. 54)

Even in the golden era of Greek culture it was common practice in Sparta, for example, to destroy babies and children with disabilities because they were viewed as a burden on their families and as a means of "upgrading" the race (Obermann, 1965; Rubin & Roessler, 1978). Although Aristotle and other Greek philosophers began to question negative societal attitudes toward persons with disabilities, the view that people with disabilities are a burden on society persisted, even as it does today among some circles. Centuries later the Romans engaged in the same barbaric practice and were known to dispose of "some deformed and unwanted children . . . in sewers, located, ironically, outside the Temple of Mercy" (Garrett, 1969, p. 31).

Evidence that the burdensome view of persons with disabilities still exists in modern society is provided by studies of employment attitudes. In general, it can be concluded that negative attitudes toward persons with disabilities have severely limited their employment opportunities (Satcher & Hendren, 1991). This is particularly true of human-services occupations, where employees have contact with consumers and the employees' "appearance" presumably enters into hiring decisions. Businesses engaged in sales or service are less likely to hire persons with disabilities than manufacturing firms (Harris and Associates, 1987; Satcher & Hendren, 1991).

## Charitable View

In Western society at least, a second view of persons with disabilities, that of charitable concern for their welfare, emerged as a forceful theme when Jesus Christ drew attention to this population through his teachings. As a result, Christian churches accepted the plight of persons with disabilities as one of their charitable causes. This view of persons with disabilities held that they were among the "deserving poor." Providing food, shelter, and other services for people with disabilities became an important activity of the developing Church and other charitable organizations. Unfortunately, the provider-receiver relationship that was created as a result too often serves as a model for modern efforts to assist persons with disabilities. This second view of persons with disabilities, although motivated by sincere concern for their welfare, frequently translates into sympathy, pity, and a paternalistic attitude toward persons with disabilities (Bowe, 1978).

The charitable treatment of persons with disabilities received a setback in the Middle Ages, due in part to the poor economic conditions and the severe religious attitudes of the times (Rubin & Roessler, 1978). According to Scotch (1984), during the Middle Ages persons with disabilities were often placed in institutions that offered little more than custodial care. The belief that disabilities were the result of supernaturalism returned in full force. "Disabled people were to be feared or ridiculed, objects of persecution on the one hand and court jesters on the other" (Bowe, 1978, pp. 7–8). Frequently they were placed in asylums with "other individuals who did not play a productive role in the social and economic life of the community" (Scotch, 1984, p. 15). It was not until 1260 that one of the first separate institutions for persons with disabilities was established in Paris, an asylum for blind soldiers. Charitable treatment of persons with disabilities gained strength during the Renaissance, and the Elizabethan English Poor Laws of 1597–1601 provided financial support to persons with disabilities who were living at home and unemployed (Rubin & Roessler, 1978).

One of the first institutions for persons with disabilities in the United States was a school for blind persons established in Baltimore, Maryland, in 1812. A school for the deaf was founded in Hartford, Connecticut, by 1817, and in 1893 the first school for children with physical disabilities was founded in Boston, Massachusetts (Obermann, 1965). By the late nineteenth century a number of voluntary charitable organizations had been established in the United States that were concerned with the welfare of persons with disabilities. The Salvation Army, which organized in England, established an office in the United States in 1879. This was followed by The American Red Cross in 1881 and Goodwill Industries in 1902 (Scotch, 1984).

Although involved in establishing special schools for the blind, deaf, and mentally ill in the 1800s, state and federal governments did not become significantly involved with the needs of persons with disabilities until the twentieth century (Hohenshil & Humes, 1979). Then, "because of the negative by-products of industrialization, the tragedies of World War I, and a growing humanitarian philosophy, the United States government began to accept its responsibility for the vocational rehabilitation of both disabled veterans and the civilian disabled" (Rubin & Roessler, 1978, p. 44). State worker compensation laws providing medical treatment and financial compensation for injured workers were first passed in 1909, and by 1921, 45 states and territories had worker compensation laws. The first pillar of a federal vocational rehabilitation program was set in place when the Smith-Sears Veterans Rehabilitation Act was passed in 1918 mandating vocational training for veterans with disabilities. This was followed by the Smith-Fess Act of 1920, which provided limited services for people with physical disabilities (including vocational counseling). The Smith-Fess Act provided for federal funding to participating states on a fifty-fifty basis. By 1935 all the states had vocational rehabilitation programs in operation. Also in 1935, passage of the Social Security Act gave the vocational rehabilitation program permanent authorization. In 1940 the program was expanded to include previously unserved populations and the federal government's share of the funding was increased to 75 percent. Further expansion and strengthening of the federal rehabilitation program occurred in 1943 with the Barder-LaFollette Act and with the Vocational Rehabilitation Acts of 1954, 1965, and 1968 (Scotch, 1984).

Funk (1987) described the 40-year period from 1920 to 1960 as follows:

> From a broad disability/human rights perspective, the era reflects an increasing humanization of certain classes of disabled people based on qualities of "deservedness" and "normalcy" and "employability," and a move from total societal indifference to a recognition that the remaining "unfortunates" must receive some level of minimum care. However, the handicapped still retained their cast status in the public mind as dependent, unhealthy deviants, who would, in the great majority, always require segregated care and protection. (pp. 13–14)

Currently, about one third of all adults with disabilities receive federal (Supplemental Security Income, Medicaid, Social Security Disability Insurance, Medicare) and state benefits because of their disabilities (Bowe, 1988).

## Egalitarian View

While the concept of rehabilitation was an important step in the evolution of attitudes toward persons with disabilities, it was still based on a deficiency model and a view that society was performing a charitable act by providing services to deserving individuals. The focus of efforts by charitable organizations and governmental programs until the late 1960s was on rehabilitating persons with disabilities, not on adapting the environment to meet their needs. Furthermore, some rehabilitation statutes actually operated to restrict the activities of persons with disabilities. According to Laski (1978), these statutes:

> reflected common stereotypes of disabled persons as dependent and inferior. Laws characteristically excluded handicapped persons from services, benefits and protections provided, as a matter-of-course, to all persons. Specialized legislation, enacted to protect the disabled was premised on notions of charity rather than enlightenment and implemented so as to segregate the disabled and suffocate their ability to participate in society. (p. 1)

By the late 1960s a third view of persons with disabilities was emerging in the United States, a view that they are a disparate but identifiable group of individuals whose civil rights have been severely restricted, often through the efforts of well-meaning supporters. Central to this view was the philosophy that civil rights of persons with disabilities were being denied if government supported institutions were not architecturally designed to accommodate them.

> Advocates argued that disabled people should receive not special education at a special school, but supplemental services as part of a regular educational program in a regular classroom shared with able-bodied students; not sheltered workshops for the construction of handicrafts and the repair of discards, but participation in the mainstream labor market; not separate arrangements for transportation, recreation, and access to public facilities, but equal access to facilities and services used by the general public. By rejecting separate facilities, whether equal or unequal, disability rights advocates rejected the association of disabled persons with the "deserving poor" and launched a civil rights movement demanding full integration into the mainstream of American life, a movement parallel to those demanding equal rights without regard to race, gender, or age. (Scotch, 1984, pp. 10–11)

For many persons with disabilities, their civil rights movement is the most recent in a series of movements that have sought rights for laborers, people of color, women, and gay men and lesbian women (Driedger, 1989).

According to Scotch (1984), the groundwork for this egalitarian view of persons with disabilities was laid when the National Federation for the Blind and other groups lobbied state legislatures in the 1930s for guide dog and white cane laws. Guide dog and white cane laws were precedent-setting because they nullified restrictions placed on persons with disabilities by the larger society (e.g., allowing the use of guide dogs in public places where dogs are prohibited) and required able-bodied persons to adjust to their presence (e.g., drivers must take precautions upon seeing a white cane in use). The fact that young people who became disabled as the result of World War II were living longer and were more mobile than earlier generations of persons with disabilities also contributed to a climate for recognizing disability rights (Driedger, 1989). Further groundwork was laid with the Architectural Barriers Act of 1968, the first federal civil rights-oriented statute affecting persons with disabilities. This act required that a barrier-free design be employed in all new federal building construction.

For many years the formation of a cohesive social or political group representing persons with disabilities was impeded by their diverse experiences and communication differences. With the social movements of the 1960s, however, came a recognition that they shared a common experience of oppression and exclusion, and a disability civil rights movement began to take form. Initially, informal and formal interaction took place among individuals sharing similar disabilities, and later interaction and political activity took place across disability lines (Scotch, 1984). The decade from 1965 to 1975 has been referred to by Abeson (1976) as the "era in which the battle cry for public advances changed from charitable solicitations to declarations of rights" (p. 5) on behalf of people with disabilities.

In 1972 the most comprehensive piece of legislature affecting people with disabilities up to that date was signed into law by President Richard Nixon. It was entitled The Rehabilitation Act of 1973 and was intended to expand and improve the federal rehabilitation program. Section 504 of the Act, however, included language borrowed from Title VI of the Civil Rights Acts of 1964 and has been referred to by Scotch (1984) as a civil rights law for persons with disabilities. The single sentence that constitutes Section 504 reads: "No otherwise qualified handicapped individual in the United States . . . shall, solely by reason of his (sic) handicap, be excluded from the participation in, be denied the benefits of, or be subjected to discrimination under any program or activity receiving Federal financial assistance." Bowe (1978), a leading disability rights activist, referred to Section 504 as "the single most important civil rights provision ever enacted on behalf of disabled citizens in this country" (p. 205). Unfortunately, however, the disability rights provided by the Rehabilitation Act of 1973 were limited to programs receiving Federal assistance and did not apply to the private sector.

The Education of Handicapped Children Act (PL 94-142), which was signed into law by President Gerald Ford in November, 1975, also included important provisions for disability rights. This law stipulated that states must provide full educational opportunities to all children with disabilities and included federal funding toward this end. In addition to provisions for parents and child advocates to appeal educational decisions, the law mandated the concept of mainstreaming. In essence, this requirement stipulates that whenever possible, children with disabilities must receive their education in regular classrooms with nondisabled students.

The list of rights won by people with disabilities through disability rights legislation during the period from 1965–1975 is indeed impressive. In addition to the right to public-supported education, the list includes:

> The right of institutionalized handicapped persons to be free from unusual and cruel treatment; the right of institutionalized handicapped persons to be freed from employment without reimbursement and without rehabilitative purpose; the right to avoid involuntary institutionalization on the part of persons who represent neither a danger to society nor to themselves; the right of the handicapped to exercise the power to vote; the right of the handicapped both to marry and to procreate; the right of the handicapped to travel on the nation's public conveyances; and the right of the handicapped to access to America's buildings by means of removal of environmental barriers. (Abeson, 1976, p. 5)

For a period of time in the early 1980s, it appeared as if the disability rights movement in the United States had reached a plateau. According to Scotch (1984), the disability rights movement peaked in effectiveness in 1978, and he cited failure by Congress to pass an extension to the Civil Rights Act prohibiting discrimination on the basis of disability in all employment to support his position. He also suggested that many government officials sympathetic to disability rights had been removed from government agencies following the 1980 presidential election. By the end of the 1980s, however, a number of federal and state laws had been enacted that were designed to promote and enhance the career development of students with disabilities. Brolin and Gysbers (1989) listed the Job Training Partnership Act of 1982, the 1983 Amendments to the Education of the Handicapped Act of 1975, the Carl D. Perkins Vocational Education Act of 1984, the Developmental Disabilities Act Amendments of 1984, and the Rehabilitation Act Amendments of 1986 as evidence of continuing concern for the employment and civil rights of persons with disabilities. Unfortunately, although Brolin and Gysbers (1989) documented increased recognition by legislators throughout the 1970s and 1980s that better educational and rehabilitation services were needed for persons with disabilities, they also concluded that "students with disabilities are not attaining greater vocational and independent living success than they did in previous years" (p. 158).

Disability rights groups continued to lobby the Congress, and, by the late 1980s, support for a comprehensive disabilities rights bill was gaining strength. In 1990, the Congress passed the Americans with Disabilities Act (ADA, Public Law 101-336), "the most sweeping civil-rights bill in more than 25 years" (Karr, 1990, p. B1). The ADA was signed into law by President Bush on July 26, 1990, and began to take effect two years later. The purposes of the ADA are:

1. to provide a clear and comprehensive national mandate for the elimination of discrimination against individuals with disabilities;

2. to provide clear, strong, consistent, enforceable standards addressing discrimination against individuals with disabilities;

3. to ensure that the Federal Government plays a central role in enforcing the standards established in this Act on behalf of individuals with disabilities; and

4. to invoke the sweep of congressional authority, including the power to enforce the fourteenth amendment and to regulate commerce, in order to address the major areas of discrimination faced day-to-day by people with disabilities. (Karr, 1990, p. B1)

The ADA prohibits discrimination against persons with mental or physical disabilities in the private sector in four different areas: (a) employment, (b) telecommunications, (c) transportation, and (d) public services and accommodations. With respect to employment, the ADA specifies that effective July 16, 1992, employers with 25 or more employees had to "make reasonable accommodation to the known limitations of qualified persons with disabilities and to ensure that their hiring practices are nondiscriminatory" (Satcher & Hendren, 1991, p. 15). According to Youngstrom (1992), reasonable accommodations could include "hiring a reader for a blind employee; adjusting schedules so an employee can see a therapist in the middle of the day; and writing instructions for people who become anxious at oral directions" (p. 26). Effective July 26, 1994, this policy was applied to employers with 15 or more employees. The law also provides access to public buildings, telephone service, mass transportation, and government services for persons with disabilities.

This overview of laws pertaining to persons with disability is, by necessity, brief. For a readable, more extensive synopsis of 11 of the most important laws concerning rehabilitation and disability, including the ADA, we refer the reader to Perlman and Kirk (1991). For an even more comprehensive and detailed review of more than 50 laws related to this topic that were passed prior to the mid 1980s, we suggest obtaining the publication entitled *Summary of Existing Legislation Affecting Person with Disabilities* (1988) from the U.S. Department of Education.

Three branches of the disability rights movement have emerged since the 1970s: (a) the independent living movement; (b) consumer organizations; and (c) self-help groups. The goal of the independent living movement is to "mainstream" living arrangements for persons with disabilities so that they are no longer segregated in special housing. The purpose of consumer organizations of persons with disabilities is to monitor rehabilitation, transportation, and housing services provided by the government and nonprofit rehabilitation organizations. Self-help organizations of persons with disabilities are designed to do just that, provide self-help services directly or by putting political pressure on the government (Driedger, 1989).

The disability rights movement has by no means been limited to the legislative action in the United States. According to Driedger (1989),

> Organizations composed entirely of persons with various disabilities—physical, mental and sensory—have sprung up in 100 countries since the mid-1970s. . . . One of the results of this recognition was a gathering of disabled people in

Singapore in 1981 to form Disabled Peoples' International (DPI). DPI's mandate is to be the voice of disabled people and it believes that disabled people should be integrated into society and participate with the same rights as everyone else. With membership in sixty-nine countries, it is activist-oriented, it looks to lobby governments and the UN, and it educates the public about the aspirations and abilities of disabled people. (p. 1)

In March, 1988, a historic event occurred at Gallaudet University, the nation's only liberal arts college for the deaf, that provided evidence persons with disabilities could successfully organize to represent their own best interests. Drawing on the civil rights movement of the 1960s, protesting students at Gallaudet forced the resignation of a hearing campus president, who did not know sign language, and the appointment of a deaf replacement (Lewin, 1988).

Despite these successes by disability rights activists, it is important to recognize that all three views of persons with disabilities are represented in modern society. Further, there are those within the rehabilitation counseling profession that suggest securing rights for persons with disabilities has actually worked to the detriment of individuals in this group. For example, Nelson (1989) states that ". . . the perspective of justice has distorted our moral responsibility toward the disabled" (p. 228). In chapter 6, Kuehn has more to say about the tension that has developed between those counseling professionals who want to rehabilitate persons with disabilities and those who want to liberate them. In Chapter 3 we will explore further the current status of persons with disabilities in the United States.

## Psychology's Treatment of People with Disabilities

The counseling profession's involvement with persons with disabilities can be traced to the vocational rehabilitation movement that emerged in the second decade of the twentieth century. The National Civilian Rehabilitation Conference first convened in 1924 and was renamed the National Rehabilitation Association in 1927. Vocational rehabilitation over the next three decades moved from an educational emphasis, to a social work approach and to a vocational guidance approach (Cull & Hardy, 1972). The National Rehabilitation Counseling Association was established as a division of the NRA to meet the specialized needs of rehabilitation counselors, a profession struggling to identify itself. According to Rubin and Roessler (1978), the rehabilitation counseling profession is still attempting to define its role and function. The two major foci of rehabilitation counselors to date have been on helping clients accept their disability and gain meaningful employment.

By the mid-1950s research psychologists began to take an interest in disabilities and their psychological impact, and rehabilitation psychology emerged as a specialization. Rehabilitation psychologists have focused their research on persons with disabilities and their self-perceptions and on nondisabled individuals and their perceptions of persons with disabilities. Considerable research has also focused on the clinical process—developing a helping relationship, predicting work adjustment, and promoting successful rehabilitation (Fenderson, 1984).

Rehabilitation psychology was not formally recognized as a division (Division 22) of the American Psychological Association (APA) until 1958 (at that time entitled the National Council on Psychological Aspects of Disability). While research psychologists formed a division to study the psychological effects of disabilities, however, the APA itself neglected to offer leadership in the area of disability rights. By the mid to late 1970s, psychologists with disabilities within the APA began to lobby for greater access to APA conventions (i.e., to remove the architectural and communication barriers at convention centers). Their efforts resulted in the establishment of the Task Force on Psychology and the Handicapped by the APA Board of Social and Ethical Responsibility for Psychology in 1979. This task force attempted to draw the attention of psychologists to barriers faced by psychologists with disabilities. In their final report published in 1984 (Task Force, 1984) the Task Force recommended the establishment of a permanent Committee on Psychology and Handicaps. The committee was renamed the Committee on Disabilities and Handicaps in 1986 and was placed under the aegis of the APA Board of Social and Ethical Responsibility. In 1991 it was again renamed, this time as the Committee on Disability Issues in Psychology, with oversight by the Board for the Advancement of Psychology in the Public Interest. At that time its responsibilities were broadened to include sensitizing and educating the APA membership about the role psychology can play to assist all persons with disabilities, not just psychologists with disabilities, to realize their potential (Tomes, 1992).

While a large number of helping professions (e.g., rehabilitation psychologists, rehabilitation counselors, occupational therapists, physical therapists, nurses, school psychologists, teachers) have focused their attention on people with disabilities, their efforts have primarily been to rehabilitate people with disabilities, not liberate them. According to Roberts (1989), the medical rehabilitation model that emerged in the 1940s actually contributed to negative images of persons with disabilities, even among members of this population themselves. Roberts (1989) suggests that millions of persons with disabilities who could not be rehabilitated to "normal" functioning have come to perceive themselves as rehabilitative failures (p. 233).

It seems ironic that a profession that prides itself in sensitivity to individual needs has been so slow to recognize disability rights and so ineffective in promoting them. Only recently have a few psychologists spoken out for disability rights, and the major profession representing psychologists has yet to take a strong, proactive stance on the issue. Rigler (1992) chastises the APA for failing to act ethically on behalf of both psychologists and clients with disabilities. With respect to psychologists with disabilities, she points out that:

> Such people are often barred by attitudinal, architectural or communications barriers from making professional contributions to or attending APA-accredited or -sponsored programs, internships or conferences. Their employment prospects

and post-hiring opportunities are dramatically limited. . . . If they have an interest in disability-related issues, they are often denied interviews in all but medically dominated, rehabilitation settings. . . . Even our vaunted new APA building contains barriers to people with disabilities, due to inadequate prior consultation with such people. (Rigler, 1992, p. 4)

Furthermore, as Bruce and Christiansen (1988) point out, even when some therapists do attempt to advocate on behalf of people with disabilities, they can exacerbate prejudicial attitudes.

They are largely unaware that in communicating their concerns they may inadvertently convey the prejudicial attitudes they are fighting and help reinforce the barriers they are trying to remove. . . . even in the professional literature, problems with the pejorative use of language persist. (p. 190)

Writing in *The Vocational Guidance Quarterly,* a journal for professional vocational counselors, Grealish and Salomone (1986) charge counselors with responsibility for maintaining the status quo with respect to people with disabilities:

Good intentions notwithstanding, however, as able-bodied citizens, you have tended to support (often by inaction) the attitude that an individual with a disability should be the object of sympathy and charity but not of equality and friendship. (p. 147)

Unfortunately, some psychologists and counselors have been found to share some of the same biases toward people with disabilities as are held by the lay public. Nathanson (1979) reviewed the research on attitudes that helping professionals, counselors in particular, have toward persons with disabilities. Some of the feelings he attributes to counselors of persons with disabilities include discomfort, fear, pity, guilt, frustration, and sorrow. Nathanson (1979) suggests that because counselors are human, their deeply held and often subconscious feelings and thoughts can have a profound effect on the counseling relationship with clients with disabilities.

According to the Bureau of the Census (1987), only about one in three persons with disabilities is employed. This low employment rate can be blamed in part on discrimination against people with disabilities by employers. May and Vieceli (1983) suggest, however, that employer attitudes will not change as long as counselors devote so little time and energy to job placement services and "counselors take the more comfortable path of delivering less threatening services to clients" (p. 45). They go on to suggest that the barriers to placing clients with disabilities in suitable occupations include counselor bias against job placement (considered unprofessional and "dirty work"), administrative pressure to increase the number of placements with little regard for their quality, and lack of placement training for rehabilitation counselors. Rigler (1992) points out that psychologists who work in inaccessible environments are discriminating against people with disabilities and are therefore acting unethically.

Many rehabilitation counselors share the biased attitudes toward people with disabilities that are held by employers. Several studies indicate that counselors feel people with disabilities are not motivated to work, they have little job training, and little or no work experience (Zadny, 1979; Zadny & James, 1978, 1979). Blaming people with disabilities for their lack of job training and work experience is an example of "blaming the victims" for the problems they face. The perception that people with disabilities are not motivated to work is simply not true for the majority. Harris (1987) found that although one third of all adults with disabilities receive federal and state benefits due to their disabilities, 67 percent of these beneficiaries would rather work even if they had to give up their government aid. Furthermore, when they are able to obtain employment, "handicapped workers' records on production, job performance, cost to employ, needs for job redesign, absenteeism, job turnover, and safety are as good, and in some cases, better than their nonhandicapped counterparts" (Mithaug, 1979).

The recently enacted ADA has implications for psychologists, particularly industrial/organizational psychologists who help select applicants for employment.

> Under the new law, psychologists will have to ensure that their employment and promotion tests don't unfairly screen out people because of their disabilities. They will have to demonstrate that tests measure "essential job functions"; disabled people can't be refused a position if they have trouble doing peripheral tasks or if they could perform core tasks with "reasonable accommodation." And psychologists will have to find alternate ways to give people with all kinds of physical and mental disabilities standardized tests—and score them.
> (Youngstrom, 1992, p. 26)

Counselors and psychologists are also affected by the accessibility provisions of the law; those in private practice as well as public service have to make their services accessible to individuals with various types of disabilities. This includes the possibility of providing a sign language interpreter as well as providing physical access to their office. It is clear that counselors and psychologists need to develop greater sensitivity to the experiences of persons with disabilities if they are to provide "equal opportunity" services and not just charitable assistance to this population.

## Treatment of Elders

> We ought not to heap reproaches on old age, seeing that we all hope to reach it. (Bion quoted in Diogenes Laertius, *Lives and Opinions of Eminent Philosophers.* Third century A.D.)

> How good we all are, in theory, to the old; and how in fact we wish them to wander off like old dogs, die without bothering us, and bury themselves. (Edgar Watson Howe, *Ventures in Common Sense,* 1919)

## Society's Treatment of Elders

According to Hendricks and Hendricks (1981), attitudes toward and treatment of the elderly have varied across the three major types of human societies, namely, nomadic, agricultural, and industrial. In hunting and gathering societies, life was precarious and marginal. Under such circumstances, the elderly were often left to die on their own when they could no longer contribute to the food supply or keep up with the nomadic movements of the group. However, some elderly persons who were a source of valued knowledge related to the group's physical and cultural survival were no doubt supported by other members of the group as long as possible.

In agricultural societies where property rights often became inherited and immutable, power and prestige were accorded elderly persons (usually men) who held these rights. Thus, the status of elders was generally much improved in agricultural societies over their status in nomadic tribes. However, sociologist Leo Simmons (1945), in his study of aging in 71 "primitive" nomadic and agricultural societies, found that although some degree of prestige for elders was prevalent in all societies, it applied to a "prime of life" old age and not to disability in old age. He also found that in all of the societies studied that older people obtained support from others by rendering, in turn, essential services to the young and strong. In many of the societies studied, when elders could no longer contribute a valued service they were left to fend for themselves. It should be noted that the need to contribute to society did not necessarily work against older people in the ancient Greek and Roman societies. Kebric (1988) cites overwhelming evidence that many people lived active, productive lives into their seventies and eighties during the days of the Greek and Roman empires. In Greek society, men were expected to serve in the military until age 60.

Although earlier societies may have accorded elders a measure of prestige, there is also recorded evidence that negative stereotypes of the elderly have been with us since the pre-Christian era. Aristotle, in Treatise on Rhetoric, describes old age as a time of conservatism and small-mindedness. Authors during the Middle Ages and the Renaissance reflected a similar theme. Pope Innocent III, in the thirteenth century, referred to old men as stingy, avaricious, sullen, and quarrelsome. Shakespeare's depiction of the elderly in his Second Sonnet is anything but flattering where he describes the end of a man's life as second childishness marked by loss of teeth, hearing, and virility (Hendricks & Hendricks, 1981). The negative stereotypes of the elderly were not restricted to men. In a review of terminology used historically to refer to older people, Covey (1988) found that gender was a critical factor in selecting terminology.

> The English language has a long history of separating old men from old women. Terms for old men tend to be focused on their being old-fashioned, uncouth, conservative, feeble, stingy, incompetent, narrow-minded, eccentric, or stupid. Terms for old women are focused on mysticism, bad temper, disagreeableness,

spinsterhood, bossiness, unattractiveness, spitefulness, and repulsiveness. . . . Although women have longer lifespans than men, women are viewed as being old much earlier than men. Thus women have been subjected to old-age labels much earlier in life and for much longer periods during their life-spans. (pp. 291–292)

In the United States, elders commanded power and respect during the colonial period, due in part to their role as property owners. Fischer (1978) suggests respect for old age in colonial America also may have been due to the fact that it was comparatively rare (see data on changing American demographics in Chapter 1). According to Fischer (1978), the undermining of the esteem with which older Americans were held began about the time of the American revolution. He identifies 1770 to 1820 as a period of decline in hierarchically oriented institutions and a questioning of the hierarchies of sex, race, and age in particular. Furthermore, he cites the strong American cultural value of individualism as one of the forces that began to undermine the privileged status enjoyed by the elderly in the eighteenth century.

Historian Andrew Achenbaum (1978) examined experiences of the elderly from 1790 to 1970 and found marked differences between the way elders were perceived and treated in colonial and modern America. Prior to the Civil War, those elderly who were physically able to work were expected to do so. They were also greatly valued for their moral wisdom and practical sagacity. After the Civil War, however, Americans

begannto challenge nearly every favorable belief about the usefulness and merits of age that had been set forth by republican and romantic writers and that still appeared in contemporary literature. . . . By the outbreak of World War I, if not before, most Americans were affirming the obsolescence of old age. (Achenbaum, 1978, p. 39)

While there is disagreement about the factors that precipitated the decline in prestige accorded elders, most authors agree that the industrial revolution contributed significantly to the increasingly negative attitudes toward the elderly in the United States. During the evolution from an agricultural to an industrial society, the elderly lost prestige as economic power moved from land to currency, and greater emphasis was placed on change, mobility, and competition (Cowgill & Holmes, 1972; Hendricks & Hendricks, 1981). The shift from an economy based on agriculture to one based on production, service, and technology usurped the power that older family members held as property owners. The development of large-scale business and organizations had a profound effect on American values and life-styles. Efficiency became the sine qua non of successful enterprise, and individuals within a corporate structure became dispensable (Achenbaum, 1978).

Perceptions of elders and their contribution to the labor force began to change. Businesses began discharging employees at a predetermined age rather than on the basis of their productivity. "Between 1861 and 1915, the federal government and especially private industry began to design and implement policies that discharged workers because they were considered too old to stay on the job" (Achenbaum, 1978, p. 48). The first federal retirement law was passed by Congress in 1861 when they mandated that naval officers must retire at age 62. The first private pension plan, motivated in part by a desire to remove older workers from the labor force, was implemented by the American Express Company in 1875. As a result of these subsequent laws and policies mandating a retirement age, the proportion of the labor force made up by persons over age 65 declined steadily from 1900 to 1970 (Achenbaum, 1978).

The rapid changes that accompanied the industrial revolution helped to promote a valuing of youth. The young could better adapt to the many changes, it was assumed, and wisdom previously attributed to elders was supplanted in importance by intelligence attributed to the young. Advertisements that played upon a desire to appear and behave youthfully began to make their appearance after the Civil War (Achenbaum, 1978).

As U.S. society moved away from an agrarian base and the value of elderly parents began to decline, responsibility for caring for the elderly began to shift from the extended family to the government. Recognizing the need to provide medical care for the elderly, Presidential candidate Teddy Roosevelt in 1912 endorsed the Progressive Party's call for federal medical insurance. The concept of national medical insurance was dropped, however, when Woodrow Wilson won the election. The concept was reintroduced later in the decade by other Progressive reformers, but was again opposed by medical societies and the American Federation of Labor (Fein, 1992). Thus, many elderly people who were forced to retire and whose families were no longer willing or capable of acting as a safety net, faced extended and sometimes terminal illness without adequate medical care.

Between World War I and World War II, theories developed and were supported by circumscribed research that physical decay, mental decline, deviant psychological functioning, and personal isolation accompanied old age.

> Americans between 1914 and 1949 described the status of the aged more pessimistically than did their predecessors. . . . Americans after World War I perceived and voiced concern that current demographic and socioeconomic conditions were making old age per se a national problem as well as a personal misfortune. (Achenbaum, 1978, p. 109)

Levin and Levin (1980) suggest this developing view of the elderly as a societal "problem" is another example of blaming the victim. Thus, elders, who had mandatory retirement policies forced upon them by the federal government and private industry became a societal problem because they were not able to support themselves. Numerous surveys between 1914 and 1940 by civic groups, the U.S. Bureau of Labor, and state legislatures revealed that urbanization, industrialization, and the shortened working period of life were the real culprits of financial hardship experienced by elderly (Achenbaum, 1978).

Initial efforts after World War I to cope with economic insecurity of the elderly included the federal compulsory old age and disability insurance program for civil service employees enacted in 1920 and the expansion of retirement plans in the private sector at about the same time. Evidence that traditional solutions died hard can be found in the fact that five states enacted laws requiring children to support their indigent parents. Other states, however, began to pass old age assistance programs in the late 1920s, a trend that was accelerated by the depression (Achenbaum, 1978).

The Great Depression of the 1930s was hard on many people, but particularly hard on the elderly. Elders were the first to lose their jobs and the last to be hired. In addition, many lost life-long savings when banks were unable to fulfill their obligations to depositors. Several bills introduced in Congress during the early 1930s were aimed at meeting the economic needs of the elderly, but they failed to become law, due in part to pressure from groups that perceived old-age pensions to be un-American. It is interesting to note, in fact, that the United States was one of the last Western industrialized nations to grant retirement pensions. The first was Germany in 1889. Most of the others passed such legislation in the next 25 years (Rich & Baum, 1984).

Finally, the Congress passed, and President Franklin Roosevelt signed into law (on August 14, 1935), the Social Security Act of 1935. Although Title I of the Act granted states considerable flexibility in determining the amounts of assistance elders would receive, it did include a provision with important ramification for the self-esteem of individuals receiving funds.

> By permitting applicants to appeal administrative decisions, the federal government made old-age assistance a right that could be legally enforced. Public relief in old age was no longer a gratuity. (Achenbaum, 1978, p. 135)

However, the Social Security Act did not include any provisions for medical benefits. Although Roosevelt originally envisioned national health insurance for the elderly as part of the Social Security bill, his Cabinet-level Committee on Economic Security convinced him that to include it could jeopardize any form of social assistance for the elderly. Once again elders were left without a safety net for health problems. President Harry Truman took up the national health insurance banner when he proposed an economic bill of rights for all American citizens on September 6, 1945. However, the American Medical Association, invoking the fear of communism, successfully fought against the concept of national health insurance (Fein, 1992).

It should be noted that after 1941, elders began to organize to fight discrimination against them. Older citizens began to form lobby groups to push for legislation to assist the elderly. Groups like the National Association of Retired Federal Employees, the National Retired Teachers Association, and The Gray Panthers became active lobbyists and played a major role in the establishment of a number of programs for elders. The American Association of Retired Persons (AARP) currently has a membership of over 27 million persons age 50 and over. "Originally formed to promote life insurance and other group benefits, AARP has slowly developed into a powerful political force" (Hess, 1991).

Since the passage of the Social Security Act, the federal government has evolved into a major clearinghouse for ideas related to aging. The first National Conference on Aging was held in 1950 with subsequent White House conferences on aging in 1961, 1971, and 1981. These conferences set forth recommendations concerning housing, nutrition, transportation, and other areas. Medicare and Medicaid, hospital insurance programs for the elderly, were passed in 1965, and Congress insured all elderly of a minimal income by passing the Supplementary Security Income program in 1972 (Achenbaum, 1978).

While Social Security and other programs have produced an overall improvement in the economic security of elderly citizens, the effects have not been evenly distributed across all groups of people. For example, people who supplement benefits from income from savings or pension plans are better off than those on social security alone. Also, persons who minimally satisfy requirements for social security payments receive significantly lower retirement incomes than do those who made larger contributions to the system. As Margolis (1990) suggests:

> Social Security has never fulfilled its ample promise. From the working poor's perspective, the program's ideological reach has consistently exceeded its practical grasp. The reason is no secret: To the notion of equal entitlement, society has appended a typically American extenuation—the idea of just deserts, which tends to reward winners and penalize losers. (p. 23)

In linking benefits to a citizen's wage-based payments into the social security trust fund, the government has overlooked the contributions of the unpaid housewife and the volunteer worker. This policy also overlooks the widespread employment discrimination experienced by women, people with disabilities, African Americans, Hispanics, and others that depress their wages and thus their social security benefits (Margolis, 1990). As a result, "old-age dependence remains a serious predicament, especially for minorities and women" (Achenbaum, 1978, p. 151).

It seems clear that since World War II, Americans have become increasingly sensitive to the plight of elders. Yet a Louis Harris poll in 1975 (Harris, 1975) revealed that most people still hold the images of the elderly that prevailed prior to World War II. "Americans continue to disparage the elderly's usefulness even though recent research lends substantial support for a concept of old age that recognizes the diversity in older person's abilities and conditions and that emphasizes positive as well as negative aspects of senescence" (Achenbaum, 1978, p. 163).

In summary, treatment of elders in Western society has been a function of their role in the economy. The most power and prestige were accorded elders in agricultural societies and least in nomadic and industrial societies. The United States has responded more slowly than other nations to security problems of the elderly arising out of the industrial revolution. However, since the passage of The Social Security Act in 1934, a number of programs have been established to address these problems.

Negative stereotypes of elders are as old as human existence and persist despite recent research to the contrary. As we shall see in Chapter 3, these stereotypes have often served as the rationale for discriminating against the elderly.

## Psychology's Treatment of Elders

Although humans have probably been concerned about the aging process since prehistoric times, the formal study of aging by psychologists is relatively new. According to Birren (1964), "an empirically based psychology of aging did not appear until about 1835 with the work of Quetelet, and it showed a very slow growth in factual information until after World War II" (p. 9). In reviewing the history of the psychology of aging, Birren (1961) identifies three phases: Early Period (1835–1918); Beginning Systematic Studies (1918–1940); and Period of Expansion (1946–1960). The Early Period is typified by descriptive studies of human aging, descriptions of how human senses develop and change with advancing age. This was followed by the Beginning Systematic Studies during which numerous studies were conducted relating age to physical ability, reaction time, drive, mental ability, and other measures. Much of the research and writing of this period, as exemplified by G. Stanley Hall's (1923) *Senescence,* focused on the psychological decline of the aging individual.

The Period of Expansion was just that; more psychology of aging research was published in the 1950–1959 decade than had been published in the preceding 115 years (Birren, 1961, p. 127). It was also during this period (1945 to be exact) that the Division on Maturity and Old Age of the American Psychological Association was organized. Other significant events during this time included the convening of the National Conference on the Psychological Aspects of Aging (1953) and the publishing of the *Handbook of Aging and the Individual.* However, the declining ability of the aged remained a central theme of the research published during this period. In fact, a review of research on the psychology of aging by Levin and Levin (1980) revealed a continuing theme of decline in sensory and perceptual processes, psychomotor performance, cognitive processes, drives and personality research. Similarly, a review of research on the creativity of artists and scientists leads to a rather pessimistic view of productivity in the later years.

> Beginning somewhere in the 20s, output first increases fairly rapidly until a peak is reached, usually sometime in the 30s or 40s, after which a gradual decline sets in. This age curve holds even after introducing all varieties of statistical controls for potential artifacts and spurious relationships. . . . Hence the age decrement in creativity after the mid-life optimum seems very real. Indeed, evidence strongly suggests that the longitudinal changes in creative achievement are cross-culturally and transhistorically invariant. (Simonton, 1990, p. 627)

Notwithstanding this consistent finding, Simonton (1990) identified a number of reasons why creative individuals can anticipate continued productivity during the latter part of their life. This led him to conclude that "aging need not silence outstanding creativity in the last years" (p. 630).

Although experimental psychologists have shown some interest in the effects of aging on mental capacities since the turn of the century, applied psychologists have only recently turned their attention to the psychological needs of elders. In a review of research on utilization of psychological services by the elderly, Gatz, Karel, and Wolkenstein (1991) found substantial evidence of underutilization despite that fact that mental health needs do not decrease with age and despite evidence that psychotherapy is effective with older people. Although some underutilization can be explained by the stigma older people attach to psychological services, another important factor is therapist resistance to working with the elderly (Kent, 1990). At an April, 1992, conference cosponsored by the APA's Practice Directorate, the National Institute of Mental Health, and the Retirement Research Foundation, several myths emerged as the reasons why psychologists have resisted serving the needs of elders (Moses, 1992). The prevailing myths or stereotypes held by psychologists are that "mental health issues disappear after mid-life, or that depression, anxiety and other problems are to be expected in the elderly and aren't worth treating" (p. 34). Related to this is the view that the mental health needs of elders have been neglected because it was assumed that the older people are developmentally static, and coping mechanisms learned in their youth should suffice in old age (Mardoyan & Weis, 1981). Other reasons why psychologists have not addressed the needs of elders can be hypothesized. For example, applied psychologists traditionally have been more interested in the needs of children and young adults than in the needs of older adults (Piggrem & Schmidt, 1982). Also, in the absence of a national health insurance that guarantees remuneration for working with the elderly, many mental health practitioners have simply focused their services on more lucrative populations.

However, underutilization cannot be explained in totality in terms of resistance on the part of mental health workers. It is true that most elderly people are socialized to handle their own problems and to not be a burden on others; therefore, they are reluctant to request counseling and other mental health services (Atkinson, 1980). In a survey of 100 elderly persons, Kunkel and Williams (1991) found that:

> recourse to a counselor or psychologist was considered to be neither relevant nor worthwhile except in the most extreme circumstances. The independence and guardedness themes suggested by other researchers among elderly persons were strongly present in this sample. . . . Few elderly persons in this sample thought that counselors were appropriate sources of help for retirement difficulties, fear of death, or sexual problems. . . . Many elderly persons may be part of a cohort that tends to view counseling services as irrelevant and even contrary to life experience. (p. 319)

However, there is reason to believe that this reluctance to use psychological services is changing with each new group of retiring cohorts and that future generations of elderly people will seek services on their own, rather than be referred by doctors, courts, home-health agencies, and adult children (Kent, 1990).

Notwithstanding the "reduced need" explanation for underutilization, there is a widely held belief among many mental health experts that psychological impairment increases with old age. Feinson (1991, p. 125) cited a number of quotes from policy-making individuals and commissions that document this belief. For example, The President's Commission on Mental Health concluded that "depression escalates decade by decade," the former director of the Center for the Study of Mental Health and Aging at the National Institute of Mental Health stated that "the prevalence of mental illness and emotional distress is higher among those over 65 than in the general population," and an official at the National Center for Health Statistics testified that "I have been told that depression is very prevalent among the elderly." However, after reviewing epidemiological studies conducted in the United States since 1950, Feinson (1991) concluded that:

> The one consistent finding from all cross-sectional studies conducted during the past forty years is that, to the extent that a relationship exists between impairment and age, more disorders are found among younger, rather than older, age groups! (p. 133)

Due in part to the negative views about serving the elderly held by psychologists, training programs seldom provide course work on aging. Birren and Woodruff (1973) found that there was only one psychologist trained to work with the elderly for every 76,000 elderly persons; the ratio for the general population was one psychologist for every 3,400 people. Surveys of counselor education programs reveal that only a minority of them offer any coursework on counseling older people (Myers, 1989; Salisbury, 1975). Nonetheless, a substantial number of practitioners do see some elderly clients, despite the fact that few have had any training for working with this client population (Gatz et al., 1991). Several conferences convened by the American Psychological Association have addressed the need for more training in this area. A conference was convened in 1981 in Boulder, Colorado, that resulted in a number of recommendations but no action plans. According to Dr. John Santos, a trustee of the Retirement Research Foundation, "APA just fell asleep at the wheel. . . . APA failed to set up mechanism for helping psychologists develop curricula and service in this field" (quoted in Moses, 1992). An APA conference convened in Washington, D.C., in April, 1992, also resulted in a number of recommendations for training for gerontological practice, but it remains to be seen if the American Psychological Association puts them into action.

The American Counseling Association (ACA), on the other hand, has taken several steps to promote training of counselors who have at least a minimum competence in gerontological issues. According to Myers (1992), the ACA (or more accurately, its predecessor, the American Association for Counseling and Development) conducted five national projects on aging between 1977 and 1991 with total funding from the U.S. Administration on Aging for these projects exceeding $1 million. All five projects were focused on developing models and resources for preparing counselors to work with older persons. The most recent of the five projects identified "both generic competencies designed for training all counselors in gerontological issues and specialty competencies for training of gerontological counselors" (Myers, 1992, p. 37) and resulted in a proposal for a specialty credential in gerontological counseling that was accepted by the National Board for Certified Counselors (NBCC) in 1989. Gerontological competencies identified in these projects also contributed to the standards for training in gerontological counseling adopted by the Council for Accreditation of Counseling and Related Educational Programs (CACREP) in March, 1992. Further, the ACA has submitted standards to CACREP that were designed to infuse gerontological counseling into the common core preparation areas required for accreditation of counselor training programs. "This model would make it possible for all counselors (in accredited programs, at least) to graduate with some knowledge of the needs of older people and of ways to work successfully with them" (Myers, 1992, pp. 35–36).

With the aging of a significant proportion of our society and the lengthening of the life span has come a growing recognition by psychologists in the 1980s and 1990s that they must begin serving the elderly population. By sheer numbers elders are making us increasingly aware of their special needs. Psychologists can make a significant contribution to their well being through both research and direct service efforts. Addressing researchers, Schaie (1993) points out that contemporary psychology should be concerned about ageism in contemporary psychology because: (a) the rapid growth of the elderly in the 1990s has focused considerable research attention on this population; (b) the increased funding for research in this area has attracted researchers with little previous experience with research on aging, researchers whose ageist language may reinforce societal stereotypes; and (c) psychological research is playing an increasingly important role in developing public policy. Similarly, direct service psychologists should be concerned about how their ageist attitudes and behavior may impact elders as more and more services are targeted for this age group.

> Ageism may be manifested by psychologists in many ways, including (a) assumptions of restrictions on behavior due to age, (b) positive or negative stereotypes about the elderly, (c) belief that age is usually or always a relevant dimension to variables under study, and (d) the untested assumption that data from one age group generalize to others. (Schaie, 1993, p. 49)

In Chapter 16 we will discuss some of the steps that psychology must take to address the psychological needs of elders.

# Treatment of Women

## Society's Treatment of Women

Women have been largely neglected in historical texts, existing mostly in passing references or as the wives, mothers, or lovers of great men. Only recently have historians begun to untangle the reality of women's lives throughout history from the fiction of myth and literature (Schulenburg, 1979). Virginia Woolf (1957) best summarized the problems in understanding women's place in history:

> If woman had no existence save in the fiction written by men, one would imagine her a person of utmost importance; very various; heroic and mean; splendid and sordid; infinitely beautiful and hideous in the extreme; as great as man, some think even greater. But this is woman in fiction. In fact, as Professor Trevelyan points out, she was locked up, beaten, and flung about the room. A very queer, composite being thus emerges. Imaginatively she is of the highest importance; practically she is completely insignificant. She pervades poetry from cover to cover; she is all but absent from history. . . . Some of the most inspired words, some of the most profound thoughts in literature fall from her lips; in real life she could hardly read, could hardly spell, and was the property of her husband. . . . It was certainly an odd monster that one made up by reading the historians first and the poets afterward—a worm winged like an eagle; the spirit of life and beauty in a kitchen chopping up suet. But these monsters, however amusing to the imagination, have no existence in fact. (pp. 45–46)

Women's actual status in society has varied tremendously across time and across cultures (Leavitt, 1971). However, the generalization that must be derived from any study of women through the ages is that women's status has usually been inferior to men's (Nielsen, 1978).

Leavitt (1971) argued that the key to understanding women's status anywhere is her degree of participation in the economy of the society, as well as her control over the products she produces. Every known society employs some type of sexual division of labor, but this segregation of tasks per se is not the cause of the inferior status of women. Rather, it is the *nature* of the division of labor by sex that affects the relative status of men and women and that influences their relationships within each society (Nielsen, 1978).

## Primitive Societies

In early hunting and gathering societies in the Old Stone Age, and in the modern-day world where such societies still exist, women's status within the clan was roughly equal to men's (Leavitt, 1971). In primitive societies the division of labor by sex originated because of women's limited mobility due to child-bearing and -rearing responsibilities. Men ranged widely as hunters, while women's responsibilities included gathering vegetables and grains. Women, however, contributed equally to the subsistence of the clan; their contribution to the food supply was stable, and at least as important as men's. In fact, in some societies the clan depended primarily on the food gathered by women, with the meat provided by men being seen as a luxury (Martin & Voorhies, 1975).

With the domestication of animals and the agricultural advances in the New Stone Age, ten to twelve thousand years ago, came the beginnings of social changes that had a tremendous impact on women's status. Men are generally credited with the discovery of the domestication of animals, a development that evolved naturally from their earlier hunting activities (Deckard, 1983). Women's food-gathering activities also subsequently led to important cultural advances:

> It is generally accepted that owing to her ancient role as the gatherer of vegetable foods, woman was responsible for the invention and development of agriculture. Modern analogies indicate that so long as the ground was prepared by hoeing and not by ploughing women remained the cultivator. (Hawkes & Woolley, 1963, p. 265)

Women are also credited with the invention of pottery, weaving and the loom, and various tools related to their work activities, such as tools for grinding wheat (Deckard, 1983). Most early horticultural and herding societies maintained their dependence on vegetables and grains as their primary food source, and so women's status remained fairly high (Deckard, 1983).

In the clan societies of this time, women's status was probably the highest ever achieved. The existence of matrilineal clans, that is, communities in which kinship and descent were calculated through the women, were common in primitive agricultural societies (Deckard, 1983). More recent examples of this type of kinship system can be found among Native American tribes such as the Hopi (Leavitt, 1971).

Even in herding societies, where men's influence was greater and descent through the male line (i.e., patriliny) was typical, women were not necessarily demeaned or dominated in the ways they were later in history. Male dominance, or patriarchy, seems to have been stimulated by the increasing sexual division of labor and the decreasing importance of women's contribution to the economy of the community resulting from the invention of the plow (Leavitt, 1971). The plow changed agriculture from a female to a male occupation; women's hardest labor was ended, but women also lost control of the food supply; consequently their economic value diminished.

Increased agricultural productivity produced a situation where, for the first time in history, communities had surpluses of food and thus wealth. Accumulation of these surpluses were then consolidated by individual chiefs who sought ways to transfer their wealth and authority to their descendants. In clan societies, especially matrilineal societies, children were community property and paternity was unimportant. With the accumulation of private as opposed to community property, and the desire to preserve wealth through one's line, came the tendency to regard women as property, and the necessity of secluding women to ensure legitimate sons (Gough, 1975).

It was not only women who were treated as property. The development of private property and surplus wealth also produced slave societies (Deckard, 1983). As slaves provided more and more of the productive work, women's value to the economy declined further; both slave and free women were used for sexual pleasure.

## Ancient Greece and Rome

In Athenian Greece, 80 percent of women were slaves, sometimes performing the hardest work in the fields but more often employed in the household; however, even the wives of the ruling-class men were treated as property and had few rights (Childe, 1971). The golden era of Greek democracy applied only to the free male ruling-class. Ruling-class women were secluded, prohibited from participating in the political system, required to have a legal guardian, usually father or husband, and could not obtain a divorce except under extreme circumstances (Childe, 1971).

The great Greek philosophers and writers held that women were inherently inferior and evil. The Pandora legend exemplifies the woman-hatred (misogyny) that was widespread even among the intellectuals of ancient Greece. Aristotle, whose influence on religious and scientific thought, and on our culture generally, has been profound, felt that women were defective men. He classed women and children together, concluding that neither had a fully developed rationality; in his view, both women and children ought to be ruled by men (Schaffer, 1981). Women's status was slightly better within Roman culture; women were not excluded from political and social life, and their status was less obviously inferior (Hunter, 1976). However women were still seen as the source of misery and suffering, and women's emancipation was viewed in Roman literature as a causal factor in the decline and fall of Rome (Hunter, 1976). These themes of women as inferior and woman as a source of evil and suffering appear throughout history in various forms.

## Medieval Societies

In medieval times, slavery was replaced by systems of serfdom. Serfs were slightly better off than the slaves of ancient times, but were still bound to the land and their masters. Society was ordered into classes: King, greater nobility, lesser nobility, and the serfs, with women varying in status according to their husband's or father's place in society. Christian doctrine was a strong source of support for the views on the inferiority of women at this time. Christ himself demonstrated a high regard for women and nothing appeared in his original teachings denigrating women. But St. Paul was the major influence on the early and medieval church, and the Christian Church has historically held a low opinion of women as a result (Chafetz, 1978):

> The head of the woman is the man . . . for a man is the image and glory of God. . . . I suffer not a woman to teach, nor to usurp authority over the man, but to be in silence. . . . (St. Paul, quoted in Deckard, 1983, p. 197)

As in ancient Greece, medieval women of the nobility had little freedom. Nunneries were one of the few places where women could get an education and find respite from men's oppression. Despite the glorification of the "weaker sex" within the medieval code of chivalry, female serfs worked as hard as their male counterparts.

In the late medieval period, some women of the growing middle class achieved a measure of independence as merchants and as weavers and spinners (thus, the term "spinster" for older, unmarried women) (Deckard, 1983). As capitalistic economies evolved, upper-class women's lives improved, although they were still regarded as inferior to men. Women generally had a more significant role in feudal societies than indicated in most historical texts, even though they were legally subjugated. For example, female serfs played a leading role in peasant uprisings and rebellions, perhaps because of their double oppression. Rebellious peasants often met at night, and such night assemblies were claimed to be "witches' sabbaths" because of women's roles in them. Both men and women were tortured and burned as witches, but women were persecuted in greater numbers and with more vigor; the terms "woman" and "witch" became virtually equivalent (Nelson, 1979). Women's so-called "evil nature" was a source of both hatred and fear by the male rulers and nobility. Women who refused to accept their subordinate status, or who obtained knowledge or power that was considered the domain of men (e.g., women who practiced the healing arts), were particularly vulnerable to charges of witchcraft and sorcery. Witch burnings were an effective means of social control (Nelson, 1979).

The Renaissance produced many advances in the status of upper-class women, including increased educational opportunities for women. Women of the lower classes did not fare as well. However, a considerable number of noblewomen of this time had a significant impact on history (e.g., Queen Isabella of Spain, Catherine de Medici, and Elizabeth I), and enlightened views on women were increasingly expressed. Thomas More, in his *Utopia,* specifically stated that women should receive an education equivalent to men's, adding the caveat that some books are more appropriate to one sex than another. The Protestant Reformation and the subsequent rise in religious bigotry cut short the progress stimulated by the Renaissance (Deckard, 1983).

## The Enlightenment

The Age of Revolutions, generally regarded as a time when freedom and democracy began to flower in western Europe and the United States, was also a time of advances for women, but not because the major philosophers of the time advocated that equality be extended to women. In fact, most liberal philosophers still held reactionary positions on women. Rousseau, one of the French Enlightenment's most important theorists, said:

> Nature herself has decreed that woman, both for herself and her children, should be at the mercy of man's judgement. . . . When the Greek women married, they disappeared from public life; within the four walls of their home they devoted themselves to the care of their household and family. This is the mode of life prescribed for women alike by nature and reason. (Rousseau, quoted in Hunter College Women's Studies Collective, 1983, p. 71)

"Liberty, equality, and brotherhood" meant just that—liberty and equality for men, usually only property-owning men.

The Enlightenment did stimulate the writings of the first feminist philosophers. In 1792 Mary Wollstonecraft, in *A vindication of the rights of woman,* spoke out against the oppression of women and argued for equal educational opportunities for upper-, middle-, and working-class women:

> Men, indeed, appear to me to act in a very unphilosophical manner when they try to secure the good conduct of women by attempting to keep them always in a state of childhood. . . . It is a farce to call any being virtuous whose virtues do not result from the exercise of its own reason. This was Rousseau's opinion respecting men: I extend it to women. (Quoted in Hunter's College Women's Studies Collective, 1983, p. 71)

One of the few male liberal philosophers who spoke out in support of the equality of women was John Stuart Mill. Mill and his wife, Harriet Taylor, collaborated on many works, including *On the subjection of women.* Mill argued that women were not innately inferior, and ascribed women's inferior social status to environmental factors such as a lack of educational opportunities.

The Industrial era of the nineteenth and twentieth centuries was again a time of advances for women. The women's movement in the United States arose out of the abolitionist movement, and the history of both civil rights campaigns have been interconnected to the present day (Davis, 1981).

## Women in America

Prior to the first women's movement, women in the United States had few rights; many women came to the United States as indentured slaves. White women were sold from London prisons or kidnapped from the streets; black women were kidnapped from Africa (Deckard, 1983). Married women did not "exist" legally apart from their husbands; they could not testify in court, their property belonged to their husbands, and they did not even have a right to their own children. In frontier settlements in early America, women enjoyed the rough "equality" borne of economic and social necessity:

> Women were just as indispensable as men since a household which lacked their homemaking skills, as well as nursing, sharp shooting and hunting when needed, was not to be envied. As colonial society became more complex this tradition became obscured, but its roots remained in American life and thinking; as the frontier moved westward in a changing world, the idea that women were the equals of men traveled with it, with far-reaching results. (Flexner, 1975, p. 9)

Indeed, the western states have always been at the forefront of the fight for women's equality, with Wyoming the first state to give women the right to vote in 1869.

Black female slaves in the southern states held a position very similar to the slaves in Athenian Greece; the same analogy could be extended to their White mistresses and the ruling-class women in Greece. The latter's status was higher, but still subordinate to men. The paradox between the antebellum

South's notions of chivalry and their beliefs about women's nature, the treatment of Black women in slavery, and the disadvantagement of free Black and poor and working-class White women, is captured in Sojourner Truth's famous statement. At a women's rights meeting in Ohio in 1851, a male clergy member ridiculed the demand for women's right to vote by arguing that women were weak, dependent, and helpless. Sojourner Truth responded:

> The man over there says women need to be helped into carriages and lifted over ditches, and to have the best place everywhere. Nobody ever helps me into carriages or over puddles, or gives me the best place—and ain't I a woman? Look at my arm! I have plowed and planted and gathered into barns and no man could lead me—and ain't I a woman? I could work as much and eat as much as a man—when I could get it—and bear the lash as well! And ain't I a woman? I have borne 13 children, and seen most of 'em sold into slavery, and when I cried out with my mother's grief, none but Jesus heard me—and ain't I a woman? (Quoted in Flexner, 1975, p. 91)

The first Women's Rights Conference was held at Seneca Falls, New York, in 1848. The catalyst for this action was the refusal of male abolitionists to seat female delegates at the World Anti-Slavery Convention in London in 1840 (Flexner, 1975). Although much disagreement arose over whether women should demand the right to vote (it was seen as too radical by many), the conference delegates did unanimously agree to use every means possible to end discrimination against women (Flexner, 1975).

By the 1860s women had made progress in certain areas such as securing the right to control their own wages. Progress in education and work came more slowly, and the right to vote for women was not won in the United States until the Nineteenth Amendment became law in 1920. Suffragists in the United States, after decades of work and continuing frustration, adopted some of the militant techniques of the British suffragists prior to the passage of the Nineteenth Amendment (Flexner, 1975). The Equal Rights Amendment was originally brought before Congress in 1923 and then reintroduced every year until it passed in 1972, only to go down to defeat in 1982 (Deckard, 1983).

Despite the advances made by women in the twentieth century in terms of their social roles, legal rights, and access to the political process, inequities persisted. The extreme disparity between what has been called the "happy housewife" myth and the reality of women's lives in the 1950s gave rise to the second women's movement (Amundsen, 1971). Betty Friedan, in her classic *The Feminine Mystique* (1963), gave voice to the dissatisfaction felt by many middle-class American women that reflected the gap between social ideology and social reality.

Dramatic legal progress was not obtained for women until the 1960s and 1970s. The Equal Pay Act of 1963, first introduced in 1945, required that women be paid at the same rate as men, but did nothing to make job discrimination illegal (Deckard, 1983). Title VII of the comprehensive Civil

Rights Bill of 1964 went much further, and finally gave women legal recourse for discriminatory practices (Bird, 1971). Even though the sex discrimination section of this bill was introduced as a way to kill the bill (it was assumed by opponents of civil rights for minorities that the inclusion of women would cause the bill to be laughed off the floor), Title VII has had far-reaching effects (Deckard, 1983). Other legal "victories" for women's rights included the 1967 Executive Order 11246, prohibiting sex discrimination in employment by federal contractors, and the passage of Title IX in 1972, prohibiting sex discrimination in educational institutions.

## Psychology's Treatment of Women

The academic discipline of psychology was slow to attend seriously to female psychology and women's experiences, and the psychological literature was so full of blatant sexism that, in 1971, Naomi Weisstein was prompted to write of it: "Psychology has nothing to say about what women are really like, what they need and what they want, essentially because psychology does not know" (p. 209). Weisstein's central thesis, indicated by the title of her article "Psychology constructs the female, or the fantasy life of the male psychologist" was that, due to the androcentric (i.e., male-centered) bias in the field, psychological research and theory had little connection to women's reality.

At the dawn of the discipline, usually traced to the late 1870s, psychologists were concerned with establishing a "scientific" field of study of the individual. The "woman question" was regarded as a social issue and therefore outside the purview of the nascent field (Shields, 1975).

> The business of psychology was the description of the "generalized adult mind," and it is not at all clear whether "adult" was meant to include both sexes. When the students of German psychology did venture outside of the laboratory, however, there is no evidence that they were sympathetic to those defending the equality of male and female ability. (p. 739)

### The Search for Sex Differences

Although German psychology under Wundt chose to ignore women, the functionalist movement in the United States in the late nineteenth and early twentieth centuries stimulated a great deal of research on sex differences in human functioning. Functionalists, heavily influenced by evolutionary theory, sought mainly to establish the superiority of White males; their attention was focused primarily on racial differences that supported White supremacy, but investigations of sex differences aimed at proving the subordinate role of women were a natural byproduct of such thinking (Shields, 1975).

Researchers in the functionalist tradition first began to search for the "proof" of women's inferiority by examining sex differences in cranial capacity (Gould, 1981). Women's heads are on the average smaller than men's, and this was originally thought to be the physiological mechanism of women's diminished capacity (Shields, 1975). Broca, an early researcher on brain functioning and cranial capacity, said:

> In general, the brain is larger in mature adults than in the elderly, in men than in women, in eminent men than in men of mediocre talent, in superior races than in inferior races. . . . Other things being equal, there is a remarkable relationship between the development of intelligence and the volume of the brain. (Broca, 1861; quoted in Gould 1981, p. 83)

This avenue of research came to a dead-end after several grand and notable failures: when adjusted for size of the body, women's brains were found to be *larger* than men's; no clear relationship could be established between achievement in life and cranial capacity after death; and repeatedly, the brains of highly eminent men (e.g., Walt Whitman and Anatole France) were found to be embarrassingly small (Gould, 1981).

Research on sex differences then proceeded through comparative examinations of whatever aspect of brain organization, structure, or functioning might provide the illusive evidence for the widely-held and obvious conclusion of female intellectual inferiority. The legacy of this androcentric, biased approach to the scientific study of women is with us today, manifested in studies of sex differences in cerebral dominance and laterality (Unger, 1979).

Psychologists of the functionalist movement also focused their attention on the purported biological mechanisms of sex differences in temperament, including the presumed biological complementarity of the sexes and the effects of "maternal instinct" on women's "nature." As to the former, men were seen as having different metabolisms than women, resulting in two different and complementary natures:

> The feminine passivity is expressed in greater patience, more open-mindedness, greater appreciation of subtle details, and consequently what we call more rapid intuition. The masculine activity lends a greater power of maximum effort, or scientific insight, or cerebral experiment with impressions, and is associated with an unobservant or impatient disregard to minute details, but with a more stronger (sic) grasp of generalities. (Geddes & Thomson, 1890, quoted in Shields, 1975, p. 746)

Three presuppositions about sex differences, though disproved repeatedly, continued to influence eminent psychological researchers, as did the concept of maternal instinct, an assumption strongly held in American society and predating the advent of formal psychology (Shields, 1975). In essence, ". . . women's emotional nature (including her tendency to nurturance) was a direct consequence of her reproductive physiology" (Shields, 1975, p. 749). This maternal tendency was seen as having a significant and detrimental impact on women's development. The long-standing impact of these sexist and unproven assumptions are illustrated in the comments made by Bruno Bettelheim, over 100 years after the ideas had first been introduced: ". . . as much as women want to be good scientists or engineers, they want first and foremost to be womanly companions of men and to be mothers" (Bettelheim, 1965, p. 15).

Some oppositional voices were "crying in the wilderness." In 1910, Helen Thompson Wooley characterized the extant research on sex differences as ". . . logic martyred in the cause of supporting a prejudice, unfounded assertions, and even sentimental rot and drivel. . . ." (Quoted in Shields, 1975, p. 739). Leta S. Hollingworth effectively dismantled the carefully constructed arguments of that period on the intellectual inferiority of women in an article entitled "Social devices for impelling women to bear and rear children" (1916; Sherif, 1979). Nevertheless, the dominant sexist attitudes persisted within psychology.

The early functionalist influence on psychology, and the consequent search for the biological mechanisms of sex differences, was eventually supplanted by the behaviorist tradition in this country in the 1930s. Behaviorists, searching for the universal laws governing behavior, were not concerned with sex differences, and so there came a hiatus in the study of female psychology in the United States (Shields, 1975). However, psychoanalytic theory was in ascendance in Europe, and eventually Freudian theory dominated the study of women.

## Freud and His Followers

Although some of Freud's most famous clients were women, he was far less certain about female developmental processes than about male development. His theory of girls' development was presented fully 20 years after his more famous exposition of the Oedipal theory for boys; his writings on women reflect a trend common in psychological writings even today, that is, extending men's experiences to women's (Hare-Mustin, 1983; Schaffer, 1981). Psychoanalytic theory rests squarely on the dictum "anatomy is destiny" (for women but not for men) and corresponding assumptions about the biological inferiority of women. Thus Freud, despite having written only 3 articles on women, has had a significant and negative impact on both past and contemporary psychological views of women (Rohrbaugh, 1979).

Freud's central thesis was that girls, lacking a penis, are never as motivated as boys by castration anxiety to resolve the central developmental dilemma of the Oedipal complex. Girls therefore tend to be more susceptible to psychological disturbances, as well as to lag behind boys developmentally (Rohrbaugh, 1979). On the consequences of these developmental differences, Freud had this to say:

> I cannot escape the notion (though I hesitate to give it expression) that for women the level of what is ethically normal is different from what it is in men. Their super-ego is never so inexorable, so impersonal, so independent of its emotional origins as we require it to be in men. (1925; Quoted in Rohrbaugh, 1979, p. 87)

In other words, women generally fail to develop a strong super-ego or conscience. Further, women are seen as developing various personality characteristics as a result of their differential development, penis-envy in particular, and also including narcissism, vanity, jealousy, passivity, and masochism (Schaffer, 1981). Margaret Mead (1974) summarized one perspective on Freud when she commented that it was a pity that Freud, although contributing so much to psychology, understood so little about women (Mead, 1974).

Among Freud's followers were many critics: Helene Deutsch, Karen Horney, Alfred Adler, Clara Thompson, and Carl Jung all disagreed with various aspects of Freud's views on women (Schaffer, 1981). Adler, for example, posited that society requires men to assume positions of unnatural dominance over women. Karen Horney wrote extensively about the social and cultural biases in Freud's thinking, and explicitly rejected the psychoanalytic notion of women as masochistic (Schaffer, 1981). In critiquing Freud, Horney also stressed his tendency to look at women from an exclusively male perspective; ". . . like all sciences and all valuations, the psychology of women had hitherto been considered only from the point of view of men" (1926; Quoted in Rohrbaugh, 1979, p. 108).

Such critiques of androcentric bias did not prevent later theorists, most notably Erik Erikson, from making the same mistakes. Erikson's (1968) schema outlining stages of identity development was developed out of boys' and men's experiences. The theory was later expanded to account for women's development, but women received attention primarily in terms of their perceived deviance from the male model of development. Erikson (1964) hypothesized that a woman's identity becomes clear only after her decision about a marriage partner; he saw a woman's role as a mother crucial to her development of an identity. Moreover, women were seen as becoming neurotic and feeling deprived, lonely, and unfulfilled, unless their "inner space" (i.e., womb) was filled (via motherhood).

## Bias in Psychology

Psychodynamic theory and its offshoots are not the only culprits behind the bias against women in psychology. Every research area within the field can be exposed in similar ways. One further example will suffice as an illustration of this "masculine bias" in scientific psychology. In the area of research on achievement motivation, elaborate theories evolved detailing the factors predictive of educational and vocational success (Atkinson & Feather, 1966; McClelland, Atkinson, Clark, & Lowell, 1953). These theories, as with many other theories in different domains, have been presented as equally applicable to men and women. Yet studies on achievement motivation consistently yielded different results for women than men, and women's responses in such studies were not congruent with the hypothesized theories of achievement motivation (Rohrbaugh, 1979). Only upon careful reading of this literature can the reader determine the truth. The data on women were so confusing that they were consequently largely ignored by the major theorists and researchers.

Thus we can identify four main themes characterizing psychology's historical treatment of women: a) neglect of female psychology entirely; b) blatant sexism, including searches for the presumed mechanisms of women's inferiority; c) ignorance of women's unique experiences and the consequent unthinking extension of theories of male functioning and development to women; and d) feminist analyses geared toward understanding women's personality patterns, behavior, and male-female relationships in social context. The latter theme, as we will see in the next chapter, is unfortunately still not in ascendance in mainstream psychology, despite the recent explosion of research and writing by feminist psychologists (Gilbert, 1992; Sherif, 1979).

# Treatment of Gay Men and Lesbian Women
## Society's Treatment of Gay People

> Attitudes toward gay people have varied considerably throughout the history of Western culture from the ancient civilizations of Greece and Rome, where homoeroticism was considered quite unremarkable, to the intolerance and persecution characteristic of both the Middle Ages and the Twentieth century. Regardless of opposition or tolerance, some groups of people in every age turns out to be gay, the greatest difference between periods is not the proportion of the population that is gay, but in the way sexual preference is expressed. (Moses & Hawkins, 1982, p. 4)

Gay people, even more so than women, have been invisible in history; most of what we know about homosexuality and attitudes toward homosexuality is derived from religious and legal sanctions against homosexual behavior (Bullough, 1976). We know very little, for example, about the everyday experience of gay people in different historical periods, and what evidence exists largely concerns gay men (Bullough, 1979). The attitudes of society, as illustrated in the preceding quote, have ranged the gamut from tolerance to harsh oppression; the norm in Western societies has been hostility and condemnation.

Gay people in the past (and, to a great degree, in the present) have kept their sexual orientation a secret. When gay people have surfaced in the historical record, it is often because of exposure and persecution, resulting in a distortion of the historical picture. For example, Oscar Wilde is one of the few "known" gay men in nineteenth century England because of his prosecution and imprisonment as a result of his liaison with Lord Alfred Douglas (Bullough, 1979). His name and life-style have been equated with homosexuality, yet his life is undoubtedly unrepresentative. In this chapter we are therefore largely confined to a discussion of broad societal attitudes because of the furtive nature of gay life, and the relative neglect and active avoidance of the topic by past historians.

Although gay people have always been present as a significant minority, and at certain times homosexual behavior has been viewed with tolerance or even as an acceptable developmental stage for men, at no time has exclusive homosexuality been acceptable for the majority of the population. Societal views toward gay people can be roughly categorized in terms of views of homosexual behavior as tolerable, as sin, as crime, and as sickness. The first three views will be addressed in this section, the last in the section on psychology's attitudes toward homosexuality.

## Tolerant Attitudes toward Homosexuality

Before detailing the overwhelmingly negative societal attitudes toward gay people, we will focus on some examples of societal views of homosexuality as a normal variant of sexual behavior. Plato was one of the first writers to propose an explanation of the origins of homosexuality. In his *Symposium* Plato explained that people originally had four arms and four legs until the gods divided these individuals into two. The "double people" contained all male, all female, or both male and female elements, and sexual orientation could be explained in terms of "trying to find one's other half" (Bullough, 1976). Plato's attitudes are more a reflection than a cause of the tolerant attitudes of the Ancient Greeks toward gay people.

In classical Greek Society homosexual or "homoerotic" attachments were viewed as a normal and acceptable stage of development, especially for men.

> Many Greeks represented gay love as the only form of eroticism which could be lasting, pure, and truly spiritual. The origin of the concept 'Platonic Love' (which postdates Plato by centuries) was not Plato's belief that sex should be absent from gay affairs but his conviction that only love between persons of the same gender could transcend sex. The Attic lawgiver Solon considered homosexual eroticism too lofty for slaves and prohibited it to them. In the idealistic world of the Hellenistic romances, gay people figured prominently as star-crossed lovers whose passions were no less enduring or spiritual than those of their non-gay friends. . . . Even among primitive peoples some connection is often assumed between spirituality or mysticism and homosexuality. Only in comparatively recent times have homosexual feelings come to be associated with moral looseness. (Boswell, 1980, p. 27)

Women in Ancient Greek Society were not encouraged as men were to have homoerotic attachments; women of all classes led severely restricted lives. Very little solid evidence exists about female homosexuality. The scraps of information that survive about gay women take the form of the writings of Sappho, a sixth century B.C. poet from the Greek island of Lesbos (thus the term "lesbian" for gay women and "sapphic" as a description of love between women). Sappho was the head of a school for girls on Lesbos, and her poetry clearly praises love between women (Bullough, 1979). Bullough (1979) points out the fact that Sappho was married and describes the parallel to the lives of many women today who do not "come out" as gay until sometime after their marriage. One of the reasons for the paucity of information about Sappho appears to be the purposeful destruction of most of her poetry later, in the Christian era, because of the antigay attitudes of the Christian Church (Bullough, 1976).

The neglect of the topic of homosexuality throughout history, and especially the systematic erasure of evidence (e.g., Sappho's poems) about gay people's lives or positive attitudes toward homosexuality, makes the discussion of tolerant attitudes difficult. However, some evidence does exist from cross-cultural research performed on supposedly "inferior" people that helps to illuminate the topic; discussions of the sexual customs of "heathens" or "primitive peoples" are very much more candid than Western observers' descriptions of their own cultures (Bullough, 1979).

Ford and Beach (1951) published a comprehensive survey of sexual activities across cultures and concluded that no absolute norms for sexual behavior could be identified; no one culture's attitudes toward homosexuality can be viewed as representative. Even though their data probably suffered from under-reporting of homosexual activity, they found that, of the societies where data existed about attitudes toward homosexuality, fully 64 percent viewed it as normal, at least for some portion of the population (Ford & Beach, 1951). Some Native American subcultures, for example, fostered positive or tolerant attitudes toward gay men and lesbian women (Allen, 1989). "Many American Indian tribes had institutionalized homosexuality, at least of the male variety, into the role of the *berdache* (the male woman), while other primitive groups have chosen their Shamans from them" (Bullough, 1979, p. 2).

Finally, some idea can be gained of the pervasiveness of homosexual behavior across time and societies, of the neglect and active avoidance of the subject by mainstream historians, and of the contributions made by gay men and lesbian women to society, by examining the lives of eminent individuals in Western Civilization who were gay. Because the lives of prominent politicians, royalty, soldiers, artists, and writers have been open to a scrutiny not focused on the "average" person, eminent gay men and women are hardly representative. Yet their exposure by recent historical writings allows gay men and lesbian women today to gain a sense of their own history that has previously been unavailable to them (Duberman, Vicinus, & Chauncey, 1989).

Rowse's (1977) book, *Homosexuals in History,* describes in some detail the lives of famous gay male artists, among them Leonardo da Vinci and Michelangelo; gay kings and other royalty, such as Richard the Lion Heart, Henri III of France, James I of England, Frederick the Great, and Ludwig II of Bavaria; military commanders such as Alexander the Great and Julius Caesar are also mentioned; scientists such as Erasmus and Francis Bacon; musicians such as Tchaikovsky; and other eminent gay men, such as T. E. Lawrence and John Maynard Keynes. Writers proliferate among known gay men and lesbian women, largely because their written work often contains references to or illuminates their personal lives. The philosophers George Santayana and Ludwig Wittgenstein, and the writers Cocteau, Oscar Wilde, Marcel Proust, Andre Gide, Lytton Strachey, E. M. Forster, Walt Whitman, Hart Crane, Herman Melville, and W. H. Auden were all gay (Bullough, 1979; Rowse, 1977). Prominent lesbian women in history are harder to identify, and largely consist of writers and poets, for example, Virginia Woolf, Collette, Elizabeth Bowen, Vita Sackville-West, Gertrude Stein, Alice B. Toklas, Willa Cather, and May Sarton (Foster, 1956; Rule 1975). One of the few examples in the older historical record of the daily existence of two lesbian women can be obtained from the intriguing story of "The Ladies of Llangollen," two Irish noble women who lived in Wales in the eighteenth century (Martin & Lyon, 1972).

## Homosexuality as Sin

Some writers regard the Judeo-Christian religious tradition as the most significant force in determining Western attitudes about gay people (Bullough, 1979). "The church bears heavy responsibility for our present attitudes toward sex deviates and their problems, and for the severe penalties with which the law has requited them for their offenses" (Wysor, 1974, p. 65). Boswell (1980), however, refutes this stance and argues persuasively that religious beliefs merely served to justify the oppression and persecution of groups, especially gays, who are held in contempt because of personal hostility and prejudice. Regardless of the exact role, cause, or justification of intolerance, Western religious views are an important factor to explore in any discussion of gays in history.

The interpretation of scriptural references to homosexuality has been a source of ongoing controversy. Wysor (1974) has noted, from extensive research, that:

> Exactly seven references in the entire Bible (refer) to what is interpreted by some as activity involving homosexuality. Six of these seem to refer to such activity among men, and one appears to refer to women. However, these have been quite sufficient to help generate over two thousand years of condemnation and judgment against persons who express their emotional and sexual natures man to man or woman to woman. (pp. 22–23)

The earliest reference in the Bible specifically condemning homosexuality (although not using the word) can be found in Leviticus: "Thou shalt not lie with mankind, as with womankind: it is an abomination" (quoted in Bullough, 1979, p. 19). However, it is the story of Sodom that has had the greatest influence on attitudes toward gays; the term "sodomy," referring to anal intercourse, was derived from this biblical passage.

The destruction of Sodom and Gomorrah is commonly interpreted as resulting from the sin of homosexuality on the part of the townspeople. Yet many scholars have pointed out that:

> None of the biblical condemnations of homosexuality refer to Sodom, nor, more important, do any of the biblical references to Sodom explain just exactly what crimes the residents were guilty of having committed. In fact, when the Bible does spell out the sins for which Sodom (and Gomorrah, Admah, and Zeboin) were destroyed, they are listed as pride, unwillingness to aid the poor and needy,

haughtiness, and the doing of abominable things, all actions and attitudes which many other biblical peoples and cities demonstrated. Though the doing of abominable things might refer to sexual activities, their greatest sin was clearly pride, contentment, and ignoring the needy, none of which was unforgivable. (Bullough, 1979, pp. 20–21)

Bailey (1955) argued that the antihomosexual aspects of the story of Sodom were added much later than the original writing, probably as part of an anti-Greek campaign by the Jews in Palestine (homosexuality being tolerated and even adulated in Greek culture). Evidence from early Talmudic writings indicates that the Jews, although hostile to homosexuality, were by no means actively and virulently antihomosexual (Bullough, 1979). And of course there is no mention in any of the Christian scriptures of Christ saying anything about homosexuality (Bullough, 1979).

Nonetheless, various Christian theologians were virulently antigay, among them St. Paul, St. Augustine, and St. Thomas Aquinas. In the medieval period, it was Aquinas who originally proposed a separate category of "sins against nature," figuring homosexuality prominently in a list of such sins that also included bestiality, intercourse in an unnatural position, and masturbation (Bullough, 1979). Later, during the Reformation, Martin Luther and other Protestant theologians, while disagreeing with much of Catholic doctrine, continued the arguments of the early Church fathers against homosexuality (Bullough, 1979). Many of the same arguments, based on dubious scriptural interpretation, can still be heard today.

Boswell (1980), the author of the most complete scholarly analysis of religious views of homosexuality, summarized his views on the matter of scriptural justification of antigay sentiment:

In the particular case at issue, the belief that the hostility of the Christian Scriptures to homosexuality caused Western society to turn against it should not require any elaborate refutation. The very same books which are thought to condemn homosexual acts condemn hypocrisy in the most strident terms, and on greater authority; and yet Western society did not create any social taboos against hypocrisy, did not claim hypocrites were "unnatural," did not segregate them into an oppressed minority, did not enact laws punishing their sin with castration or death. No Christian State, in fact, passed laws against hypocrisy per se, despite its continual and explicit condemnation by Jesus and the church. In the very same list which has been claimed to exclude from the Kingdom of heaven those guilty of homosexual practices, the greedy are also excluded. And yet no medieval states burned the greedy at the stake. (p. 27)

Reverend Troy Perry, a gay activist, has made a thought-provoking response to those who base antigay sentiments on the Bible. He feels that such persons:

. . . are exercising considerable judgement over which Biblical teachings to accept and which to disregard. Perry often refers to Leviticus, where the recommendation is made that two men who engage in a homosexual act should be stoned. He observes that in the same book of the Bible, it is said to be wrong for a woman to wear a scarlet dress or for anyone to eat shrimp. And yet people who wear scarlet and eat shrimp continue to cite Leviticus as their authority for condemning homosexuality. (Weinberg, 1972, p. 10)

Many other examples of selective reading of the scriptures to support personal attitudes are readily available.

## Homosexuality as Crime

Religious views influenced legal codes throughout history, but laws against gays have also, in turn, influenced attitudes toward homosexuality. Modern American and European legal systems have been profoundly influenced by early Roman laws, especially the laws of Christian Rome (Bullough, 1979).

Bullough (1979) identifies the key Roman law about homosexuality affecting succeeding generations and dating from about A.D. 390, as the law prescribing the death penalty for anal intercourse. The intention of this rarely enforced law was evidently to curb male prostitution. Later this mandate became codified in the sixth-century collection of Roman laws sponsored by the Emperor Justinian, and the *corpus juris civilis* served as the foundation for the laws of the Christian Church (canon law) as well as European and English civil law (Bullough, 1979). A curious twist to the original condemnation of homosexuality was added by Justinian in the sixth century A.D., ". . . calling for repentance and confession by homosexuals, warning that God would condemn the sinner, and adding if they did not repent, society as a whole would be punished" (Bullough, 1979, p. 32). Such a warning naturally resulted in the scapegoating of gays; plagues, famines, and other disasters were commonly attributed to the "sin" of homosexuality, and gay people were sought out, castrated, and put to death in times of crisis.

Interestingly, the tendency to scapegoat gays is apparent throughout the historical record, from Ancient Roman times to today, and warrants a brief digression into the relationship between laws and social repression. Just as the emancipation of women was proposed as a cause for the decline and fall of Rome, so too was homosexuality, despite the fact that homosexual behavior was outlawed and severely punished during Roman times.

> The civilization of the Roman Empire was vitiated by homosexuality from its earliest days. A question, uncomfortable to our contemporary lax moralists, may be raised: Is not the common practice of homosexuality a fundamental debilitating factor in any civilization where it is extensively practiced, as it is a wasting spiritual disease in the individual? (Cantor, 1963, quoted in Bullough, 1979, p. 89)

In the medieval period, accusations of witchcraft were often associated with claims of homosexual activity, and heretics were also usually charged with sodomy (Bullough, 1979). The term "faggot," an epithet still employed for gay men, is derived from the term "fagot," a bundle of twigs, sticks, or branches bound together; men accused of same-sex sexual activity were often used as kindling for burning witches (Grahn, 1984).

> Stigmatizing one's enemies with charges of homosexuality is a standard practice, and some in the past have raised it to great art. In his *Divine Comedy,* Dante describes many of the inhabitants of Hell as homosexual, most of them people who happened to be his political opponents. (Bullough, 1979, p. 92)

The Knights Templar, a powerful and wealthy organization in France in the fourteenth century, were destroyed primarily through accusations of homosexuality. This practice continued and more recently was evidenced in Nazi Germany, and in the McCarthy-era Red-baiting in the 1950s in this country (Bullough, 1979). In Nazi Germany, hundreds of thousands of homosexuals or men accused of homosexuality were incarcerated in the concentration camps and brutalized with special ferocity. Many of these homosexuals remained in jail after the war because West Germany did not eliminate antigay laws from the books until 1969 (Plant, 1986). Senator Joe McCarthy, in 1950, declared homosexuality as much of an issue as Communism, and initiated a campaign to get 3,500 "sex perverts" out of jobs in the Federal Government (Bullough, 1979).

The tradition of antihomosexual laws continued from Roman through medieval times in the form of legal prescriptions against "sodomy" and "crimes against nature." Although homosexual activity was  one of the activities clearly indicted, the laws themselves were vague; sodomy referred to a variety of sexual activities, including any form of heterosexual intercourse other than the position of a woman on her back. These ambiguities of language produce problems in deciphering the historical record. For example, Havelock Ellis, an early sex researcher, equated "buggery" and "sodomy" when he happened upon these terms. "Buggery" is currently employed as a derogatory term for anal intercourse. Yet the word originally applied to members of a heretical group in the late medieval period who were often burnt at the stake for their heresy, not for homosexual activity (Bullough, 1979). Only later were the terms "buggery" and "sodomy" equated.

In the sixteenth century, at the height of the Reformation and the resulting conflicts between Protestants and Catholics, negative attitudes about sexual activity in general, and homosexuality in particular, again resulted in sanctions appearing in the civil laws. Various cases of legal action against homosexual behavior appeared in England, but often antigay hostility was not the most prominent factor. For example, in the reign of Charles the First, the Earl of Castlehaven was charged with sodomy and rape and subsequently executed. The Earl was Catholic, and anti-Catholic hostility on the part of the jurors was proposed as a more important reason for his conviction than the sodomy charges (Bullough, 1979).

The issue of homosexuality per se was revived in the seventeenth century. English legal commentators, for example, spent much time justifying antigay laws, usually drawing on Biblical sources to support their views.

> Buggery is a detestable and abominable sin, amongst Christians not to be named, committed by carnal knowledge against the ordinance of the Creator,

and order of nature, by mankind with mankind, or with brute beast, or by womankind with brute beast. (Bullough, 1979, p. 35)

This passage demonstrates the continuing view of homosexual behavior as a "crime against nature," the classification of homosexual behavior with various forms of "unnatural" heterosexual behavior, and also highlights the relative neglect of female homosexuality by the law. Women were, by definition, not considered capable of "buggery," except via anal intercourse with a man. The origins of this attitude seem to be the biblical induction against a man "spilling his seed" except to procreate. Male semen, as the key to conception, was of vital importance; consequently, the sin was viewed as relatively minor when women engaged in lesbian activity (Bullough, 1979). Undoubtedly, the low regard in which women were held also accounts for the lack of attention to lesbian activity (Deckard, 1983).

In France, with the introduction of the Napoleonic code, came the view that any consenting sexual activity by adults in private was outside the purview of the law (Bullough, 1979). "Deviant sexual acts were treated as a crime only when they implied an outrage on public decency, when there was violence or absence of consent, or when one of the parties was under age or not regarded as able to give valid consent for one reason or another" (Bullough, 1979, p. 37). Despite the legal changes, public opinion in France and all of Europe remained hostile to gays. The Napoleonic code was adopted in whole or in part by many countries in Europe and in some Latin American countries. The one notable exception was Germany, long an active antagonist of France. Germany, under Prussian leadership in the nineteenth century, maintained the harsh Prussian laws against homosexuality; the death penalty was kept on the books until the twentieth century. By the late nineteenth century only England and Germany retained their repressive laws against homosexual behavior, although the legal changes elsewhere in Europe often did not reduce the oppression experienced by gays.

Yet in every country there were some proponents of more liberal attitudes toward homosexuality. In England, for example, Jeremy Bentham, the founder of English utilitarianism, wrote extensively in the 1800s against regarding any kind of sexual activity as evil in and of itself, and outlined guidelines for judging the morality of sexual activity. His central thesis was that public opinion should not be used as the final arbiter of sexual conduct, and he argued persuasively for changing the law (Bullough, 1979). Unfortunately, his writings were never published, probably due to the attitudes of the time.

In the late 1800s in England, Parliament hurriedly passed a series of laws originally designed to protect children from sexual abuse and prostitution. The wording of these laws inadvertently resulted in the prohibition of any sexual act between adult males, even if consenting and taking place in private. Oscar Wilde, as mentioned previously, was the first victim of this new act. Friedreich Krupp (1851–1902), the scion of the powerful armaments firm in Germany, also suffered because of his exposure as a homosexual at about the same time.

Because accusations of sodomy were so difficult to prove, many gay men escaped legal prosecution. But, as in the case of Krupp, who committed suicide because of the scandal, many people were ruined by the accusation alone (Bullough, 1979).

In the United States, actual convictions for sodomy were rare, but not unknown. Laws in the United States banning homosexual activity were largely instituted on the state or local level. The first recorded conviction for homosexual activities in the colonies occurred in 1637 in Plymouth, Massachusetts; the first execution for sodomy occurred several years later (Bullough, 1979). State courts often had difficulties defining the exact meaning of "crimes against nature," and, for example, the Texas courts in the 1860s judged that sodomy could not be punishable until it was defined. Thereafter, numerous court decisions in Texas and in other states were focused on identifying the various definitions of punishable crimes under the sodomy laws, and eventually included oral intercourse and heterosexual and homosexual anal intercourse as crimes. Iowa only explicitly introduced sodomy as a crime in 1897; California finally passed laws clarifying what was meant by "crimes against nature" in 1915, including fellatio and cunnilingus as well as anal intercourse (Bullough, 1979). California clearly prohibited lesbian activity as well as gay male activity, but also included heterosexual oral-genital contacts as well. These types of laws remained on the books in California into the 1970s and can still be found in other states in the 1990s. The current status of such laws will be addressed in the next chapter.

## Psychology's Treatment of Gay People

Thomas Szasz pointed out that ". . . what was defined as sin in the moral order became sickness in the evolution of the medical model and both definitions have equally destructive effects" (1979, quoted in Woodman & Lenna, 1980, p. 3). Essentially, the fields of psychology and psychiatry merely translated religious attitudes about homosexuality into medical terms, and these negative attitudes have long biased the "scientific" investigation of gay men and women.

### Studies of Sexual "Degenerates"

The earliest social scientific studies of gay people were conducted by sociologists studying criminal behavior and "degeneracy." Many of the sociological writings of the nineteenth century attempted to explain the causes of homosexuality or, as it is sometimes still called, "sexual deviance," in an attempt to discern whether it was "curable" (Bullough, 1976; 1979).

> Most of the early students of sexual behavior believed that homoerotic behavior and other "perversions of nature" were biological in origin, stemming from such things as degeneration of genes, abnormal or incomplete embryonic development, incomplete social evolution, and disorders of the brain or sex glands or both. In order to determine what had gone wrong with these people and to be able to identify possible degenerates, there were a number of attempts to isolate their distinctive features. (Moses & Hawkins, 1982, p. 7)

Attempts to distinguish sexual deviates from "normal" people included a wide variety of what now seem amusing tests, including skull measurement and examination of distribution patterns of body hair (Moses & Hawkins, 1982). A sexual degenerate was seen, in the popular evolutionary terms of the time, as a "throw-back"—"degeneracy was a reversal of progressive evolution . . . a sexual degenerate was thus a primitive, animal-like person who might do anything" (Bullough, 1979, p. 9).

Some challenges to the prevailing views did appear. Karl Ulrichs, a gay man himself, argued that homosexual urges were inborn, and therefore "natural," and posited a pattern of development for gay people whereby "inverts" as he called them (he created the term as a positive label for gays) had the physical features of one sex but were born with the sexual instincts of the other sex. He felt that the development of a "Third sex" resulted in an "inversion" of sexual attraction for gay people, but that gays were not "degenerates" as a result (Bullough, 1979).

## Early Sex Researchers

The most important of the early social scientific and medical studies of gay people were conducted by Richard von Krafft-Ebing in the late nineteenth century (Bullough, 1979). Krafft-Ebing combined several prevailing views on "sexual inversion" and collected over 200 case studies in his famous *Psychopathis Sexualis* of "abnormal" or "pathological" individuals to support his theses. He claimed that ". . . frequent abuses of the sexual organs (masturbation) or . . . an inherited abnormal constitution of the nervous system" (Bullough, 1979, p. 11) produced a perversion of the sexual instinct and "unnatural practices" such as homosexuality. His views on homosexuality were directly related to his religious view that the purpose of sex was reproduction, and therefore any other type of sexual activity was an "unnatural practice" (Bullough, 1979). Interestingly, the term "homo-sexuality" was first introduced to an English audience by one of Krafft-Ebing's translators, Charles Gilbert Chaddock (Halperin, 1989).

> Sexual inversion, the term used most commonly in the nineteenth century, did not denote the same conceptual phenomenon as homosexuality. "Sexual inversion" referred to a broad range of deviant gender behavior, of which homosexual desire was only a logical but indistinct aspect, while "homosexuality" focused on the narrower issue of sexual object choice. (Chauncey, 1982, quoted in Halperin, 1989, p. 38)

Havelock Ellis, the other prominent sex researcher of the period, worked from a premise very different from Krafft-Ebing's. Ellis, considered the forerunner of modern sex researchers, took a sympathetic and descriptive stance in relation to his subject. Ellis regarded homosexual behavior as a part of a spectrum of sexual activity and, although not a defender of gay people, he was a sex reformer who advocated repealing laws banning sexual activity between consenting adults in private (Bullough, 1979). Various other lesser-known sexologists of the nineteenth century also promoted the view that homosexuality was not a perversion, including John Addington Symonds and Magnus Hirschfeld (Bullough, 1979).

## Freud and His Followers

Unlike his biased attitudes toward women and his subsequent negative impact on the psychology of women, Freud's views on homosexuality were fairly tolerant, and he had a mixed influence on attitudes toward gay people. Freud felt that homosexual behavior was a normal aspect of development, although he also thought that most people moved beyond it to heterosexuality in adulthood (Bullough, 1979). A letter he wrote to a distressed mother of a gay son illustrates his views:

> Homosexuality is assuredly no advantage, but it is nothing to be ashamed of, no vice, no degradation, it cannot be classified as an illness; we consider it to be a variation of the sexual function produced by certain arrest of sexual development. (Quoted in Moses & Hawkins, 1982, p. 8)

Freud demonstrated this same tolerance toward other variants of sexual behavior, but actually paid little attention to homosexuality in his writings (Bullough, 1979).

It was Freud's followers who developed his preliminary ideas on the environmental rather than biological causes of variant sexual behavior that ultimately had a harmful effect on gays. The implication of the belief that gayness is environmentally caused, and an immature stage of adult development, led inevitably to attempts on the part of analytically trained psychiatrists and psychologists to "cure" gay people. The dynamic view, focused mostly on gay men, was that homosexuality was:

> . . . a flight from incest. In the absence of a father, or in the presence of a weak one, a boy child who fell in love with his mother and sought to become her lover repressed his desire most effectively by suppressing sexual feeling toward all women. . . . The boy, suppressing his desires for the father, sought to be like the woman who accepted his father, but, unable to reconcile the incestuous sin of a father love, sought the father in other roles. (Bullough, 1979, pp. 13–14)

The psychoanalytic approach toward gays, promoted more by his followers than by Freud, has resulted in psychology's focus on curing rather than understanding gay women and men. Gay men and lesbian women were thus viewed, by different writers, as neurotic, mentally ill, ". . . egocentric, . . . lonely, unhappy, tormented, alienated, sadistic, masochistic, empty, bored, repressed, and neurotic" (Moses & Hawkins, 1982, p. 8).

Weinberg and Williams (1974), in their study of research on homosexuality, have pointed out the negative ramifications of the psychoanalytic case study approach to research on homosexuality. First, they criticized the psychoanalytic research as biased. Homosexual behavior was presumed from the start to be immature and productive of maladjustment, an assumption that was not subjected to empirical tests, at least by the psychoanalytically-oriented psychiatrists and psychologists. Because pathology was presumed, only its possible causes were investigated. Second, the gay people who have been studied within this research tradition have been patients who cannot be assumed to be representative of all gays any more than nongay psychiatric patients can be presumed to be representative of all nongays. And finally, Weinberg and Williams, (1974) criticized the literature on homosexuality as culture bound. As we have previously seen, cross-cultural studies cast grave doubt on the assumptions made about the pathology of homosexual behavior (Ford & Beach, 1951). Maladjustment among gay people is more likely caused by society's reactions to them than by inherent pathology. It was not until the Kinsey Studies (Kinsey, Pomeroy, & Martin, 1948; Kinsey, Pomeroy, Martin, & Gebhard, 1953), described in Chapter 1, that homosexual behavior was examined from a descriptive viewpoint and more representative, nonclinical samples of gay people were obtained.

## Heterosexuals versus Homosexuals

When researchers within psychology and psychiatry finally approached the issue of *whether* gay people differed from nongay people on measures of pathology (rather than *presuming* pathology), interesting results emerged. Research findings have often been directly influenced by the preexisting assumptions of the investigators.

Bieber et al. (1962), for example, in a psychoanalytic study of gay men, found that a "close-binding intimate mother" was much more common for gay than nongay men. This retrospective case study is, of course, open to methodological critique. More important, however, are the criticisms of the conclusions derived from Bieber et al.'s data. Because gay men were found to have come from homes differing in child-rearing practices, the assumption of the pathology of gay men was viewed as supported. Yet Davison (1977) noted that ". . . one cannot attach a pathogenic label to a pattern of child-rearing unless one *a priori* labels the adult behavior pattern as pathological" (p. 198). This tautological thinking on the part of the researchers, that is, presuming pathology, looking for differences in early life experiences, and then using those demonstrated differences to support the original theory of pathology, is commonplace within the research literature on homosexual behavior.

Contrary to the above example, some psychologists have conducted research on gay people from a nonpathological perspective, and their research has yielded results opposite of the views of the psychoanalysts. Evelyn Hooker (1957), in a landmark study, found no differences in mental health between gays and nongays. Hammersmith and Weinberg (1973) found positive correlations between an acceptance of a gay identity and mental health, while Weinberg (1970), and Evans (1970), and Dean and Richardson (1964) also found no evidence of pathology on the part of gay men as compared to nongay men. We will explore the current status and implications of this research in the next chapter.

# References

Abeson, A. (1976). Overview. In F. J. Weintraub, A. Abeson, J. Ballard, & M. L. LaVor (Eds.), *Public policy and the education of exceptional children.* Reston, VA: The Council for Exceptional Children.

Achenbaum, W. A. (1978). *Old age in the new land: The American experience since 1790.* Baltimore: Johns Hopkins University Press.

Allen, P. G. (1989). Lesbians in American Indian cultures (pp. 106–117). In M. B. Duberman, M. Vicinus, & G. Chauncey Jr. (Eds.) (1989). *Hidden from history: Reclaiming the gay and lesbian past.* New York: New American Library.

Amundsen, K. (1971). *The silenced majority.* Englewood Cliffs, NJ: Prentice-Hall.

Atkinson, D. R. (1980). The elderly, oppression, and social-change counseling. *Counseling and Values, 24,* 86–96.

Atkinson, J. W., & Feather N. T. (Eds.) (1966). *A theory of achievement motivation.* New York: Wiley.

Bailey, D. S. (1955). *Homosexuality and the Western Christian tradition.* London: Longman's.

Bettelheim, B. (1965). The commitment required of a woman entering a scientific profession in present-day American society. In J. A. Mattfield & C. G. Van Aken (Eds.), *Women and the scientific professions.* Cambridge, MA: M.I.T. Press.

Bieber, I., Dain, H. J., Dince, P. R., Diellech, M. G., Grand, H. G., Gandlach, R. H., Kremer, M. W., Rifkin, A. H., Wilbur, C. G., & Bieber, T. B. (1962). *Homosexuality: A psychoanalytic study.* New York: Random House.

Bird, C. (1971). *Born female.* New York: Pocket Books.

Birren, J. E. (1961). A brief history of the psychology of aging. *The Gerontologist, 1,* 69–77, 127–134.

Birren, J. E. (1964). *The psychology of aging.* Englewood Cliffs, NJ: Prentice Hall.

Birren, J. E., & Woodruff, D. S. (1973). Academic and professional training in the psychology of aging. In C. Eisdorfer & M. P. Lawton (Eds.), *The psychology of adult development and aging.* Washington, DC: American Psychological Association.

Boswell, J. (1980). *Christianity, social tolerance, and homosexuality.* Chicago: University of Chicago Press.

Bowe, F. (1978). *Handicapping America: Barriers to disabled people.* New York: Harper & Row.

Bowe, F. (1980). *Rehabilitating America.* New York: Harper & Row.

Bowe, F. (1985). Disabled adults in America: A statistical report drawn from census bureau data. Washington, DC: President's Committee on Employment of the Handicapped.

Bowe, F. (1988). Recruiting workers with disabilities. *Employment Relations Today, 15,* 107–111.

Brolin, D. E., & Gysbers, N. C. (1989). Career education for students with disabilities. *Journal of Counseling & Development, 68,* 155–159.

Bruce, M. A., & Christiansen, C. H. (1988). Advocacy in word as well as deed. *The American Journal of Occupational Therapy, 42,* 189–191.

Bullough, V. L. (1976). *Sexual variance in society and history.* New York: Wiley.

Bullough, V. L. (1979). *Homosexuality: A history.* New York: New American Library.

Chafetz, J. (1978). *Masculine, feminine, or human?* Itasca, IL: Peacock.

Childe, G. (1971). *What happened in history?* Baltimore: Penguin.

Committee on Education and Labor, U.S. House of Representatives. (1991). *Legislative history of Public Law 101-336: The Americans with Disabilities Act* (Serial No. 102-A). Washington, DC: U.S. Government Printing Office.

Covey, H. C. (1988). Historical terminology used to represent older people. *The Gerontologist, 28,* 291–297.

Cowgill, D. O., & Holmes, L. (1972). *Aging and modernization.* New York: Appleton-Century-Crofts.

Cull, J. G., & Hardy, R. E. (1972). *Vocational rehabilitation: Profession and process.* Springfield, IL: Charles C. Thomas.

Davis, A. Y. (1981). *Women, race & class.* New York: Vintage Books.

Davison, G. C. (1977). Homosexuality and the ethics of behavioral intervention. *Journal of Homosexuality, 2,* 195–204.

Dean, R. B., & Richardson, H. (1964). Analysis of MMPI profiles of 40 college-educated overt role homosexuals. *Journal of Consulting Psychology, 28,* 483–486.

Deckard, B. S. (1983). *The women's movement: Political, socioeconomic, and psychological issues* (3rd edition). New York: Harper & Row.

Driedger, D. (1989). *The last civil rights movement.* London: Hurst & Company.

Duberman, M. B., Vicinus, M., & Chauncey Jr., G. (Eds.) (1989). *Hidden from history: Reclaiming the gay and lesbian past.* New York: New American Library.

Erikson, E. H. (1968). *Identity, youth, and crisis.* New York: Norton.

Evans, R. B. (1970). Sixteen personality factor questionnaire scores of homosexual men. *Journal of Consulting and Clinical Psychology, 34,* 212–215.

Fein, R. (1992). Prescription for change. *Modern Maturity, 35* (4), 22–35.

Feinson, M. C. (1991). Reexamining some common beliefs about mental health and aging. In B. B. Hess & E. W. Markson (Eds.), *Growing old in America* (4th Edition, pp. 125–135). New Brunswick, NJ: Transaction Books.

Fenderson, D. A. (1984). Opportunities for psychologists in disability research. *American Psychologist, 39,* 524–528.

Fischer, D. H. (1978). *Growing old in America.* New York: Oxford University Press.

Flexner, E. (1975). *Century of Struggle: The woman's rights movement in the United States* (Revised Edition). Cambridge, MA: Belknap Press/Harvard University Press.

Ford, C. S., & Beach, F. A. (1951). *Patterns of sexual behavior.* New York: Harper.

Foster, J. H. (1956). *Sex variant women in literature.* New York: Vantage Press. [Reprinted: Baltimore: Diana Press, 1975]

Friedan, B. (1963). *The feminine mystique.* New York: Dell.

Funk, R. (1987). Disability rights: From cast to class in the context of civil rights. In Alan Gartner & Tom Joe (Eds.), *Images of the disabled, disabling images* (pp. 7–30). New York: Praeger Publishers.

Garrett, J. F. (1969). Historical background. In D. Malikin & H. Rusalem (Eds.), (pp. 29–38) *Vocational rehabilitation of the disabled.* New York: New York University Press.

Gatz, M., Karel, M. J., & Wolkenstein, B. (1991). Survey of providers of psychological services to older adults. *Professional Psychology: Research and Practice, 22,* 413–415.

Gilbert, L. A. (1992). Gender and counseling psychology: Current knowledge and directions for research and social action (pp. 383–416). In S. D. Brown & R. W. Lent (Eds.), *Handbook of counseling psychology.* New York: Wiley.

Gough, K. (1975). The origin of the family. In R. R. Reither (Ed.), *Toward an anthropology of women.* New York: Monthly Review Press.

Gould, S. J. (1981). *The mismeasure of man.* New York: Norton.

Grahn, J. (1984). *Another mother tongue: Gay words, gay worlds.* Boston: Beacon Press.

Grealish, C. A., & Salomone, P. R. (1986). Devaluing those with disability: Take responsibility, take action. *The Vocational Guidance Quarterly, 34,* 147–150.

Hall, G. S. (1923). *Senescence: The last half of life.* New York: D. Appleton.

Halperin, D. M. (1989). Sex before sexuality: Pederasty, politics, and power in classical Athens (pp. 37–53). In M. B. Duberman, M. Vicinus, & G. Chauncey Jr. (Eds.) (1989). *Hidden from history: Reclaiming the gay and lesbian past.* New York: New American Library.

Hammersmith, S. K., & Weinberg, M. S. (1973). Homosexual identity: Commitment, adjustment, and significant others. *Sociometry, 36,* 56–79.

Hare-Mustin, R. T. (1983). An appraisal of the relationship between women and psychotherapy: 80 years after the case of Dora. *American Psychologist, 38,* 593–601.

Harris and Associates (1987). *The ICD survey of disabled Americans: Bringing disabled Americans into the mainstream. A nationwide survey of 1,000 disabled people.* New York: Author.

Harris, L. (1975). *The myth and reality of aging in America.* Washington, DC: The National Council on Aging.

Hawkes, J., & Woolley, L. (1963). *Prehistory and the beginning of civilization.* New York: Harper & Row.

Hendricks, J., & Hendricks, C. D. (1981). *Aging in mass society: Myths and realities.* Cambridge, MA: Winthrop.

Hess, B. B. (1991). Growing old in the 1990s. In B. B. Hess & E. W. Markson (Eds.), *Growing old in America* (4th Edition, pp. 5–22). New Brunswick, NJ: Transaction Books.

Hohenshil, T. H., & Humes, C. W. (1979). Roles of counseling in ensuring the rights of the handicapped. *Personnel and Guidance Journal, 58,* 221–227.

Hooker, E. (1957). The adjustment of the male homosexual. *Journal of Projective Techniques, 21,* 18–31.

Hunter College Women's Studies Collective (1983). *Women's realities, women's choices: An introduction to women's studies.* New York: Oxford University Press.

Hunter, J. (1976). Images of women. *Journal of Social Issues, 32,* 7–17.

Karr, A. R. (1990, May 23). Disabled-rights bill inspires hopes, fears. *Wall Street Journal,* pp. B1, B2.

Kebric, R. B. (1988). Old age, the ancient military, and Alexander's army: Positive examples for a graying American. *The Gerontologist, 28,* 298–302.

Kent, K. L. (1990). Elders and community mental health. *Generations, 14,* (1), 19–21.

Kinsey, A. C., Pomeroy, W. B., Martin, C. E. (1948). *Sexual behavior in the human male.* Philadelphia: Saunders.

Kinsey, A. C., Pomeroy, W. B., & Martin, C. E., & Gebhard, P. H. (1953). *Sexual behavior in the human female.* Philadelphia: Saunders.

Kunkel, M. A., & Williams, C. (1991). Age and expectations about counseling: Two methodological perspectives. *Journal of Counseling & Development, 70,* 314–320.

Laski, F. (1978, May). *Legal strategies to secure entitlement to services for severely handicapped persons.* Paper presented at the Conference on Habilitation of Severely Handicapped Adults, Public Interest Law Center, Philadelphia, PA.

Leavitt, R. R. (1971). Women in other cultures. In V. Gornick & B. K. Morgan (Eds.), *Woman in Sexist Society* (pp. 393–427). New York: New American Library.

Levin, J., & Levin, W. C. (1980). *Ageism: Prejudice and discrimination against the elderly.* Belmont, CA: Wadsworth.

Lewin, T. (1988, March 13). Rights movement for disabled seen. *Santa Barbara News-Press,* p. 3.

Mardoyan, J. L., & Weis, D. M. (1981). The efficacy of group counseling with older adults. *Personnel and Guidance Journal, 60,* 161–163.

Margolis, R. J. (1990). *Risking old age in America.* Boulder, CO: Westview Press.

Martin, D., & Lyon, P. (1972). *Lesbian/woman.* New York: Bantam.

Martin, M. K., & Voorhies, B. (1975). *Female of the Species.* New York: Columbia University Press.

May, V. R., & Vieceli, L. (1983). Barriers to placement: Strategies and resolution. *Journal of Rehabilitation, 49* (3), 43–46.

McClelland, D. C., Atkinson, J. W., Clark, R. A., & Lowell, E. L. (1953). *The achievement motive.* New York: Appleton-Century-Crofts.

Mead, M. (1974). On Freud's view of female psychology. In J. Strouse, (Ed.), *Women and analysis.* New York: Grossman.

Mithaug, D. E. (1979). Negative employer attitudes toward hiring the handicapped: Fact or fiction? *Journal of Contemporary Business, 8*(4), 19–26.

Moses, A. E., & Hawkins, R. O. (1982). *Counseling lesbian women and gay men.* St. Louis: Mosby.

Moses, S. (1992). More clinicians needed to help a graying America. *Monitor, 23*(8), 34.

Myers, J. E. (1989). *Infusing gerontological counseling into counselor preparation: Curriculum guide.* Alexandria, VA: American Association for Counseling and Development.

Myers, J. E. (1992). Competencies, credentialing, and standards for gerontological counselors: Implications for counselor education. *Counselor Education and Supervision, 32,* 34–42.

Nathanson, R. B. (1979). Counseling persons with disabilities: Are the feelings, thoughts and behaviors of helping professionals helpful? *Personnel and Guidance Journal, 58,* 233–237.

Nelson, M. (1979). Why witches were women. In J. Freeman (Ed.), *Women: A feminist perspective* (pp. 451–468). (2nd Edition). Palo Alto, CA: Mayfield.

Nelson, R. M. (1989). Ethics and the physically disabled. In B. W. Heller, L. M. Flohr, & L. S. Zegans (Eds.), *Psychosocial interventions with physically disabled persons* (pp. 222–230). New Brunswick, NJ: Rutgers University Press.

Nielsen, J. (1978). *Sex in society: Perspectives on stratification.* Belmont, CA: Wadsworth.

Obermann, C. E. (1965). *A history of vocational rehabilitation in America.* Minneapolis: Denison.

Perlman, L. G., & Kirk, F. S. (1991). Key disability and rehabilitation legislation. *Journal of Applied Rehabilitation Counseling, 22,* 21–27.

Piggrem, G. W., & Schmidt, L. D. (1982). Counseling the elderly. *Counseling and Human Development, 14,*(20), 1–12.

Plant, R. (1986). *The pink triangle: The Nazi war against homosexuals.* New York: New Republic.

Rich, B. M., & Baum, M. (1984). *The aging: A guide to public policy.* Pittsburgh: University of Pittsburgh Press.

Rigler, A. L. (1992). Disability issues stance tests our ethical integrity. *APA Monitor, 23*(11), 4.

Roberts, E. V. (1989). A history of the independent living movement: A founder's perspective. In B. W. Heller, L. M. Flohr, & L. S. Zegans (Eds.), *Psychosocial interventions with physically disabled persons* (pp. 231–244). New Brunswick, NJ: Rutgers University Press.

Rohrbaugh, J. B. (1979). *Women: Psychology's puzzle.* New York: Basic Books.

Rowse, A. L. (1977). *Homosexuals in history.* New York: Carroll & Graf.

Rubin, S. E., & Roessler, R. T. (1978). *Foundations of the vocational rehabilitation process.* Baltimore: University Park Press.

Rule, J. (1975). *Lesbian images.* New York: Doubleday.

Salisbury, H. (1975). Counseling the elderly: A neglected area in counselor education and supervision. *Counselor Education and Supervision, 14,* 237–238.

Satcher, J., & Hendren, G. R. (1991). Acceptance of the Americans with Disabilities Act of 1990 by persons preparing to enter the business field. *Journal of Applied Rehabilitation Counseling, 22* (2), 15–18.

Schaffer, K. F. (1981). *Sex roles and human behavior.* Cambridge, MA: Winthrop.

Schaie, K. W. (1993). Ageist language in psychological research. *American Psychologist, 48,* 49–51.

Schulenburg, J. T. (1979). Clio's European daughters: Myopic modes of perception. In J. A. Sherman & E. T. Beck (Eds.), *The prism of sex: Essays in the sociology of knowledge* (pp. 33–54). Madison, WI: University of Wisconsin Press.

Scotch, R. K. (1984). *From good will to civil rights.* Philadelphia: Temple University Press.

Sherif, C. W. (1979). Bias in psychology. In J. A. Sherman & E. T. Beck (Eds.), *The prism of sex* (pp. 93–133). Madison, WI: University of Wisconsin Press.

Shields, S. (1975). Functionalism, Darwinism, and the psychology of women: A study in social myth. *American Psychologist, 30,* 739–754.

Simmons, L. W. (1945). *The role of the aged in primitive society.* New Haven: Yale University Press.

Simonton, D. K. (1990). Creativity in the later years: Optimistic prospects for achievement. *The Gerontologist, 30,* 626–631.

U.S. Department of Education (1988). *Summary of Existing Legislation Affecting Persons with Disabilities* (Publication No. E-88-22014). Washington, DC: U.S. Department of Education, Clearinghouse on the Handicapped.

Task force on psychology and the handicapped (1984). Final report of the task force on psychology and the handicapped. *American Psychologist, 39,* 545–550.

Tomes, H. (March, 1992). Disabilities are major public interest issue. *APA Monitor.*

Unger, R. K. (1979). Toward a redefinition of sex and gender. *American Psychologist, 34,* 1085–1094.

United States Bureau of the Census. (1987). Unpublished tables from March 1987 Current Population Survey. In *Chartbook on disability in the United States.* Washington, DC: National Institute on Disability and Rehabilitation Research.

Weinberg, G. (1972). *Society and the healthy homosexual.* New York: Anchor.

Weinberg, M. S. (1970). *The male homosexual: Age-related variations in social and psychological characteristics.* Social Problems, 17, 527–537.

Weinberg, M. S., & Williams, C. J. (1974). *Male homosexuals: Their problems and adaptations.* New York: Oxford University Press.

Weisstein, N. (1971). Psychology constructs the female, or the fantasy life of the male psychologist. In V. Gornick & B. K. Moran (Eds.), *Woman in sexist society* (pp. 207–224). New York: New American Library.

Woodman, N. J., & Lenna, H. R. (1980). *Counseling with gay men and women.* San Francisco: Jossey-Bass.

Woolf, V. (1957). *A room of one's own.* New York: Harcourt, Brace Jovanovich. (Original work published 1929).

Wysor, B. (1974). *The lesbian myth.* New York: Random House.

Youngstrom, N. (1992). ADA is super advocate for those with disabilities. *Monitor, 23*(7), 26.

Zadny, J. J. (1979). Planning for job placement. In D. Vandergoot and J. D. Worrall (Eds.), *Placement in rehabilitation: A career development perspective.* Baltimore, MD: University Park Press.

Zadny, J. J., & James, L. F. (1978). A survey of job search patterns among state vocational rehabilitation clients. *Rehabilitation Counseling Bulletin, 22,* 60–65.

Zadny, J. J., & James, L. F. (1979). The problem with placement. *Rehabilitation Counseling Bulletin, 22,* 439–442.

# 3
# Evidence of Continuing Discrimination

In this chapter we examine the evidence of continuing discrimination against persons with disabilities, elderly people, gay people, and women. Discrimination against these groups continues to take many forms, ranging from negative stereotypes to physical violence.

## Persons with Disabilities

Despite recent legislation on their behalf, discrimination against people with disabilities persists in social, economic, and environmental forms and abuses.

### Social Discrimination

As with all minority groups, discrimination against persons with disabilities has its roots in negative attitudes and stereotypes. Vargo (1989) reviewed the research on attitudes of the general public toward persons with disabilities and concluded that: (a) these attitudes are generally negative; (b) some cultures are more accepting of persons with disabilities than others (in general, highly industrialized countries are more accepting than agrarian societies); and (c) in cultures where low social status is assigned to being female, women with disabilities must overcome more serious obstacles than men with disabilities. He also pointed to the Bible and the media as sources of negative attitude formation. With respect to the Bible, Vargo cited passages in both the Old and New Testaments implying that physical and mental disorders are punishments inflicted by God for not complying with religious laws. With respect to the media, he suggested that "disability as characterized in drama, literature, and movies is nearly always clothed in metaphor and that the metaphor most often used is symbolic of . . . 'monstrosity' " (Vargo, 1989, p. 283).

Livneh (1982) developed a system of 12 categories for classifying sources of negative attitudes toward persons with disabilities. According to Livneh (1982) people form negative attitudes due to sociocultural conditioning, childhood influences, psychodynamic mechanisms, perceptions of disabilities as punishment, image, marginality associated with a minority group, symbolic parallelism between disability and death, prejudicial-provoking behaviors by people with disabilities, disability-related factors (levels of functionality severity), visibility, and observer-related factors (sex, age, ethnocentrism, authoritarianism). He concludes that attempts by researchers and clinicians to change negative attitudes toward people with disabilities have been unsuccessful because they have not addressed the multifarious and long-term nature of their source.

Mental health professionals are not immune from discrimination against people with disabilities. Several studies have found that counselors have significant biases against individuals with a variety of disabling conditions (Schofield & Kunce, 1971; Wicas & Carluccio, 1971). There is also some evidence that counselors who hold negative attitudes toward people with disabilities are, in general, less effective counselors than those who perceive people with disabilities more favorably (Cook, Kunce, & Getsinger, 1976).

A national survey cited by Bowe (1980) suggests most people support special efforts for people with disabilities, at least in the abstract. When asked if they supported special efforts (e.g., accessibility modifications, affirmative action in employment) on behalf of people with disabilities, 79 percent of the respondents answered yes. This figure was almost double the percentage responding affirmatively for special efforts on behalf of women (47%) and ethnic minorities (44%).

Yet social discrimination continues to be problematic for people with disabilities, suggesting Americans support a special effort for people with disabilities as long as it is in the abstract and they are not directly affected by it. Neighborhood resistance to the opening of group homes for the mentally retarded or mentally ill is a prime example of social discrimination. Bowe (1980) cites lack of knowledge about disabilities, stereotyping, and unnecessary selection requirements (for employment, membership, etc.) as other examples of social discrimination. Formal and informal labeling of people with mental disabilities is still another form of social discrimination (Lombana, 1982). Further, there is evidence that a social-acceptability hierarchy exists for disabilities, with the more visible and functionally disabling conditions judged to be the least acceptable (Bruce & Christiansen, 1988).

Unfortunately, people with disabilities are subject to the same sources of attitude formation as are people who have no disabilities. As a result, some people with disabilities accept a number of intrapersonal and interpersonal misconceptions that seriously hamper their social and emotional development (Vargo, 1989). According to Vargo (1987), these misconceptions include the following:

1. My disability is a punishment.
2. All of my difficulties are caused by my disability.
3. Asking for help is a sign of personal weakness.
4. It is impossible for a disabled person to be happy.
5. I'm of less value as a person because I'm not able-bodied.

6. No one can possibly understand how I feel.
7. I can't continue to live like this.
8. I can't do things the way I used to, so why do anything at all?
9. I could never succeed in anything.
10. Life can't possibly be fulfilling for me. (p. 284)

The effect of stereotypes that significant others hold of children with disabilities can be particularly pernicious and, combined with other factors, can contribute to a vicious cycle:

> A physical appearance that may alter initial reactions to the child, data on aptitudes and achievement that are not accurate, the assignment of benign academic tasks by those who plan for and work with the student, and the student's own sensitivity to his or her lack of acceptance and success may interact to produce behavior and performance that confirm the doubts of both the student and those who are closest to him or her. (Williams & Lair, 1991, p. 196)

## Economic Discrimination

There is very clear evidence of a relationship between disability and unemployment, low earnings, and poverty. The unemployment rate is somewhat deceiving because it does not include those people who have been out of work so long that they have given up looking for a job (according to Bowe, 1980, most people with disabilities have given up looking for jobs because they cannot obtain the education needed for employment, secure transportation to and from work, or obtain access to places of work). For both men and women ages 16 to 64 with a work disability, the unemployment rate in 1988 was 14.2 percent; for men with no work disability the unemployment rate was 6.2 percent and for women with no work disability the comparable figure was 5.2 percent. More telling figures are the data on fulltime employment by work disability status. Only 23.4 percent of the men and 13.1 percent of the women with a work disability were employed full time in 1988: for men and women with no work disability the respective figures were 74.8 percent and 47.1 percent (U.S. Bureau of the Census, 1989). Similarly, Harris and Associates (1986) found in a survey of 1000 people with disabilities that 66 percent were unemployed but wanted to work. The effect of a work disability on fulltime employment is even more severe for those individuals who are members of an ethnic minority group. Only 10.8 percent of Black persons with a work disability and 13.9 percent of those of Hispanic origin were employed fulltime in 1988 compared to 26.2 percent of White persons with a work disability.

According to Satcher and Hendren (1991), high unemployment rates among persons with disabilities is a function of the negative attitudes that employers have about them. For example, employers frequently believe that persons with disabilities are accident-prone and will increase worker's compensation costs, are frequently absent from work, have low rates of productivity, and will not relate well with co-workers (Freedman & Keller, 1981).

Although 26 states and the District of Columbia had laws barring discrimination against people with disabilities by employers prior to the recent enactment of the ADA of 1990 (as did the federal government for employers receiving federal funds), discrimination still occurred (LaFraniere, 1985). Discrimination against persons with disability also occurred despite Section 503 of the Rehabilitation Act of 1973, which has for the past 20 years required that any employer doing business with the federal government to take affirmative action to hire persons with disabilities.

Employers have been particularly reluctant to make adjustments to their work settings to accommodate people with disabilities because they assume it will be too expensive. By the mid-1980s, a legal precedent had been set requiring that an employer must make reasonable adjustments to minimize such dangers (Moskowitz, 1985). More recently, the ADA requires that "employers with more than 15 employees must make reasonable accommodation to the known limitations of qualified persons with disabilities and to ensure that their hiring practices are nondiscriminatory" (Satcher & Hendren, 1991). Karr (1990) cites the experiences of companies already in compliance with the disabilities-access rule as evidence that concerns about the cost of accommodating people with disabilities is overblown; a study at Syracuse University found that when access features are designed into new construction they add less than 1 percent, of average, to the total cost.

Although the effect of the ADA remains to be seen, as recently as the late 1980s people with disabilities have found it difficult to find employment. It remains to be seen if the Americans with Disabilities Act of 1990, which extends nondiscrimination against persons with disabilities to employment in the private sector, can have an impact on these employment statistics.

Persons with disabilities who are able to secure employment earn average incomes that are considerably lower than average incomes for persons with no work disability. The average annual income in 1987 for men with a work disability was $15,497 compared to $24,095 for men with no work disability. For women with disabilities the average annual income in 1987 was $8,075 compared to $13,000 for women with no work disability (U.S. Bureau of the Census, 1989). As might be expected due to the effects of double oppression, the mean earnings for Black persons with a work disability ($11,876) and persons of Hispanic origin who have a work disability ($12,213) are lower than White persons with a work disability ($15,869).

In addition to lowering labor force activity and earnings, the existence of a work disability also significantly decreases the chances of being covered by an employer-provided health plan. Only 52.1 percent of men with a work disability were covered by employer-provided health insurance in 1987, compared to 65.9 percent of men with no health disability. Similar figures for women were 40.1 percent and 52.6 percent, respectively.

Due to the low numbers of people with work disabilities who are employed and the low salaries for those who have secured employment, many people with work disabilities live on incomes below or near the poverty level. According to the U.S. Bureau of the Census (1992), 23.1 percent of all men and 32.5 percent of all women with a work disability between the ages of 16 and 64 lived below the poverty level in 1991. For persons with a severe disability, the comparable figures are 29.7 percent and 40.5 percent, respectively. These figures compared to 13.9 percent of all women and 9.4 percent of all men between 16 and 64 in the general population. According to Bowe (1980), almost half (47 percent) of the population with severe disabilities under age 35 receive public income-maintenance funds; for those with severe disabilities aged 55–64, the proportion is 71 percent (Bowe, 1980).

Bowe (1980) also cites evidence from Social Security Administration Surveys in 1965 and 1971 that indicate a worsening of the economic situation for people with disabilities. He points out, for example, that a smaller proportion of people with disabilities were employed in 1971 than in 1965.

The problems of economic discrimination are compounded for ethnic minorities with disabilities. For example, American Indian people with disabilities who live on reservations, state and federal agencies facing tight budgets often attempt to shift the responsibility for funding programs away from themselves. According to Joe (1988), "these jurisdictional questions and misinformation from service providers has and continues to plague the rights and accessibility to resources by disabled people in many American Indian communities" (p. 254). She points out that in addition to state-federal jurisdictional problems, American Indians with disabilities often do not receive mandated services due to inadequate financial resources, lack of culturally relevant programs, lack of public transportation, and the remoteness and isolation of most Indian reservations. Small reservations are particularly affected by these barriers to services. Also, although children with moderate or mild disabilities have profited from the passage of PL 94-142, American Indian adults with disabilities and children with severe or multiple disabilities seldom receive any services unless they are institutionalized in state hospitals or nursing homes, often far from their families and cultural support systems (Joe, 1988).

## Environmental Discrimination

> Some of the more glaring reflection of negative societal attitudes are seen in architectural designs. . . . Inaccessible housing, street corners without curb cuts, poor transportation services, signs and signals yielding only visual or only audio cues, and architectural designs that thwart an individual's full appreciation of societal membership in effect say to the individual with a disability: "you don't count," "you're not important to this society," and "you have little value." (Grealish & Salomone, 1986, p. 148)

In every community there is evidence of continuing environmental discrimination (in the form of environmental barriers) against people with disabilities. Physical barriers exist in the form of rampless entry ways, steep flights of stairs, narrow or revolving doors, drinking fountains, elevator controls, and telephones that are too high, and corridors that are too narrow. Communication barriers exist in the form of audio-only announcements (inaccessible to the deaf) and visual-only announcements (inaccessible to the blind) in stores, hotels, transportation centers, employment settings, and public buildings. Nor are personnel in these settings trained to assist deaf and blind people. Transportation barriers exist in subway, train, and bus systems that are inaccessible to the orthopedically handicapped.

Although Section 504 of the Rehabilitation Act of 1973 requires the removal of architectural, communication, and transportation barriers that affect people with disabilities in federal agencies and agencies supported by federal money, most of the mandated changes have yet to be achieved. Although enacted in 1973, the DHEW regulations for the Rehabilitation Act were not released until 1977. Because of the huge price tag alleged to be involved in making these accommodations, many state and local agencies have dragged their feet in implementing the regulations. Further, the regulations only apply to those agencies receiving assistance from the federal government (Bowe, 1980).

It is likely to be a long time before the accessibility mandates of the ADA will have an impact on some parts of the country, particularly on rural areas (Rural disabled, 1992). Given the economic conditions of recent years, many small town governments and businesses are unwilling to make such changes as replacing street corner curbs with ramps, installing elevators, and providing wheel-chair accessible buses. Also, the ADA requires only that existing services be brought into compliance with the law. Areas in which no public transportation is provided are not required to develop a new transportation service for people with disabilities.

## Abuse

Ammerman, Van Hasselt, and Hersen (1988) reviewed the child abuse literature and found that children with disabilities were overrepresented among those physically abused. In addition to overrepresentation of children with disabilities among those who are abused, the Ammerman et al. (1988) review revealed an alarmingly high incidence rate of abuse among children with disabilities. They identified the following as characteristics of children with disabilities commonly associated with abuse: (a) prematurity, low birthweight, and medical complications; (b) disruption of mother-infant attachment; (c) parental stress; and (d) vulnerability in infancy. According to Blatt and Brown (1986), the abuse of children with disabilities in institutional settings is almost four times as high as it is in the community.

Persons with disabilities are also vulnerable to sexual abuse. Sullivan, Vernon, and Scanlan (1987) reviewed four studies of sexual abuse of children with a hearing disability and found that 54 percent of the boys and 50 percent of the girls had been sexually abused. Another study reported that an astonishing 96 percent of children with hearing impairments and other disabilities being evaluated at Boys Town's Center for Abused Handicapped

Children had been sexually abused (Brookhouser, Sullivan, Scanlan, & Garbarino, 1986). Davis (1989) found that 75 percent to 80 percent of mentally retarded women living in various community residences had been sexually assaulted. The developmentally disabled are particularly vulnerable; the California Department of Developmental services, office of Human Rights, estimates that 50 percent to 90 percent of persons with developmental disabilities are sexually abused (Crossmaker, 1991). A survey of 245 women with disabilities revealed that 40 percent had experienced some form of abuse, including 12 percent who had been raped (Ridington, 1989). Mental illness is a disability that puts people at high risk for abuse. The U.S. Senate Subcommittee on the Handicapped (1985) examined 31 facilities for people with mental disabilities and found numerous cases of rape and sexual abuse and sexual harassment of patients by staff and other patients. These and other data clearly suggest that both children and adults with disabilities are at greater risk of sexual abuse and sexual assault than are those without disabilities (Sobsey & Mansell, 1990). Furthermore, Sobsey and Varnhagen (1991) concluded after reviewing previous research and conducting their own survey that "even when abuse is reported, police, courts, and social agencies are often unwilling to pursue charges when the victim is disabled" (p. 208).

When combined with the review that follows regarding abuse of elders, many of whom are persons with disabilities, these data provide strong documentation that persons with disabilities are at high risk of physical, sexual, and emotional abuse.

# Elders

## Social Discrimination

People continue to hold negative stereotypes about elders that are used to justify other forms of discrimination (e.g., if they are unproductive and inflexible they should be forced to retire). A meta-analysis by Kite and Johnson (1988) of studies through 1985 revealed that attitudes toward older people were more negative than those toward younger people. Despite the increased publicity and concern over the rights of elders, Schwalb and Sedlacek (1990) surveyed college students in 1979 and again in 1988 and found that "the overall attitudes of college students toward older people were generally negative in both the 1979 and 1988 samples" (p. 129). They concluded that college students' attitudes toward older people do not seem to be changing. Richman (1977) analyzed the content of 100 jokes about the elderly and 160 jokes about children and found that 66 percent of the former were negative while over 70 percent of the latter were positive. In a Louis Harris (1975) poll, adult Americans typically perceived persons over age 65 as not very sexually active, not very open-minded and adaptable, not very useful members of their community, and not very bright and alert.

Despite recent research that indicates elders are able to function physically and mentally longer and with much more capability than the pre World War II research suggested, negative stereotypes persist among both the lay public and mental health professions. Butler (1979) identifies a number of myths and stereotypes of unproductivity, disengagement, inflexibility, and senility, all of which he identified as myths since they lack support from research findings. Levin and Levin (1980) reviewed two types of studies related to the functioning of elderly people. One set of studies examines the perceptions various age groups (children, college undergraduates, adults, the elderly) have of the sexual activity, job performance, intelligence, resistance to change, and disengagement from society of elderly persons. The other set of studies examined survey and behavioral indices of elderly functioning in these areas. In each area the second set of studies refuted the stereotypes found in the first set. They concluded from this analysis that images of the aged are "based more on myth than reality, more on fiction than on fact" (p. 79) but that negative stereotypes are "passed from generation to generation through the process of socialization much like other cultural phenomena" (p. 85). Similarly, Hess (1980), reviewed hundreds of research reports and concluded that "many negative stereotypes are clearly not supported by the research data" (p. 532).

Nowhere are stereotypes of elders more extreme than in the arena of sexuality. Sexual stereotypes of the elderly include the perception that they are sexless, that their expressions of passion are gross and disgusting, that they are in danger of a heart attack when they engage in sex, and that sexually active elders are "dirty" old men and women. These stereotypes in turn impact how friends, relatives, and care-providers treat elders. Friends and relatives often directly and indirectly discourage elderly people from talking about sex or engaging in sexual behavior. According to Brown (1989), "nursing homes and institutions deny the elderly their rights to sexual relationships by segregating men from women, depriving them of the privacy necessary for intimacy, labeling sexual behavior as deviant and administering drugs as well as social pressure to prevent it" (p. 76).

Social discrimination against elders is not restricted to negative attitudes; it can also be observed in the form of overt behavior, as in the case of housing discrimination. Civic organizations and informal neighborhood groups often oppose housing developments for the elderly, ostensibly because they will alter the character of the community (Mitric, 1985) or detract from property value (McAllister, 1985).

Mental health practitioners also hold stereotypes of elders that cause them to discriminate against older clients with respect to the type of treatment they provide. According to Blank (1974), psychotherapy is the treatment of choice with depressed elders yet "There are such negative feelings about the value of psychotherapy for aged persons that it is seldom used" (p. 148). Cohen (1990) points out that even the language of geriatric advocates tends to portray elders with disabilities as incapable of exercising control over their lives. Cohen (1990) surveyed numerous recent issues of the *Gerontologist, Generations,* and federal monographs, and came up with the following terms used by mental health workers: "Elderly-at-risk, frail elderly, impaired elderly, institutionalized elderly, homebound elderly, chair-bound elderly, bedridden elderly, wheelchairbound elderly, vulnerable elderly, dependent elderly, patient (rather than consumer), and 'the Alzheimer' (referring to the person who has the disease) (p. 14). He argues that terms like these rob older persons with disabilities of their motivation to assert themselves. Thus, even well intentioned advocates may be contributing to a new ageism that restricts the capability of elders.

## Economic Discrimination

Paradoxically, elders are currently among the most affluent and, at the same time, most poverty-stricken groups in the United States. Due to rising salaries, the success of private and public pension plans, and the inflation of property values over the past five decades, many recent retirees are enjoying a higher standard of living than at any time in the history of the United States. Hess (1991) credits the decision by Congress to link changes in Social Security benefits to inflation and the introduction of health insurance for the elderly as reasons why "the incidence of poverty among America's aged has dropped from over one in three before 1960 to slightly under the national rate of 14 percent today" (p. 8). As a group, the median income for people over 65 rose 21 percent in inflation-adjusted dollars during the 1980s compared to 6 percent for all Americans.

These figures, plus the rapidly rising Medicare costs, have created a new stereotype of elders as "fat cats living the good life at the expense of everybody else" (Lewis, 1992b, p. 14). As a result, entitlements for the elderly are being blamed for the growing federal deficit, when "the major culprits are system-wide escalation of health costs and the 1981 tax cut" (New AARP study, 1992, p. 3). Furthermore, the rising federal deficit and the shrinking funds for programs that benefit children and adolescents are being blamed on the mandated increases in Social Security.

> Critics of Social Security and Medicare blamed the deteriorating condition of children and families on the "graying of the federal budget" (more than half of all federal domestic goes to the elderly) and raised the specter of intergenerational warfare between young and old. . . . The generational equity campaign continues to portray the elderly as selfish, politically powerful, and potentially dangerous. (Cole, 1991)

However, the view of elders as budgetary piranhas ignores the fact that the most costly entitlement programs are largely self-funded; many current retirees have been paying into Social Security since its inception. As Hess (1991) points out:

> It should also be realized that before the 1980s, the Social Security Trust Funds had never before been included in the regular federal budget, where they now serve to make the U.S. budget deficit appear *smaller* than it actually is. . . . If . . . one takes only the programs funded from general revenues (that is,

excluding Medicare and Social Security), the elderly are not overly coddled, receiving a share of federal outlays considerably lower than their representation in the total population. The fact that assistance for poor children and their families is vastly under funded is an issue that should be addressed directly on its own merits and not made into a zero-sum situation in which the benefits available to one group must come at the cost of reducing programs for other needy populations. (p. 8)

The economic gains made by a minority of recently retired elderly are in direct contrast to the experiences of many older persons, particularly single women, ethnic minorities, the seriously ill, and the "old old" (people over 85). Only 15.5 percent (3.2 million) of elderly households had annual incomes in 1990 that exceeded $40,000. By comparison, 28 percent (5.7 million) had incomes under $10,000 a year and 3.7 million lived below the poverty level in 1990. Another 8.1 million have incomes no more than twice the poverty rate. The poverty and low income figures are particularly disturbing for women and ethnic minorities. Two million elderly women living alone (more that one in four) had incomes below the poverty level and seven out of ten women aged 65 or older had incomes under $10,000 in 1988 (Hess, 1991). For older Hispanic and African American women, the poverty rate was 49 percent and 60 percent, respectively (Lewis, 1992b).

Furthermore, the federal figures on the elderly and poverty are misleading in that figures to compute the poverty level are adjusted by age.

> Because the elderly are considered to be relatively Spartan food consumers, the line for elderly poverty has been set below that for other age groups. Depending on which groups are being compared, the difference can run as high as 11 percent. To put it another way, it is possible for someone to live *under* the poverty line at age 64 and *over* it the following year, even if that person's income has not increased one cent beyond the cost-of-living index. (Margolis, 1990, p. 11)

Notwithstanding the large number of elderly below or near the poverty level, the recent "fat cat" image of older people has been used as a rationale for proposals to reduce or eliminate entitlement programs that benefit elders. Americans for Generational Equality (AGE) was formed in 1985 to "promote greater public understanding of problems arising from the aging of the U.S. population and to foster increased public support for policies that will serve the economic interest of next century's elderly" (Gerber et al., 1989). The organization credits the entitlements received by the current generation for the ballooning federal deficit and argues that resources should be held in reserve for the future generation of old. Thomasma (1989) points out that as the numbers of older people increase over the next 50 years, the United States will face a "tremendous economic and political crisis in providing health care and long-term care for the elderly" (p. 170). According to Cole (1991), the competition for limited federal resources has raised a number of moral questions, some of which could serve as the basis of future ageist social policies:

> Is it fair to spend such a large proportion of our health expenditures on the dying elderly? Do these expenditures actually benefit them? Should we be devoting so

much of our biomedical research and technology to the diseases of aging? Questions of distributive justice inevitably lead to questions of social meaning. How do we justify funds spent on a population that is not economically productive? What "good" are old people anyway? (p. 27)

Ageist social policies are being proposed that basically would ration available resources by age; the impact of these proposals would include "a lack of respect for the aged in return for all they have done for the younger generations, the creation of institutional dumping grounds for elderly, unjust decision-making for incompetent persons, and cutting off care for many elderly persons who could profit from it and return to a norm life" (Thomasma, 1989, p. 170). Proposals that seek to allocate health care on the basis of age are a form of economic discrimination that will reinforce (and be reinforced by) social discrimination against the elderly.

In addition to misperceptions that elders garner a disproportionate share of the country's wealth, concerns are being raised about their self-centered political activities. Rosenbaum and Button (1989) describe three hypotheses that have been raised about the impact of the growing elderly population on the politics of Sunbelt states. The "gray participation" hypothesis assumes that as the aging population increase, their political activism will increase. The "gray power" hypothesis assumes that the retirement community will form a voting bloc that supports services to the elderly. And the "gray peril" hypothesis assumes that elders will resist local government taxing and spending programs other than those that provide immediate benefit to the elderly. In their survey of Florida's local public officials, however, Rosenbaum and Button (1989) found that although older persons are active in Florida's local politics, the retirement population is "far less organized and active in local political advocacy on its own behalf than either the gray power or gray peril hypotheses would assume" (p. 305).

Elders are often the first to lose their jobs in economic downswings. Although recent federal legislation increased the mandatory retirement age from 65 to 70, it did not eliminate occupational discrimination for those 70 and above and people 65 to 70 are still pushed into retirement by unchallenging work (particularly among blue collar jobs), company pressure, self-fulfilling prophecy, and economic incentives provided, ironically, by the government (Levin & Levin, 1980). Older workers are often given the choice to retire early or take a drop in rank and pay. According to a survey by the Equal Employment Opportunity Commission Survey in 1983, most older people don't realize they can press age discrimination complaints. An increasing number do, however. In 1983, 21,000 age discrimination suits were filed, up four-fold from 1979 (Morse, 1985).

Once they lose their jobs, the elderly and older workers find it difficult to obtain new employment. A survey by the Bureau of the Census found 5.1 million workers displaced in 1979, 750,000 of whom were between 55 and 64. Five years later in 1984 almost one-third of these 750,000 had still not found jobs, the highest rate of continued displacement for any age group (Rajeswary, 1985). Without jobs, many elderly have to rely on Social Security benefits for their primary source of income. For a majority of the elderly population, Social Security benefits account for more than half of their income. Further, one in five of all elderly (two in five Blacks) receive 90 percent or more of their income from Social Security.

Unemployment, low income, and poverty figures are most dismal for women and ethnic minorities as subgroups of the elderly population. Elderly living alone (generally women) are among the very poor. According to the Council of Economic Advisers (Seaberry, 1985), women constituted 71.1 percent of poor elders but only 59.1 percent of the total elderly population. The oldest of the elderly are also the poorest because they earned less than more recent retirees and often have used their savings for costly medical expenses, etc. In 1981 the poverty rates varied from 6 percent for White males living in families to 61 percent for Black females living alone (U.S. Bureau of the Census, 1983b).

Although some elderly people retired in the 1980s and early 1990s with excellent pension plans that help account for the more affluent members of this population, the security of some of these pension plans is now threatened. According to Mayer (1993), the Pension Benefit Guaranty Corporation, a government agency that insures 85,000 private defined-benefit pension plans covering over 40 million employees, will be as much as $19 billion in the red by 1997. There are other reasons to be concerned about the financial security of future retirees, even those who have lived relatively affluently most of their adult life. Defined-benefit pension plans (where a level of income is guaranteed at retirement) are increasingly being phased out by many major companies in favor of defined-contribution plans (retirement income based on how the employee invests his/her pension funds). Since most employees lack both the training and the time to properly manage their pension funds and consequently invest them in secure but low-interest portfolios, future retirees are likely to have even less expendable income than current retirees. Also, as more and more large companies downsize, move to other countries, or simply shut down, a greater percentage of the population is employed by small companies that do not offer pension plans of any kind. Smaller businesses (80 percent of all employees work for firms of 100 or fewer people) provide pension plans for only 43 percent of their full-time employees, while larger companies provide pension plans for 90 percent of their full-time employees (Gerber et al., 1989). Older workers who lose their jobs due to companies downsizing, leaving, or closing often use "contingent" jobs as an income bridge until they reach retirement (Lewis, 1992a). Contingent work consists of part-time, temporary, contract, and free-lance jobs that pay less, provide fewer benefits, and offer less security than full-time jobs. According to Lewis (1992a):

> What is new about part-time, temporary and other contingent workers is the way
> they're being used by employers these days: as commodities to be plugged into
> the workplace on an "as-need" basis, and then to be dispensed with very much

like water cooler refills or Dixie cups. . . . Corporations are moving toward a new . . . job strategy that, in effect, cuts labor costs by converting full-time jobs to contingent jobs. (p. 2)

For workers over 50, this switch from full-time to contingent jobs means a loss of income, benefits, and security at a time in life when they should be most affluent and padding their pension funds for retirement years. The knowledge that they are "disposable" workers also threatens their self-esteem at a time when peers have moved to the top of their career ladders.

Unfortunately, Social Security and other federal and state programs for elders are also in trouble. The federal budget draft for fiscal 1986, for example, included proposed cuts in Medicare, Medicaid, food stamps, and federal retirement programs. While these cuts and those mandated for the Gramm-Rudman Act may have little effect on middle- and upper-class retirees, some lower income workers will be severely effected in old age (Marriott, 1984). A worst case scenario could place increasing numbers of elders below the poverty level for many years to come.

## Victimization

### Crimes against Elders

Although recent research suggests crimes against elders are not as common as they were thought to be earlier, the elderly are clearly the targets of criminals for selected types of crimes (Doyle, 1990). Purse thieves often see elderly women as easy targets, and it is not uncommon that the victim is injured during the commission of the crime. Cashing a Social Security check can be a particularly dangerous time for an elderly person to be alone on a city street.

Crimes against the elderly are not restricted to conventional criminal acts like robbery. Swindlers often prey upon elders, employing "pigeon drops" to filch their lifetime savings. Because of their strong desire to remain in their own home combined with their diminished ability to perform home maintenance and repair, the elderly may be particularly susceptible to home repair fraud. Older Americans may be the preferred targets of confidence men. "The variety of schemes used is endless but often involves tricking the victim into handing over a large sum of cash—for example, to help a phony bank examiner catch a dishonest teller or to secure a share of some found money or a lost inheritance" (Doyle, 1990, p. 302). Many such crimes go unreported due to the victim's embarrassment, and little solid information is available about their frequency.

Particularly pernicious is the health-care fraud perpetuated by health-care providers charged with looking after the physical well-being of the elderly. The House Select Committee on Aging concluded in 1984 that health fraud steals $10 billion a year from Americans 65 or older. Elders suffering chronic pain are a prime target (Colburn, 1985). Of 110,000 heart-pacemakers implanted in elderly Americans in 1985, one in three may have been unnecessary according to the Senate Special Committee on Aging. While some of the unnecessary implants are due to incompetent doctors, the Senate Committee Chair, Senator

John Heinz, is also quoted as saying "This committee's investigation, I'm sorry to say, reveals a Pandora's box full of crooked manufacturers, greedy doctors, and defective products" (UPI, 1985, A11). Although a law enacted by Congress in 1989 and effective January 1, 1991, limits doctors not participating in Medicare from charging patients more than 20 percent over the Medicare rate, "thousands of Medicare patients are being overcharged by their doctors" (McLeod, 1992). These excessive charges affect the elderly patient directly because he/she must make up the difference between what the doctor charges and what Medicare will pay; they also affect all Medicare patients and all taxpayers by draining Medicare resources.

Although elders may not experience more violent crimes than younger persons, fear of such crimes have a particularly debilitating effect on the elderly. While we all face the danger of criminal acts, the singling out of the older persons for certain criminal acts is a form of oppression of elders as a group (Butler, 1979).

## Elder Abuse

Elder abuse has only recently been recognized as a form of oppression experienced by large numbers of older Americans. According to Myers and Shelton (1987), the public first became aware of child abuse in the 1960s and spouse abuse in the 1970s but did not become aware of elder abuse until the 1980s. Even then it received little attention from mental health professionals, law enforcement officials, and legislatures compared to the attention given to child abuse and spouse abuse. By the early 1980s, however, it became apparent that abuse of elders was common and widespread.

The House Select Committee on Aging, chaired by the late Representative Claude Pepper, began hearing testimony on abuse of older Americans by their family members and other careproviders in 1978. Since those initial hearings, the Committee has issued three reports: (a) "Elder abuse: The hidden agenda" published in 1980; (b) "Elder abuse: A national disgrace" published in 1985; and (c) "Elder abuse: A decade of shame and inaction" published in 1990 (it should be noted that the U.S. House of Representatives allowed the House Select Committee on Aging to expire in 1993 after nearly two decades of serving as a forum for airing issues vital to older persons). The first report revealed that elder abuse was not an isolated or localized problem involving a few frail elderly. Instead, the Committee characterized it as a full-scale national problem that existed at a frequency and rate similar to that of child abuse. The second report revealed that instead of diminishing, elder abuse is increasing dramatically from year to year. The third and most recent report found further evidence that elder abuse is on the increase. While in 1980 they reported that 1 out of every 25 (roughly 1 million) older Americans were abused annually, in 1990 they found that 1 out of every 20 (about 1.5 million) older Americans are victims of abuse each year. Another estimate is that 1 in 10 elderly persons living with a family member is abused each year (Lau & Kosberg, 1978).

Abuse occurs in all types of settings, including domestic homes, private nursing facilities, and public hospitals. Abuse of elders also takes many different forms.

> The most shocking is the physical battering of an older person by the family member who is responsible for providing care. Less flagrant but perhaps equally devastating forms are threats of physical assault, verbal assaults, and financial exploitation. Prescription and over the counter drugs such as tranquilizers or sleeping pills that are given to older persons in order to make them more manageable are sources of potential abuse. Excessive alcohol consumption may be overlooked by family members or even encouraged for the same reason. Involuntary constriction—tying an older person to a bed or chair—is sometimes inappropriately used to maintain control. In some instances sexual abuse has been inflicted on older women. (King, 1984, p. 3)

Physical abuse is generally defined as assault, battery, assault with a deadly weapon or force, unreasonable physical constraint, sexual assault, or physical or chemical restraint under specified conditions. Other common types of elder abuse include neglect, abandonment, intimidation, and fiduciary abuse. The House Select Committee on Aging (1990) found that "physical violence, including negligence, and financial abuse appear to remain the most common forms of abuse, followed by abrogation of basic constitutional rights and psychological abuse" (p. XII). Abuse in institutional settings often takes the form of overmedication. "Older persons in institutions take an average of 10 to 12 drugs per day, in contrast to 4 to 7 per day for older persons living in communities" (Myers & Shelton, 1987).

Most experts agree that reported cases are just the tip of the iceberg. Elder abuse is often ignored by third parties due to our negative stereotypes of aged people. Friends, relatives, and caretakers often ignore self reports of violence and assume they are the result of a wandering mind. Bruises and cuts are often attributed to an aging body and ambulation problems (Kosberg, 1983). Also, elders are reluctant to report that their child is abusing them because of the shame it will bring to the family and because they are afraid of losing whatever support they do receive from the abusing child. The House Select Committee on Aging (1990) found that elder abuse is less likely to be reported than is child abuse, perhaps due in part to the fact that there is no objective third party to report elderly abuse as there is with child abuse (Ifill, 1986). For child abuse, it is estimated that about 1 out of 3 cases is reported, while for elder abuse only 1 out of every 8 cases is reported. The House Select Committee on Aging (1990) found the latter figures to be particularly alarming because in 1980 1 out of every 5 cases was reported.

The decreasing proportion of reported cases suggests that elder abuse is becoming even more of a hidden problem at the same time that increased attention is focused on it. Prior to 1980, only 16 states had adult protective service laws mandating that elder abuse be reported. During the 10-year period from 1980 to 1990, mandatory reporting laws were passed in 26 additional states; reporting of elder abuse is now mandatory for selected professionals in 42 states and the District of Columbia (Select Committee, 1990). The California mandatory reporting law is typical of that in many states. The California law stipulates that adult care custodians and health practitioners (including psychologists, psychiatrists, social workers, and marriage and family counselors) *must* report incidents of physical abuse, and *may* report incidents of other types of abuse, that are inflicted upon elderly or dependent adults. No one who is required to report known or suspected instances of abuse can be held liable for their report. Failure to report an instance of elder or dependent adult abuse can result in a fine of $1,000 or six months in jail or both. Individuals who make abuse reports even though they are not required to cannot be held liable unless it can be proven that they knowingly made a false report.

The victim of elder abuse is often physically or mentally impaired and frequently lives with the abuser (King, 1984). The House Select Committee on Aging (1990) found that most victims were age 75 or older and that women are more likely to be abused than men. According to Robert Butler (1983), "the most vulnerable elders seem to be poor frail women, unmarried or widowed" (p. xl), but the victims of elder abuse can be male or female, rich or poor, married or unmarried, and from any ethnic or racial background.

Contrary to the stereotype of the abusing institutional care provider, the abuser is often an adult child or relative of the abused elder. Only about 1 out of every 4 abusers are care providers who are unrelated to the elderly victim (Select Committee, 1990). A number of factors combine to create the conditions under which an individual will abuse their elderly parent.

> The likely abuser will usually be experiencing great stress. Alcoholism, drug addiction, marital problems and long-term financial difficulties all play a role in bringing a person to abuse his or her parents. The son of the victim is the most likely abuser, followed by the daughter of the victim. It is interesting to note that the abuser, in many cases, was abused by the parents as a child. (Select Committee, 1990, p. XII)

Giordano and Giordano (1984) reviewed the theoretical explanations for elder abuse and arrived at seven hypotheses. They were family dynamics, impairment and dependence, personality traits of the abuser, filial crisis, internal stress, and two particularly relevant to the thesis of this book, external stress and negative attitudes toward the elderly.

Perhaps even more insidious and more common than physical abuse is the psychological neglect and abuse suffered by many elderly people (Giordano & Giordano, 1984). Those living in nursing homes are often ignored and isolated by staff who have neither the time nor inclination to interact with their charges in a constructive way. Those living with relatives are often treated as burdens on young families and made to feel guilty for their state of dependence (Kosberg, 1983). In recent years the stress on family care-providers has led to "granny dumping," abandonment of elderly persons with disabilities on hospital emergency room doorsteps in desperation. According to Hey and Carlson

(1991), such abandonment is much more routine than had been thought and provides graphic evidence that our long-term care policies in this country are inadequate.

Abuse of elders is a national disgrace and responsibility for this growing problem rests at a number of different levels. At the national level, the 96th, 97th, 98th, 99th, 100th, and 101st sessions of Congress share in the blame for failing to pass the Prevention, Identification and Treatment of Elder Abuse Act (or similar measure). Two bills were enacted by the 98th Congress, The Child Abuse Amendments of 1984 (PL 98-457) and the Older Americans Act Amendments of 1987 (PL 98-459), which contained provisions for abused elders. Unfortunately, no appropriations were ever made available for the provisions relating to elder abuse. At the state level,

> each State in 1989 spent about $3.80 per elderly resident for protective services. The picture is a bit brighter for child abuse victims, for whom the States, on the average, spend about $45. Nearly one fourth (10 of 42) of States reporting spent less than a dollar per elderly resident for these services in 1989. (Select Committee, 1990, p. XIII)

Furthermore, "while the average amount per elderly resident for protective services has increased from $1.52 to $3.80 over the last 10 years, much of that has been eaten away by 62 percent increase in prices due to inflation over the same period" (Select Committee, 1990, p. XII).

At the local level, all of us can feel some share of the responsibility for ignoring the problem. In addition to the more obvious forms of discrimination against elders, benign neglect of our elderly and their problems in living can be viewed as a form of discrimination and victimization (Atkinson, 1980). The United States clearly has the technology and resources to ease the life stresses placed upon the elderly due to failing health, loss of income, lack of transportation, difficulty living independently, isolation, victimization, and other problems. The fact that we are unwilling to prioritize the needs of elders over defense and space spending, for example, is evidence of discrimination by benign neglect. The fact that when we do respond to the needs of the elderly, it is often with high visibility material assistance rather than with low visibility social assistance (personal involvement, emotional nurturance, respect) provides further evidence of discrimination by benign neglect.

## Women

"Americans are condescendingly sure that women in this country are much better off than women anywhere else" (Hewlett, 1986; p. 139). This statement probably best captures mainstream opinion in the United States today. It is *assumed* that women have achieved equality; women now have only to sort out the problems and responsibilities that have come with that success. Some writers have even referred to a "post-feminist era" (Faludi, 1991); nothing more need be done to advance women's rights. Unfortunately the reality is far different from commonly-held beliefs.

After the significant and far-reaching legal and social advances of the liberal 1960s and 1970s we entered a regressive era in the 1980s and early 1990s. Conservative political groups have become increasingly powerful politically, and some of the major goals of such groups are strongly antifeminist (Faludi, 1991). As a result of changes in the political climate, many of the advances in women's rights and civil rights programs have been stalled or even reversed. For example, conservative forces successfully fought against the ratification of the Equal Rights Amendment (Deckard, 1983). Some conservative groups also oppose affirmative action, sex education, interference with the family in the form of programs combating child abuse, battered women's shelters, and funding for child care programs, all issues intimately related to women's social status (Faludi, 1991). Two past administrations (1981–1993) consistently opposed most women's rights issues. The Equal Employment Opportunity Commission (EEOC), the agency responsible for enforcing anti sex discrimination laws, has been all but dismantled (Faludi, 1991), and two past presidents had poor records of appointing women to influential offices, despite the appointment of the first female Supreme Court Justice by Reagan. President Reagan, in particular, had a record of appointing antifeminist when his appointments were female (Deckard, 1983). Although the Clinton administration is strongly committed to women's issues, the problems and reverses in women's status require substantial and enduring redress. The following section documents the continuing problems faced by American women, despite the real and significant social advances that have been made in this century.

## *Social Inequality*

As we saw in Chapter 2, attitudes toward women and women's relative status within a given society fluctuate over time, in response to social and economic trends. The 1970s were a time when it became less socially acceptable to espouse the sexist notion of women's inherent biological inferiority; yet in the 1980s and 1990s, at least in some sectors of society, sexist thinking is actively promoted.

More commonly, people ascribe to the "different but equal" view. That is, women and men are social equals but have different roles, both equally valuable. On the surface this belief (and there are many variations of the theme) appears to be egalitarian. Upon closer inspection, another variant of sexist ideology is revealed. Women's special place and special roles invariably turn out to be inferior and devalued. For example, occupational segregation by sex is often justified on the basis of women's and men's different strengths; yet feminine characteristics are often reframed to encourage women to participate in low-paid drudge work. In American society, feminine characteristics lead women "naturally" to the "women's jobs" of beautician, secretary, child-care worker, and waitress, and away from such masculine work as physician. Conversely in Russia, feminine characteristics lead women "naturally" to predominate in the medical specialty of general practitioner (women account for 74% of all physicians in the former U.S.S.R.), a relatively low-paid, low status area of medicine, while masculine characteristics lead Russian men naturally to the higher-status specialties. We will discuss occupational segregation in greater depth in the next section of this chapter; for now, it is important to note how social ideologies in the form of "women are not inferior, but . . ." are sexist at the core and serve to promote and maintain women's inferior status (Deckard, 1983).

The ongoing subtle and often not-so-subtle sexism that prevails in American culture manifests itself in many forms. Research has repeatedly demonstrated that even very young children have already acquired stereotypical views of masculine and feminine characteristics, and the occupational choices open to each gender (Betz, in press; Gettys & Cann, 1981). Overall, some loosening in traditional gender-role stereotypes have been observed, but we are still far from equality.

Attitudes toward women's roles, especially work roles, have been changing markedly (Russo & Denmark, 1984), but certain other fundamental assumptions remain largely unchanged. We shall see in the next section how traditional assumptions about women's gender-roles and responsibilities in the family continue to interact complexly with changing expectations for women, producing new problems for women, men, and society.

## Economic Disadvantagement

A major cause of the economic disadvantages for women is the differential pay they receive for similar work. American women earn, on the average, 64 cents on the dollar compared to men, and this wage gap has remained virtually unchanged for the past forty years (Faludi, 1991; Kahn-Hut, Daniels, & Colvard, 1982). The earnings gap between men and women is also the largest such difference in the industrialized countries of the world (Hewlett, 1986). The wage disparity is even more severe for racial/ethnic minority women and women who are disadvantaged in other ways, for example the physically disabled (Faludi, 1991; Howe, 1977; U.S. Women's Bureau, 1975). For example, Hispanic women and older women have seen their wages gap *decrease;* African-American women's earning power has changed very little (Faludi, 1991). Even college educated women are not doing well; they still earn 59 percent of what college educated men earn (Faludi, 1991).

What are the reasons for this disparity in earnings? A long-standing myth has been that women work for "pin money" (the term refers to extra pocket money for trinkets, e.g., pins, rather than earnings necessary for survival) and are not seriously attached to the work force (Farmer & Backer, 1977). In fact, most women work out of economic need, because they are single, divorced, or widowed, or if married because their earnings are required by the family for subsistence (Hewlett, 1986). Ongoing discrimination, even though illegal, continues; but the reasons for the wage gap are complex and extend beyond overt discrimination to include inadequate maternity benefits and child care, occupational segregation by sex, devaluation of women's work, as well as outright pay inequities.

## Maternity and Child Care Support

One of the most significant social changes in this century has been the increasing entry of married women and mothers into the paid labor force (Kahn-Hut, Daniels, & Colvard, 1982). Currently, nearly 70 percent of all women, over 50 percent of married women, 61 percent of women with children, and 52 percent of mothers with preschool-aged children work outside the home (Betz, in press). The overwhelming majority (nearly 95%) of all women will participate in the work force at sometime in their lives (Betz, in press). The failure of our society to provide adequate and affordable child care has been a significant drawback for working women, and a formidable barrier to mothers of young children, often blocking participation in the paid labor force completely. Good high-quality private child care is very costly and can easily consume a substantial part of a working mother's earnings. Many single or divorced mothers of young children are virtually forced to go on welfare in order to survive, even when they would rather be working (Deckard, 1983). Employed women experience a double burden, working their paid jobs and also working as caretakers of spouses, children, and home.

Our country has an extremely poor record on the issues of maternity and child care:

> The United States is the only industrialized country that has no statutory maternity leave. One hundred and seventeen countries (including every industrialized nation and many developing countries) guarantee a woman the following rights: leave from employment for childbirth, job protection while she is on leave, and the provision of a cash benefit, to replace all or most of her earnings. (Hewlett, 1986, p. 96)

Further, despite lip service given to Americans' priority on the family, all efforts at developing Government programs for child care have failed. In 1971, President Nixon vetoed the Comprehensive Child Care Act, and recent administrations have been unsupportive or even hostile toward any child care programs ("Adding up the victories," 1986; Faludi, 1991). Some businesses and major corporations are beginning to experiment with flex-time, parental leaves for fathers as well as pregnancy leaves for mothers, and child care programs for employees, both these efforts are scarce and totally inadequate to the scope of the problem (Hewlett, 1986).

In stark contrast, most European countries provide subsidized child care, child allowances, and other sources of support for women and their families, with consequent beneficial effects on women's economic status (Hewlett, 1986):

> It is also no coincidence that the country with the most developed benefits and services for working women—Sweden—is also the country with the smallest

wage gap, while the country with the least developed benefits and services—the United States—is also the country with one of the largest wage gaps. (p. 99)

The consequence of this scarcity in support services is that women must bear the full burden of their double duty as worker and mother, and this double burden is then reflected in their earnings. Women are forced to go on welfare, take part-time instead of full-time work, and lose wages due to maternity or child care responsibilities, drastically lowering their earnings and future earning power.

## Occupational Segregation and Comparable Worth

Although lack of adequate child care services is certainly one factor in the wage gap, occupational segregation by sex is clearly a more significant contributor (Hewlett, 1986). Faludi (1991) argued that occupational segregation by sex accounts for at least 45 percent of the wage gap. The extent of occupational segregation by sex is dramatic: The majority of employed women are clustered into only 20 occupational areas; only 7 percent of employed women in America work in managerial-level positions; only 1 in 10 women earns more than $20,000 per year; and fully 60% of working women earn less than $10,000 (Faludi, 1991; Hewlett, 1986). Three-quarters of all employed women work in traditionally-female jobs such as nurse, secretary, teacher, and beautician (Hewlett, 1986).

We have already seen, in the historical overview in Chapter 2, that job segregation by sex is common to almost all societies; but we have also seen that such segregation need not necessarily lead to gender inequality in society. The current sex segregation in our economy, coupled with the denigration of "women's work," is both a consequence and continuing cause of the social and economic disadvantagement of women. Traditionally-female jobs, that is, jobs where the majority of workers are women, are almost always lower-paying and lower status occupational pursuits. Howe (1977) employed the term "pink collar" workers to characterize the dead-end, low status nature of such women's jobs as beautician, waitress, and secretary. In 1980, 97.6 percent of all secretaries were women; in 1983 women comprised 70 percent of all retail and personal sales workers and 80 percent of all administrative support workers (Kahn-Hut, Daniels, & Colvard, 1980). In contrast, women represented only 8 percent of precision, craft, and repair workers, and 6.8 percent of all apprentices (Betz & Fitzgerald, 1987). "Between 1976 and 1986, the lowest job rungs in the civil service ladder went from 67 to 71 percent female. . . . At the same time at the top of the ladder, the proportion of women in senior executive services had not improved since 1979—it was still a paltry 8 percent" (Faludi, 1991, p. 366).

Even where it appears that women are making significant inroads, the realities are discrepant with widely-held perceptions. Despite dramatic increases in their absolute numbers in management positions in business and industry, White women and women and men of color have faced serious obstacles to advancement within the ranks of management (Morrison & Glinow, 1990).

Overall, women comprise 50 percent of entry-level management, 25 percent of middle management, but only 1 percent to 2 percent of upper-management positions (Hewlett, 1986).

> There is considerable evidence that White women and people of color encounter a "glass ceiling" in management. The glass ceiling is a concept popularized in the 1980s to describe a barrier so subtle that it is transparent, yet so strong that it prevents women and minorities from moving up the management ladder. Only 2% of 1,362 senior executives were women . . . only 3.6% of board directorships and 1.7% of corporate officerships in the Fortune 500 were held by women; the Fortune 500 and the health industry indicated that 4.4% of board members were women and that 3.8% and 8.5% of their corporate officers, respectively, were women. (Morrison & Glinow, 1990, p. 200)

Recent research suggests that even the limited progress made by women in upper-level management positions is now eroding (Faludi, 1991).

Further compounding women's economic status is that the legal mandate of "equal pay for equal work," even if it were being enforced, would not resolve the economic problems encountered by women. In 1980, a registered nurse with over 14 years of education earned less than deliverymen; secretaries with 13+ years of education and comparably higher-level job responsibilities earned less than truck drivers with an average of a ninth-grade education (Kahn-Hut, Daniels, & Colvard, 1982). The concept of equal pay for *comparable* work has been introduced for resolving some of these discrepancies. Comparable work proponents advocate assessing the skills, education, and responsibilities required in various jobs and adjusting pay scales to reflect equal pay for work of comparable worth or social value (Kahn-Hut, Daniels, & Colvard, 1982). It is still too early to accurately gauge the future of this new concept for correcting past and present sex discrimination in the work force, except to say that the concept has not been well received thus far.

## Wage Discrimination

Wage discrimination persists within fields as well; women consistently earn less than men for the same work. For example, early in their careers, at a time when such disparities should be lowest, male lawyers earn $27,563 per year while comparably-aged female lawyers earn $20,573. Female bus drivers earn $9,903 while their male colleagues earn $15,611 a year (Hewlett, 1986). These wage differences are reflected in virtually all vocational areas. In addition to being paid less than men for the same jobs, women also tend to be clustered in the lower levels of even traditionally-female occupations. For example, in the field of education, women are 86 percent of elementary school teachers but only 26 percent of school administrators (Betz & Fitzgerald, 1987).

Women are now receiving undergraduate degrees at parity with men, and the percentage of women receiving Ph.D.s is at an all-time high (Deckard, 1983). However, the most rapid progress has been made in areas traditional for women, whereas progress in highly nontraditional majors and career areas, although marked, is still fairly slow. For example, in engineering women are now receiving about 14 percent of the Bachelor's degrees, up from about 1 percent in the 1970s (National Science Foundation, 1990). However, women receive only 7 percent of the engineering doctorates; fewer than 4 percent of engineers working in the field are women; and, although the wage gap between women and men is smaller in the scientific/technological fields than in other vocational areas, women engineers still earn less than men at comparable levels, and the unemployment rate for female scientists and engineers is twice as high as men's (National Science Foundation, 1990). Again, racial/ethnic minority women and women with a disability experience a double or triple burden of disadvantagement; the wage gap and unemployment figures for these groups in the scientific/technical career areas is worse than for White women (National Science Foundation, 1986).

Statistics on female academics demonstrate the same pattern of wage discrimination and occupational segregation. Although 51 percent of instructors in institutions of higher education are women, most of these women are "ghettoized" in a limited number of fields and in unstable, lower paying positions, a situation that has not changed for years (Higher Education and National Affairs, 1986). At every level and in all fields women earn less than their male counterparts, are less likely to be tenured, and the relatively few female administrators are most likely to be concentrated in traditionally-female areas such as home economics and nursing (Higher Education and National Affairs, 1986).

## Economic Consequences of Unequal Treatment

An alarming development in recent years, an upshot of the wage gap and discriminatory practices, has been labeled "the feminization of poverty" (Pearce, 1979). When women combine their relatively lower earnings with a higher-earning male, as in a marriage, their economic situation is markedly better than when they must survive independently. When women are the sole supporters of dependents, especially children, their economic situation is precarious. "The feminization of poverty" refers to the increasing percentage of women living below the poverty level due to their disadvantaged economic status; the major factors in this dramatic rise in the number of female-headed households subsisting below poverty level are occupational segregation and the wage gap. However, changes in the divorce laws over the past two decades appear to be exacerbating the problem (Weitzman, 1985).

The statistics on the effects of divorce on the economic status of husband and wife are striking: Divorced women (and their children) experience an immediate 73 percent drop in their standard of living after a divorce, while men experience a 42 percent gain in their economic status (Weitzman, 1985). Although Weitzman's (1985) statistics have been questioned (they are undoubtedly on the high side), the social, interpersonal, and personal consequences of this phenomenon remain and are as unsettling as the economic repercussions:

> When the downward change in the family standard of living followed the divorce and the discrepancy between the father's standard of living and that of the mother and children was striking, this discrepancy was often central to the life of the family and remained as a festering source of anger and bitter preoccupation. The continuation of this discrepancy over the years generated continuing bitterness between the parents. Mother and children were likely to share in their anger at the father and to experience a pervasive sense of deprivation, sometimes depression, accompanied by a feeling that life was unrewarding and unjust. (Wallerstein & Kelly, p. 231, 1980, quoted in Weitzman, 1985, p. 353)

## Gender-role Stereotyping

The point of this discussion thus far has been to highlight the continuing effects of past discrimination on women's social and economic status and to emphasize that women have not yet attained equality in employment. But, as previously discussed, the present state of affairs is not entirely due to overt sex discrimination; it will take many years for the recent female graduates pursuing traditionally-male career areas to make an impact in the job market. Further, discrimination does not have to exist overtly to produce a situation where many women are still underutilizing their talents and abilities in career pursuits. First, as we have seen, there has been some loosening of the traditional gender-role stereotypes, and more female models in a wider range of occupational roles exist, but boys and girls continue to be trained in different ways. As Bem and Bem (1970/1984) have so aptly put it:

> Even if all discrimination were to end tomorrow, nothing very drastic would change. For job discrimination is only part of the problem . . . it does not, by itself, help us to understand why so many women "choose" to be secretaries or nurses rather than executives or physicians. Discrimination frustrates choices already made. Something more pernicious perverts the motivation to choose. That "something" is an unconscious ideology about the nature of the female sex, an ideology which constricts the emerging self-image of the female child and the nature of her aspirations from the very beginning; an ideology which leads even those Americans who agree that a black skin should not uniquely qualify *its* owner for a janitorial or domestic service to act as if possession of a uterus uniquely qualifies *its* owner for precisely such service. (p. 12)

Even when women are able to surmount their gender-role conditioning to enter challenging and demanding educational programs, they are still in need of additional support and encouragement. Freeman (1979) has identified the "Null Environment" as a major problem for women in academic and vocational pursuits. This concept refers to the inherent discrimination against women that results, in academic situations where *neither* men nor women are actively encouraged or discouraged, from the differential socialization and external environments experienced by women and men. Freeman (1979) feels that women enter higher education with a "handicap" that a "null" academic environment does nothing to minimize or decrease, resulting in the inadvertent discouragement of women because of lack of *encouragement*. Thus educators, and by extension counselors, may discriminate against women "without really trying." Women need active encouragement, not simply the absence of discrimination, to surmount the barriers posed by traditional feminine gender-role socialization.

## Victimization

One of the most damaging manifestations of sexism in any society is the physical, sexual, and emotional abuse of women that results from virulent misogynist attitudes intertwined with women's relative powerlessness. The long-term emotional, interpersonal, and social costs of violence against women are considerable. Sexual assault is a constant (and statistically real) fear for most American women, regardless of age, physical attractiveness, race, or class (Collier, 1982). Some groups of women within society are more vulnerable to assault than others, but no woman is "safe." Rape, sexual harassment, childhood sexual abuse, and other forms of violence against women have little to do with sexuality; sexual assault is motivated by domination and power.

Current statistics indicate the widespread nature of the problem: One in four women will be raped in her lifetime; one in two women will be physically battered by her spouse or significant other; conservatively, 25 percent of women experience some form of sexual harassment on the job—the figures are much higher for women in highly nontraditional occupations; and 10 percent to 30 percent of women are survivors of child sexual abuse, the perpetrator usually being male and someone close to the child (Courtois, 1986; Deckard, 1983; Fitzgerald, 1993; Walker, 1979). Countless other women have suffered emotional abuse, often for years. Because crimes of violence against women are grossly underreported, these statistics may very well be on the low side. While rape crisis centers, battered women's shelters, and support services for survivors of incest and child sexual abuse have done much to serve survivors of violence and inform the public, the root of the problem remains.

The social myths that exist about the seven areas of violence against women (i.e., battering, rape, girl child incest, pornography, prostitution, sexual harassment on the job, and sexual harassment between client and professional, e.g., doctor or therapist) reveal the underlying sexism behind these actions (Walker, 1979). One of the core myths about sexual and physical assaults on women is that the "victim" was responsible for the assault. With rape we often see the false and mistaken accusation of a seductive appearance on the part of the rape victim, an assumption also made about children victimized by sexual assault; and in the case of wife (woman) battering, we see the label "masochistic" placed on the victim to justify the assault (Collier, 1982; Martin, 1976). Victims (or, more positively, "survivors") of sexual harassment are accused of "sleeping their way to the top" or dressing too provocatively at work, and male therapists who sleep with their clients are often excused as having been "seduced" (Collier, 1982).

Another common myth (as false as the first) is that the abuser is mentally ill or, in the case of rape, has been overcome by a powerful sex drive (Collier, 1982). In fact, rapists have not been found to be different from nonrapists on measures of psychological functioning *except* in their tendency to act out their impulses via sexual assault; further, most rapes are premeditated (Collier, 1982). "The stereotype of the harasser is of the uneducated manual worker, the uncouth traveling salesman, the boorish office 'lech'. Professional individuals with impeccable credentials and multiple degrees are assumed to be beyond reproach, despite multiple examples to the contrary" (Fitzgerald, 1993). The common theme behind all of these forms of violence toward women and abuse of women is that they are methods of establishing dominance and control over women. Controversy exists in this area as to the exact reasons behind sexual and physical assaults. What can be said with some confidence is that women do not freely choose to be victimized, and women's and men's socialization, along with women's relative powerlessness in society, are central causative factors in violence toward women (Betz & Fitzgerald, 1993; Collier, 1982).

### *Women and the Mental Health System*

As we saw in Chapter 2, the sexism embedded in society at large penetrated and influenced the development of scientific psychology. These biases within psychology have had profound consequences for the diagnosis and treatment of women by mental health practitioners.

### Bias in Diagnosis

Women are much more likely than men to be treated for mental illness (Gove & Tudor, 1973; Williams, 1983); the sex ratio varies depending on the diagnosis, and also on the type of treatment facility, but women are clearly in the majority. Various explanations have been promulgated for this preponderance of women diagnosed as having mental problems: women are weaker and therefore more susceptible to psychological disturbance than men; women's traditional gender roles are inherently mentally unhealthy; women are labeled as ill more often than men, but no genuine sex difference in the incidence of mental illness exists; and women subjected to excessive stress and tension manifest their disturbance via emotional symptoms congruent with their gender role, while men's disturbance is manifested in physical symptomology (Williams, 1983).

Phyllis Chesler (1972) in her classic book *Women and Madness,* for example, advanced the argument that mental illness in women is a result of underconformity or overconformity to the feminine sex role:

> Men do not usually seem as "sick" if they act out the male role fully—unless, of course, they are relatively powerless contenders for "masculinity." Women are seen as "sick" when they act out the female role (are depressed, incompetent,

frigid, and anxious) and when they reject the female role (are hostile, successful, sexually active, and especially with other women). (p. 118)

A meta-analysis of 26 studies examining the relationships of gender roles to mental health produced results congruent with Chesler's thesis: "masculinity," as measured by various gender-role inventories, is more consistently and significantly associated with psychological measures of mental health than is "femininity" (Basoff & Glass, 1982).

A different but related argument has been advanced by writers who, taking note of the differences in rates of mental illness in married and unmarried men and women, have suggested that social roles are a significant factor in susceptibility to mental distress (Williams, 1983). Bernard (1971) demonstrated that men are happier when married than women; single women score higher than married women on various indices of psychological well-being than married women; and women make more adjustments in marriage than do men. These findings correspond with findings from psychological studies, indicating higher rates of mental illness for married women than single women or married men (Gove, 1980). Marriage seems to have a disadvantageous effect on women (Gove, 1973).

Arguments over the reasons for gender differences in the prevalence of mental illness may be moot. As Johnson (1980) pointedly argues:

> To speak of the overall mental health of two sexes is too sweeping a generalization . . . diagnoses are frequently of questionable reliability . . . often based on ambiguous symptoms, subject to a variety of interpretation. . . . Furthermore, a report of symptoms is not synonymous with mental illness; a person can acknowledge symptoms, but be coping with them. (pp. 363–364)

Johnson goes on to argue that we must look at the complex confluence of female socialization, societal attitudes toward women and women's roles, and external stressors, including the treatment of women by clinicians, in order to understand and assist women therapeutically.

The most recent controversy about gender bias has revolved around two new diagnoses affecting women. In the most recent edition of the Diagnostic and Statistical Manual of Mental Disorders, third edition, revised (DSM-III-R), the standard guide for the diagnosis of mental problems, two gender-related diagnoses, "self-defeating personality disorder" (originally titled "masochistic personality disorder") and the premenstrual syndrome, "late luteal phase disorder," were included after considerable controversy, as unofficial diagnoses in the appendices. These diagnoses are now being considered as fully-endorsed mental disorders in the next edition, DSM-IV. Many feminist psychologists view the attempts to officially sanction such diagnoses as a major step backward for women:

> While the criteria for this diagnostic category [self-defeating personality disorder] are couched in non-sexist language, the behaviors described reflect the cultural conditioning experienced by females, hence labeling as masochistic the social and

religious values taught women. Furthermore all the criteria reflect characteristics of women victims of violence. Therefore it is entirely possible that using such a diagnosis . . . will violate the civil rights of women by causing irreparable injury and undue hardship to women and victims of violence (most of whom are women). (Rosewater, 1985, p. 1)

To pathologize behaviors reflecting conformity to societal expectations and exhibited by a substantial majority of women is clearly problematic. Caplan (1991) exposes the underlying sexism behind this diagnosis by proposing a parallel diagnosis pathologizing conformity to the traditional masculine gender role: the diagnosis of "delusional dominating personality disorder" is no more scientifically supportable than the self-defeating personality disorder diagnosis. There are serious problems with the "late luteal phase disorder" as well, among them that the diagnosis is not supported by research, symptoms associated with the premenstrual syndrome are adequately covered in existing diagnoses, and that possible psychological and emotional effects of a medical condition experienced by women will be pathologized (Caplan, 1993).

## Bias in Treatment

The classic study of bias on the part of mental health practitioners treating women was conducted by Broverman, Broverman, Clarkson, Rosenkrantz, and Vogel (1970). In this study 79 clinicians were asked to rate the characteristics of mentally healthy adults, mentally healthy women, and mentally healthy men. Clinicians' ratings of the characteristics of mentally healthy men and adults were found to be virtually identical; ratings of "mentally healthy" women were significantly different from the ratings of men, tending toward the stereotypical feminine gender-role traits held by the dominant culture. That is, healthy women, as compared to healthy men and adults, were characterized as being ". . . more submissive, less independent, less adventurous, more easily influenced, less aggressive, less competitive, more excitable in minor issues, having their feelings more easily hurt, being more emotional, more conceited about their appearance, less objective, and disliking math and science" (Broverman et al., 1970, p. 4). The Broverman et al. study has been interpreted to demonstrate a "double-standard" in mental health for women; masculine gender traits are more closely associated with depictions of mental health, yet women are socialized to display "feminine," less "healthy" characteristics and may be deemed aberrant if they reject the feminine role (Collier, 1982; Sherman, 1980). A replication of the Broverman et al. (1970) research with a larger but similar sample yielded findings consistent with the earlier results; in 1985, males and females were still being described in gender-stereotypical ways (O'Malley & Richardson, 1985). However, O'Malley and Richardson also reported a "loosening" of stereotypes in that clinicians attributed *both* masculine and feminine traits to mentally healthy "adults."

The controversy stimulated by the landmark Broverman et al. (1970) study continues today. Although a number of investigations have yielded results supporting the contention that clinicians hold biased views toward women (e.g., Aslin, 1977; Dremen, 1978), are misinformed about women (e.g., Bingham & House, 1973), and actually respond in biased ways towards women (e.g., Abramowitz, 1977), other studies have failed to find such evidence of differential attitudes or treatment by gender (e.g., Davenport & Reims, 1978; Johnson, 1978). The two primary arguments against the existence of gender bias in counseling can be summarized as follows: (a) some evidence for bias in attitudes may exist, but this is not evidence that these attitudes have a detrimental effect on women in counseling (e.g., Stricker, 1977); and (b) no empirical evidence of gender bias exists (e.g., Smith, 1980). Stricker (1977) argued that the research providing evidence for a double standard in mental health was itself biased and the conclusions about such a double standard were based on questionable data, while Smith's (1980) meta-analysis of the research literature revealed no demonstrable bias against women, or bias for stereotypical roles for women, on the part of counselors or psychotherapists.

One major problem with studies of gender bias is that, because the Broverman et al. (1970) study is so well-known, the validity of therapists' responses in studies of bias is questionable. It is therefore increasingly difficult to disentangle real changes in counselor attitudes toward women from possible experimental demands for social desirability. Further, problems abound in performing methodologically sound investigations in this area. Richardson and Johnson (1984) concluded that there *is* a basis in the empirical literature for claims of gender bias, but they recommend that the nature of such research be modified. Farmer (1982) also concluded that, although weak, there does exist evidence for gender bias in counseling. It will undoubtedly be far more productive if researchers focus attention on what *aspects* of counselor gender-role related attitudes and behaviors influence female (and male) clients negatively, rather than continue with the past preoccupation with demonstrating (or disproving) the overall existence of gender bias.

The articles in Part IV cover guidelines for counseling women and many of the newly evolving approaches to working with female clients in "sex-fair" ways. Suggestions for training and ongoing professional development in this area are outlined in the last chapter.

## Gay Men and Lesbian Women

The long-standing historical pattern of social, legal, medical, psychological, and religious discrimination against gay people, reviewed briefly in Chapter 2, continues in various forms to this day. The majority of the American population hold negative, homophobic attitudes toward gay people (Moses & Hawkins, 1982). Internalized homophobia remains with us, too. Nonetheless, research strongly suggests that the psychological problems experienced by gay people are profoundly influenced by the hostile and derogatory societal attitudes and the internalization of those homophobic attitudes (Alexander, 1986; Alexander & Casas, 1985).

Only recently have social scientists moved from studying the presumed pathology of gay men and lesbian women and begun focusing on the correlates and precursors of homophobia in an attempt to understand the problems of gay people. Compared to those holding more favorable attitudes, people expressing negative attitudes toward gays generally: (a) have had little personal contact with lesbians or gay men; (b) are less likely to have had any homosexual contact or label themselves as gay; (c) are more likely to see their peers as holding homophobic attitudes; (d) are more likely to live in areas of the country where homophobia flourishes, especially the midwest and south, and rural areas and small towns; (e) are older and less educated; (f) are more likely to subscribe to a conservative religious ideology; (g) hold more restrictive views about gender roles; (h) have more negative views about sexuality in general; and (i) are more authoritarian (Herek, 1984; Melton, 1989).

Interestingly, surveys show that only 25 percent to 30 percent of Americans claim to know a lesbian woman or gay man (Herek, 1986). Of course, given the large percentage of gay people in the population, it is safe to assume that *everyone* knows at least one or more gay people; the 25 percent to 30 percent figure represents those who are familiar with an openly gay man or woman. Of the survey respondents who knowingly have had contact with a gay person, the majority have positive attitudes about gays as a result of their contact (Herek, 1986). Antigay sentiment is clearly based on unfounded assumptions and untested stereotypes.

Homophobic individuals are more likely to hold racist and sexist attitudes, underscoring the common sources of all forms of oppression (Dunbar, Brown, & Amoroso, 1973). Some evidence also suggests that nongay men are more homophobic than nongay women (Morin & Garfinkle, 1978). It is unclear whether the issue has to do with fear of same-sex homosexuality (i.e., most research asks respondents for attitudes about homosexuality in general, which is usually taken as meaning gay males), or whether these findings are related to fear of femininity, violation of the male gender role, and/or other gender-role issues (Morin & Garfinkle, 1978).

Herek (1984), in his review of the research on homophobia, also points out that people hold positive and negative views about gays for different reasons; understanding the complexity of these issues is important if efforts at attitude change are to be successful. Attitudes toward gays may develop out of personal experience with gay men or lesbian women and the resultant generalization of these experiences, because of defensiveness and the need to project some inner conflict or anxiety onto gays, or attitudes may be symbolic, representing firmly held beliefs or convictions (Herek, 1984).

Finally, in addition to outright homophobia, researchers have identified "heterosexual bias" as a problem for gay people. Even people who hold liberal attitudes about lesbian women and gay men may believe, either subtly or overtly, that heterosexuality is inherently superior to or more "natural" than homosexuality (Morin, 1977). This "heterosexual bias," then, precludes a true commitment to the validity of the gay life-style, and represents at best tolerance toward, rather than a proactive affirmation of, gay people. Thus, homophobic attitudes may range from repulsion through pity to tolerance; only when public and personal attitudes are truly *accepting* will gay people attain equality in this society.

## Social Discrimination

Surveys on public attitudes toward gays reveal both some trends toward tolerance and ongoing negative attitudes. Levitt and Klassen (1974) conducted two attitude surveys, in 1970 and 1974. In 1970 they found that over 75 percent of their sample of Americans believed that homosexual activity was wrong if no love was involved, and 70 percent felt homosexuality was wrong even if the participants loved each other. The large majority of the respondents felt that gays should not be allowed to hold positions of responsibility and authority such as school teacher, minister, medical doctor, lawmaker, and judge (Levitt & Klassen, 1974). Other findings supported the existence of a hostile, destructive atmosphere for gay people in our society. Their 1974 survey was quite similar, revealing limited social progress in this period (Levitt & Klassen, 1974). The overwhelming majority of people still believed that homosexuality was wrong and tended to agree with such statements as: "Homosexuals are dangerous as teachers or youth leaders, because they try to get sexually involved with children"; and "Homosexuality is a social corruption that can cause the downfall of a civilization." Other widely held beliefs included the assumption that gay people act like members of the opposite sex, and that gay men and lesbian women can be identified on the basis of their appearance (Levitt & Klassen, 1974).

Interestingly, this survey was conducted about the same time as the current gay liberation movement began (Bullough, 1979). Homosexual rights organizations are not a recent phenomenon; the first gay rights organization was formed by Magnus Hirschfield in 1897 in Germany (Lauritsen & Thorstad, 1974). However, the work of the early homosexual rights movements achieved no lasting effect on antihomosexual attitudes, and the movement was ended by the Nazis in the 1930s (Lauritsen & Thorstad, 1974).

Secret gay groups have existed in various countries and at different times, most notably, in this country, the Mattachine Foundation, later the Mattachine Society, organized originally in 1950 (Bullough, 1979). The Daughters of Bilitis, a lesbian organization, was founded in 1955, published a magazine called the *Ladder,* and provided a beginning for much of the leadership of the lesbian movement of the 1970s (Bullough, 1979).

The contemporary gay rights movement grew out of the earlier secretive societies and was officially born in 1969 as a result of a spontaneous demonstration by gay men in reaction to police harassment at The Stonewall Inn, a popular gay men's bar in Greenwich Village (Bullough, 1979). Out of the "Stonewall riots" and succeeding demonstrations, the Gay Liberation Front, a civil rights organization, was formed (Teal, 1971). Although parallels can be found between the movement for the civil rights of gay people and other civil rights movements, the meaning of the Stonewall confrontation for gay men and lesbian women was also somewhat different than was, for example, the Watts riots of 1969 for Black people. Because of their stigmatized place in society, and their ability to remain hidden, few gay men or lesbian women were willing to be public about their sexual orientation (Bullough, 1979). With the advent of the new wave of the gay rights movement and the resultant public support and affirmation of gays, many more gay people were willing to become visible, creating an overt, as opposed to the earlier covert, movement for social reform. However, as was the case with earlier movements, social progress has been slow.

The same authors of the aforementioned 1970 attitude survey conducted a follow-up survey on public attitudes about homosexuality in 1974 (Levitt & Klassen, 1974). The results of the two surveys are similar, revealing limited social progress in this period despite the active and public work on the part of the gay liberation movement. In 1974 the overwhelming majority of Levitt and Klassen's sample still believed that homosexuality was wrong, and the majority tended to agree with such statements as: "Homosexuals are dangerous as teachers or youth leaders, because they try to get sexually involved with children"; and "Homosexuality is a social corruption that can cause the downfall of a civilization." Other widely held beliefs included the assumption that gay people act like members of the opposite sex, and that gay men and lesbian women can be identified on the basis of their appearance (Levitt & Klassen, 1974).

A 1977 Gallup poll revealed somewhat more positive attitudes, with 56 percent of Americans agreeing that gay people should have equal rights in job opportunities. These more accepting attitudes did not extend to the employment of gay people in certain types of positions; 65 percent of the sample believed that gays should not be allowed to be elementary teachers, 54 percent thought gay men and lesbian women should be denied jobs as members of the clergy, and 44 percent and 38 percent, respectively, agreed that gays should not be medical doctors or members of the armed forces (Gallup, 1977). Only 43 percent of this sample advocated legalization of homosexual activity, and 14 percent felt that gay people should be allowed to adopt children (Gallup, 1977). In a *Psychology Today* poll of a sample of liberals, 70 percent of the heterosexuals polled felt that "homosexual men are not fully masculine" (Tavris, 1977).

A national poll conducted in 1989 (reported in Fassinger, 1991) yielded even more evidence of positive changes in attitudes toward gays, though not widespread acceptance:

> The overwhelming majority of the nongay public, 81%, is opposed to discrimination based on sexual orientation, but 57% disapprove of gays living together as a married couple and 18% think homosexuality should be illegal. Two thirds believe discrimination has decreased during the past 10 years, but almost one fifth reported that they would withdraw support for a gay candidate for political office, even if they agreed with everything the individual said. Nongays would more easily accept a gay friend than a gay child, and one third would 'try to change' a gay child. (p. 163)

Despite these encouraging results from 1989, the overall climate in the United States is noticeably more antigay in the early 1990s:

> Gay bashing is our new national pastime. From the Republican presidential campaign to the state of Oregon, homophobia has taken center stage. It is the last prejudice, a bias that public officials and everyday citizens are displaying without fear of instant condemnation or repudiation. . . . Imagine if a candidate for president or vice president said Jews or Catholics should not be in the cabinet, that women or African-Americans do not deserve rights. That candidate would be forced to withdraw. Not so when the prejudice is against lesbians or gay men. (Rothchild, 1992, p. A9)

Several notable reversals in civil rights for gays have occurred in the past year or two. Oregon attempted to pass an antigay measure, similar laws are being proposed in other states, and Colorado did, in fact, pass a statute forbidding gay antidiscrimination legislation. It is virtually impossible to imagine any law *denying* basic civil rights to any other group in this society even being proposed, let alone passed.

Shortly after his inauguration, President Clinton proposed to end the ban on gays in the military, a move that has been applauded by gays and civil rights groups; the consequent uproar in response to his proposal, however, is reflective of a retreat from tolerance. Despite overwhelming evidence to the contrary, the military and majority of the public at large continue to argue against the suitability of gays for military service (Herek, 1993). One of the most dramatic episodes to date has been the opposing testimony to the Senate Armed Services Committee by Marine Colonel Fred Peck, testifying on behalf of the current ban, and his gay son, arguing for admitting gays into the military. The linchpin in Colonel Peck's reasoning for continuing discrimination was his concern for his son and other gay people, who, he argued, would be in mortal danger from fellow military personnel (Smolowe, 1993). The question of whose problem it was, gays or the virulently homophobic armed forces, was evidently never considered. Research indicates, however, that ". . . lesbians and gay men are not inherently less capable of military service than are heterosexual women and men; that prejudice in the military can be overcome; that heterosexual personnel can adapt to living and working in close quarters with lesbian and gay male personnel; and that public opinion will be influenced by the way this issue is framed" (Herek, 1993).

The AIDS epidemic, too, has had a profound effect on attitudes toward gay people (Rudolph, 1989). AIDS has been identified as the "gay plague," has been labeled by some as punishment for immoral behavior, and has exacerbated already existing biases about gay people (Rudolph, 1989). Opposition to gay rights activities is also being justified by the AIDS crisis. Black (1986) reports graffiti highlighting this tendency: observed scrawled on a wall outside a New York University Conference on Gay/Lesbian Health was the slogan *Gay Rights = AIDS.*

Some methodological problems exist with both the research on correlates of homophobic attitudes and surveys about public attitudes toward gays. First, many surveys do not clearly differentiate between attitudes toward gay men and attitudes toward lesbian women. Second, questions are often phrased globally, reflecting general cultural beliefs and failing to reflect individual attitudes and the more specific ways in which gays are responded to negatively in everyday situations. And third, questions about the extent to which the survey data are representative abound (Morin, 1977; Morin & Garfinkle, 1978). Yet some conclusions can be drawn. Widespread disapproval and stigmatization of lesbian women and gay men clearly exists in American society, and these negative attitudes are strong and persistent. The recent AIDS epidemic has undoubtedly contributed to justifying and maintaining such negative attitudes. And, finally, cultural and social influences on the development of biased attitudes toward gays are as important to understanding the problems of gay men and lesbian women as is the study of gay adjustment, behavior, and reactions.

## Legal Discrimination

The legal status of gay people in this country is largely dependent on local and state statutes, varying considerably depending on geographic location. No federal statutes exist protecting lesbian women and gay men from employment, housing, or child custody discrimination, and half of the states have laws on the books prohibiting various types of consensual sexual behavior, which are used largely against gay people (Hunter, Michaelson, & Stoddard, 1992). Although some employers have voluntarily implemented antidiscrimination policies, gays are rarely legally protected from employment discrimination.

Periodic challenges to the so-called "sodomy" laws have been made on a state-by-state basis with some successes, for example in New York and Pennsylvania in 1980, causing the elimination of these restrictions (Moses & Hawkins, 1982). However, a 1986 Supreme Court decision served as a major setback for gay rights. In *Bowers v. Hardwick,* the Supreme Court made its first major ruling on a gay rights issue, overturning a federal appellate court decision in Georgia and refusing to extend constitutional protection to private homosexual acts between consenting adults (Hager, 1986). Essentially, this ruling denied the same protection enjoyed by nongays to gay people. The vote was close (5 to 4), and Justice Harry A. Blackmun vehemently chastised the Justices in the majority, calling the decision an opening for the state to ". . . invade the houses, hearts and minds of citizens who choose to live their lives differently" (Hager, 1986, pp. 1, 13).

Because lesbian women and gay men lack legal protection, gays are vulnerable to many other types of discriminatory behavior. For example, in *Gaylor v. Tacoma School District,* the Supreme Court refused to hear a case involving the dismissal, solely on the grounds of being gay, of a public school teacher who had years of outstanding work performance behind him (Moses & Hawkins, 1982). Though employment protection exists for gay people in some cities and states (a full listing is available from the National Gay Task Force), many other gays are economically vulnerable. Because many financial benefits accrue from legally sanctioned marriages, gay couples experience profound disadvantages.

> Some states have domestic partner laws, but most gay and lesbian couples cannot assume the basic rights of non-gay couples (e.g., insurance benefits, filing joint income tax returns, next-of-kin rights when a partner is hospitalized, and legal custody of children). The combination of the AIDS epidemic (prompting the need for legally sanctioned medical decisions and wills) and the "gayby boom" of increasing numbers of gay and lesbian parents has led to a push for legal protection of family rights (Fassinger, 1991, p. 162).

Finally, gays have not had much success in court in attempts to retain custody of their children after a divorce. Because custody is decided on the basis of the "best interest of the child," and lesbianism or gayness is usually viewed as inherently unhealthy, gay people are vulnerable to losing their children solely on the basis of their sexual orientation (Falk, 1989).

## Violence against Gays

One of the alarming consequences of the rampant homophobia in our society is the relative impunity with which individuals can harass, assault, and persecute gay people. Herek (1986; 1989) documented the existence and prevalence of antigay violence, and the particular ferocity and seriousness of these attacks. In statewide surveys, anywhere from 15 percent to 25 percent of the gays polled reported being survivors of physical violence directly related to their gayness (Herek, 1986); the overwhelming majority of lesbian women and gay men have experienced antigay threats and verbal abuse (Herek, 1989).

The perpetrators of antigay violence are usually young men in groups; gay men are more likely to be the targets of physical assault while lesbian women are more often sexually assaulted and harassed. The seriousness of the problem is highlighted by the following:

> Attacks against gay people often are characterized by an intense rage on the part of the attackers; thus there tends to be more violence than other physical assaults.

Commenting on this phenomenon, sociologists Brian Miller and Laud Humphreys observed, "Seldom is a homosexual (murder) victim simply shot. He is more apt to be stabbed a dozen times, mutilated, *and* strangled." (Herek, 1986, p. 3)

Herek (1986) also notes that violence against lesbian women and gay men is increasing in frequency and attributes this increase to the public fears of gay people fueled by the AIDS crisis. Attacks on gay military personnel have received attention in tandem with the debates about gays in the military. In a recent incident, a U.S. Navy sailor was beaten to death by a shipmate because he was gay; he was bludgeoned so badly that his body could only be identified by his tatoos. On being sentenced, the murderer declared no remorse, and said he would do it again because he was "disgusted for homosexuals" ("Sailor in beating death," 1993).

In addition to their susceptibility to senseless assaults and violence, gay *survivors* of violence must cope with the homophobic attitudes of medical personnel, police, and lawyers (Herek, 1989). The experience of these survivors is not unlike that of rape survivors. Often gay people are ". . . blamed by others for their assault, (and) accused of inviting the attack or deserving it" (Herek, 1986, p. 4). Because of their vulnerability to arbitrary dismissal from jobs or eviction from their residences, gay men and lesbian women who have been assaulted are unlikely to report their assault to law enforcement officials, fearing public exposure of their sexual orientation; as many as 80 percent of antigay assaults go unreported (Herek, 1986).

## Gays and the Mental Health System

After decades of discriminatory treatment of gays by the mental health system, there have been some important changes in the "official" status of homosexuality within psychology and psychiatry. Generally, there has been a movement toward the treatment, in therapy and counseling, of the *problems* of lesbian women and gay men, rather than the condition of homosexuality (Stein & Cohen, 1986), and to gay-affirmative counseling (Dworkin & Gutierrez, 1992). However, while this trend is positive, it does not necessarily reflect the attitudes and behaviors of all practitioners; gay clients are still often faced with subtle and even blatant homophobia, heterosexual bias, and misinformation about gays in counseling and therapy.

### Bias in Diagnosis

A landmark in psychiatry's treatment of gay people occurred in 1973 when the American Psychiatric Association decided to remove homosexuality as a diagnosis from their *Diagnostic and Statistical Manual of Mental Disorders*. Although protesters of this decision accused the American Psychiatric Association of succumbing to political pressure by gay rights organizations, the reality was just the opposite (Krajeski, 1986). Bias in psychology and psychiatry had historically justified the assumption, never scientifically proven, that homosexuality per se was pathological. The 1973 decision to depathologize homosexuality, followed by a similar move on the part of the American Psychological Association in 1975, simply corrected a long-existing and unscientific injustice (Krajeski, 1986).

The diagnosis of homosexuality was replaced, in the next version of the *Diagnostic and Statistical Manual of Mental Disorders III* (APA, 1980), with the diagnosis "ego-dystonic homosexuality." This diagnostic label has been employed with individuals who expressed dissatisfaction with their homosexual behavior and a desire to change their sexual orientation. It was grouped with other "Psychosexual Disorders" such as exhibitionism, masochism, and pedophilia in the DSM-III. Although an improvement over the previous diagnostic system, the inclusion of the diagnosis of ego-dystonic homosexuality in the DSM-III reinforced prevailing biases in society at large, shared by many mental health professionals. The emphasis on the individual rather than the social causes of distress remained, and gay people continued to be placed in a position inferior to that of nongays. An example of this perhaps subtle point is that there was never an official diagnosis of "ego-dystonic heterosexuality." The very idea appears absurd, but only because of the cultural context of the stigmatization of gays.

The upshot of the "ego-dystonic homosexuality" diagnosis was that many professionals continued to "treat" gay clients for their gayness by promoting programs to change sexual orientation, and thereby encourage gay people to personalize and internalize their oppression, rather than work through these issues with the goal of developing a positive gay identity. Ego-dystonic homosexuality has now been eliminated from the diagnostic nomenclature in the current edition of the diagnostic manual (DSM III-R); however, this has not prevented practitioners from continuing to use the diagnosis unofficially. The ethical issues related to sexual orientation change programs will be discussed more fully in the following section on bias in treatment.

## Bias in Treatment: Attitudes of Counselors and Therapists

The research on homophobia indicates that professionals, including mental health professionals, generally hold more positive attitudes about gay men and lesbian women than the public at large, but therapists' attitudes are not totally accepting (Levitt & Klassen, 1974; Moses & Hawkins, 1982). A large proportion of therapists and counselors appear to agree that homosexuality is not an illness; but attitude surveys also suggest that mental health professionals do see homosexuality and lesbianism as signs of some type of disturbance or developmental arrest, and many view the goal of changing sexual orientation as valid (Garfinkle & Morin, 1978; Martin, 1982). Therapists are generally uninformed about gay and lesbian life-styles and issues (Graham, Rawlings, Halpern, & Hermes, 1984), tend to hold many of the societal stereotypes about lesbian women and gay men (Casas, Brady, & Ponterotto, 1983), and may exhibit distorted judgment about the clinical concerns of gay people (Davison

& Friedman, 1981). Rudolph (1988), in Chapter 15, argues that inconsistency and ambivalence perhaps best describe the mental health establishment's perspective on counseling lesbians and gay men.

It is of vital importance to effective counseling and therapy for mental health professionals to work on their own attitudes and inform themselves about gay life-styles and related information. Gays seek counseling at a higher rate than nongays (Rudolph, 1988); therefore, some substantial percentage of any practitioner's client load will be gay, whether the counselor or therapist knows that those clients are gay or not. Paulsen (1983) reported that former gay clients of therapists perceived as holding negative views toward lesbians and gay men often experienced greater psychological distress after therapy. Nonetheless, there have been few research studies on therapist homophobia, and very little on the subject is available in the counseling and clinical literature; the topic is rarely addressed in training programs (Graham, Rawlings, Halpern, & Hermes, 1984) and is all but absent from the counseling literature (Betz & Fitzgerald, 1993). This lack of introspection on the part of counselors and therapists is particularly striking in the psychodynamic literature where Kwawer (1980) reported that not one article on "countertransference issues" with gay clients appeared.

Results of a recent survey of psychologists support the need for greater attention to therapist attitudes toward, and treatment of, gay men and lesbian women (Garnets, Hancock, Cochran, Goodchilds, & Peplau, 1991). Ninety-nine percent of the psychologists in the survey reported providing services to at least one lesbian or gay man; approximately 6 percent of the average caseload were gay men while 7 percent were lesbian women (Garnets et al., 1991). A majority of the respondents provided critical incidents illustrating the treatment of gay men and lesbian women in therapy. Examples of biased, inadequate, or inappropriate practice with gay clients included: believing that homosexuality per se is pathological; attributing client problems to their sexual orientation; failing to recognize the effects of homophobia on gay clients; assuming that all clients are heterosexual; focusing on sexual orientation when it is not relevant; demanding that clients change their sexual orientation; trivializing or demeaning a client's gay identity; inappropriately terminating a client upon disclosure of the client's sexual orientation; lack of understanding about gay identity; gross insensitivity to the importance of a client's relationships; and numerous other examples of ignorance and bias.

In addition to misinformation, stereotyping, and homophobia, a more subtle but still more damaging and widespread therapist bias is "compulsory heterosexuality" (Rich, 1980); some of the negative examples provided above reflect this prejudice. A form of heterosexual bias, Rich's concept of compulsory heterosexuality describes the implicit and unquestioned belief in the normality and inevitability of heterosexuality, resulting in the neglect in the literature, and by extension in the minds of mental health practitioners, of the very existence of gay people. Lesbian women have been more vulnerable to this lack of acknowledgment of their existence than gay men, as illustrated by an apocryphal tale about Queen Victoria. Upon being presented with a law criminalizing consenting adult homosexual activity, Victoria was unable to imagine that such a law had anything to do with "the ladies." She replied to her ministers: "Women don't do such things," and all references to lesbian women were expunged from the law (Weintraub, 1987).

Gay clients presenting themselves for counseling or therapy do not always reveal their sexual orientation to their therapists. "Compulsory heterosexuality" refers to the assumption on the part of the counselors, therapists, and society at large that everyone is heterosexual. Such an assumption can cause serious damage to gay clients who are still "in the closet" (Cohen & Stein, 1986).

## Bias in Treatment: Ethical Issues

One of the overriding issues in the psychotherapeutic treatment of gay people concerns treatments designed to change sexual orientation. The controversy applies to therapists and counselors of *all* theoretical orientations, but has been particularly heated within the behavioral tradition. Therefore, the following discussion focuses mainly on behavioral interventions, but the reader should keep in mind the generalizability of the issues.

The behaviorists, while disagreeing vehemently with psychoanalytic views in general, did agree with the Freudians about the environmental origin of homosexuality (although the mechanisms theorized to cause homosexual behavior were thought about very differently) and also focused on curing rather than studying gay people (Bullough, 1979). The behaviorists have traditionally stated that they ascribe to a "value-free" stance and have focused on treating the client's presenting concern. Thus, the argument goes, the *client* has control over the goals of treatment, and the therapist or counselor is not passing judgment on the client's problem. Numerous behavioral sexual reorientation procedures have been developed, mostly for gay men (Adams & Sturgis, 1977). These behavioral treatments have taken the form of aversive techniques, including the use of chemicals to produce noxious reactions and electrical shocks, geared to reduce sexual responses to same-sex stimuli, and positive conditioning techniques designed to increase heterosexual arousal (Adams & Sturgis, 1977). Social skills training programs to enhance heterosexual dating skills are another example of behavioral approaches to the modification of homosexuality (Adams & Sturgis, 1977).

In the 1970s some behaviorists raised serious questions about the behavioral treatment, or indeed any other treatment, of gays designed to change sexual orientation. Davison (1976; 1977) and Begelman (1975) were at the forefront of the debate over the ethics of behavioral reorientation treatment of gays.

> I believe that clinicians spend time developing and analyzing procedures only if they are concerned about a problem. This seems to be the case with homosexuality. And yet, consider our rhetoric that typically speaks of social labeling of behavior rather than viewing a given behavior as intrinsically normal

or abnormal. Consider also the huge literature on helping homosexuals (at least males) change their sexual preference, and the paucity of literature aimed at helping the labelers change their prejudicial biases and encouraging the homosexual to develop as a person without going the change route. (Davison, 1977, p. 199)

Thus, one criticism of sexual reorientation treatments is that there is no cure without a disease. Second, the availability of procedures encourages their use in treatment. And, third, a charge of bias has been leveled (Davison, 1976; 1977; Begelman, 1975). "How can we honestly speak of non-prejudice when we participate in therapy regimes that by their very existence—and regardless of their efficacy—condone the current societal prejudice and perhaps also impede social change?" (Davison, 1977; p. 199)

Begelman (1975), arguing in much the same vein as Davison, has also pointed out the countertherapeutic effects of treating gay people *for their gayness:*

> . . . behavior therapists contribute significantly to preventing the exercise of any *real* option in decision-making about sexual identity, by further strengthening the prejudice that homosexuality is a "problem behavior," since treatment may be offered for it. As a consequence of this therapeutic stance, as well as a wider system of social and attitudinal pressures, homosexuals tend to seek treatment *for being homosexuals.* Heterosexuals, on the other hand, can scarcely be expected to seek voluntary treatment for being "heterosexual," especially since all the social forces arrayed—including the availability of behavior therapy for heterosexuality—attest to the acknowledgment of the idea that whatever "problems" heterosexuals experience are not due to their sexual orientation. (Begelman, 1975, p. 180)

Thus, despite the ostensibly "positive" view of behaviorally-oriented therapists and counselors toward gay people, *in fact* gay men and lesbian women have been treated differently within this theoretical tradition. Gay-affirmative writers and researchers stress that individuals presenting themselves with the desire to change their sexual orientation are actually going through a stage in the "coming out" process in the development of a positive gay identity (Cass, 1979).

Gay adolescents are especially at risk of being damaged by efforts to change sexual orientation (Coleman & Remafedi, 1989). Intense homophobia, both external and internal, profoundly complicates the process of achieving a stable and mature personal and sexual identity on the part of teenagers; thus, gay teenagers may present with a desire "to be normal" (i.e., heterosexual). Lack of sensitivity and inappropriate treatment can be equally damaging. The gravity of the matter can be seen in recent statistics indicating that confusion over sexual orientation is a significant contributor to teenage suicide (Gibson, 1988). Working with adolescents grappling with issues of sexual orientation is challenging enough, but the process is further confounded by ethical issues such as parental consent and confidentiality (Sobocinski, 1990). School counselors, who are the most likely mental health practitioners to be in a position to assist gay youths, may themselves be at risk of sanctions from school administrators for providing ethical, gay-affirmative counseling services. Readers are referred to Sobocinski's (1990) helpful overview of ethical issues and dilemmas in counseling gay and lesbian adolescents.

In conclusion, it can be seen that most of the problems experienced by lesbian women and gay men are a direct result of societal oppression and the internalization of homophobia, and homophobic attitudes have parallels with other prejudicial attitudes such as sexism, racism, and ageism. Further, there is an intimate connection between antigay attitudes and gender-role beliefs, underscoring the relationship of homophobia and sexism. And finally, to be effective, counselors and therapists must not only inform themselves about gay lifestyles and treatment issues, but must also address their own homophobia and heterosexual biases in order to work therapeutically with gay clients.

Chapters 13–15 explore more thoroughly some of the issues most relevant to counseling gay men and lesbian women, while Chapter 16 contains recommendations for counselor preparation, continuing professional development, and for counseling research.

# References

Abramowitz, C. V. (1977). Blaming the mother: An experimental investigation of sex-role bias in countertransference. *Psychology of Women Quarterly, 2,* 25–34.

Adams, H. E., & Sturgis, E. T. (1977). Status of behavioral reorientation techniques in the modification of homosexuality: A review. *Psychological Bulletin, 84,* 1171–1188.

Adding up the victories and defeats: a box score. (1986, November 23). *Los Angeles Times,* p. VI, 1.

Alexander, R. A. (1986). *The relationship between internalized homophobia and depression and low self-esteem in gay men.* Unpublished doctoral dissertation, University of California, Santa Barbara.

Alexander, R. A., & Casas, J. M. (1985). Unpublished manuscript, University of California, Santa Barbara.

American Psychiatric Association. (1980). *Diagnostic and statistical manual of mental disorders* (3rd Ed.) Washington, DC: Author.

Ammerman, R. T., Van Hasselt, V. B., & Hersen, M. (1988). Maltreatment of handicapped children: A critical review. *Journal of Family Violence, 3,* 53–72.

Aslin, A. L. (1977). Feminist and community mental health center psychotherapists' expectations of mental health for women. *Sex Roles, 3,* 537–544.

Atkinson, D. R. (1980). The elderly, oppression, and social-change counseling. *Counseling and Values, 24,* 86–96.

Basoff, E. S., & Glass, G. V. (1982). The relationship between sex roles and mental health: A meta-analysis of twenty-six studies. *The Counseling Psychologist, 10,* 105–112.

Begelman, D. A. (1975). Ethical and legal issues of behavior modification. In M. Hersen, R. Eisler, & P. M. Miller (Eds.), *Progress in behavior modification.* New York: Academic Press.

Bem, S. L., & Bem, D. J. (1984). Homogenizing the American women: The power of an unconscious ideology. Reprinted in A. M. Jagger & P. S. Rothenberg (Eds.), *Feminist Frameworks* (pp. 10–22) (2nd Edition). New York: McGraw-Hill (Originally published in 1970).

Bernard, J. (1971). The paradox of the happy marriage. In V. Gornick & B. K. Moran (Eds.), *Women in Sexist Society* (pp. 145–162). New York: New American Library.

Betz, N. E. (In press). Basic issues and concepts in career counseling for women. In W. E. Walsh & S. H. Osipow (Eds.), *Career counseling for women.* Hillsdale, NJ: Erlbaum.

Betz, N. E., & Fitzgerald, L. F. (1987). The career psychology of women. New York: Academic Press.

Betz, N. E., & Fitzgerald, L. F. (1993). Individuality and diversity: Theory and research in counseling psychology. *Annual review of psychology, 44,* 343–381.

Bingham, W. C., & House, E. W. (1973). Counselors view women and work: Accuracy of information. *Vocational Guidance Quarterly, 21,* 262–268.

Black, D. (1986). *The plague years.* New York: Simon & Schuster.

Blatt, E. R., & Brown, S. W. (1986). Environmental influences on incidents of alleged child abuse and neglect in New York state psychiatric facilities: Toward an etiology of institutional child maltreatment. *Child Abuse and Neglect, 10*(2), 171–180.

Blank, M. L. (1974). Raising the age barrier to psychotherapy. *Geriatrics, 29*(11), 141–144, 147–148.

Bowe, F. (1980). *Rehabilitating America.* New York: Harper & Row.

Brookhouser, P. E., Sullivan, P., Scanlan, J. M., & Garbarino, J. (1986). Identifying the sexually abused deaf child. The otolaryngologist's role. *Laryngoscope, 96,* 152–158.

Broverman, I. K., Broverman, D. M., Clarkson, F. E., Rosenkrantz, P. S., & Vogel, S. R. (1970). Sex-role stereotypes and clinical judgments of mental health. *Journal of Consulting and Clinical Psychology, 34,* 1–7.

Brown, L. K. (1989). Is the sexual freedom for our aging population in long-term care institutions? *Journal of Gerontological Social Work, 13* (3/4), 75–93.

Bruce, M. A., & Christiansen, C. H. (1988). Advocacy in word as well as deed. *The American Journal of Occupational Therapy, 42,* 189–191.

Bullough, V. L. (1979). *Homosexuality: A history.* New York: New American Library.

Butler, R. N. (1979). *Why survive? Being old in America.* New York: Harper & Row.

Butler, R. N. (1983). Foreword. In J. I. Kosberg (Ed.), *Abuse and maltreatment of the elderly: Causes and interventions.* Boston: John Wright.

Caplan, P. (1991). Delusional dominating personality disorder (DDPD). *Feminism and Psychology, 1,* 171–174.

Casas, J. M., Brady, S., & Ponterotto, J. G. (1983). Sexual preference biases in counseling: An information processing approach. *Journal of Counseling Psychology, 30,* 139–145.

Cass, V. C. (1979). Homosexual identity formation: A theoretical model. *Journal of Homosexuality, 4,* 219–235.

Chesler, P. (1972). *Women and madness.* New York: Avon.

Cohen, C. J., & Stein, T. S. (1986). Reconceptualizing individual psychotherapy with gay men and lesbians. In T. S. Stein & C. J. Cohen (Eds.), *Contemporary perspectives on psychotherapy with lesbians and gay men* (pp. 27–56). New York: Plenum.

Cohen, E. S. (1990). The elderly mystique: Impediment to advocacy and empowerment. *Generations, 14*(supp), 13–16.

Colburn, D. (November 27, 1985). Pain, placebos, and profit. *The Washington Post,* HE9.

Cole, T. (1991). The specter of old age: History, politics, and culture in an aging America. In B. B. Hess & E. W. Markson (Eds.), *Growing old in America* (4th Edition, pp. 23–37). New Brunswick, NJ: Transaction Books.

Coleman, E., & Remafedi, G. (1989). Gay, lesbian, and bisexual adolescents: A critical challenge to counselors. *Journal of Counseling and Development, 68,* 36–40.

Collier, H. V. (1982). *Counseling Women.* New York: Free Press.

Cook, D. W., Kunce, J. T., & Getsinger, S. H. (1976). Perceptions of the disabled and counseling effectiveness. *Rehabilitation Counseling Bulletin, 19,* 470–475.

Courtois, C. A. (1986, April). *The new scholarship on child sexual abuse: Counseling adult survivors.* Paper presented at the Annual Meeting of the American Educational Research Association, San Francisco.

Crossmaker, M. (1991). Behind locked doors—Institutional sexual abuse. *Sexuality and Disability, 9,* 201–219.

Davenport, J., & Reims, N. (1978). Theoretical orientation and attitudes toward women. *Social Work, 23,* 306–309.

Davis, M. (1989). Gender and sexual development of women with mental retardation. *The Disabilities Studies Quarterly, 9*(3), 19–20.

Davison, G. (1977). Homosexuality and the ethics of behavioral intervention. *Journal of Homosexuality, 2,* 195–204.

Davison, G. C. (1976). Homosexuality: The ethical challenge. *Journal of Consulting and Clinical Psychology, 44,* 157–162.

Davison, G., & Friedman, S. (1981). Sexual orientation stereotype in the distortion of clinical judgment. *Journal of Homosexuality, 6,* 37–44.

Deckard, B. S. (1983). *The women's movement: Political, socioeconomic, and psychological issues* (3rd edition). New York: Harper & Row.

Doyle, D. P. (1990). Aging and crime. In Kenneth F. Ferraro (Ed.), *Gerontology: Perspectives and issues* (pp. 294–315). New York: Springer Publishing Company.

Dremen, S. B. (1978). Sex-role stereotyping in mental health standards in Israel. *Journal of Clinical Psychology, 34,* 961–966.

Dunbar, J., Brown, M., & Amoroso, D. (1973). Some correlates of attitudes toward homosexuality. *Journal of Social Psychology, 89,* 271–279.

Dworkin, S. H., & Gutierrez, F. J. (1992). Introduction: Opening the closet door (pp. xvii–xxvii). In S. H. Dworkin & F. J. Gutierrez (Eds.), *Counseling gay men and lesbians: Journal to the end of the rainbow.* Alexandria, VA: American Association of Counseling and Development.

Falk, P. J. (1989). Lesbian mothers: Psychosocial assumptions in family law. *American Psychologist, 44,* 941–947.

Faludi, S. (1991). *Backlash: The undeclared war against American women.* New York: Crown.

Farmer, H. S. (1982). Empirical evidence for sex bias in counseling weak. *The Counseling Psychologist, 10,* 87–88.

Farmer, H. S., & Backer, T. E. (1977). *New career options for women: A counselor's sourcebook.* New York: Human Science Press.

Fassinger, R. E. (1991). The hidden minority: Issues and challenges in working with lesbian women and gay men. *The Counseling Psychologist, 19,* 157–176.

Fitzgerald, L. F. (1993). The last great open secret: The sexual harassment of women in the workplace and academic. *Federation of behavioral, psychological, and cognitive sciences.* Washington, DC: Author.

Freedman, S. M., & Keller, R. T. (1981). The handicapped in the work force. *Academy of Management Review, 6,* 449–458.

Freeman, J. (Ed.) (1979). *Women: A feminist perspective* (2nd Edition). Palo Alto, CA: Mayfield.

Gallup, G. (1977). Gallup poll on gay rights: Approval with reservations. *San Francisco Chronicle,* July 18, pp. 1–18.

Garfinkle, E. M., & Morin, S. F. (1978). Psychologists' attitudes toward homosexual psychotherapy clients. *Journal of Social Issues, 34,* 101–112.

Garnets, L., Hancock, K. A., Cochran, S. D., Goodchilds, J., & Peplau, L. A. (1991). Issues in psychotherapy with lesbians and gay men. *American Psychologist, 46,* 964–972.

Gerber, J., Wolff, J., Klores, W., & Brown, G. (1989). Lifetrends: The future of baby boomers and other aging Americans. New York: McMillan Publishing Co.

Gettys, L., & Cann, A. (1981). Children's perceptions of occupational sex stereotypes. *Sex Roles, 7,* 301–308.

Gibson, P. (1988). Gay male and lesbian youth suicide. In *Report of the secretary's [Department of Health and Human Services] task force on youth suicide* (pp. 3–110 to 3–142). Washington, DC: U.S. Government Printing Office.

Giordano, N. H., & Giordano, J. A. (1984). Elder abuse: A review of the literature. *Social Work, 29,* 232–236.

Gove, W. R. (1973). Sex, marital status, and mortality. *American Journal of Sociology, 79,* 45–67.

Gove, W. R. (1980). Mental illness and psychiatric treatment among women. *Psychology of Women Quarterly, 4,* 345–362.

Gove, W. R., & Tudor, J. F. (1973). Adult sex roles and mental illness. *American Journal of Sociology, 78,* 812–835.

Graham, D. L. R., Rawlings, E. I., Halpern, H. S., & Hermes, J. (1984). Therapists' needs for training in counseling lesbians and gay men. *Professional Psychology, 15,* 482–496.

Grealish, C. A., & Salomone, P. R. (1986). Devaluing those with disability: Take responsibility, take action. *The Vocational Guidance Quarterly, 34,* 147–150.

Hager, P. (1986, July 1). Ruling upholds ban on homosexual conduct. *Los Angeles Times,* 1, 13.

Harris and Associates (1986). *The ICD survey of disabled Americans: Bringing disabled Americans into the mainstream. A nationwide survey of 1,000 disabled people.* New York: Author.

Harris, L. (1975). *The myth and reality of aging in America.* New York: National Council on Aging.

Herek, G. M. (1984). Beyond "homophobia": A social psychological perspective on attitudes toward lesbians and gay men. *Journal of Homosexuality, 10,* 1–21.

Herek, G. M. (1986, October 9). *Violence against lesbians and gay men.* Statement presented to the United States House of Representatives, Committee on the Judiciary, Subcommittee on Criminal Justice.

Herek, G. M. (1989). Hate crimes against lesbians and gay men: Issues for research and policy. *American Psychologist, 44,* 948–955.

Herek, G. M. (1993). Sexual orientation and military service: A social science perspective. *American Psychologist, 48,* 538–549.

Hess, B. B. (1980). Stereotypes of the aged. In B. B. Hess (Ed.), *Growing old in America.* New Brunswick, NJ: Transaction Books.

Hess, B. B. (1991). Growing old in the 1990s. In B. B. Hess & E. W. Markson (Eds.), *Growing old in America* (pp. 3–22). New Brunswick, NJ: Transaction Publishers.

Hewlett, S. A. (1986). *A lesser life: The myth of women's liberation in America.* New York: William Morrow.

Hey, R. P., & Carlson, E. (1991). 'Granny dumping:' New pain for U.S. elders. *AARP Bulletin, 32*(8), 1, 16.

Higher Education and National Affairs (1986). *Women academics still experience discrimination.* Washington, DC: American Council on Education.

Howe, L. K. (1977). *Pink collar workers.* New York: Avon.

Hunter, N. D., Michaelson, S. E., & Stoddard, T.B. (1992). *The rights of lesbians and gay men: The basic ACLU guide to a gay person's rights.* Carbondale, IL: Southern Illinois University Press.

Ifill, G. (1986, March 2). To millions of elderly Americans neglect is just one more form of abuse. *Washington Post,* pp. B1, B10.

Joe, J. R. (1988). Government policies and disabled people in American Indian communities. *Disability, Handicap & Society, 3,* 253–262.

Johnson, M. (1978). Influence of counselor gender on reactivity to clients. *Journal of Counseling Psychology, 25,* 359–365.

Johnson, M. (1980). Mental illness and psychiatric treatment among women: A response. *Psychology of Women Quarterly, 4,* 363–371.

Kahn-Hut, R., Daniels, A. K., & Colvard, R. (1982). *Women and work: Problems and perspectives.* New York: Oxford University Press.

Karr, A. R. (1990, May 23). Disabled-rights bill inspires hopes, fears. *Wall Street Journal,* pp. B1, B2.

King, N. R. (1984). Exploitation and abuse of older family members: An overview of the problem. In J. J. Costa (Ed.), *Abuse of the elderly.* Lexington, MA: D. C. Heath.

Kite, M. E., & Johnson, B. T. (1988). Attitudes toward older and younger adults: A meta-analysis. *Psychology and Aging, 3,* 233–244.

Kosberg, J. I. (1983). *Abuse and maltreatment of the elderly: Causes and interventions.* Boston: John Wright.

Krajeski, J. P. (1986). Psychotherapy with gay men & lesbians. In T. S. Stein & C. J. Cohen (Eds.), *Contemporary perspectives on psychotherapy with lesbians and gay men* (pp. 9–26). New York: Plenum.

Kwawer, J. S. (1980). Transference and countertransference in homosexuality—Changing psychoanalytic views. *American Journal of Psychotherapy, 34,* 72–80.

LaFraniere, S. (January 27, 1985). Virginia's mentally ill caught in tug of war. *The Washington Post,* B1–B5.

Lau, E., & Kosberg, J. (1978). Abuse of the elderly by informal care providers: Practice and research issues. Paper presented at the 31st Annual Meeting of the Gerontological Society, Dallas, Texas, November 20, 1978.

Lauritsen, J., & Thorstad, D. (1974). *The early homosexual rights movement.* New York: Times Change Press.

Levin, J., & Levin, W. C. (1980). *Ageism: Prejudice and discrimination against the elderly.* Belmont, CA: Wadsworth.

Levitt, E., & Klassen, A., Jr. (1974). Public attitudes toward homosexuality: Part of a 1970 national survey by the Institute of Sex Research. *Journal of Homosexuality, 1,* 29–43.

Lewis, R. (1992a). Disposable workers: New corporate policies put many older employees at risk. *AARP Bulletin, 33* (5), 2.

Lewis, R. (1992b). Ups and downs of the 1980s: New income data refutes "fat cat" age stereotype. *AARP Bulletin, 33* (2), 1, 14–16.

Livneh, H. (1982). On the origins of negative attitudes toward people with disabilities. *Rehabilitation Literature, 43,* 338–347.

Lombana, J. H. (1982). Counseling handicapped children and youth. *Counseling and Human Development, 15*(4), 1–12.

Margolis, R. J. (1990). *Risking old age in America.* Boulder, CO: Westview Press.

Marriott, M. (December 16, 1984). Plan to cut aid for aged draws fire. *Washington Post,* A16C.

Martin, A. (1982). Some issues in the treatment of gay and lesbian patients. *Psychotherapy: Theory, research and practice, 19,* 341–348.

Martin, D. (1976). *Battered wives.* New York: Pocket Books.

Mayer, M. (1993). Pensions: The naked truth. *Modern Maturity, 36*(1), 40–44.

McAllister, M. (March 16, 1985). McLean group opposes project for elderly. *Washington Post,* E4, E5.

McLeod, D. (1992). Overcharge . . . Critics: Feds slighting Medicare patients. *AARP Bulletin, 33,*(2), 1, 4–5.

Melton, G. B. (1989). Public policy and private prejudice: Psychology and law on gay rights. *American Psychologist, 44,* 933–940.

Mitric, J. M. (September 21, 1985). Housing for elderly opposed. *Washington Post,* E37, E40.

Morin, S. F. (1977). Heterosexual bias in psychological research on lesbianism and male homosexuality. *American Psychologist, 32,* 629–637.

Morin, S. F., & Garfinkle, E. M. (1978). Male homophobia. *Journal of Social Issues, 34,* 29–47.

Morrison, A. M., & Glinow, M. A. (1990). Women and minorities in management. *American Psychologist, 45,* 200–208.

Morse, S. (August 13, 1985). Early retirement: Tarnishing the golden years. *The Washington Post,* C5.

Moses, A. E., & Hawkins, R. O. (1982). *Counseling lesbian women and gay men.* St. Louis: Mosby.

Moskowitz, D. B. (September 16, 1985). Rights of handicapped expanded. *Washington Post.*

Myers, J. E., & Shelton, B. (1987). Abuse and older persons: Issues and implications for counselors. *Journal of Counseling and Development, 65,* 376–380.

National Science Foundation. (1990). *Women and minorities in science and engineering.* Washington, DC: Author.

New AARP study: Health costs, '81 tax cut fuel U.S. deficit. (1992). *AARP Bulletin, 33*(9), 3.

O'Malley, K. M., & Richardson, S. (1985). Sex bias in counseling: Have things changed? *Journal of Counseling and Development, 63,* 294–299.

Paulsen, J. (1983, April). *Homophobia in American psychiatrists.* Paper presented to the Group for the Advancement of Psychiatry, Philadelphia.

Pearce, D. (1979). Women, work and welfare: The feminization of poverty. In K. W. Feinstein (Ed.), *Working women and families* (pp. 103–124). Beverly Hills, CA: Sage.

Rajeswary, I. (July 27, 1985). Aging former steelworker recounts job-hunt plight. *The Washington Post,* A7.

Rich, A. (1980). Compulsory heterosexuality and lesbian existence. *Signs: Journal of Women in Culture and Society, 5,* 631–660.

Richardson, M. A., & Johnson, M. (1984). Counseling women. In S. D. Brown & R. W. Lent (Eds.), *Handbook of Counseling Psychology* (pp. 832–877). New York: Wiley.

Richman, J. (1977). The foolishness and wisdom of age: Attitudes toward the elderly as reflected in jokes. *Gerontologist, 17,* 210–219.

Ridington, J. (1989, March). *Beating the "odds": Violence and women with disabilities* (Position paper 2). Vancouver: DAWN (DisAbled Women's Network) Canada.

Rosenbaum, W. A., & Button, J. W. (1989). Is there a gray peril?: Retirement politics in Florida. *The Gerontologist, 29,* 300–306.

Rosewater, L. B. (1985). *A critical statement on the proposed diagnosis of masochistic personality disorder.* Unpublished manuscript.

Rothschild, M. (1992, September 21). Gay bashing becomes new national pastime. *Arizona Republic,* p. A9.

Rudolph, J. (1988). Counselors' attitudes toward homosexuality: A selective review of the literature. *Journal of Counseling and Development, 67,* 165–168.

Rudolph, J. (1989). The impact of contemporary ideology and AIDS on the counseling of gay clients. *Counseling and Values, 33,* 96–108.

Rural disabled find barriers slow to fall. (1992, October 6). *Santa Barbara News Press,* p. 1.

Russo, N. F., & Denmark, F. L. (1984). Women, psychology, and public policy: Selected issues. *American Psychologist, 39,* 1161–1165.

Sailor in beating death of gay would 'do it again'. (1993, May 26). *Arizona Republic,* p. A5.

Satcher, J., & Hendren, G. R. (1991). Acceptance of the Americans with Disabilities Act of 1990 by persons preparing to enter the business field. *Journal of Applied Rehabilitation Counseling, 22*(2), 15–18.

Schofield, L. F., & Kunce, J. T. (1971). Client disability and counselor behavior. *Rehabilitation Counseling Bulletin, 14,* 158–165.

Schwalb, S. J., & Sedlacek, W. E. (1990). Have college students' attitudes toward older people changed? *Journal of College Student Development, 31,* 127–132.

Seaberry, J. (February 7, 1985). Poverty still a problem for elderly. *Washington Post,* Elc, E2a.

Select Committee on Aging. (1990). *Elder Abuse: A decade of shame and inaction* (Comm. Pub. No. 101-752). Washington, DC: U.S. Government Printing Office.

Sherman, J. A. (1980). Therapist attitudes and sex-role stereotyping. In A. M. Brodsky & R. Hare-Mustin (Eds.), *Women and psychotherapy,* (pp. 35–66). New York: Guilford.

Smith, M. L. (1980). Sex bias in counseling. *Psychological Bulletin, 87,* 392–407.

Smolowe, J. (1993, May 24). Hearts and minefields. *Time,* pp. 41–42.

Sobocinski, M. R. (1990). Ethical principles in the counseling of gay and lesbian adolescents: Issues of autonomy, competence, confidentiality. *Professional Psychology: Research and Practice, 21,* 240–247.

Sobsey, D., & Mansell, S. (1990). The prevention of sexual abuse of people with developmental disabilities. *Developmental Disabilities Bulletin, 18,* 51–66.

Sobsey, D., & Varnhagen, C. (1991). Sexual abuse and exploitation of disabled individuals. In C.R. Bagley & R. J. Thomlison (Eds.), *Child sexual abuse* (pp. 203–216). Toronto: Wall & Emerson, Inc.

Stein, T. S., & Cohen, C. J. (Eds.). (1986). *Contemporary perspectives on psychotherapy with gay men and lesbians.* New York: Plenum.

Stricker, G. (1977). Implications of research for psychotherapeutic treatment of women. *American Psychologist, 32,* 14–22.

Sullivan, P. M., Vernon, M., & Scanlan, J. M. (1987). Sexual abuse of deaf youth. *American Annals of the Deaf, 132,* 256–262.

Tavris, C. (1977, January). Men and women report their views on masculinity. *Psychology Today, 35.*

Teal, D. (1971). *The gay militants.* New York: Stein and Day.

Thomasma, D. C. (1989). Moving the aged into the house of the dead: A critique of ageist social policy. *Journal of the American Geriatrics Society, 37,* 169–172.

United States Bureau of the Census. (1983b). *Population Profile of the United States: 1982* (Current Population Reports, Series P-23, No. 130). Washington, DC: U.S. Government Printing Office.

United States Bureau of the Census. (1989). *Labor force status and other characteristics of persons with a work disability: 1981 to 1988* (Current Population Reports, Series P-23, No. 160). Washington, DC: U.S. Government Printing Office.

United States Bureau of the Census. (1992). *Poverty in the United States: 1991* (Current Population Reports, Series P-60, No. 181). Washington, DC: U.S. Government Printing Office.

United States Senate Subcommittee on the Handicapped. (1985). Staff report on the institutionalized mentally disabled. *Joint Hearings of the Subcommittee on the handicapped.* Washington, DC: U.S. Government Printing Office.

UPI. (May 11, 1985). Fraud, abuse reported in pacemaker business. *Washington Post,* A11.

Vargo, J. W. (1987, May). *'And sometimes I wonder about thee': A misconception hypothesis approach to viewing attitudes toward people with disabilities.* Paper presented at the meeting of the Canadian Guidance and Counselling Association, Toronto.

Vargo, J. W. (1989). 'In the house of my friend': Dealing with disability. *International Journal for the Advancement of Counselling, 12,* 281–287.

Walker, L. E. (1979). *The battered woman.* New York: Harper & Row.

Weintraub, S. (1987). *Victoria: An intimate biography.* New York: E. P. Dutton.

Weitzman, L. J. (1985). *The divorce revolution: The unexpected social and economic consequences for women and children in America.* New York: The Free Press.

Wicas, C. A., & Carluccio, L. W. (1971). Attitudes of counselors toward three handicapped groups. *Rehabilitation Counseling Bulletin, 15,* 25–34.

Williams, J. H. (1983). *Psychology of women* (2nd Edition). New York: Norton.

Williams, W. C., & Lair, G. S. (1991). Using a person-centered approach with children who have a disability. *Elementary School Guidance & Counseling, 25,* 194–203.

Women's Bureau. (1975). *1975 Handbook on Women Workers.* Washington, DC: U.S. Department of Labor.

# PART 2

## The Client with a Disability

McDowell, Bills, and Eaton (1989) point out that "Persons with disabilities need what every individual needs—respect, encouragement, satisfying experiences, and the opportunity to develop his or her abilities" (p. 151). From Chapters 1, 2, and 3, however, we know that persons with disabilities are not treated the same as individuals without disabilities. This suggests that in addition to meeting the normal developmental needs that are experienced by all individuals, the counselor may need to address the influence of segregation and discrimination on their client when working with an individual with a disability.

In this part we present readings that examine the psychological and/or sociopolitical considerations relevant to counseling clients with disabilities. In Chapter 4, Livneh and Sherwood critique a number of contemporary counseling theories and interventions for counseling clients with disabilities. These theories might be considered traditional counseling approaches since the focus is on the client's adaptation to and coping with disability. Although the framework for their discussion is based on the phases of adaptation to traumatic disability, we believe their analysis of theories and interventions has implications for counseling persons with congenital disabilities as well as adventitious disabilities since both groups share many common needs and experiences. Their discussion of the somatopsychological approach is particularly instructive since most counselors outside the rehabilitation specialty may not be familiar with this approach. We find their argument that interventions should be matched to stage of adaptation convincing.

In Chapter 5, Humes, Szymanski, and Hohenshil broaden the view of counseling persons with disabilities somewhat by suggesting that the client's disability should not be the sole focus of counseling and by proposing that society (rather than the client with a disability) may need adjustment. This might be labeled a nontraditional or emerging approach to counseling persons with disabilities. Humes et al. also point out the important role that counselors and other professionals in schools can play in fostering social interaction between students with disabilities and their peers and in preparing students with disabilities for a future as fully participating and contributing members of society. The authors place special emphasis on the responsibility of counselors to assist students with disabilities as they plan for the transition from school to community.

In Chapter 6, Kuehn provides a comprehensive and thought-provoking analysis of the agendas that could influence the professional practice of rehabilitation counseling in the 1990s. Although his comments are directed specifically toward rehabilitation counselors, most of what he has to say has implications for all professional counselors and psychologists who serve persons with disabilities. In particular, his indictment of conflicting and dependence fostering rehabilitation policies and practices applies to all mental health services for persons with disabilities. He suggests that policies and practices granting special resources and services for persons with disabilities (i.e., traditional rehabilitation counseling policies and practices) may increasingly come into conflict with policies and practices designed to protect their civil rights. He concludes by suggesting that rehabilitation (and other) counseling practices should move in the direction of fostering greater independence on the part of clients with disabilities.

## Reference

McDowell, W. A., Bills, G. F., & Eaton, M. W. (1989). Extending psychotherapeutic strategies to people with disabilities. *Journal of Counseling & Development, 68,* 151–154.

# 4

# Application of Personality Theories and Counseling Strategies to Clients with Physical Disabilities

*Hanoch Livneh and Ardis Sherwood*

A dearth of information exists regarding the application of the insights gained from psychological theories of human personality and behavior to understanding the psychosocial impact of physical disability. Not surprisingly, theoretically derived intervention strategies to facilitate psychosocial adjustment to disability are also sparsely encountered in the counseling and rehabilitation literature. Over the past four decades, assumptions concerning the interdependence of physical illness and disability, and the process of psychosocial adjustment have undergone substantial developments and modifications (see, for example, Duval, 1982; Shontz, 1971; Wright, 1983). These notions, ranging from concepts that are embedded in intricate personality theories to impressions that are portrayed through sketchy reports, have the potential of occupying an essential role in the understanding of adaptation to major traumatic events and the provision of rehabilitation care and service delivery to people with disabilities.

To complicate things, adaptation to disability is not a static concept. It is a dynamic and often protracted process that is composed of several fluctuating and overlapping phases (Falek & Britton, 1974; Fink, 1967; Shontz, 1965). Various clinically observed phase models of adaptation to disability were proposed in the past (Bray, 1978; Cohn, 1961; Weller & Miller, 1977). Briefly, the most commonly observed (or inferred) phases of adaptation to traumatic disability include the following:

1. *Shock.* The initial psychic numbness associated with the impact of a sudden and severe physical impairment.

Reprinted from *Journal of Counseling & Development, 69,* 525–540, 1991. © ACA. Reprinted with permission. No further reproduction authorized without written permission of American Counseling Association.

2. *Anxiety.* A panic-like reaction of initial recognition of the enormity of the traumatic event.
3. *Denial.* An attempt at mobilizing psychological defenses to ward off the painful realization of the resultant condition.
4. *Depression.* An initial and full realization of the loss of one's prior physical/sensory abilities (e.g., mobility, sight).
5. *Internalized anger.* A reaction of self-directed resentment accompanied by feelings of guilt and self-blame.
6. *Externalized hostility.* A reaction of other-directed anger as a form of retaliation against imposed physical limitations.
7. *Acknowledgement.* Intellectual recognition of the implications of the disability and gradual acceptance of its permanence and resultant functional limitations.
8. *Adjustment.* Affective internalization of the functional implications of the disability along with behavioral adaptation to newly perceived life situation.

The psychosocial reactions experienced by a person with a disability at these various phases call for differential intervention strategies specifically tailored to the individual's particular needs. Moreover, although the sequence of the adaptation phases appears to be, at least partially, internally determined, appropriately timed external interventions (e.g., psychosocial, behavioral, environmental) may have a decidedly positive effect upon the nature and duration of those phases and the ways of coping with them (Livneh, 1986).

The intent of this article is to assist the reader in exploring the substantive and clinical utilities of the most commonly used theories and intervention strategies for counseling people with disabilities. The theories selected for this review are not intended to constitute a complete set of theories applicable to working with persons with disabilities, nor should they be regarded as being held in higher professional esteem than are the theories that are not included. The decision rule used for theory adaptation was twofold. First, theories were selected based on their familiarity to most readers (i.e., their inclusion in popular text books such as Corey [1986], Corsini & Wedding [1989], and Patterson [1986]). And second, only theory-driven intervention strategies that have been previously successfully adapted to counseling clients with disabilities were selected. In addition, the principles, concepts, and constructs selected for discussion from each theory should not be construed as an attempt to provide the reader with an exhaustive list of the theory's constructs. Rather, these should be viewed as an effort at describing a selected, albeit, highly relevant set of concepts from personality theories that have direct application to the rehabilitation of clients with disabilities.

The theories slated for discussion are arranged largely according to their historical importance in the counseling field. The analysis includes theories that (a) emphasize psychodynamic motivational mechanisms (e.g., Psychoanalysis,

Individual Psychology), (b) focus on the humanistic-affective perspective (Person-Centered Therapy, Gestalt Therapy), (c) concentrate on cognitive issues (Rational-Emotive Therapy, Cognitive Therapy, Reality Therapy), and (d) are concerned with the behavioral domain (Operant, Classical Behavioral Therapy). The article concludes with an examination of the Somatopsychological approach, a model that uniquely addresses the psychosocial experience of people with physical disabilities.

The discussion of each approach is organized into four parts. First, the most relevant concepts of the theory that are related to the understanding of the dynamics underlying adaptation to disability are presented. These are followed by a discussion of the general intervention strategies that seem most appropriate to counseling people with disabilities. The intent of the second section (general intervention strategies) is to (a) acquaint the reader with areas of congruency between the most salient goals of each theory and those appropriate for counseling people with disabilities and (b) provide the reader with a general understanding of the application of each theory's primary intervention modalities to rehabilitation settings. The third portion focuses on specific counseling procedures that are associated with the process of adaption to physical disability. Disabilities differ along several dimensions (e.g., sensory versus physical, congenital versus adventitious, time of onset, level of severity), and this section examines those counseling interventions that are generally regarded as more appropriate within the context of the temporal process of psychosocial adaptation to disability (Dunn, 1975; Halligan, 1983; Hohmann, 1975).

The eight phases of adaptation to disability previously delineated are used as benchmarks for discussion. To assist the reader further in gaining a better insight into the nature and adaptation to physical disability, the discussion provides references to spinal cord injury, a disability of a sudden and traumatic nature that typically occurs in early adulthood. Finally, criteria for therapeutic change assessment are briefly delineated. Whenever feasible, the assessment of change in rehabilitation settings is related to those outcome criteria that are more frequently advocated by practitioners from each theoretical orientation.

Prior efforts to highlight the application of personality theories to persons with disabilities (i.e., Duval, 1982; English, 1971; McDaniel 1976; Riggar, Maki, & Wolf, 1986; Thomas, Butler, & Parker, 1987) have differed considerably from this discussion. The focus of Duval (1982), English (1971), and McDaniel (1976) was on a limited number of the more traditional personality theories (e.g., Psychoanalytic, Body Image, Individual Psychology), with the intention of providing the reader with a general appreciation of the role played by the most salient personality constructs in understanding the psychology of physical disability.

The more recent work of Riggar et al. (1986) and Thomas et al. (1987) shares more commonalities with this discussion. Their work, however, provides a more generic treatment of personality and counseling theories and their assumptions, main constructs, goals, and techniques but only limited discussion of specific counseling interventions directed at people with physical disabilities. Two unique features of this article are (a) assisting the reader in gaining a greater understanding of the relationship between specific counseling strategies and particular psychosocial patterns (phases) of adaptation to disability and (b) offering the reader a brief exposure to client outcome criteria advocated by rehabilitation practitioners of various counseling persuasions. In this respect, this article may be regarded as an extension and refinement of the prior work initiated by English and McDaniel almost 20 years ago, culminated by the recent contributions of Riggar et al. (1986) and Thomas et al. (1987).

# The Psychoanalytic Approach

## Concepts

The most relevant concepts of the orthodox psychoanalytic approach to understanding the psychosocial implications of physical disability are (a) the ego's defense mechanisms, (b) body image, (c) mourning and grief, and (d) the importance of early developmental stages.

The ego's *defense mechanisms* (e.g., repression, regression, reaction formation, projection, rationalization, denial) are regarded by psychoanalytic theory as unconscious processes, in the service of the ego, whose major goal is warding off anxiety through the distortion or denial of certain internal and external realities. In this capacity, defense mechanisms serve people with disabilities in their attempt to cope with the adversity generated by the onset of a physically disabling condition. Insofar as psychoanalytic theory underscores the importance of the person's acceptance of the permanence of the disability, successful adaptation is regarded as possible only when the person with disability acknowledges his or her limitations and minimizes the use of maladaptive defenses (Duval, 1982). Chief among these maladaptive defense mechanisms are the following: (a) denial, which is viewed as a defensive retreat from painful realization of the implications of the condition; (b) projection, which is associated with the externalization of hostility toward people, objects, and environmental conditions (e.g., blaming others for disability onset or for lack of progress); and (c) turning against the self or internalization, which is manifested through the displacement of anger toward one's self, invariably leading to feelings of self-blame, guilt, and possible self-injurious episodes (Cull & Hardy, 1975).

*Body image* may be viewed as the unconscious mental representation of the body (Schilder, 1950). The body image is formed relatively early in life but is constantly changing as a result of information received by way of visual and spatial stimuli, postural, and tactile impressions and internal sensations. Chronic diseases, physical traumas, and disabling conditions provoke abnormal sensations that interfere with the image of an intact body. Likewise, disability may produce regression that rekindles childhood conflicts related to body perception (Menninger, 1953). These sensations readily become a part of the total experience of the individual, and, consequently, the person may exhibit inappropriate reactions (e.g., anxiety, guilt, anger) to the impairment (McDaniel, 1976). Because the primary causes of behavior are regarded by psychoanalytic formulations as internally determined and because the loss of physical integrity is theorized to have a negative impact on the body image, attitudes toward oneself and others are also adversely influenced.

*Mourning* and *depression* (melancholia) were first explored by Abraham (1916/1948) and Freud (1917/1950) in the context of orthodox psychoanalytic object relations theory. According to this theory, the loss of a loved object (e.g., person, body part, country) is seen as triggering what Freud (1917/1950) termed the "work of mourning" and viewed as a process that, when completed, results in a free and uninhibited ego. During the initial phases of this process, however, depression is explained in terms of an aggression-turned-inward mechanism. This model argues that the strong ambivalence toward the lost object can be resolved only by turning against oneself (i.e., internalization) the hostility felt toward that object. In other words, in the case of a physical disability, the aggressive tendencies originally engendered by the loss of a body part or function and directed toward it can only be abated by internalizing them and blaming oneself for the onset of the condition. Shontz (1971), in contrast, maintained that regression in the service of the ego may actually facilitate ego growth, when such regression follows successful coping with the mourning necessitated by the bodily loss.

*Early developmental stages* are considered by psychoanalytic thinking to be crucial in the development of adult personality traits. In fact, personality is believed to be formed during the first 5 to 6 years of childhood. Because each of the postulated early psychosexual stages (i.e., oral receptive, oral sadistic, anal sadistic, anal retentive, and phallic) has a particular conflict that must be resolved before the individual can pass on to the next stage, any difficulties in passing from one stage to the next would have implications for future personality development. More specifically, frustration of needs, overindulgence of needs, and traumatic events may each lead to fixation at that particular developmental stage. Hence, disablement, especially when occurring in early childhood, has an adverse impact on later personality formation and often paves the way to immature and passive-aggressive behaviors (English, 1971). Likewise, parental overprotection of the infant who is disabled (e.g., overindulgence of needs) might result in adults who exhibit dependent, unmotivated, and narcissistic personalities.

The parallelism between physical disability and symbolic castration, a potentially useful concept for understanding the psychology of disability, has been suggested by psychoanalytic thinking, yet has failed to be adequately explored. Castration anxiety may be rekindled by a wide array of analogous and symbolic losses, including losses of extremities, vision, and internal organs. Freudian theory, accordingly, would postulate that such losses in adult life are capable of triggering the archaic Oedipal taboo and its associated fear of castration. Similarly, bodily losses may be unconsciously perceived as the punishment inflicted upon oneself because of certain sexual transgressions (Cubbage & Thomas, 1989; Wright, 1983).

## General Intervention Strategies

Applications of psychoanalytic intervention to rehabilitation settings are virtually nonexistent. This is obviously a manifestation of the protracted duration of treatment required, the necessity for advanced professional training, and the financial burden involved. Yet, understanding of psychoanalytic concepts and methods may assist the counselor in better appreciating the complexity of the personality, especially as it strives to adjust to the real and symbolic losses of physical functioning (Thurer, 1985).

The process of rehabilitation and physical restoration often rekindles conflicts associated with body image (McDowell, Coven, & Eash, 1979). Kolb and Woldt (1976), for example, in a modified analytic-gestalt procedure, advocated assisting the person with disability first to contact his or her physique through fantasy exercises, self-exploration, and psychodrama by focusing on those regions where bodily sensation is hindered (e.g., paralyzed or amputated extremities) and, second, to contact other people through mutual body exploration and nonverbal communication, so as to exchange sensory and affective experiences.

## Adaptation to Disability-Related Interventions

The extensive training required for psychoanalytic practitioners, the expense of therapy, and the prolonged style of treatment make it difficult to incorporate this therapeutic approach into the phase model of adaptation to disability. In addition, psychoanalytic-oriented practitioners seek to reconstruct one's personality structure and, accordingly, concentrate most of their efforts on clients with psychopathological reactions that require uncovering early developmental issues. Conversely, clients with physical disabilities more typically require adaptive or ameliorative interventions, which are targeted directly at the functional loss at hand.

Despite the obvious discrepancies in philosophy and goal setting between the rehabilitation approach and orthodox psychoanalysis, psychoanalytic-based methods may assist clients who have successfully come to terms with their disability, its permanence, and its induced functional limitations (clients in the acknowledgement and adjustment phases) so that they may gain a better insight into their needs, motivations, and aspirations. Understanding the personal meaning the client attaches to the affected body parts and functions and the defense mechanisms used to ward off anxiety and other unpleasant emotions can be instrumental in assisting the client on his or her road to recovery.

## Criteria for Change

Change, in psychoanalytic theory, is judged subjectively by the client (e.g., restored feelings of well-being) and, clinically, by the therapist (e.g., an achieved balance between internal impulses and social restrictions, and degree of self-insight achieved by the client). Knight (1941) proposed a more specific set of criteria, three of which seem to be relevant in rehabilitation settings. These criteria include (a) increased productiveness, (b) improved interpersonal relationships, and (c) the ability to handle ordinary psychological conflicts and reasonable reality stress. The last criterion has obvious implications for assessing the client's success in coping with the ordinary barriers and frustrations imposed by the disability.

# The Individual Approach

## Concepts

The most commonly used concepts of Adler's (1917/1927) Individual Therapy for understanding the impact of physical disability on personality are
(a) inferiority (or organ inferiority), (b) compensation, (c) the striving for superiority and (d) life-style.

*Inferiority feelings* may result from either organ (i.e., congenital or early acquired structural or functional anomalies of a physical or mental nature) or status inferiority (i.e., infants are born feeling weak, incomplete, and unfulfilled, especially in comparison to adults). *Compensation,* as a particular innate defense mechanism, acts to overcome these real or imagined inferiority feelings by attempting to strengthen one's ability in the same (direct or primary compensation) or a different (indirect or secondary compensation) area. *Striving for superiority* is an innate drive to attain perfection. Adaptive striving is guided by social interest and recognition of others' needs. Nonadaptive striving is discerned by pathological and false feeling of power, coupled with ignoring other people's needs. McDaniel (1976) further suggested that the exemptions and privileges of disability, along with the manipulation of others, may offer a substitute for the original goal of superiority. The *life-style,* or plan of life, gradually emerges during the first 5 years of life. This self-consistent unity represents the individual's organismic ideas and goals and seeks to achieve superiority out of early experienced inferiority feelings. It is the overriding unique mental pattern that directs the person's feelings, cognitions, and behaviors in relation to life's tasks (Adler, 1917/1927; Dreikurs, 1967; Rule, 1987).

According to Adler (1917/1927), three major factors that lead to abnormal inferiority feelings and faulty life-styles are a child's experiencing early physical deformities (e.g., imperfect organs, chronic childhood diseases), pampering the child by overprotecting him or her or paying him or her too much attention, and neglecting or rejecting the child by not paying enough attention to his or her needs. If disability occurs during early childhood, it would likely factor in the development of the life-style. If, however, the onset of disability is later in life, the individual's already formed life-style should exert a strong influence on the perception and the process of adjustment to disability (Rule, 1984).

## General Intervention Strategies

The overriding goal of Adlerian Therapy is assisting clients to develop their life-style so that they will be able to direct a more socially useful and productive style of life. Accordingly, life-style counseling, as applied to a client with disability, seeks to enable the client to move from a position of noncoping (i.e., felt inferiority) to that of coping (i.e., overcoming inferiority) through striving toward a subjectively determined sense of significance (Rule, 1987). In this capacity, life-style information often broadens the counselor's understanding of how the client might cope with physical disability. The counselor focuses on how the client's life-style notions and goals (how the client's personal meaning is attached to the disability) are contributing to (through compensation) or undermining (through despair and retreat) the acceptance of, and adjustment to the disability (Rule, 1984).

The Adlerian life-style counseling process is composed of four phases (Dreikurs, 1967; Mosak, 1977). The application of the therapeutic plan to counseling clients with disabilities and the facilitation of the acceptance and adjustment to the disability is described by Rule (1984, 1987) as follows:

1. *Establishing and maintaining a relationship with the client.* The counselor seeks to gain insight into the client's frame of reference and encourage the client to explore the implications of the disability. Specific information on the client's medical history and current status is also gathered.
2. *Investigating the client's life-style.* The counselor obtains relevant information to explore with the client how he or she is currently functioning in the three areas of social living, work (or school), and interpersonal relationships. In this phase, the client is often asked, "What would be different if you were well (able-bodied) or if the problem did not exist?" Finally, the counselor obtains from the client information on remembered childhood experiences and early family life. The importance of early memories in Adlerian Therapy is well documented. These selective memories serve as anchoring points that reflect the most meaningful conclusions, goals, and expectations crystallized during this early period and shed light on the client's predisability stages of life-style formation within the psychosocial context of family constellation.
3. *Interpreting the client's life-style.* During this phase, the counselor cautiously probes to identify the client's network of life-style notions, goals, and expectations, and endeavors to convey these impressions to the client. The goal is to enable the client to gain insight, especially as it relates

to "life-style blinders" that will promote acceptance of the disability. Hence, clients are encouraged to assume responsibility for identifying linkages between the life-style information and daily situations, with particular emphasis upon disability-associated issues.

4. *Reorienting and reeducating the client.* The focus during the final phase is on behavior change. Clients are helped to resolve difficulties and formulate future-oriented goals. They are also directed toward alternative ways of understanding and valuing themselves. The guiding principle is removal of life-style barriers to acceptance of, and adjustment to disability. These barriers often include inferiority feelings stemming from comparison with able-bodied people, feelings of social isolation, and felt dependency. The counselor, therefore, should focus on decreasing the client's feelings of inferiority (other-comparison) and increasing feelings of social belongingness (Dreikurs, 1967; Rule, 1984).

## *Adaptation to Disability-Related Interventions*

The application of Adlerian therapeutic methods to the different phases of the process of adaptation to disability is, to some extent, affected by some of the same limitations previously discussed under psychoanalytic methods (e.g., duration of therapy, emphasis on early recollections, and reconstruction of the life-style). Nevertheless, Adlerian Therapy has its greater impact when first used during the client's experiencing of depressive and internalized anger reactions. During this time, the counselor focuses on the client's noncoping behaviors (i.e., feeling inferior, experiencing depression, socially withdrawing) and seeks to assist the client in developing effective strategies for coping and attaining a sense of personal significance and social belongingness (Rule, 1987).

In the later phases of acknowledgement and adjustment, the counselor strives to help the client view the disability within the broader context of his or her life-style goals and aspirations. More specifically, therapeutic goals are directed toward (a) enabling the client to gain a better insight into the personal meaning he or she associates with the disability; (b) facilitating the client's acceptance of the newly created barriers imposed by the disability, and incorporating these limitations into his or her life-style and future goals; and (c) reeducating the client to achieve constructive behavioral change in the areas of social, educational, interpersonal, and vocational functioning (Rule, 1984).

Adaptation of Adlerian procedures to the client with spinal cord injury who manifests signs of an extended depression may take the following form. The client's depression is first anchored (i.e., investigated) within the client's life-style perspective. Because depression is often associated with feelings of inferiority and the latter, in turn, are based on assessment or comparison with others or one's prior situation, the focus then becomes reorienting and educating the client to relinquish these comparisons. In addition, clients are assisted in developing a sense of social usefulness and coping skills required to function independently and successfully in the community.

## Criteria for Change

Change is typically assessed through the client's attained social usefulness. No objective measures are used to judge this outcome. Agreement by an outside observer (e.g., significant other, employer), the counselor, and the client's introspective self-report, however, can be jointly used to estimate the degree of disability acceptance (as process assessment indicator) and social usefulness (as outcome assessment indicator).

# The Person-Centered Approach

## Concepts

The central constructs of Rogers's (1951) Person-Centered theory that seem to be useful in understanding the psychological implications of physical disability to the individual are (a) the salience of the phenomenological field, (b) the self-concept, and (c) the denial and distortion of threatening experiences. The concept of counselor-produced facilitative conditions is also of significant importance.

Person-Centered proponents argue that individuals are capable of experiencing reality (i.e., the external and internal environments) only as it is filtered through their *phenomenological field,* or subjective perception. The self-concept, it is further claimed, is the differentiated and organized portion of this field, which is composed of a series of perceptions, values, and attitudes commonly referred to as "I," or "me" (Ford & Urban, 1963; Rogers, 1951). "What one would like to be," on the other hand, is referred to as the ideal self. When a discrepancy exists between the ideal self and the self-concept or when incongruence is experienced between the organismic experience (the innate actualizing tendency) and one's self-concept, this is felt as a threat and may consequently evoke anxiety.

As related to the impact of disability on the individual, advocates of Person-Centered counseling argue that it is not the disability per se that psychologically affects the person but rather the subjective meaning and personal attitudes associated with it (the phenomenological perception). Disability represents a threat to the self-concept, and it may ultimately result in lowered self-esteem (Roessler & Bolton, 1978). It also acts to widen the gap between the actual and ideal selves. To cope with this threat and ward off anxiety, the individual might deny the existence of impact of the disability or distort reality, for example, by misconstruing the permanence or degree of severity associated with the disability (Cook, 1987).

## General Intervention Strategies

There are important limitations to the traditional Person-Centered approach to counseling clients with disabilities. Although most experts would undoubtedly agree on the value of the counselor's providing and communicating early facilitative conditions, such as empathic understanding, respect, genuineness, warmth, and positive regard, to assist the client with a disability to establish a more positive self-concept, it is the need for a more active and direct approach, in the latter phases of the counseling process, that seems to limit the applicability of the Person-Centered approach to rehabilitation settings (Cook, 1987; Thomas, Butler, & Parker, 1987). See (1985) provided a list of the discrepancies between classical Person-Centered Therapy and the requirements of rehabilitation counseling and described the limitations of the use of this approach in rehabilitation settings. Among these deficiencies are the Person-Centered approach's (a) reluctance to set specific goals (apart from self-actualization), (b) aversion to diagnosis and evaluation, (c) questions concerning the value of advice giving, (d) lack of concern with the external environment, (e) nature of being process oriented rather than outcome oriented, and (f) tendency not to focus on client behavior or skill development.

Yet, Person-Centered counseling is not without its merits for counseling people with disabilities. Clients may still profit, especially early in the counseling encounter, from gaining insight into their perceptions and feelings of being disabled, and come to accept their disability emotionally without devaluing themselves or resorting to defensive maneuvers concerning the existence of their condition.

### Adaptation to Disability-Related Interventions

Rogerian methods, or more appropriately, therapeutic conditions, are most useful during the early and intermediate phases of adaptation to disability. During this time, clients often manifest feelings of anxiety, confusion, depression, and self-blame, and the Person-Centered counselor can provide the client with salubrious reassurance, support, and physical comfort (Walters, 1981). The counselor encourages the recently injured client to express feelings that are associated with the traumatic loss and when appropriate clarifies them to the client (Herman, Manning, & Teitelman, 1971). During these phases, the counselor's ability to listen and attend empathetically to the client's fears and concerns is of paramount importance (Dunn, 1975). When the spinal cord injured client is allowed to vent feelings of insecurity, guilt, and shame in the protective environment offered by the counselor, he or she is eventually inclined to recognize the impact of the disability upon his or her self-concept and acknowledge the discrepancy created between his or her current situation and future hopes and aspirations (i.e., the ideal self). This gained awareness, in turn, is used by the client to reach a progressively better understanding of those positive inner resources and strengths that will pave the way toward eventual acceptance of the disability and coping with its ramifications.

## Criteria for Change

In Person-Centered approach, it is the client who determines when sufficient change has been achieved. The client sets his or her own goals and expectations of counseling and decides when the goals have been met. Subjective indexes of felt change may include (a) moving toward openness to experience and acceptance of disability, (b) perceiving self with disability more realistically and less anxiously, (c) seeing self as a process characterized by change and fluidity rather than by the rigidity and immobility imposed by the disability, (d) becoming increasingly more trusting of the self with a disability, rather than a disabled self, and (e) acting with confidence and assertiveness. Despite the Person-Centered counselor's dislike of personality measures, more objective indexes may be used. These include self-concept ratings and "real" self-"ideal" self congruence measures interspersed along crucial junctures of the counseling process.

# The Gestalt Approach

## Concepts

The most critical concepts of Gestalt theory for understanding the psychosocial adaptation to physical disability are (a) the holistic view of the individual, (b) the emphasis on awareness and the present, (c) personal responsibility, and (d) the principles of polarities and closure.

In Gestalt theory (Perls, Hefferline, & Goodman, 1951) the person is viewed as a composite whole, which is composed of connected, integrated parts. The holistic principle asserts that body, mind and soul, sensations, thoughts, emotions, and perceptions are all elements of the total organism and are essential to understanding the individual. Integration of fragmented components to a unified whole is the driving force behind the transition from dependency to self-sufficiency. Gestalt principles are directed toward the person's development as a whole, and emphasize his or her striving toward growth, self-realization, and potentialities rather than social adjustment (Coven, 1977b; Jung, 1978). The rehabilitation perspective, likewise, stresses a holistic approach to therapy and advocates a system that completely addresses the physical, psychosocial, and vocational aspects of the person.

Gestalt theory emphasizes *awareness* and the *present*. Awareness is regarded as important in its role in achieving organismic self-regulation (i.e., homeostasis). It is also seen as a crucial therapeutic tool (Allen, 1985; Simkin & Yontef, 1984). The "here-and-now" orientation refers to the significance of existing and fully experiencing in the present. Attention is paid to immediate behavior (Perls, 1969). Rehabilitation, similarly, is performed in the here-and-now. It focuses on the client's coming in contact and becoming aware of present feelings, experiences, and behaviors (Coven, 1977a). The concept of personal *responsibility* further assumes that people have the capacity to become responsible for what they do and how they feel. Congruent with the rehabilitation mission, clients with disabilities are perceived to have the ultimate responsibility for choosing (a) how they would want to live with a disability, (b) the new behaviors with which they would be willing to experiment, and (c) how and when to become self-sufficient and independent (Coven, 1977a).

Last, the principles of *polarities* and *closure* should be mentioned. The principle of polarities (or opposites) states that thinking in opposites, and differentiation into opposites, is an essential quality of human mentality. Polarization, however, can take a more psychopathological shift that may lead to splits between two or more elements in a psychological process and may consequently manifest itself in disturbed behavior (Perls, Hefferline, & Goodman, 1951). These splits within the self assume discordant poles (e.g., victim versus oppressor, healthy versus sick, independent versus dependent) and serve to impede the person's awareness (Allen, 1985). Persons with disabilities are subject to strong feelings of fragmentation, especially with respect to the development of independence. The client's disabled part might overshadow the awareness of other positive assets of the person. Also, people with disabilities may readily develop ambivalent attitudes, and simultaneously acknowledge and deny their disability. Therefore, it can be reasonably assumed that traumatic losses adversely affect the continuing struggle to restore balance to one's private world (Coven, 1977a).

The principle of closure suggests that the mind strives to finish an uncompleted task or situation (i.e., eliminate a state of "unfinished business"). The closure principle may be viewed as a derivative of the homeostasis principle. According to this view, the mind operates to restore a loss of balance by meeting the arising needs that disrupt the state of equilibrium. Disability is but one such condition that disrupts homeostasis. People with disabilities struggle to restore equilibrium to their world because the loss that ensues the disability alters the ways in which needs are customarily met.

### General Intervention Strategies

Gestalt Therapy procedures offer rich opportunities for practitioners who counsel clients with disabilities. This section provides the reader with a few prototypical examples of the application of Gestalt Therapy techniques to rehabilitation settings. The goals of Gestalt Therapy may be briefly summarized as (a) increasing client self-awareness (i.e., experiencing fully the concerns, feelings, attitudes, and disowned parts of the self); (b) enabling the client to assume responsibility for self; and (c) helping the client to deal with his or her impasse and reach a closure of the unfinished needs and concerns. To achieve these aims, Gestalt therapists typically resort to intensive group work in which various experimental games (techniques) are used to foster and provoke the client into coming to grips with his or her feelings and expose conflicts so that they can be inspected and resolved. In these groups (often composed of clients with common problems, concerns, or disabilities), clients (a) are forced into confronting and acknowledging their avoided feelings, (b) become aware of and work through their impasse, (c) assume responsibility for their actions, and (d) increase self-awareness and self-sufficiency (Allen, 1985; Coven, 1977a). More specifically, the following games and role-playing exercises are frequently adopted:

1. *The game of unfinished business.* When areas of unfinished or incomplete life situations are recognized, the client is invited to complete them. This can be accomplished through "trying out" and rehearsing ways to achieve a closure for these unfinished life situations in the here-and-now of the counseling setting. Eventually, the client with disability can confront the task of completing more taxing life situations outside the therapeutic session (Coven, 1977b). In a similar vein, the use of fantasy may be applied to unresolved grief associated with the loss of a body part or function. Allen (1985) and Coven (1977a) suggested fantasizing the lost part of the self and then saying farewell to it. This fantasy exercise offers the client the opportunity to facilitate completion of the grieving process and directly cope with its manifestations. Through fantasy projection, fantasy exercises also provide the opportunity for the client to explore hopes and wishes, while he or she realistically considers the obstacles to be encountered in the path to successful rehabilitation (Coven, 1977b).

    Dreams represent unfinished business in Gestalt theory. Clients may be requested to act out the dream, and play the part of various persons or objects appearing in the dream. As a result, they can gain gradual awareness of their innermost feelings, attitudes and conflicts (Coven, 1977a, 1977b).

2. *The game of dialogue.* When polarizations and personal conflicts are identified, the client is given the opportunity of gaining increased awareness of these issues by carrying on a dialogue between conflicting components of the self. These dialogues ordinarily evolve around top-dog versus underdog parts of the self (e.g., imposed parental demands versus personal resistance tendencies). In a rehabilitation context, the dialogue might be between the (a) able versus disabled components of the self, (b) the independent versus dependent parts, (c) the "good life" versus life with disability, or (d) coping with versus succumbing to disability (Allen, 1985; Coven, 1977b; Lofaro & Fleming, 1980). The prime objective of these games is an increase in the client's awareness of his or her assets and limitations, and acceptance of disability.

3. *The game of exaggeration.* When the client produces a particular movement, gesture, or expression that appears to be of symbolic significance, he or she is asked to exaggerate it. The exaggeration is considered by Gestalt therapists to heighten the specific emotion linked to the behavior and to clarify its meaning (Allen, 1985; Coven, 1977b). In rehabilitation settings, this technique is of particular importance because the encountered gestures and expressions are considered to reflect temporary cracks in the client's defensive maneuvers (e.g., denial of limitations).

4. *Taking responsibility and personalizing pronouns.* Clients are encouraged to use phrases such as "I take responsibility for . . ." immediately following personal actions. The use of personal pronouns such as "I" and "me," followed by assertion of responsibility for a particular act, necessitates awareness of the experience and re-owning of one's feelings, attitudes, and behaviors.
5. *Reversals.* The client is asked to play the opposite role to his or her overt behavior. This procedure is regarded as beneficial in exposing the client to attributes and experiences he or she seeks to deny or avoid.

## Adaptation to Disability-Related Interventions

Gestalt techniques are particularly useful for clients who seem to be "stuck" in the denial, depression, internalized anger, and externalized hostility phases of adaptation to disability. The counselor engages clients who deny the permanence or severity of their disability (e.g., spinal cord injury) in self-awareness exercises and mild confrontations by specifying and clarifying inconsistencies and discrepancies between verbal and nonverbal messages, cognitions, and behaviors, and the like. Finally, clients may be asked to project their disability-related problems into the future, thereby allowing them to incorporate the currently denied difficulties into their life situation in a less threatening and nonimmediate life context (Allen, 1985; Dunn, 1975).

Clients who manifest feelings of depression and internalized anger can also benefit from Gestalt Therapy exercises. Here, the focus is on empty (wheel) chair work, role playing, and games of dialogue. The client may be helped to gain awareness of inner conflicts, unfinished business (of lost body part or function), disowned and/or underdeveloped parts of the self. Farewell letter writing and role playing expressing grief, anger, and ambivalence toward the lost part assist the client to become aware of his or her inner conflicts and predisability unfinished business, and to assimilate and ultimately accept the new reality (Coven, 1977a).

Finally, for the client who experiences anger at others or toward external events, the counselor may wish to consider having the client role-play anger-causing situations. This technique allows the client to become aware of his or her unrecognized needs and wishes, and the sources he or she associates with (blames for) the onset of the disability.

A typical example of Gestalt work with a spinal-cord-injured client may be seen in instructing the client to engage in an "able-bodied" versus "disabled" person dialogue. When assuming the "able-bodied" part, the client reenacts his or her predisability wishes and needs. When shifting to the "disabled" part, the client focuses on the current level of functioning, with the associated feelings of discouragement, grief, frustration, anger, bitterness, and so on. The counselor may direct the client with a spinal cord injury to move from the wheelchair to another chair and ask the client to "address the wheelchair and talk about the plans and desires you had before you were injured, and discuss how you feel about these former plans and dreams." The client is then asked to get back in the wheelchair and respond from his or her current situation or as a person who no longer can fulfill *all* these goals and wishes. The counselor guides the client in discussing more realistic hopes and goals and the feelings that are associated with the lost aspirations. The direct communication between the two parts serves to heighten the reality of the experience and the client's awareness of current feelings. Ultimately, such a dialogue can assist a denying client to become aware of disowned feelings and perceptions, as well as assist the depressed client to come to terms with the loss and its functional implications.

### Criteria for Change

Gestalt Therapy is rather adamant about the use of outcome measurement. Judgment concerning client improvement is strictly clinical and is typically derived from subjective indices such as client change in outlook, adequate self-expression, the ability to extend awareness to the verbal level, and assuming responsibility for one's actions and feelings.

# The Rational-Emotive Cognitive Approach

## Concepts

The most singular concept of Rational-Emotive Therapy (RET; Ellis, 1973) and Cognitive Therapy (CT; Beck, 1976) that seems to be closely allied to the practice of counseling clients who are physically disabled, is Ellis's A-B-C Theory of Personality and Beck's parallel view that affect and behavior are largely determined by cognitive perceptions.

Rational-Emotive therapists regard people as having the inherent capacity to think and act both rationally and irrationally. Rational thinking is seen as leading to appropriate emotions and adaptive behaviors, resulting in healthy functioning. Irrationality, on the other hand, results in inappropriate emotions and ineffective behaviors. Such cognitions are the culprit of unhealthy or self-defeating functioning (Ellis, 1973). The A-B-C Theory of Personality, accordingly, argues that it is not the antecedent event (A), such as losing a job, that causes the consequence (C) (negative emotion or reaction), such as depression, but rather the person's belief system (B), which comprises those self-evaluative meanings or self-verbalizations that negatively magnify the person's attitude toward the event, namely, being rejected from that job.

People with disabilities are perceived no differently than people who experience any other life misfortune (e.g., loss of job, loss of home, loss of loved one). Indeed, disabilities are regarded as noxious events experienced by the individual (Ostby, 1985). Beck (Beck, 1976; Beck & Emery, 1985) visualized feelings as being influenced by cognitions through self-verbalizations, subjective perceptions, and idiosyncratic meanings attributed to various life experiences. These cognitions and self-verbalizations frequently result in negative feelings about oneself that culminate in lowered self-esteem (e.g., "Since I lost my ability to walk, I must be helpless and therefore, my future is hopeless").

## General Intervention Strategies

Both Ellis (1973) and Beck (1976) subscribed to an eclectic approach to therapy; they, however, generally stressed the use of cognitive-behavioral techniques. Proponents of both approaches have the similar goal of teaching the client to examine and modify his or her irrational perceptions and beliefs. Thus, RET and CT practitioners seek to minimize the client's misconceptions and self-defeating outlook on life and to maximize coping skills and a more realistic philosophy of life. To achieve this goal, a structural reeducative-relearning approach is adopted, whereby the client is taught to dispute irrational beliefs, eliminate them, and finally replace them with a rational belief system. Frustrations and unhappiness associated with disability are considered irrational because they stem from a belief system that wrongly equates impairment and disability with terrible and catastrophic events. Clients are taught to end the disability-associated frustrations by either modifying their environments or by learning to accept their existing life limitations when circumstances cannot be altered (Ard, 1968).

Clients are assisted in setting short-term and specific goals (e.g., maneuver wheelchair around one's living quarters, applying for a seeing-eye dog permit). The problems faced by the client with disability are broken down to smaller components, through graded task assignments. When necessary, activity schedules are developed to decrease passivity, reduce the client's ruminations about the disability, and increase motivation (Bowers, 1988). Clients are also assigned homework exercises. The written or practiced homework is subsequently brought in to be discussed during counseling sessions. Finally, with the client who is disabled, skill training may be used to compensate for social, vocational, sexual, and marital deficits (Ostby, 1985).

## Adaptation to Disability-Related Interventions

Within the phase model of adaptation to disability, RET and CT counselors seem to be best equipped to work with the depressed client. During the client's depression, the counselor often confronts and interrupts the client's unrealistic and negative beliefs and expectations concerning the disability and its implications. The counselor proceeds to assist the client in restructuring and eventually eliminating these illogical beliefs (Beck, 1967; Ellis, 1973; Halligan, 1983). When counseling a client with spinal cord injury who experiences feelings of depression, bitterness, and guilt, the counselor adopts the following model. First, an attempt is made to verify the existence of a depressive (or an internalized anger) pattern. A positive conclusion of its existence is based on the client's irrational beliefs, as indicated by his or her verbalizations and associated feelings of despair and self-depreciation. The counselor interrupts, confronts and disputes any self-defeating verbalizations and illogical beliefs, and demonstrates to the client how these ideas are exaggerated and globalized. The following dialogue is an example of a typical cognitive-behavioral client/therapist interaction.

Client:     "I'm useless because I cannot walk. I will never be able to work again if I am confined to a wheelchair. I'll spend the rest of my life at home."

Therapist:  "How are sedentary jobs affected by being in a wheelchair? Why would your ability to attend concerts, films, sporting events or even drive a car be compromised?"

Finally, RET and CT counselors can further help the client with breaking down problems perceived as temporarily insurmountable into smaller and more manageable units (Dunn, 1975; Halligan, 1983).

### Criteria for Change

Traditionally, success of RET and CT has been measured through the client's self-report and the counselor's observations and evaluations. Client's reports are assessed using the number of times and durations the client reports being upset, depressed, or anxious, the number of rational choices made, the number of positive life changes, and so on. Client change is also addressed through analysis of homework content and problem-oriented record keeping. Diagnostic instruments that measure irrational and rational ideas can also be used (e.g., Ellis's Personality Data Form). The counselor's observation of change includes subjective measures such as evaluations of illogical/logical thinking ratio. Other measures involve the client's proficiency in analyzing his or her self-verbalizations and the ability to teach RET to others.

# The Reality Therapy Approach

### Concepts

Reality Therapy (RT) counselors promote the concepts of success identity and social responsibility (Glasser, 1965). Both of these concepts are useful in understanding psychological adjustment to disability and the ensuing rehabilitation intervention. Proponents of RT perceive people as possessing a need for personal and social identity. This identity can be classified as either *success identity* or *failure identity,* and is formed during early childhood.

Glasser (1984, 1985) maintained that people are internally motivated by certain fundamental needs that are intrinsically incorporated into their genetic structure, and all human behavior is voluntarily directed toward the fulfillment of these basic needs. Primary psychological needs are the need to belong, to love and be loved, and to feel worthwhile. The fulfillment of this need is considered to be a requirement for growing up successfully and preserving that accomplishment, or for changing a failure identity into a success identity.

The implications for clients with disabilities are obvious. Disability is but one variable that might interfere with the development of a success identity or, alternatively, add weight to the formation of a failure identity. A disability that occurs early in life has the potential of exerting more of an impact on the development of a failure identity, especially when it interferes with the gratification of the need for belonging. The results might include feelings of inadequacy, not be involved with others (partially because of the failure of parents to become more involved with the child and partially because of negative peer and school environments), and not learning to act responsibly. When the success identity has been achieved through the recognition and acceptance of the person's previous accomplishments, a later onset of disability most likely will not markedly affect one's identity (Walker, 1987).

In Reality Therapy the focus is on how people can appropriately increase their control over the world by evaluating their behavior and choosing more effective and productive behaviors. Fundamental to this therapeutic goal is the concept of responsibility. Responsibility is achieved when people are able to competently fulfill their personal needs and, thus, control their world without interfering with or depriving others of the opportunity to satisfy their own needs. Autonomy, emotional strength, and fulfillment occur most often when people are willing to assume a responsible attitude toward their internal and external environment (Glasser, 1965, 1984). Clients with disabilities are seen as responsible for their lives and are expected to develop responsible goals and plans to achieve their physical, psychological, social, and vocational needs and desires. If they do so, they are regarded as mature, and psychologically healthy and adjusted.

## General Intervention Strategies

Rehabilitation counselors frequently encounter clients who have developed a failure identity. These clients either deny reality (distort the real world) or ignore it (break the rules and laws of society) (Glasser, 1984; Ososkie & Turpin, 1985). The goals of RT are to teach clients to accept the real world, assume responsibility for who they are and what they do, and develop realistic, acceptable, and responsible plans and behaviors that will enable them to achieve and maintain a success identity. During the early phases of counseling, clients are required to learn and face the reality of the disability and are guided on how to live within its framework. Disabilities are not allowed to be used as excuses for personal failures and dependency (Ososkie & Turpin, 1985; Walker, 1987). When counseling clients with disabilities, RT practitioners emphasize achievement of personal independence, and focus on the client's assets and positive attributes and potentialities. At the same time, the client and counselor jointly seek to identify and meet those unalterable demands of the social, occupational, and recreational environments that are associated with the client's inherent limitations.

Several of the principles that bind the counselor-client working relationship include the following: (a) focusing on the current behavior (because the past cannot be modified) and the client's currently faced obstacles and problems; (b) helping the client to formulate specific (and realistic) plans using a contractual agreement to modify failure behaviors (e.g., succumbing to disability) into success behaviors (e.g., coping with disability); (c) prompting the client to make a commitment to carry out the plans and assume responsibility for their outcome; (d) refusing to accept client excuses when a plan is not carried out or when it fails; and (e) eliminating punishment.

Clients with disabilities are not penalized for their failure to successfully carry out a rehabilitation plan. Instead, a new plan is formulated and implemented. Punishment can only aggravate the situation for a client who already has a failure identity or for a client who equates his or her disability with a punishment for personal wrongdoings. RT counselors do, however, use sarcasm ("verbal shock therapy") to confront clients with unrealistic and irresponsible behaviors who repeatedly fail to adhere to their contractual plans (Glasser, 1965).

## Adaptation to Disability-Related Interventions

Reality Therapy methods can be effective for clients who manifest reactions of externalized hostility and they may also be useful during the final phases of adaptation to disability, acknowledgement, and adjustment. Rehabilitation clients frequently exhibit resentment and anger toward medical staff, family members, and their peers and may occasionally engage in verbal (e.g., screaming, cursing) or physical (e.g., pushing, striking at) abuse directed at others. During this phase, RT counselors teach the client to express anger in a socially appropriate manner (Hohmann, 1975). Clients practice assuming personal and social responsibility for their behavior and its consequences (Glasser, 1965). RT counselors invariably resort to some form of contracting with the aggressive client to decrease the acting out and other abusive behaviors. At the same time, they are careful to refrain from punishing the client for his or her unacceptable behaviors and either adhere to the written contract or when necessary, formulate new plans and actions (Ososkie & Turpin, 1985). Through an integrated process of encouragement, education, confrontation, consultation, emotional involvement, and guidance, clients are shown that hostile behaviors toward others represent frustrations or failure-identity-triggered behaviors. Clients are encouraged to modify these irresponsible behaviors by practicing how to cope with their disability-associated frustrations in a more useful and responsible manner. The counselor might confront a hostile client with the following statement: "Screaming at your physical therapist will not change your muscle strength, but trying harder and practicing longer probably will. It is entirely your responsibility to continue your treatment, and you are the only person who can determine if your rehabilitation program will be successfully completed."

During the final phases of adaptation, the RT counselor may further assist the client in setting time-limited personal, social, and vocational goals, and teaching and practicing community-based problem-solving and decision-making skills (Scofield, Pape, McCracken, & Maki, 1980).

### Criteria for Change

Because RT counselors use contractual arrangements between client and counselor, counseling is terminated when the contract is fulfilled. Upon achievement of the client-determined goals, as specified in the contract, client and counselor review each of the goals and if mutual agreement is reached, counseling is discontinued.

General criteria usually involve (a) attaining responsible behavior, (b) meeting personal needs without harming self or others, (c) reaching independence in community functioning, and (d) realistically accepting the functional limitations imposed by the disability. Success in meeting these criteria is judged by both counselor and client.

# The Behavioral Approach

### Concepts

Learning theory and its psychotherapeutic application of behavioral modification have provided the practicing counselor with numerous concepts conducive to understanding the behavior of people with disabilities. Among the concepts are (a) the principles of operant conditioning and its underlying components of positive and negative reinforcement, punishment, extinction, and shaping; (b) classical conditioning and its emphasis on learning by temporal and spatial associations, conditional, and reciprocal inhibition; (c) modeling and other forms of vicarious learning; and (d) social-cognitive approaches focusing on behavioral management, self-control, social assertiveness, and the like.

Behavioral Therapy is a reductionistic, deterministic, and experimental (i.e., laboratory-based) approach (Skinner, 1953). Human beings are perceived to be shaped and determined by external environments (both physical and sociocultural). All human behavior is learned and, therefore, can be unlearned; behavior is orderly and lawful and, hence, can be controlled. Emphasis is placed upon the role of the environment in producing and maintaining behavior.

Adjustment to disability is viewed as operating on the same learning principles that govern all other human behaviors (Duval, 1982). The onset of a disability coincides with loss of certain functions. It often results in the inability to engage in customary behaviors and attain past reinforcements (Rice, 1985). From an operant perspective, Fordyce (1971) viewed depression as the deprivation of previously sustaining reinforcers. A consequence of a sudden onset of a disability can be the immediate loss of many anticipated reinforcers and a gradual onset of a disability can eventuate in a progressive removal of desired reinforcers.

The disability can create several obstacles that may induce the person with a disability to appropriate various adaptive mechanisms. First, the client may need to eliminate maladaptive behaviors that can be associated with the onset of disability. For example, clients with spinal cord injury may manifest dependent behavior and fantasies of returning to old and no longer appropriate jobs. Second, clients may need to acquire new and adaptive behaviors (e.g., wheelchair ambulation, specific vocational skills). Third, clients may need to relearn old behaviors lost as a result of disability onset (e.g., relearning to speak in aphasic stroke patients) (Rice, 1985).

Rehabilitation, accordingly, is viewed as involving the elimination or reduction of older and no longer appropriate modes of behavior, and the acquisition of new and adaptive behaviors that are more compatible with the disability and the functional requirements placed upon the individual.

## General Intervention Strategies

The overriding goal of Behavioral Therapy is to eliminate maladaptive behaviors and replace them with constructive and appropriate behaviors. To achieve this goal, operant conditioning methods follow the principles of reinforcement, extinction, and so forth, to enable the client to reduce and abandon unwanted behaviors (e.g., aggressive reactions, fears, and anxieties), and gradually acquire new appropriate behaviors of coping that harmonize with the functional limitations of the disability. Inappropriate behaviors are reduced or extinguished by the withdrawal of the reinforcers that sustain them (e.g., attention giving to pain patients). These maladaptive behaviors are replaced by disability-appropriate behaviors (e.g., engaging in physical therapy, exercise, learning new job-related skills).

In a thoughtful treatise on the application of operant approaches to rehabilitation settings, Greif and Matarazzo (1982) advocated the following steps when working with clients with disabilities: (a) define behavioral goals and skills to be mastered; (b) analyze the stimulus contingencies under which behaviors occur, and the positive and negative consequences that succeed counseling; (c) shape the desired behaviors by rewarding the client for gradually approximating more skillful behaviors; (d) reinforce only targeted behaviors and ignore behaviors incompatible with the targeted behaviors; (e) adjust the rehabilitation plan by continuously assessing the client's level of skilled performance; and (f) teach the client the skills of self-monitoring and self-reinforcement.

An extended system of positive reinforcement to reward appropriate behaviors is a token economy (Ayllon & Azrin, 1968). This procedure, which is frequently practiced in rehabilitation workshops and hospital units, arranges for conditional positive reinforcers (tokens that are later exchanged for primary reinforcers) to follow desirable behaviors elicited by clients. Targeted behaviors may include self-care, successful job-related performances, appropriate social interactions and so on.

Additional operant procedures that may benefit counselors who practice in rehabilitation settings include time-out, overcorrection, and covert conditioning. Time out, or the removal of clients from the area (e.g., workshop, rehabilitation unit) in which the inappropriate behavior has been reinforced, entails a brief social segregation of the client. Time-out is used as a variant of aversive control and clients with destructive behavior are isolated for several minutes in a small separate room. This procedure is repeated as long as these unacceptable activities are still a part of their behavioral repertoire. Overcorrection is another method used to discourage undesirable behaviors. Two sequential steps follow the inappropriate behaviors. First, the client remedies the efforts of the wrongdoing ("restitution") and, second, overcorrects it by extensive rehearsal of the appropriate behavior (Foxx & Azrin, 1973). Overcorrection has been particularly effective in reducing disruptive and aggressive behaviors in institutionalized settings. In covert conditioning, which combines elements of both operant and classical conditioning, clients are taught to vividly imagine extremely unpleasant consequences (e.g., felt pain, image of a cirrhotic liver) each time they think of a certain maladaptive behavior (e.g., drinking alcoholic beverages). The pairing of the negative image (consequence) with the thought leading to the undesirable behavior (antecedent) is regarded as an aversive procedure that gradually leads to extinction of the maladaptive behavior. Similar principles apply to associating positive images with desirable behaviors (Cautela, 1966).

In rehabilitation settings in which the counselor might frequently encounter clients with negative self-regard and highly dependent behaviors that materially interfere with the rehabilitation process, covert conditioning is of substantial merit (Livingston & Johnson, 1979). In the process of counseling clients with disabilities, any progress toward the successful performance of a rehabilitation goal can be self-rewarded. Covert self-reinforcements often include positive self-statements (e.g., "I am doing great"), mental image (e.g., visualizing oneself functioning independently in a specific community setting) or a feeling of well-being.

Classical conditioning methods, such as systematic desensitization, thought stopping, implosive therapy, and flooding are used less frequently in rehabilitation settings, but their potential for altering clients' maladaptive behaviors is rather substantial. The principle of reciprocal inhibition is at the base of Wolpe's (1958) systematic desensitization, in which anxiety-evoking situations are typically paired with inhibitory (antagonistic responses), such as relaxation or assertion. In rehabilitation settings, reducing anxiety through relaxation training is often used to combat the anxiety experienced in connection with disability issues that can prevent the client from participating in various life activities.

A variant of this method, biofeedback training, empowers the client to gain control over sensory, musculoskeletal, or internal responses (e.g., bladder control, heart rate, seizure activities) that accompany anxiety (Levenkron, 1987). Similarly, assertiveness training is frequently used to extinguish anxiety elicited by interpersonal situations. Clients with disabilities are taught to stand up for their rights in an appropriately firm manner and develop more effective social coping skills.

Thought stopping is a behavioral technique wherein a client's disturbing thoughts are terminated by either an aversive stimulus or by the simple use of the word "stop" (Groden & Cautela, 1981). Eventually, the client assumes responsibility for ceasing these thoughts by personally using the stop command. Thought-stopping techniques have been used to enable terminally ill patients to successfully disrupt unwanted thoughts and feelings associated with the dying process (Sobel, 1981). Patients were taught to control their disturbing thoughts by focusing on events, images, and memories that elicited positive feelings. The implications of these studies for counseling people with physical disabilities are obvious.

Another behavioral approach is that of Bandura's (1977) theory of social learning or modeling. This perspective relies on the use of imitative learning either directly, by observing other people's behavior and its consequences, or through vicarious experience. Modeling in rehabilitation settings emphasizes the client's assets. Consequently, clients are instructed to observe models with similar disabilities who have mastered various tasks, despite the existence of a physical impairment.

A final behavioral procedure to be discussed is self-management or self-control. As an outgrowth of operant conditioning, self-management assists clients in developing the ability to regulate their behaviors and exercise self-control in daily activities (Livingston & Johnson, 1979; Sawyer & Crimando, 1984). A self-management program customarily adopts a wide range of environmental manipulations and behavioral techniques that include, but are not limited to, the following: (a) self-observation and systematic self-monitoring, (b) behavioral initiation and the commencement of alternative responses to those deemed maladaptive, and (c) self-reward with a personally meaningful positive reinforcer that is contingent upon successfully performing a targeted activity. The application of self-management procedures to rehabilitation settings can assist clients with disabilities in decreasing the impact of disability-related problems while increasing the potential for client growth (Sawyer & Crimando, 1984).

## Adaptation to Disability-Related Interventions

As the previous section demonstrates, the possibilities inherent in applying behavioral methods to counseling people with disabilities are numerous. Although behavioral interventions are more congruent with clients who are active and motivated and are particularly effective during the final phases of adaptation to disability, the application of these interventions to earlier phases should not be overlooked. For example, the reinforcement of behaviors that are incompatible with denial (e.g., rewarding physical activities and compliance with medications and treatment regime) can be used with clients who deny the implications of their disability (Dunn, 1975). Behavioral interventions for clients who are depressed include (a) reinforcement of positive self-statements, (b) lack of reinforcement (ignoring) of negative self-statements, (c) reinforcement of interpersonal contacts, and (d) assertiveness skills training (Walters, 1981). During the phase of externalized hostility, the emphasis shifts toward teaching the client relaxation techniques that help to defuse anger and applying aversive therapy methods to clients who manifest destructive and other-injurious behaviors. As suggested, behavioral therapy is one of the primary strategies of choice for clients who fully recognize their disability. During the acknowledgement phase, the counselor focuses on (a) modeling new, appropriate behaviors, (b) teaching and reinforcing new activities (personal, social, and vocational), and (c) teaching skills training for employment applications, job interviewing, and work performance (Russell, 1981; Scofield et al., 1980). For example, when working with a client with a spinal cord injury who has accepted the disability and its implications, the counselor can (a) mobilize the assistance of a long-term wheelchair user to model negotiation of possible environmental work-setting barriers; (b) reward and encourage the acquisition of the newly learned behaviors through verbal statements such as, "This was great; you have improved by 100% since your performance last week"; and (c) teach self-management techniques through the use of self-regulation ("I can attend the football game when I successfully complete my homework assignment") and self-reinforcement techniques.

## Criteria for Change

Behavioral Therapy approaches almost invariably adopt specific, observable, and measurable goals and criteria for behavioral change. The counselor's observations and judgments, based on changes observed in the therapeutic situation, and on changes reported by the client and significant others to have occurred outside the session, are the prima facie evidence of behavioral change. Client extinction of maladaptive behaviors, followed by acquisition of adaptive behaviors as reported by the client and significant others in real life situations, are the criteria adopted for assessment of change. For example, the percentage of time or number of occasions a client engages in a certain maladaptive behavior (e.g., abusive language directed at rehabilitation unit personnel) is expected to decrease over time as a result of the therapeutic intervention. Behaviorally anchored personality schedules and inventories (e.g., the Willoughby Personality Schedule; Willoughby, 1969) are also used to measure precounseling to postcounseling levels of functioning.

# The Somatopsychological Approach

## Concepts

The Somatopsychology theory of Barker, Wright, Myerson, and Gonick (1953), Dembo, Leviton, and Wright (1956), and Wright (1983) originated from Lewin's (1935) field theory. Proponents of this theory argue that behavior is the result of a unique interaction between the individual's intrapsychic (mental) processes and external (environmental) condition (see also Duval, 1982). The theory has been formulated toward understanding the psychological mechanisms adopted by people with physical disabilities. Physique and behavior are perceived to be interrelated and mutually dependent. Behavioral (i.e., functional) limitations and social rejection interact in forcing the person with disability into a subordinate position in which goals are frequently inaccessible.

Moreover, it is the personal meaning of the disability, in association with the stimulus value the disability holds for others in the life space of the person with disability, that is of significance in understanding the psychosocial adjustment to disability. Indeed, people with disabilities frequently assume an inferior status position because of both internal mechanisms and external conditions. Internal mechanisms may include (a) engaging in "as if" behaviors (i.e., denying or covering up the disability); (b) dually identifying with both disabled and able-bodied groups; (c) idolizing standards of normal performance; or (d) focusing attention upon deficit behaviors. External influences include negative attitudes directed toward persons with disabilities, such as ascribing to them a minority group status, with its accompanying feelings of prejudice, stereotyping, and social marginality (Wright, 1983).

## General Intervention Strategies

Wright (1983) recommended a fourfold intervention approach to counseling persons with disabilities. These interventions include the following:
(a) enlarging the scope of values (extending the client's horizons beyond those charted by the disability and realizing values other than those affected by the disability); (b) subordinating physique (permitting other values, which hold satisfaction and significance in the life of the client, to assume greater potency); (c) containing disability effects (preventing the spread of disability-connected limitations into nondisability-related areas); and (d) transforming comparative status values into asset values (effecting a shift in perspective from other-comparison to the intrinsic positive qualities and potentialities of the client).

Wright (1983) further suggested that the counselor prepares clients with disabilities to face the challenges necessitated by social encounters through interventions that facilitate (a) role-playing difficult situations in group settings, (b) experiencing real-life situations with a "knower" (an experienced person with disability who is proficient in handling disability matters in social situations), and (c) experiencing real-life situations with other novices through participation in social excursions with people who have similar disabilities.

Inherent in these coping strategies is the emphasis on (a) what a person with a disability can do, (b) the life areas in which the person can participate, (c) the active role the person assumes in shaping his or her life, and (d) the premise that people with disabilities can lead meaningful and productive lives (Wright, 1975).

## Adaptation to Disability-Related Interventions

The Somatopsychological approach is the only system that was especially developed for rehabilitation settings. As such, it has a wider applicability to the process of adaptation to disability. In counseling people with disabilities, somatopsychologists characteristically initiate their interventions with clients who exhibit depressive reactions and proceed until the client reaches the hopeful milestone of full adjustment to the disability. During the phases of depression and internalized anger, the somatopsychologist typically concentrates on preventing the generalization of disability associated limitations to other nonaffected life areas. In this regard, the orientation is somewhat reminiscent of the work of cognitive therapists (Wright, 1983). In the later phases of externalized hostility and acknowledgement, the therapeutic focus shifts to exploring and clarifying personal values. During this period, the counselor seeks to replace the client's physique-based values (e.g., athletic prowess) with values of social and spiritual nature. Also, clients are taught to take pride in inherent and current personal achievements rather than relying on comparisons with others or predisability accomplishments (Scofield et al., 1980; Wright, 1983). During these final phases, counseling methods include role-playing of authentically encountered predicaments, observing successful and experienced role models, and practicing of real-life situations in various community-based settings (e.g., school, work). These latter procedures rely more heavily on principles adopted from behavioral methods of counseling.

The client with spinal cord injury is assisted in exploring his or her current values, and when these values are deemed no longer appropriate or realistic, an attempt is made to help the client explore other values. The counselor can simultaneously validate the client's ideals and suggest alternate modes to express these values with the following dialogue: "I realize the importance you attached to your physical strength. That is why you chose to operate heavy machinery for the past 10 years. Now you can no longer do it. However, your hobby of fixing small appliances can be handy. You can refine it and being in a wheelchair should pose no obstacle." The client can then be introduced to another wheelchair user who successfully engages in the proposed occupation or a similar occupation. Eventually, the client will be expected to independently perform those activities necessitated by the new job.

### Criteria for Change

Somatopsychological practitioners do not advocate any measures for assessing counseling success. It might, however, be conjectured that assessing change, when it occurs, resides primarily with the client. Based on the above characteristics of the coping framework, clients with disabilities may be considered psychologically improved or adjusted when (a) their scope of values has shifted in the direction of values not linked to personal loss or disability, (b) non-physique-related values assume greater significance for the person, (c) the impact of disability is limited to only those areas directly connected with the disability, and (d) the client upholds asset evaluation, and focuses on his or her inherent strengths and gradual progress.

## Summary

The intent of this article has been to provide the reader with a descriptive account of the merit of some of the most popular personality and counseling theories in the field of rehabilitation counseling. More specifically, the discussion used eight personality theories to explore the most cardinally relevant concepts, interventions strategies, adaptation to disability-related methods, and therapeutic change criteria that are related to understanding and counseling people with disabilities.

Counselors who seek to assist clients with disabilities through the process of adaptation to disability often follow the phase model framework and, thereby, subscribe to an eclectic approach to counseling. When the counselor elects to use the phase model, it is important that he or she realize that the sequence of the adaptation phases is not irreversible, nor is it made of discrete and nonoverlapping stages (Gunther, 1969). Furthermore, not all people with disabilities exhibit all the observed phases of adaptation to disability. Despite these circumstances, thoughtful and well-balanced counseling interventions can serve as useful clinical tools in helping clients to successfully cope with disabilities and their vicissitudes. The counselor's choice of specific approaches depends on (a) the client's needs; (b) the degree of psychosocial impact; (c) the onset, nature, course, and progression of the disability; (d) the client's support system; and (e) the counselor's knowledge and mastery of the different intervention strategies.

As a general rule, interventions that tend to be affective and nondirective in nature (e.g., the Person-Centered approach, Gestalt Therapy) seem to be more useful in the early phases of the adaptation process. Strategies of a more cognitive-behavioral and active-directive orientation (e.g., Rational-Emotive

Therapy, Cognitive Therapy, Reality Therapy, Behavioral Therapy) seem to be more effective in the latter phases of the adaptation process.

The relevance and appropriateness of these counseling approaches to the rehabilitation context can only be determined by each individual practitioner. There are no hard and fast rules that are easily applicable across disabled populations or treatment settings. As Thomas, Butler, and Parker (1987) aptly argued, counselors who work with clients with disabilities should select those concepts, approaches, and intervention strategies that are congruent with their own personal philosophy, theoretical orientation, and academic and vocational training. But just as importantly, the chosen approach should also be relevant to the client's specific counseling requirements. The counselor should devote particular consideration to the type, nature, onset, and duration of the disability prior to the selection of a certain strategy. Finally, these approaches ought to blend well with the broader life context in which the client lives, works, and is being served.

# References

Abraham, K. (1984). The first pregenital stage of the libido. In *Selected papers of Karl Abraham* (pp. 248–278). London: Hogarth Press. (Original work published 1916).

Adler, A. (1927). *Study of organ inferiority and its psychical compensations.* New York: Nervous and Mental Disease Publishing Co. (Original work published 1917).

Allen, H. A. (1985). The Gestalt perspective. *Journal of Applied Rehabilitation Counseling, 16*(3), 21–25.

Ard, B. N. (1968). Rational therapy in rehabilitation counseling. *Rehabilitation Counseling Bulletin, 12,* 84–88.

Ayllon, T., & Azrin, N. H. (1968). *The token economy.* New York: Appleton-Century-Crofts.

Bandura, A. (1977). Self-efficacy: Toward a unifying theory of behavioral change. *Psychological Review, 84,* 191–215.

Barker, R. G., Wright, B. A., Myerson, L., & Gonick, M. R. (1953). *Adjustment to physical handicap and illness: A survey of the social psychology of physique and disability* (2nd ed.). New York: Social Science Research Council, Bulletin 55.

Beck, A. T. (1967). *Depression: Cause and treatment.* Philadelphia: University of Pennsylvania Press.

Beck, A. T. (1976). *Cognitive therapy and the emotional disorders.* New York: International Universities Press.

Beck, A. T., & Emery, G. (1985). *Anxiety disorders and phobias: A cognitive perspective.* New York: Basic Books.

Bowers, W. A. (1988). Beck's Cognitive Therapy: An overview for rehabilitation counselors. *Journal of Applied Rehabilitation Counseling, 19,* 43–46.

Bray, G. P. (1978). Rehabilitation of spinal cord injured: A family approach. *Journal of Applied Rehabilitation Counseling, 9,* 70–78.

Cautela, J. R. (1966). Treatment of compulsive behavior by covert sensitization. *Psychological Record, 16,* 33–41.

Cohn, N. (1961). Understanding the process of adjustment to disability. *Journal of Rehabilitation, 27,* 16–18.

Cook, D. (1987). Psychosocial impact of disability. In R. M. Parker (Ed.), *Rehabilitation counseling: Basics and beyond* (pp. 97–120). Austin, TX: Pro Ed.

Corey, G. (1986). *Theory and practice of counseling and psychotherapy* (3rd ed.). Monterey, CA: Brooks/Cole.

Corsini, R. J., & Wedding, D. (Eds.). (1989). *Current psychotherapies* (4th ed.). Itasca, IL: F. E. Peacock.

Coven, A. B. (1977a). The Gestalt approach to rehabilitation counseling. *Rehabilitation Counseling Bulletin, 20,* 167–174.

Coven, A. B. (1977b). Using Gestalt psychodrama experiments in rehabilitation counseling. *The Personnel and Guidance Journal, 56,* 143–147.

Cubbage, M. E., & Thomas, K. R. (1989). Freud and disability. *Rehabilitation Psychology, 34,* 161–173.

Cull, J. G., & Hardy, R. E. (1975). *Counseling strategies with special populations.* Springfield, IL: Charles C Thomas.

Dembo, T., Leviton, G. M., & Wright, B. A. (1956). Adjustment to misfortune: A problem of social-psychological rehabilitation. *Artificial Limbs, 3*(2), 4–62.

Dreikurs, R. (1967). *Psychodynamics, psychotherapy, and counseling.* Chicago: Alfred Adler Institute.

Dunn, M. E. (1975). Psychological intervention in a spinal cord injury center: An introduction. *Rehabilitation Psychology, 22,* 165–178.

Duval, R. J. (1982). Psychological theories of physical disability: New perspectives. In M. G. Eisenberg, C. Griggins, & R. J. Duval (Eds.), *Disabled people as second-class citizens* (pp. 173–192). New York: Springer.

Ellis, A. (1973). *Humanistic psychotherapy: The Rational-Emotive approach.* New York: McGraw-Hill.

English, R. W. (1971). The application of personality theory to explain psychological reactions to physical disability. *Rehabilitation Research and Practice Review, 3,* 35–47.

Falek, A., & Britton, S. (1974). Phases in coping: The hypothesis and its implications. *Social Biology, 21,* 1–7.

Fink, S. (1967). Crisis and motivation: A theoretical model. *Archives of Physical Medicine and Rehabilitation, 48,* 592–597.

Ford, D. H., & Urban, H. B. (1963). *Systems of psychotherapy.* New York: Wiley.

Fordyce, W. E. (1971). Behavioral methods in rehabilitation. In W. S. Neff (Ed.), *Rehabilitation psychology* (pp. 74–108). Washington, DC: American Psychological Association.

Foxx, R. M., & Azrin, N. H. (1973). The elimination of autistic self-stimulatory behavior by overcorrection. *Journal of Applied Behavior Analysis, 6,* 1–14.

Freud, S. (1950). Mourning and melancholia. In S. Freud *Collected papers.* London: Hogarth Press. (Original work published 1917).

Glasser, W. (1965). *Reality therapy.* New York: Harper & Row.

Glasser, W. (1984). Reality therapy. In R. J. Corsini (Ed.), *Current psychotherapies* (3rd ed., pp. 320–353). Itasca, IL: F. E. Peacock.

Glasser, W. (1985). *Control theory: A new explanation of how we control our lives.* New York: Harper & Row.

Greif, E., & Matarazzo, R. G. (1982). *Behavioral approaches to rehabilitation.* New York: Springer.

Groden, G., & Cautela, J. R. (1981). Behavior therapy: A survey of procedures for counselors. *The Personnel and Guidance Journal, 60,* 175–180.

Gunther, M. S. (1969). Emotional aspects. In D. Ruge (Ed.), *Spinal cord injuries* (pp. 93–108). Springfield, IL: (Charles C Thomas).

Halligan, F. G. (1983). Reaction depression and chronic illness: Counseling patients and their families. *The Personnel and Guidance Journal, 61,* 401–406.

Herman, C. D., Manning, R. A., & Teitelman, E. (1971). Psychiatric rehabilitation of the physically disabled, the mentally retarded and the psychiatrically impaired. In F. H. Krusen, F. J. Kottke, & P. M. Ellwood (Eds.), *Handbook of physical medicine and rehabilitation* (pp. 761–768). Philadelphia, PA: W. B. Saunders.

Hohmann, G. W. (1975). Psychological aspects of treatment and rehabilitation of the spinal cord injured person. *Clinical Orthopaedics, 112,* 81–88.

Jung, H. (1978). Gestalt therapy in rehabilitation counseling. *Psychosocial Rehabilitation Journal, 2,* 26–34.

Knight, R. P. (1941). Evaluation of the results of psychoanalytic therapy. *American Journal of Psychiatry, 98,* 434–446.

Kolb, C. L., & Woldt, A. L. (1976). The rehabilitative potential of a Gestalt approach to counseling severely impaired clients. In W. A. McDowell, S. A. Meadows, R. Crabtree, & R. Sakata (Eds.), *Rehabilitation counseling with persons who are severely disabled* (pp. 48–58). Huntington, WV: Marshal University Press.

Levenkron, J. C. (1987). Behavior modification in rehabilitation: Principles and clinical strategies. In B. Caplan (Ed.), *Rehabilitation psychology desk reference* (pp. 383–416). Rockville, MD: Aspen.

Lewin, K. (1935). *A dynamic theory of personality.* New York: McGraw-Hill.

Livingston, R. H., & Johnson, R. G. (1979). Covert conditioning and self-management in rehabilitation counseling. *Rehabilitation Counseling Bulletin, 22,* 330–337.

Livneh, H. (1986). A unified approach to existing models of adaptation to disability. Part I: A model of adaptation. *Journal of Applied Rehabilitation Counseling, 17,* 5–16, 56.

Lofaro, G. A., & Fleming, J. (1980). Experimental disability: A Gestalt perspective. *Rehabilitation Counseling Bulletin, 23,* 209–217.

McDaniel, J. W. (1976). *Physical disability and human behavior* (2nd ed.). New York: Pergamon.

McDowell, W. A., Coven, A. B., & Eash, V. C. (1979). The handicapped: Special needs and strategies for counseling. *The Personnel and Guidance Journal, 57,* 228–232.

Menninger, K. A. (1953). Psychiatric aspects of physical disability. In J. F. Garrett (Ed.), *Psychological aspects of physical disability* (pp. 8–17). Washington, DC: Office of Vocational Rehabilitation, Department of Health, Education and Welfare.

Mosak, H. H. (1977). *On purpose.* Chicago: Alfred Adler Institute.

Ososkie, J. N., & Turpin, J. O. (1985). Reality therapy in rehabilitation counseling. *Journal of Applied Rehabilitation Counseling, 16*(3), 34–38.

Ostby, S. S. (1985). A Rational-Emotive perspective. *Journal of Applied Rehabilitation Counseling, 16*(3), 30–33.

Patterson, C. H. (1986). *Theories of counseling and psychotherapy* (4th ed.). New York: Harper & Row.

Perls, F. (1969). *Gestalt therapy verbatim.* Moab, UT: Real People Press.

Perls, F., Hefferline, R. F., & Goodman, P. (1951). *Gestalt therapy.* New York: Julian Press.

Rice, J. M. (1985). A behavioral perspective. *Journal of Applied Rehabilitation Counseling, 16*(3), 26–29.

Riggar, T. F., Maki, D. R., & Wolf, A. W. (Eds.). (1986). *Applied rehabilitation counseling.* New York: Springer.

Roessler, R. T., & Bolton, B. (1978). *Psychosocial adjustment to disability.* Baltimore, MD: University Park Press.

Rogers, C. R. (1951). *Client-Centered therapy.* Boston: Houghton Mifflin.

Rule, W. (Ed.). (1984). *Lifestyle counseling for adjustment to disability.* Rockville, MD: Aspen Systems.

Rule, W. R. (1987). Acceptance and adjustment to disability: An Adlerian orientation. In G. L. Gandy, E. D. Mertin, R. E. Hardy, & J. G. Cull (Eds.), *Rehabilitation counseling and services: Profession and process* (pp. 219–233). Springfield, IL: (Charles C) Thomas.

Russell, R. A. (1981). Concepts of adjustment to disability: An overview. *Rehabilitation Literature, 42,* 330–338.

Sawyer, H. W., & Crimando, W. (1984). Self-management strategies in rehabilitation. *Journal of Rehabilitation, 50,* 27–30.

Schilder, P. (1950). *The image and appearance of the human body.* New York: Wiley.

Scofield, M. E., Pape, D. A., McCracken, N., & Maki, D. R. (1980). An ecological model for promoting acceptance of disability. *Journal of Applied Rehabilitation Counseling, 11*(4), 183–187.

See, J. D. (1985). Person-Centered perspective. *Journal of Applied Rehabilitation Counseling, 16*(3), 15–20.

Shontz, F. C. (1965). Reactions to crisis. *The Volta Review, 67,* 364–370.

Shontz, F. C. (1971). Physical disability and personality. In W. S. Neff (Ed.), *Rehabilitation psychology,* (pp. 33–73). Washington, DC: American Psychological Association.

Shontz, F. C. (1980). Theories about the adjustment to having a disability. In W. M. Cruickshank (Ed.), *Psychology of exceptional children and youth* (4th ed., pp. 3–44). Englewood Cliffs, NJ: Prentice-Hall.

Simkin, J. S., & Yontef, G. M. (1984). Gestalt therapy. In R. J. Corsini (Ed.), *Current psychotherapies* (3rd ed., pp. 279–319). Itasca, IL: F. E. Peacock.

Skinner, B. F. (1953). *Science and human behavior.* New York: Free Press.

Sobel, H. (1981). Toward a behavioral thanatology in clinical care. In H. Sobel (Ed.), *Behavioral therapy in terminal care: A humanistic approach.* Cambridge, MA: Ballinger.

Thomas, K. R., Butler, A. J., & Parker, R. (1987). Psychosocial counseling. In R. M. Parker (Ed.), *Rehabilitation counseling: Basics & beyond* (pp. 65–95). Austin, TX: Pro Ed.

Thurer, S. (1985). Rehabilitation counseling: A psychodynamic perspective. *Journal of Applied Rehabilitation Counseling, 16*(3), 4–8.

Walker, G. (1987). Rehabilitation counseling with dual diagnosis clients. *Journal of Applied Rehabilitation Counseling, 18*(1), 35–37.

Walters, J. (1981). Coping with leg amputation. *American Journal of Nursing, 81,* 1349–1352.

Weller, D. J., & Miller, P. M. (1977). Emotional reactions of patient, family, and staff in acute-care period of spinal cord injury: Part I. *Social Work in Health Care, 2,* 369–377.

Willoughby, J. R. (1969). The Willoughby Personality Schedule. In J. Wolpe, *The practice of behavior therapy* (Appendix 1, 2, pp. 279–282). New York: Pergamon Press.

Wolpe, J. (1958). *Psychotherapy by reciprocal inhibition.* Stanford, CA: Stanford University Press.

Wright, B. A. (1975). Social-psychological leads to enhance rehabilitation effectiveness. *Rehabilitation Counseling Bulletin, 18,* 214–223.

Wright, B. A. (1983). *Physical disability—A psychosocial approach.* New York: Harper & Row.

# 5

# Roles of Counseling in Enabling Persons with Disabilities

*Charles W. Humes, Edna Mora Szymanski,*
*and Thomas H. Hohenshil*

"People with disabilities, *like all citizens,* [emphasis added] are entitled to participate in and contribute to the general life of the community" (Wright, 1983, p. xvi). The significance of this entitlement is realized when one reviews the long history of segregation and second-class treatment accorded by various societies and cultures to people with disabilities (Hohenshil & Humes, 1979). Although legislation, technology, and social movements of the last two decades have opened up many new opportunities for people with disabilities (Bruininks & Laikin, 1984; Rubin & Roessler, l987), numerous barriers and challenges remain (Hahn, 1985; Rubin & Rubin, 1988).

It is generally agreed that counseling can assist individuals in personal growth and realization of potential (C. Patterson, 1986). Thus, counseling can be seen as enabling fuller participation in and contribution to the general life of the community. Societal, systemic, and architectural barriers continue to impede the full participation of people with disabilities in society (Rubin, Garcia, Millard, & Wong, 1988), thereby magnifying the challenge to counseling professionals who work with such individuals.

A variety of counseling specialties (e.g., school counseling, mental health counseling) have evolved to address the needs of individuals in particular life stages or situations. Rehabilitation counseling is one such specialty that focuses on disability related issues (Thomas, Butler, & Parker, 1987). Because disability can affect all life stages and situations (Danek & Finnerty-Fried, 1985; Wright, 1983), a number of counseling-related professions, along with other educational and health-related professions, are often involved in facilitating full participation of persons with disabilities in society (Orelove & Sobsey, 1987; Power, Dell Orto, & Gibbons, 1988; Tooman, Revel, & Melia,

1988). In this article we discuss the role of counseling and its relation with other professions in facilitating career preparation and social integration of people with disabilities through the following topics: (a) disability and nomenclature issues, (b) counseling in the school years, and (c) rehabilitation counseling.

## Disability and Nomenclature Issues

In recent years models of disability have shifted. Hahn (1985) identified the following three disability models that emerged successively in this century: medical, economic, and sociopolitical. The sociopolitical model, which is most useful for counseling, defines disability as the product of the interaction between the individual and the environment (Hahn, 1985). Consistent with this model has been an evolution of acceptable language usage in reference to individuals with disabilities. It is no longer acceptable to use an impairment as an adjective describing the person (e.g., handicapped person, retarded student) or as a noun describing a group of persons (e.g., the retarded, the handicapped) (J. Patterson, 1988; Research & Training Center on Independent Living, 1987). Such language usage can inadvertently evoke stereotypical perceptions that obscure an individual's true characteristics (Wright, 1983). The accepted terminology (e.g., people with disabilities, person with mental retardation) emphasizes that disability is an attribute of the individual (like hair color) not a descriptor of the whole person. Likewise, despite the influence of P.L. 94-142, The Education for All Handicapped Children Act, we should move away from the prevailing nomenclature of *handicapped* in the school setting.

A client's disability should not be the sole focus of counseling interventions. Although environmental conditions contribute substantially to the individual impact of disability, they are often overlooked or underrated, thus obscuring potentially beneficial environmental interventions (e.g., adaptive equipment, environmental modifications) (Wright, 1983). Berkowitz (1985) has pointed to a tendency of counselors to "adjust" individuals when it is society that needs adjustment. Emerging ecological frameworks in rehabilitation counseling have stressed the importance of the following dimensions in assisting persons with disabilities in vocational planning and preparation: (a) individual attributes, (b) environmental attributes (current and future), and (c) individual perceptions of the client, family members, and involved professionals (Szymanski, Hershenson, & Power, 1988). Additionally, recent literature has stressed the importance of considering multiple situations and environments in assessment of persons with disabilities (Gaylord-Ross, 1986; Wright, 1983).

In summary, disability is a multifaceted construct that involves individual and environmental dimensions and affects and is affected by individual perceptions (including expectations) and interpersonal interactions (Szymanski, Dunn, & Parker, in press). The literature includes many testimonies of persons with disabilities (including gifted and talented individuals) who have achieved successful careers despite roadblocks they perceived to have been imposed by counselors (Rubenfeld, 1988; Whitmore & Maker, 1985). In order to truly enable clients with disabilities, the following disability related recommendations are made for counselors:

1. avoid using disabling language
2. always consider the effects of environment(s) and individual perceptions (including expectations) in educational and vocational planning
3. emphasize abilities rather than limitations
4. recognize the complexity of disability and consider referring to or consulting with a specialist (e.g., rehabilitation counselor, school psychologist) when necessary

## Counseling in the School Years

Formal education plays a critical role in preparing individuals to be productive members of society. Because of the criticalness of the educational years, we will briefly overview a number of topics related to counseling during the school years, including the following: legislative influences, IEP involvement, career development, transition, and school-agency relationships. First, we present the results of a recent survey on the status of counseling services in the schools for students with disabilities.

## National Survey Results

A brief survey, consisting of six yes–no responses and two rank order questions, was sent to state guidance offices in all fifty state Departments of Education to obtain a brief description of the current pattern of school counseling services for students with disabilities. Of 50 surveys, 23 (46%) were returned.

In response to a yes–no question, the majority of state respondents indicated that school counselors are currently more involved with IEP development than 10 years ago (16 respondents *versus* 5 respondents). When asked to rank order professionals as to the amount of counseling services they provided to students with disabilities, group medians suggested that most respondents ranked special education teachers first; school counselors and school psychologists tied for second with more respondents ranking school counselors first than school psychologists (6 *versus* 2). In the second rank order question, group median ranks revealed that respondents considered special education teachers to be the most involved professionals in transition issues/services (i.e., movement from school to post-school environments) followed by school counselors and rehabilitation counselors.

In response to a yes–no question, respondents indicated a perceived increase in counseling services available for parents of students with disabilities at present in comparison to 10 years ago (16 yes *versus* 5 no). In another yes-no question, 14 respondents indicated that, in their opinion, the lack of specificity with regard to school counselors in P.L. 94-142 regulations had been a detriment to role development in working with students with disabilities; 8 respondents disagreed, revealing variability of opinion. With regard to state guidance supervisors, only 4 respondents indicated that such positions had been incorporated into or reported to special education divisions or administrations. Nineteen respondents indicated that such incorporation had not occurred in their states, and one respondent objected vociferously to the notion of such incorporation; another respondent indicated that both organizational units were equal partners at the state level.

The final two survey questions dealt with preservice and inservice training issues for school counselors working with students with disabilities. The majority of respondents indicated that specific coursework in special education or counseling students with disabilities was *not* required for state certification in school counseling (14 *versus* 9), although there was considerable variability. However, respondents did indicate that their State Departments of Education had provided inservice education over the past 10 years to help school counselors work more effectively with students with disabilities (18 *versus* 4), showing a strong commitment to staff development during the past 10 years. Nonetheless, some respondents suggested that such inservice programs were not conducted in the recent past.

The overall data indicate that school counseling services for students with disabilities have improved over the past 10 years. Noteworthy is the fact that rehabilitation counselors now serve school clientele. However, it is also obvious that counseling roles have broadened and now include personnel not usually considered to be counseling professionals.

Interestingly, these counseling roles, while not specifically defined, have been acknowledged by state guidance offices. Application of the results of this survey are limited by a variety of factors, including the following: (a) the relatively low response rate, (b) the representativeness of state guidance assessment of local practices, and (c) the relatively small population surveyed. Further replications on state, regional, and local levels are recommended to continue to ascertain shifting patterns of counseling and service delivery roles for students with disabilities.

## Legislative Influences

The most pervasive influence in determining counseling roles in the schools has been P.L. 94-142, The Education for All Handicapped Children Act, and P.L. 93-112, The Rehabilitation Act of 1973, and the Carl Perkins Vocational Education Act (1984), which provided categorical funding for vocational counseling and assessment services for students with disabilities. These statutes have indicated what local school districts are to provide for students with disabilities and pose the threat of legal action for noncompliance (Hummel & Humes, 1984). Serving students with disabilities had one of the highest priorities for school districts during the past decade, and recruitment and hiring policies have been influenced substantially by the federal mandate (Hummel & Humes, 1984). School and rehabilitation counselors have been concerned by the lack of specificity in the regulations (Lombana, 1982), and how this has impacted staffing in the schools. Unfortunately, P.L. 94-142 was written without much, if any, counselor involvement (Humes, 1978). Counseling roles related to special education are defined in the regulations for school psychologists, school social workers, and speech pathologists, but not for school or rehabilitation counselors.

Despite the lack of specificity, there are explicit or implicit role functions for counselors under P.L. 94-142 as amended. Although school counselors are only casually mentioned in the regulations, it has been reported frequently that they are required to perform a variety of tasks associated with special education (Lombana, 1982). Rehabilitation counseling is now recognized as a related service in special education (House Report No. 99-860); however, rehabilitation counselors suffer from similar problems of lack of specificity with respect to the services that they provide to students with disabilities.

School psychologists have functioned traditionally as assessment specialists, but there is a steady movement toward counseling and consultation activities (Hummel & Humes, 1984). A major trend is the expansion of the school psychologist's counseling role in the provision of psychological services in career counseling programs. The term *vocational school psychology* was first postulated in 1974, and since that time the concept and services have considerably expanded (Hohenshil, 1984). In addition, preschool counseling and assessment are beginning to be viewed as increasingly important services. Here, youngsters with disabilities, as well as others "at risk," are provided with supportive services during their preschool years, when chances for successful intervention are greatest (Hohenshil & Hohenshil, 1989; Hohenshil & Humes, 1988).

The counseling role of school social workers, although specified in the P.L. 94-142 regulations, often has to do with their assigned duties in a school district. When the emphasis is on casework and home visitations, the ranks are thin. When a broader role exists, which includes counseling, the numbers increase. The school social worker role has tended to change as generic social work has changed (NASW, 1978). Social worker academic training programs no longer stress only casework but are heavily committed to counseling (Hancock, 1982). Concurrently, speech clinicians, through the influence of P.L. 94-142, have evolved from a technician status to a more generalist function that includes counseling. Furthermore, while school and rehabilitation counseling remain as related services, speech therapists have recently moved from a related service category to a special education category. Such a move enables them to provide services to students who need no special education services other than speech therapy. In contrast, special education regulations stipulate that students with disabilities can receive related services only when they require special education services (e.g., special instruction, speech therapy) (Podemski, Price, Smith, & Marsh, 1984). Clearly, this situation seriously limits counseling services to students with disabilities who do not require special instruction but who nonetheless require counseling services. While counseling roles for school psychologists, school social workers, and speech clinicians are clearly stated in the P.L. 94-142 regulations, the counseling roles of other personnel dealing with the needs of youth with disabilities are inferred. It is thus not difficult to see how perceived counseling roles in special education have proliferated.

During the past 10 years we have witnessed an increase in comprehensive counseling services for people with disabilities. Role changes have been seen both in the range of services provided and also in the types of counseling personnel involved. In school settings students with disabilities now receive a full range of services, including assessment, individual and group counseling, consultation, career information, and placement. Such students and their parents have sought the same privileges as their nondisabled peers and they have been granted, partly through attitude modification and partly through legislative and judicial requirements (Berry, 1987; Fahey, 1984; Humes & Hummel, 1984; Seligman, 1985). However, this does not imply that all services are provided in all settings.

The most dramatic development appears to be the range of personnel who now provide services. Counseling for students with disabilities is not only provided by school counselors and rehabilitation counselors but also by psychologists, social workers, speech clinicians, teachers, occupational therapists, and nurses, to name a few. Apparently, we have a trend toward a transdisciplinary approach (Szymanski, Hanley-Maxwell, & Parker, in press). Some have had formal training in counseling while others have not. Counseling from these allied specialists usually relates to direct care for the impairment and contact with parents (Seligman, 1985). Some counseling practitioners and counselor educators may reject this proliferation on the grounds that some of the personnel may not be fully trained in counseling. However, psychological intervention is usually most effective when it is related to a specific problem, is immediate, and is provided by a trusted helper. On the positive side, it has often been observed that total mental health needs will never be met by only fully credentialed personnel (Shaw & Goodyear, 1984). The collaborative consultative model, currently emerging in special education (Cannon & West, 1988), may provide an appropriate vehicle for trained school and rehabilitation counselors and school psychologists to consult with and train other individuals involved in the delivery of counseling services to students with disabilities.

## Individualized Educational Program (IEP)

The notion of an individual plan is a part of all services for persons with disabilities. It suggests that individualization will occur that will override generalized or stereotypical agendas. In rehabilitation counseling we have the Individualized Written Rehabilitation Plan (IWRP), and under residential facilities there is the Individual Service Plan (ISP) (Rubin & Roessler, 1987; Humes & Saggs, 1988). In special education the concept of *individualization* is paramount. The cornerstone of P.L. 94-142 is the IEP. It has influence due to a variety of factors, including individualized educational planning, due process requirements, and parental involvement. The IEP was, and is, a potent factor in service to students with disabilities (Podemski et al., 1984). Our national survey indicates that school counselors are more involved with IEP development than was the case 10 years ago. The prediction that school counselors would be involved in IEP development (Humes, 1978) has come to fruition. The least restrictive environment has been engineered with the cooperation and participation of school and rehabilitation counselors and school psychologists. While few school districts subscribed to the notion of a counseling IEP (Humes, 1980), the inclusion of counseling and career-related goals are now commonplace. The significance of this IEP involvement is obvious. The IEP, or individual plan, is the centerpiece of the special education process, and to the extent that reference is made therein to counseling, legitimizes the counseling process in the delivery of special education and transition services (Fahey, 1984). Career development, a major focus of counseling in the school years, is the subject of the next section.

## Career Development

There is a paucity of literature, in particular empirical studies, related to the vocational development theories and persons with congenital disabilities (Conte, 1983). However, the following points may be useful to counselors in assisting persons with disabilities in career development:

1. Any disability that limits an individual's interaction with the environment can result in developmental delay (Daniels, 1987; Turner, 1987). Such delays have been demonstrated in persons with visual impairments (Scholl, 1986), hearing and mobility impairments (Fallen & Umansky, 1985), and learning disabilities (D'Alonzo, Arnold, & Yuen, 1986). Development of critical skills may lag behind during childhood and adolescence yet reach

normal or superior levels in adulthood (Whitmore & Maker, 1986); thus age-related norms and normal academic predictors may obscure actual career potential of persons with disabilities.

2. Deficient experiences and opportunities, a frequent problem for children with severe disabilities, can limit development of independence, work personality, and ability to fully participate in career decision making (Daniels, 1987; Szymanski et al., 1988). Life-centered career education (Kokaska & Brolin, 1985), paid work experiences (Cobb & Hasazi, 1987), and social skills training (Bullis & Foss, 1986) are recognized interventions that offset some of the deficiencies that may result from limited early experiences.

3. Involvement of the student's family is critical to fostering adequate career development. Household chores and age-appropriate play activities should be encouraged (Fallon & Umansky, 1985; Szymanski et al., 1988).

Consideration of the above facets will increase the number of options open to students with disabilities and thus enhance their career development. Transition from school to work, the subject of the next section, is a major step in the career development of persons with disabilities.

## Transitional Issues

"The transition from school to working life is an outcome-oriented process encompassing a broad array of services and experiences that lead to employment" (Will, 1984, p. 2). The following points were distilled from recent transition literature to assist counselors in transition planning with persons with disabilities:

1. Adolescence is a challenging life stage that is further complicated by the presence of a disability (Daniels, 1987). Thus counselors must address potentially heightened adolescent concerns when assisting persons with disabilities in planning for transition.

2. Transition involves preparation for a change in environment (school to work or postsecondary education) and a change in life role (high school student to worker or college student). The characteristics and requirements of potential future environments must be considered in deciding on options and planning for successful transition (Szymanski et al., 1988).

3. People with disabilities do not always perceive the same obstacles or possibilities that are perceived by their families or by professionals working with them (Hoffman et al., 1987; Wright, 1983). Thus it is important for counselors to clarify the perceptions of all involved parties regarding goals, characteristics, and requirements for success of future work or school environments, and potential barriers (Szymanski et al., 1988).

4. Transition services must focus on enabling independence, self-determination, and productive participation in society by students with disabilities. Segregated service options, although once considered appropriate, are now thought to hinder acquisition of independence and productivity (Szymanski, Hanley-Maxwell, & Parker, in press).

## School-Agency Relationships

Effective transition often involves a coordinated effort of school and community agencies (Eleventh Institute of Rehabilitation Issues, 1984). Eligibility requirements, types of services, and service availability may differ considerably among involved agencies (Humes & Suggs, 1988). For example, although students may have received special education services during their school years, they are not automatically eligible for vocational rehabilitation services from state agencies (Szymanski, King, Parker, & Jenkins, 1989). Counselors will need to consider both services and eligibility requirements in planning for successful school-to-work transition for students with disabilities.

## Rehabilitation Counseling

One counseling profession specializes in the needs of persons with disabilities. By educational preparation, rehabilitation counselors are trained as specialists in the vocational behavior of persons with disabilities (Hershenson, 1988) through master's programs accredited by the Council on Rehabilitation Education (CORE). Their education is similar to that provided to other counselors trained in master's programs accredited by the Council on Accreditation of Counseling and Related Educational Programs (CACREP) (R. M. Parker, personal communication, September 26, 1988). However, rehabilitation counselors are required to have specific coursework covering medical and psychosocial aspects of disability, job preparation and placement of persons with disabilities, and other disability related concerns (CORE, 1983).

It should be noted that some agencies hire persons without preservice training or adequate experience in rehabilitation counselor titles (Hershenson, 1988). National certification for rehabilitation counselors, provided through the Commission on Rehabilitation Counselor Certification (CRCC) (CRCC, 1986) in processes that parallel those of the National Board for Counselor Certification, provides some assurance of minimum standards of education and experience.

Rehabilitation counseling is an allowable related service in special education of students with disabilities (House Report No. 99-860, 1986); therefore, rehabilitation counselors can serve as important members of transdisciplinary teams both as school district employees and as state vocational rehabilitation agency counselors (Szymanski & King, 1989). Individual school counselors need to seriously evaluate their own skills and competence in the area of disability and consider their ethical responsibilities to seek the consultation of specialists such as rehabilitation counselors when necessary.

## Summary

As noted in the national survey, a variety of professions are involved in the provision of counseling services to students with disabilities. The survey responses appear consistent with recent trends in the literature, which have suggested a transdisciplinary approach in special education and rehabilitation services in which different professions work in coordination. The determination of which professional assumes the lead role at any specific time is affected by the students' specific needs and the constraints of the situation. The involvement level of different professionals and the leadership of the transdisciplinary team is also expected to change as the individual moves through different phases of a program (Orelove & Sobsey, 1987; Tooman, Revell, & Melia, 1988). It is suggested that the transdisciplinary model can be an effective means of focusing the skills and knowledge of educational and rehabilitation professions in career preparation of persons with disabilities.

Persons with disabilities have the same rights to school and community participation as their nondisabled peers. Despite the legislative and social changes of the last two decades, numerous barriers still impede their full participation in society. Counseling services can facilitate fuller participation of persons with disabilities in education and employment. Such services, however, must always be provided in an enabling context and by counselors or counseling-related professionals practicing within the bounds of their professional knowledge and skills.

## References

Berkowitz, E. D. (1985). Social influences on rehabilitation planning: Introductory remarks. In L. G. Perlman & G. F. Austin (Eds.), *Social influences in rehabilitation planning: Blueprint for the 21st century* (pp. 11–18). A report of the Ninth Mary E. Switzer Memorial Seminar. Alexandria, VA: National Rehabilitation Association.

Berry, J. O. (1987). A program for training teachers as counselors of parents of children with disabilities. *Journal of Counseling and Development, 65,* 508–509.

Bruininks, R. H., & Laikin, K. C. (Eds.). (1985). *Living and learning in the least restrictive environment.* Baltimore: Brookes.

Bullis, M., & Foss, G. (1986). Guidelines for assessing job-related social skills of mildly handicapped students. *Career Development for Exceptional Individuals, 9,* 89–97.

Cannon, G. S., & West, J. F. (1988). Essential collaborative consultation competencies for regular and special educators. *Journal of Learning Disabilities, 28,* 56–63.

Cobb, B., & Hasazi, S. B. (1987). School-aged transition services: Options for adolescents with mild handicaps. *Career Development for Exceptional Individuals, 10,* 15–23.

Constable, R. T., & Flynn, J. P. (Eds.). (1982). *School social work: Practice and research perspectives.* Homewood, IL: Dorsey Press.

Conte, L. E. (1983). Vocational development theories and the disabled person: Oversight or deliberate omission? *Rehabilitation Counseling Bulletin, 26,* 316–328.

Council on Rehabilitation Education. (1983). *Accreditation manual for rehabilitation counselor education programs.* Chicago: Author.

D'Alonzo, B. J., Arnold, B. J., & Yuen, P. C. (1986). Teaching adolescents with learning and behavioral differences. In L. F. Masters & A. A. Mori (Eds.), *Teaching secondary students with mild learning and behavior problems* (pp. 1–42). Rockville, MD: Aspen.

Danek, M. M., & Finnerty-Friend, P. (Eds.). (1985). Transition and disability over the life span. [Special issue] *Rehabilitation Counseling Bulletin, 29*(2).

Daniels, J. L. (1987). Transition from school to work. In R. M. Parker (Ed.), *Rehabilitation counseling: Basics and beyond* (pp. 283–317). Austin, TX: Pro-Ed.

Eleventh Institute on Rehabilitation Issues. (1984). *Continuum of services: School to work.* Menomonie, WI: Research and Training Center, University of Wisconsin–Stout.

Fagan, T. (1981). Role expansion of the eighties: Counseling and vocational school psychology. *The Communique, 9,* 2–3.

Fahey, D. A. (1984). School counselors and psychological aspects of learning disabilities. *The School Counselor, 32,* 433–441.

Fallen, N. H., & Umansky, W. (1985). *Young children with special needs* (2nd ed.). Columbus, OH: Merrill.

Federal Register. (1977, August 3). *Education For All Handicapped Children Act. Implementation of Part B.*

Gaylord-Ross, R. (1986). The role of assessment in transitional, supported employment. *Career Development for Exceptional Individuals, 9,* 129–134.

Hahn, H. (1985). Changing perception of disability and the future of rehabilitation. In L. G. Perlman & G. F. Austin (Eds.), *Social influences in rehabilitation planning: Blueprint for the 21st century* (pp. 53–64). A report of the Ninth Mary E. Switzer Memorial Seminar. Alexandria, VA: National Rehabilitation Association.

Hancock, B. L. (1982). *School social work.* Englewood Cliffs, NJ: Prentice Hall.

Hawkins, M. E. (1982). State certification standards for school social work practice. *Social Work in Education, 4,* 41–52.

Hershenson, D. B. (1988). Along for the ride: The evolution of rehabilitation education. *Rehabilitation Counseling Bulletin, 31,* 204–217.

Hoffman, F. J., Sheldon, K. L., Minskoff, E. A., Sautter, S. W., Steidle, E. F., Baker, D. P., Bailey, M. B., & Echols, L. D. (1987). Needs of learning disabled adults. *Journal of Learning Disabilities, 20,* 43–52.

Hohenshil, T. H. (1984). The vocational aspects of school psychology: 1974–1984. *School Psychology Review, 13,* 503–509.

Hohenshil, T. H., & Hohenshil, S. (1989). Preschool counseling. *Journal of Counseling and Development, 67,* 430–431.

Hohenshil, T. H., & Humes, C. W. (1979). Roles of counseling in ensuring the rights of the handicapped. *The Personnel and Guidance Journal, 58,* 221–227.

Hohenshil, T. H., & Humes, C. W. (1988). Preschool assessment: Implications for counselors. *Journal of Counseling and Development, 66,* 251–252.

Hohenshil, T. H., Humes, C. W., & Anderson, W. T. (1984). School psychologists facilitating career development in secondary education. *Career Development for Exceptional Individuals, 7,* 51–58.

House Report No. 99–860. Washington, DC: U.S. House of Representatives.

Humes, C. W. (1978, August 10). Counselors' role in P.L. 94-142: *Guidepost,* pp. 5–8.

Humes, C. W., & Suggs, M. M. (1988). Group counseling with persons who are mentally retarded on work-related behaviors. *Journal of Applied Rehabilitation Counseling, 19,* 33–36.

Hummel, D. L., & Humes, C. W. (1984). *Pupil services: Development, coordination, administration.* New York: Macmillan.

Kokaska, C. J., & Brolin, D. E. (1985). *Career education for handicapped individuals* (2nd ed.). Columbus, OH: Merrill.

Leyser, Y. (1988). Let's listen to the consumer. The voice of parents of exceptional children. *The School Counselor, 35,* 363–369.

Lombana, J. H. (1982). *Guidance for handicapped students.* Springfield, IL: Charles C Thomas.

National Association of Social Workers. (1978). *NASW standards for social work in schools.* Washington, DC: Author.

Orelove, F. P., & Sobsey, D. (1987). *Educating children with multiple disabilities: A transdisciplinary approach.* Baltimore, MD: Brookes.

Patterson, C. H. (1986). *Theories of counseling and psychotherapy* (4th ed.). New York: Harper & Row.

Patterson, J. B. (1988). Disabling language: Fact or fiction? *Journal of Applied Rehabilitation Counseling, 19* (1), 30–32.

Podemski, R. S., Price, B. J., Smith, E. C., & Marsh, G. E. (1984). *Comprehensive administration of special education.* Rockville, MD: Aspen.

Power, P. W., Dell Orto, A. E., & Gibbons, M. B. (Eds). (1988). *Family interventions throughout chronic illness and disability.* New York: Springer.

Research and Training Center on Independent Living. (1987). *Guidelines for reporting and writing about people with disabilities.* Lawrence, KN: Author.

Rubenfeld, P. (1988). The rehabilitation counselor and the disabled client: Is a partnership of equals possible? In S. E. Rubin & N. M. Rubin (Eds.), *Contemporary challenges to the rehabilitation counseling profession* (pp. 31–44). Baltimore: Brookes.

Rubin, S. E., Garcia, J., Millard, R., & Wong, H. (1988). Preparing rehabilitation counselors to deal with ethical dilemmas: A major challenge for rehabilitation education. In S. E. Rubin & N. M. Rubin (Eds.), *Contemporary challenges to the rehabilitation counseling profession* (pp. 303–315). Baltimore: Brookes.

Rubin, S. E., & Roessler, R. T. (1987). *Foundations of the vocational rehabilitation process* (3rd ed.). Austin, TX: Pro-Ed.

Rubin, S. E., & Rubin, N. M. (Eds.). (1988). *Contemporary challenges to the rehabilitation counseling profession.* Baltimore: Brookes.

Scholl, G. T. (Ed.). (1986). *Foundations of education for blind and visually handicapped children and youth: Theory and practice.* New York: American Foundation for the Blind.

Seligman, M. (1985). Handicapped children and their families. *Journal of Counseling and Development, 14,* 274–276.

Shaw, M. C., & Goodyear, R. K. (1984). Prologue to primary prevention in schools. *The Personnel and Guidance Journal, 62,* 446–447.

Szymanski, E. M., Dunn, C., & Parker, R. M. (1989). Rehabilitation counseling with persons with learning disabilities: An ecological framework. *Rehabilitation Counseling Bulletin, 33,* 38–53.

Szymanski, E. M., Hanley-Maxwell, C., & Parker, R. M. (in press). Transdisciplinary planning for supported employment. In F. R. Rusch (Ed.), *Handbook of supported employment: Models, methods, issues.* Chicago: Sycamore.

Szymanski, E. M., Hershenson, D. B., & Power, P. W. (1988). Enabling the family in supporting transition from school to work. In P. W. Power, A. E. Dell Orto, & M. B. Gibbons (Eds.), *Family interventions throughout chronic illness and disability* (pp. 216–233). New York: Springer.

Szymanski, E. M., & King, J. (1989). Rehabilitation counseling in transition planning and preparation. *Career Development for Exceptional Individuals, 12* (1), 3–10.

Szymanski, E. M., King, J., Parker, R. M., & Jenkins, W. M. (1989). The state-federal rehabilitation program: Overview and interface with special education. *Exceptional Children, 56,* 70–77.

Thomas, K., Butler, A., & Parker, R. (1987). Psychosocial counseling. In R. M. Parker (Ed.), *Rehabilitation counseling: Basics and beyond* (pp. 65–95). Austin, TX: Pro-Ed.

Tolbert, E. L. (1978). *An introduction to guidance.* Boston: Little, Brown.

Tooman, M. L., Revell, W. G., & Melia, R. P. (1988). The role of the rehabilitation counselor in the provision of transition and supported programs. In S. E. Rubin & N. M. Rubin (Eds.), *Contemporary challenges to the rehabilitation counseling profession* (pp. 77–92). Baltimore: Brookes.

Turner, K. D. (1987). *Birth to six interactions: Implications for Special Education.* Unpublished manuscript, University of Texas at Austin, Special Education Department.

U.S. Department of Health, Education and Welfare. (1977, August 23). *Education of handicapped children.* Federal Register, pp. 42474–42504.

Whitmore, J. R., & Maker, J. C. (1985). *Intellectual giftedness in disabled persons.* Rockville, MD: Aspen.

Will, M. (1984). *OSERS Programming for the transition of youth with disabilities: Bridges from school to working life.* Washington, DC: Office of Special Education and Rehabilitative Services, U.S. Department of Education.

Wright, B. A. (1983). *Physical disability—A psychosocial approach* (2nd ed.). New York: Harper & Row.

# 6

# An Agenda for Professional Practice in the 1990s

*Marvin D. Kuehn*

Disability policy in the United States has evolved from the perspectives and interests of various human service-related programs. The result has been narrow, fragmented programs, many of which have evolved from policies designed for populations that work at cross-purposes. These disability programs reflect many styles of policymaking which have caused great duplication of services and confusion in administration. Ultimately, the lack of a consistent disability policy has led to unneeded competition, conflict, a splintering of professional preparation disciplines, program administration indecision, and confusion. Some programs rely on the court system and the private sector of rehabilitation to award benefits to persons with disabilities while others operate through the tax system and the public sector. Some programs compensate people who have severe physical limitations; others attempt to eliminate disability. Programs differ for civilians, veterans, and other federal workers while railroad workers have still another alternative. Within Congress, benefit provisions and the responsibility for philosophical direction of programs lies scattered across innumerable committees and subcommittees that, more often than not, fail to consult with each other (Berkowitz, 1987).

## Perspectives on Disability Policy

The predominant policy paradigm within the field of disability studies in the 1980s has become what might be called the social construction of disability, i.e., the meaning and consequences of disability for people with physical and mental impairments is defined by attitudes, practices, and institutional structures rather than by impairments themselves (Berkowitz, 1985; Skotch & Berkowitz, 1990). Public policy plays a particularly important role in this social

Reprinted from *Journal of Applied Rehabilitation Counseling, 22*(3), 6–15, 1991. Reprinted by permission of author.

**167**

construction, both in its own right as a provider of resources to many people with disabilities and as an expression of societal values and beliefs about disability.

The fundamental definition of disability accepted today by most policymakers has been in terms of an individual's physical or mental capacities as they relate to the potential for workforce participation. Some individuals having a legally-certified impairment have been excused from the expectation of remunerative work and instead can legitimately claim public benefits because this status exempts them from the expectation of gainful employment. Other individuals with disabilities have been eligible to receive vocational rehabilitation to facilitate participation in the workforce. Policies have generally sought to distinguish and assist people who might be called "truly disabled," i.e., those whose physical or mental impairments conformed to statutory definitions. The physical and social environment that constrains individuals with such impairments has not been addressed in public policy until recently; environmental factors, including discrimination, have been perceived as unfortunate but inevitable or have been frequently ignored altogether (Berkowitz, 1987; Hahn, 1985).

Much of the literature on disability policy in recent years, including the work of Berkowitz (1987), Hahn (1985), Percy (1989), and Scotch (1984), has examined policy in light of the social construction/minority-group model and the anti-discrimination and independent living programs that flow from it. A common theme in this emerging body of work is that different ways of conceptualizing disability and its relation to social and economic functioning have different policy consequences.

The dilemma for professional practitioners in the 1990s can be seen by reviewing the differing benefit and eligibility perspectives of the blind as a privileged group. For example, spokesmen for the blind made certain that blind people could qualify for disability insurance more easily than other groups. On the other hand, this same group was among the earliest advocates for civil rights legislation to protect people with disabilities. While these representatives sought both expanded benefits and the right to work without losing such benefits, they made claims both of ability and incapacity (Scotch & Berkowitz, 1990). Comparable incongruities appear in debates over the accessibility of local public transportation, mandated accommodations in education and employment, and a range of other disability issues. Nevertheless, the changing conceptual basis of disability that underlies policy positions and debates may reveal much about attitudes and about the larger social context within which disability may or may not affect social functioning. By drawing on the methods and conceptual frameworks of historians and social scientists, public policy, along with its implicit and explicit assumptions, can be an important topic in itself, and also can be an opening into the broader subject of rehabilitation services that may be needed by persons with disabilities (Berkowitz, 1987).

The passage of the Americans with Disabilities Act (ADA) reflects a new stage in American disability policy; however, important policy issues that predate the passage of ADA remain unresolved. Policy assumptions that have guided various disability income and medical assistance programs since their inception in the 1950s and 1960s are still significant issues of concern. The most detrimental presupposition is that to be eligible for income or medical assistance, the impairment must be so limiting and the employment outlook so negative that future prospects for work are inconceivable. This postulation is self-fulfilling and out of step with policy hypotheses that motivated the passage of the ADA (DeJong & Batavia, 1990).

The confusing state of disability policy in this country can be attributed in part to the fact that many of the nation's disability programs were contrived in earlier periods when the social preconception and policy presumption inferred that disabilities necessarily preclude employability and participation in the social life of the community. While the ADA should be applauded for recognizing social change and for conforming to the needs and expectations of persons experiencing disability, it has not or will not eliminate or modify the invalid assumptions of previously enacted policy. The civil rights goal of the ADA—to bring persons with disabilities into the mainstream of American life—is likely to be frustrated unless the other components that make up the nation's disability policy are also addressed.

Broadly conceived, disability policy is comprised of three general components that affect professional practice in rehabilitation counseling: (a) civil rights laws and regulations, (b) income and in-kind (e.g., medical) assistance programs, and (c) skill enhancement programs such as education and vocational rehabilitation (Berkowitz, 1987). Unfortunately, these components are not synchronous and often do not reflect current professional beliefs about the role of people with disabilities as productive citizens.

Improvements in medical rehabilitation, the development of new assistive technologies, and the evolution of changing expectations of people with disabilities have enhanced opportunities for independent living and employment (Greenwood, 1990; Haber, 1985; & Nosek, 1985). Determination of a person's medical condition, however, has become an inadequate basis for determining a person's work capability and eligibility for public programs. The independent living movement has helped us focus our attention on environmental conditions that impede or facilitate educational and employment opportunities. Thus, much of the progress that has been achieved in making the environment more accommodating for people with disabilities has minimized their medical conditions (DeJong, 1981; National Council on the Handicapped, 1986, 1988).

Each year the nation pays a high cost for these conflicting disability programs, both in practical and relative terms. For example, disability expenditures in the public and private sectors amounted to $122 billion in 1982 (Berkowitz, 1987). Almost none of that money prepared people for work or removed the architectural barriers that make so much of society inaccessible to persons with disabilities. Consequently, the focus has been on paying people not to work.

Some disability programs pay benefits to workers who have either temporarily or permanently left their jobs while others encourage workers to seek employment or to rejoin the labor force. Berkowitz (1987) indicated that worker's compensation, for example, which paid benefits to employees who had been injured on the job in 1984, cost employers $22.5 billion a year in insurance premiums; only a small fraction of this money funded the rehabilitation of injured workers. Currently, vocational rehabilitation, which attempts to restore the productivity of persons with disabilities by job placement and job training, costs the federal government about a billion dollars a year. It is by far the least expensive of the major disability programs. Social Security Disability Insurance (SSDI) has emerged as the nation's most expensive disability program (Kiernan, Sanchez, & Schalock, 1989). Unless someone makes an effort to coordinate these programs and others like them, expensive, contradictory programs that perpetuate disability dependence will continue to be the norm. At the present time, other than discussions about national health care, there is little evidence that major disability policy reforms are forthcoming. Government continues to authorize and fund programs with overlapping objectives and services without regard to program ramifications and to the discrepant system that is being created.

SSI (Supplemental Security Income), SSDI, and Title XIX programs clearly reside within a realm of programs broadly identified as part of our country's welfare system. These programs, through income maintenance or medical assistance, are part of our country's need-based distribution system as opposed to the work-based distribution system (Stone, 1984). Other programs affecting persons with disabilities are part of the special education and rehabilitation system. These programs are part of the "work-based" distribution system in that their purpose is legally protective or vocationally corrective (Berkowitz, 1987; Haveman, Halberstadt, & Burkhauser, 1984) instead of ameliorative. Ideally, these programs are designed to prepare, maintain, or return someone's capacity for participation in the workforce.

In the past, worker's compensation and social security disability insurance have formed the core of America's public policy toward disability. Both of these programs represent ameliorative responses to disability (Berkowitz, 1987). By raising people's incomes, they seek to ease the financial burden that physical and mental impairments impose on people; they do nothing about the impairments or limitations themselves.

Berkowitz (1987) contrasts ameliorative responses to disability with corrective responses. Programs that embody the corrective response seek to improve the work productivity of individuals with disabilities or to change the economic environment in which they function. In other words, corrective responses represent efforts to overcome impairments or make them less of a handicap to the affected worker. The corrective strategy toward disability has clear advantages as it focuses on the future and the investment concept of service delivery philosophy; this type of corrective response allows the person with a disability to achieve independence instead of fostering dependence on a government-sponsored program.

Today, the corrective response is desired in most professional practice settings as it focuses on vocational rehabilitation, independent living programs, and civil rights and architectural barrier laws. However, the corrective response plays a distinctly secondary role in American public policy toward disability. The ameliorative response consumes many more public dollars and attracts much more attention from Congress. Even though vocational rehabilitation, America's major corrective disability program, now costs well over a billion dollars a year in federal money alone, the SSDI program costs at least seventeen times more (Berkowitz, 1987).

In the 1980s the most publicized event in the evolution of disability policy involved a fight to keep people on the disability rolls and out of the labor force. Berkowitz (1987) stated that in order to gain access to these rolls, people had to prove to the satisfaction of a state disability examiner, an administrative law judge, or a federal judge that they were unable to do any sort of gainful work. When the Reagan administration suggested that some of these people could indeed work and removed them from the rolls, a furor erupted. Advocates for people with disabilities argued that these individuals had a legal entitlement to a disability pension and should not be forced to seek work. However, they made no mention of the efforts to facilitate the entrance of the handicapped into the work force. Thus, efforts to open up the labor force to people with disabilities and to protect their rights to retire pointed out the inconsistent philosophy driving disability policy.

If physical barriers prevent people from working or from taking part in other activities, then public policy must seek ways to remove the barriers. For those whose conditions make work impossible, public policy should promote independence and self-care. Being an individual with a disability should not be equated with being helpless (Hahn, 1985). We need to move disability policy beyond retirement and maintenance and toward the participation of everyone in American life.

## Transcending Definitions

America's disability policy can be simply defined as the aggregate of social policies (at all levels of government) intended to maintain or enhance the quality of life of people with disabilities and their families. But what does this really imply?

The term **disability** resists precise definition and measurement, and, therefore presents subtle as well as complicated problems. Clearly identifying who qualifies as a person with a disability is a task controlled or dictated by a program's goals, mission, and eligibility criteria. Disability usually represents a social judgment, and it involves a combination of physical, economic, and psychological factors that make the formation and administration of public policy difficult and complex. The responses and adjustments that different people make to the same limiting physical or mental condition contribute to the difficulty in formation of standard policy (Bowe, 1978; Haveman, Halberstadt, & Burkhauser, 1984; Nagi, 1979).

A substantial roadblock to a rational disability policy lies in the fact that disability has different meanings depending upon the eligibility requirements or purposes of a program. This interpretation problem will continue to influence professional practice and delay the articulation of a strong national disability policy.

Individuals entering the rehabilitation field to become service providers must learn the differences and implications of the definition of disability used in their respective work settings. In the worker's compensation program and in the courts, disability means "the damages that one person collects from another as a result of an insult or injury." In the SSDI program, disability refers to "a condition that links ill health and unemployment." And in the context of civil rights laws, disability connotes "handicap." In addition, policy analysts have spent a great deal of time puzzling over the distinctions among such terms as functional limitations, impairment, disability, and handicap. Despite the scholarly efforts to explain the relationships among the terms, different programs use the terms inconsistently or in some cases interchangeably (Berkowitz, 1987).

Another problem in the absence of a common definition of disability is that people involved with the judicial system, for example, continue to associate disability with damages. The lengthy and expensive judicial process requires that a person demonstrate the extent of disability (need for compensation) rather than focusing efforts on rehabilitation (employment). It concentrates money on compensation after the fact and detracts from the goal of preventing the hazard in the first place or promoting the independence and employment of the individual experiencing the disability. This definition also raises questions of fairness since those with the most money—those who need damage awards the least—may have access to the most skilled lawyers and the most effective expert witnesses (Greenwood, 1990).

Berkowitz (1987) suggested that if a person leaves the labor force as a result of a physical or mental condition, he is neither unemployed nor temporarily ill; he is disabled. Such an interpretation increases the subjectivity of the concept and makes disability policy that much more difficult to administer. Thus, the differences between temporary illness, permanent disability, and unemployment are difficult to understand.

# Political Influence on Disability Programs

Historically, one of the main reasons for the lack of congruence in disability policy is that disability programs have never attracted a political following. The contrast with programs to aid the elderly is striking. Highly visible Congressional committees monitor public policy toward the elderly, but few Congressional committees air the grievances and publicize the problems of individuals with severe disabilities (Berkowitz, 1987; DeJong & Batavia, 1990). Until the passage of the Americans with Disability Act (ADA) in 1990, few leaders of the disabled community had risen to national prominence, nor had people with disabilities received the sustained attention from print and television media as had the elderly.

It is clear that people with disabilities have a more difficult time securing entitlement to a pension and other benefits than an elderly person. Policymakers presume that the elderly have, because of their years in the labor force, earned the right to retire. It is easy to verify whether or not a person is elderly. Everyone expects to grow old, so the elderly, unlike the disabled, do not stand apart from the rest of the population. For all of these reasons, giving benefits to the elderly has gained universal acceptance. In contrast, persons with disabilities who may never have worked are not accepted as having "earned" a right to benefits in the same way as the elderly. Those individuals who have worked and who wish to retire are, in a sense, asking for a special favor—to be let out of the labor force and to draw a pension from the government (Berkowitz, 1987).

When disability policy is viewed in totality, a fundamental contradiction appears. Simply stated, a large portion of the funds allocated for disability programs actually result in disincentives to individuals with disabilities to obtain employment. At the same time, policymakers fund training programs and pass civil rights laws as inducements for people with disabilities to enter the labor force. Because disability has been subsumed under so many different departments, agencies, and labels, the contradiction goes largely unnoticed (Berkowitz, 1987; Hahn, 1985; McConnell, 1985).

Equating the term "disability" with "handicap" leads to other problems. Someone who looks or acts disabled is not necessarily unable to work. But many people identify someone in a wheelchair, for example, as handicapped regardless of abilities. Since the person with a disability cannot alter this perception, one authority refers to disability as a "product of the interaction between the individual and the environment." From this perspective, the problems associated with disability are not so much the result of personal limitations as they are the perceptions and attitudes held by society in regard to persons with disabilities (Hahn, 1985).

Disabling environments require correction at the community level, yet our disability policy frequently focuses on the individual's limitations rather than on the environmental (attitudinal as well as architectural) barriers created by society. Berkowitz (1987) stated that instead of learning about environmental barriers to employment, many rehabilitation counselors, trained in the 1950s and 1960s in the methods of counseling and psychology, often studied only the individual psyche of the person with a disability. Counselors spent time matching people to jobs rather than expanding the range of accessible jobs. They did little to lower the barriers that excluded people with disabilities from society; instead they adjusted the person to society and in this manner maintained, even legitimized, the barriers.

As many individuals of a growing advocacy-oriented, rights-conscious community of persons with disabilities have come to realize, some programs, such as public vocational rehabilitation, develop policies and procedures for reasons that often have nothing to do with the people and agencies whom they serve (Berkowitz, 1989). People with disabilities have therefore tried to gain control over disability policy, to take power away from professional administrators, and to assume both themselves. This effort has led to the passage of civil rights laws and to the creation of independent living centers which are largely run by persons with disabilities rather than by professional administrators and able-bodied, direct service providers.

The philosophy and changing attitudes of the purpose of vocational rehabilitation have had a positive influence on the professional rehabilitation counselor as well as a political impact on federal policymakers. People do not regard public vocational rehabilitation as a welfare program, and that is one reason for its success. Where welfare frequently fosters dependence, rehabilitation should promote independence and/or employment. Welfare usually represents a net cost to society; vocational rehabilitation is an investment in society's future.

The distinction between rehabilitation and welfare is illustrated through a cost-benefit analysis process that allows evaluation of success by measuring the cost of dependency. It attempts to show that the program returns more to society than it costs. This argument has been used to convince Congressional decision-makers that the state/federal rehabilitation program turns potential welfare recipients into taxpayers. This cost-benefit argument has become a potent political weapon for the vocational rehabilitation program. Congressional reports consistently note that public vocational rehabilitation returns more money than it spends. Estimates of the ratio of benefits to costs have ranged between 8:1 and 35:1 (Berkowitz, 1987).

Another reason for this program's success has nothing to do with distinguishing the program from welfare and everything to do with politics—in particular, it has to do with accommodating the interests of Congressmen and interest groups such as the blind or disabled veterans. Special interest politics tend to establish the allocation of disability projects among various populations as well as result in the strategic location of programs related to political considerations. The March of Dimes, a primary example, illustrates the focus on specific impairment, polio in this case, and the appeal of cure over care, rather than disability and the reduction of limitation in general.

## Relationship of Professionalism to Policy Formation

Even as vocational rehabilitation program administrators played politics, they strove to bring a professional ethic and approach to the rehabilitation process and rehabilitation counseling practice. They called rehabilitation "an individualized process." Since rehabilitation had no "production line," it demanded professional counselors who could oversee each individual case. Professionalization of the program's counselors and its services became another factor in the program's success which, like the other factors, was apparent quite early in the program's history (Berkowitz, 1987; Boschen, 1989; Roessler & Schriner, 1991).

Passage of vocational rehabilitation legislation in 1954 was a major event that put the public service delivery program on a professional basis. The legislation initiated new types of federal grants to establish professional training programs in universities, to subsidize research on rehabilitation methods, and to enable counselors to attend new professional development and education programs at public expense. The impact on professional practice was profound. The master's degree in rehabilitation counseling became a prerequisite for entering the profession. In essence, the 1954 law had elevated rehabilitation counseling to a profession that had been defined, created and paid for by the federal government.

As the number of rehabilitation counselors grew and related professional and educational activities increased, the need for a body of specialized rehabilitation literature was perceived. Academicians in rehabilitation counseling and rehabilitation psychology developed scholarly journals in which their research findings could be published and distributed to interested colleagues. The growth of the professional literature in rehabilitation as well as the efforts to keep others without degrees in rehabilitation counseling from obtaining employment in the public rehabilitation program helped to improve the quality of rehabilitation counseling and to protect it against abuses present in disability programs in the early years.

As the profession of rehabilitation counseling has grown and evolved, the importance of specific counselor competencies and services to be provided clients/consumers has strengthened the need for a focused disability policy in America. The professional rehabilitation counselor is now required in most states to have a masters degree and in many work settings is expected to perform many specialized functions. He or she may be a case manager, a coordinator of services, a consultant/advocate, a job developer, a placement specialist, a client assessment specialist, a vocational evaluator, and therapeutic counselor/facilitator. In the past few years, the skill of marketing has also received considerable attention. Counselors must relay to various health and human service programs the contributions the professional rehabilitation counselor can provide individuals with disabilities and also communicate the role of preparing clients for the labor market.

With such complex, wide-ranging responsibilities, rehabilitation counselors wield a great deal of power over the client and over the goals of the program and the services that may be provided. The discretionary power of counselors in the public rehabilitation service delivery system differentiates them from counselors in the SSDI and workers' compensation programs and points out a principle that determines the disability policy in many agencies. Some believe this system has evolved to encourage an approach that permits counselors to turn clients away as well as to fill an agency's rolls with motivated clients who, by achieving success in the labor market, also bring the agency success.

Cost-benefit analysis, an accommodation to the politics of disability, the creation of a self-sustaining professional culture, and the ability to purchase or deny services from other agencies have all helped to define the scope of practice of the professional vocational rehabilitation counselor (Berkowitz, 1987). Each of these factors reinforces the natural appeal of the public program as a source of hope rather than a cause of dependency. However, the result of the interplay of these factors has, in effect, created agency policy that evolved due to self-interests rather than by a well thought-out, rational plan. Even with this development, many state/federal disability programs were helped to obtain increased appropriations and expand responsibilities and services.

Professional practice, however, has not always been characterized by growth and optimism. In the early 1970s, the vocational rehabilitation program, like many social welfare programs, reached a time of transition. The optimism of the 1960s gave way to the realism and pessimism of the mid-1970s. Failure of the economy to grow as rapidly as before limited the number of new jobs available and put pressure on the federal budget. The increasing participation of women and members of the baby-boom generation into the labor force exacerbated the problem. Protected entitlement programs such as social security laid claim to diminishing federal funds. Vocational rehabilitation, not an open-ended entitlement in the federal or state budget, was far more vulnerable to budget constraints than were the other disability programs such as workers' compensation and disability insurance (Berkowitz, 1987).

In selecting their caseloads, rehabilitation counselors typically favored those with mild, as opposed to those with more severe, impairments. In 1973, Congress produced a new vocational rehabilitation bill that signaled a major change in who should be served in the public program. Emphasis was to be placed on the vocational rehabilitation of the severely disabled rather than on those individuals who could readily be placed in employment. This was an attempt to eliminate the creaming (the practice by an agency of serving only those individuals from the applicant pool most likely to be employed) and to shift the focus to more difficult cases.

The implications for professional practice became obvious. Program administrators became primarily concerned about the number of people successfully served. The problem with this approach was that individuals with severe limitations noticed their frequent exclusion from the vocational rehabilitation program. They argued that they were being screened out while agencies called this practice "screening out the undermotivated." The concept of "creaming" emerged from this practice.

## New Emphases for Professional Practice

To ensure that every individual had an opportunity to participate in the decision-making, the 1973 federal law mandated the use of an individualized rehabilitation plan (IWRP) to be signed by the counselor and the client. Congress also initiated client-assistance projects that established ombudsmen in the rehabilitation agencies to protect the rights of the consumer. Furthermore, these programs were required to be independent of the vocational rehabilitation program itself. In this manner the client-assistance programs became a source of legal advice that a disgruntled client could use to pursue a grievance through the courts (Whitehead, 1989).

The 1973 law facilitated a new relationship between the individual with a disability and the vocational rehabilitation counselor. In theory people with disabilities were to enter the public rehabilitation program, look at the options that the counselors had to offer, and then decide which of the program's services they would consume. With changes in agency priorities, attitudes, and populations served, the program's clients then became its consumers. This signaled the end of what Professor Joseph Stubbins referred to as the "clinical model of rehabilitation": the counselor no longer "dominates" the client but instead, consults with the individual with a disability and together they formulate a course of action (Berkowitz, 1987).

Individual written rehabilitation plans have become quasi-legal documents that contain promises that can be enforced in a court of law. These plans, which list services that the client must receive, are written in extremely explicit language. These plans, coupled with client-assistance programs, have created a new way of conducting rehabilitation because the counselor no longer has total control over the client.

The potential for conflict between the disabled community and the public vocational rehabilitation program remains high. Counselors value their professional autonomy, and the disabled community increasingly believes it possesses inherent rights. Counselors and individuals with disabilities often disagree over where limitations of the individual end and the failures of society begin. Only the shared goal of employment minimizes the conflict. Most clients hope to gain valuable services and ultimately a job.

Declining numbers of successful rehabilitations (individuals who obtain employment) make the program's inherent conflicts more visible and more difficult to resolve. Program goals seem at times to be incongruent and often incompatible with the needs of individuals with severe disabilities or those interested in independent living issues. This situation creates pressures on counselors as "quantity" versus needed services seems to be the goal driving many programs.

Ironically, the resurgence of conservatism has placed an emphasis on the inherent value of work and its superiority to government transfer of payments as a solution to social problems. The focus on serving the severely disabled and the conflicts between professional autonomy and the civil rights of individuals with disabilities have inhibited the overall effectiveness of many programs.

The Americans with Disabilities Act offers an opportunity for both the administration and the Congress to act positively in the face of the changing needs and aspirations of an increasingly politicized disabled population and to do so at a relatively low cost to the federal government. The political unwillingness to make fundamental changes in our disability assistance programs made the passage of the ADA all the more urgent. Even if the legal requirements of ADA are enforced vigorously, as we hope they will be, the law cannot adequately substitute for other policy changes that need to be made (DeJong & Batavia, 1990).

The federal government continues to spend more than a billion dollars a year on public vocational rehabilitation. The private sector of rehabilitation services also continues to expand. Professional practice will always need to respond to the unique work settings and the multi-faceted needs of clients. Therefore, to promote a concise, simplistic description of disability policy and the future of rehabilitation counseling is probably not desirable, nor realistic. What is important is vigilance and reassessment of purpose to maintain the philosophical assumptions that form the framework of professional rehabilitation counseling practice. We should constantly fight for the rights of consumers/clients and the integrity of the service delivery system in America.

## Factors Influencing Disability Policy

Social forces exert tremendous influence on the awarding of disability benefits and the implementation of policy. Economic recessions often lead to surges in the disability rolls because older "impaired" workers use disability programs to retire. During the 1970s, for example, when disability program officials appeared willing to loosen the definition of disability, employers used disability benefits as a way to ease out older workers and replace them with younger ones. In the 1980s, efforts to reduce social spending led to a decline in the disability rolls even without formal changes in the program (Benshoff, 1990).

Berkowitz (1987) stated that in the 1970s the size of the SSDI program became a political liability. In an age of concern about "uncontrollable" social welfare costs, expenditures for disability insurance consistently exceeded the expectations of policymakers. The growth of disability insurance put pressure on the entire social security system which at that time faced, and is continuing to face, a series of financial crises.

Changes in the nature of jobs have and will continue to accompany economic changes in society and influence disability policy. Increasingly, jobs in the service sector will tend to be highly technological, labor intensive, interpersonally interactive, and highly complex. Many jobs will be communication- and information-based and will require new expertise related to technological advances (Roessler & Schriner, 1991; Roth, 1985).

Sophisticated emergency medical and trauma services, advances in neonatal care, and improvements in medical therapeutics and diagnostics are having substantial impact on the status of disability (Zola, 1989). These services are frequently technologically expensive, e.g., incorporating ventilators for breathing, electric wheelchairs for mobility, and computer systems for communication and life skills management.

Along with more complex and expanded levels of care, individuals with severe disabilities will also require specialized services from rehabilitation practitioners. Individuals who formerly would have been confined to nursing homes or state mental hospitals are now being actively and aggressively served in a wide variety of facilities ranging from medically-oriented, coma intervention programs to community re-entry rehabilitation programs. Advances have also been made in approaches to behavior analysis, and case managers/counselors serving the TBI (traumatic brain injury) population are now working with pediatric clients as well as with clients dependent upon advanced technologies.

Traditional chemical dependency treatment has historically been cognitively-based. Individuals with sensory or certain cognitive disorders have been effectively excluded from full and meaningful participation in this type of treatment (Benshoff, 1990). Second, many chemical dependency treatment programs have been slow to respond to the accessibility needs of individuals with physical impairments, especially those clients living in rural settings who often have limited accessible transportation and physical facilities.

The increasing incidence of substance abuse in the workforce and the notoriously poor experience that many employers have had in rehabilitating substance abusers has led employers and workers compensation insurance carriers to limit the reimbursement rate for substance abuse treatment programs. Many employers have cut their maximum lifetime mental health benefits. This negative experience by employers may also create a backlash against employees with other disabilities; they may be reluctant to make accommodations for people with other disabilities for fear that the precedent will be used for other people who do not stop their substance abuse despite numerous rounds of treatment (Benshoff, 1990).

AIDS is another emerging disabling condition for which individuals are accorded rights under the Rehabilitation Act of 1973. Counselors are challenged to provide an array of services to meet the multi-faceted needs of this client population. Cohen (1990) has suggested that counselors will face unique and substantial ethical dilemmas about confidentiality and disclosure. Some rehabilitation agencies may be confronted with increased costs for healthcare benefits because of AIDS.

For older workers, the natural consequences of slower recovery and recuperation may result in greater difficulties in achieving return-to-work status. It has been well-documented that returning to work after a disabling injury is positively related to timeliness of service (Seventeenth Institute on Rehabilitation Issues, 1990). Therefore, individuals with short acute care and rehabilitation periods are more likely to have positive vocational rehabilitation outcomes (Beck, 1989).

The importance of transition-to-work programs has become a major issue that, because of the size of the population to be served, could have significant policy implications. Transition programs are a variant of supported employment which rely heavily upon the strategies of job coaching, industrial enclaves, and mobile work crews. Successful implementation of transition programs requires multi-disciplinary cooperation of schools, state VR programs, employers, parent groups, and clients. Rehabilitation counselors and educators may need to develop new strategies and thought patterns and to relinquish previously held notions about professional roles in order to provide optimal services (Benshoff, 1990).

The application of new technologies, especially ergonomics, has great potential to prevent or reduce job related injuries. While the majority of workers' compensation claims continue to be for back injuries, carpal tunnel syndrome problems are growing, particularly among women who perform repetitive hand functions. The increased use of computer technology has resulted in an escalation of visual, neuromuscular, and headache difficulties resulting from prolonged use of keyboards and video display terminals.

The development of both a medical model approach and a vocational model approach in private sector rehabilitation has pointed out two different philosophical orientations and approaches that could be influenced by national disability policy decisions. The medical model centers on the provision of intensive medical case management, generally by a rehabilitation nurse. In general this model suggests that intensive, efficient medical service will result in a more timely return to work. The vocational model, more closely akin to traditional rehabilitation endeavors, stresses the importance of vocational rehabilitation services offered by a rehabilitation counselor as a complement to medical and other services. Following this model it is assumed that the process will be more closely synchronized to the needs of the individual with a disability and also the needs of the employer, resulting in greater mutual satisfaction (Benshoff, 1990).

Perhaps one of the most significant issues that affects disability policy and professional practice is litigation. Because it is a time-consuming process, it delays rehabilitation (Holmes, Hull, & Karst, 1989). Because of the fragmentation of disability policy, the trend toward more litigation is not comprehended by many administrators, Congressmen, and members of the disabled community. Disability policy needs to reflect priority on programs that would encourage independence rather than concern about the dilemmas of dependency (income maintenance programs).

Finally, supported work initiatives have increased the scope of rehabilitation services available, and the continued growth of these programs will have monetary implications for public policy. Supported employment programs are characterized by intensive skill training and ongoing support services directly at the employment site after job placement.

## Possible Agendas for the '90s

To identify a concise agenda for professional practice in the 1990s is difficult at best. No one person has all the expertise necessary to comprehend the diverse legal, economic, and social phenomena encompassed by disability policy. An attempt to gain agreement on subjects such as the methods of compensating permanent partial disabilities, labor supply economics, the legal bases of civil rights law, and the principles of rehabilitation counseling has produced controversy and frustration (Atkins, Dew, Esser, Hansen, Mundt, Scalia, Thornton, & Wesolek, 1987). Few people understand the language of the specialists and most do not have sufficient background to view the entire rehabilitation system from a holistic perspective. Congressmen, for example, operate by means of subcommittees that are heavily dependent on experts, interest groups, and others who have learned the specialized language of policy discourse. Rarely does the level of analysis rise above individual programs to include the larger picture. The focus then becomes justification of program, not development of rational disability policy.

The concept of "independence initiatives" (Berkowitz, 1987) could be one approach that should be considered in improving disability policy. With this approach, we should not waste money trying to rehabilitate those who have spent time in the labor force and now want to retire. Others who have much to contribute to the labor force in the future should be encouraged to accept independence initiatives in the form of vouchers that could be exchanged for attendant care or the modification of transportation and architectural barriers.

Another likely agenda for professional practice is to encourage employers to accept the obligation to prevent disability by instituting disability management principles in the workplace. The importance of prompt employer intervention after an accident or illness must be emphasized. The slower and less coordinated the intervention, the more likely an employee will progress from temporary illness to long-term or chronic disability (Habeck, Williams, Dugan, & Ewing, 1989).

DeJong & Batavia (1990) suggested that to facilitate changes in disability policy and to support the improvement of professional practice several additional alternatives should be considered:

1. Provide greater economic incentives and financial support to work for persons with disabilities. Modify tax policy to offer greater deductibility of, or tax credits for, disability-related expenses.

2. Eliminate any assumption in policy decisions that a person is, or is not, totally disabled. Disability may be a non-static condition.

3. Alter the assumption that a disability necessarily reduces the capability to work. Rely less on medical eligibility criteria and give more consideration to individual functional capacity and to environmental accommodations that a person with a disability may require.

4. Create incentives to work and separate employment status from program eligibility status. Assistive devices and health care benefits should be available regardless of employment status.

These ideas are not particularly radical or new. They reflect traditional American values that emphasize individual initiative, self-determination, private responsibility, and community support (Berkowitz, 1987; DeJong & Batavia, 1990). All persons who can contribute productively to our society must be encouraged to do so. The scope of professional practice can easily embrace these values and practitioners can focus rehabilitation efforts on dignity, independence and employment. People with disabilities are likely to contribute substantially to the nation's productivity if supported by a comprehensive public policy guiding rehabilitation services.

Disability policy in America seems to be at a turning point. With recent federal budget deficit concerns, the social policy agenda has basically been placed on hold. Because structural changes often involve unanticipated consequences, the Administration and Congress have been unwilling to risk changes that will require additional funds in the short run but are likely to stimulate greater economic productivity in the long run. Prospects for expanding disability programs have been made worse by a slow-growth economy, the nation's unwillingness to accept new taxes, the financial fiasco of the savings and loan industry, and the continued rapid growth in health care costs (DeJong & Batavia, 1990).

Relative to a specific agenda for professional practice, there are at least four general themes that could foster the establishment of a more unified national disability policy. First, practitioners should target programs that improve the quality of life for persons with disabilities. For example, federal support for the special education programs mandated since 1975 by PL 94-142 has never come close to the funding formula set forth in the legislation. In addition, it is not that funds are grossly inadequate but that they support programs that work at cross-purposes. The point is not that targeting is totally absent or that it is unique to disability programs. Professionals must be sure to identify the various programs that may interface or provide benefits as they coordinate appropriate disability services. They must continually advocate for eliminating bureaucratic wastefulness and for corrective, versus ameliorative programs (Berkowitz, 1987).

Second, practitioners must be persistent in assisting agencies and related programs in developing outcome measures and quality assurance practices to evaluate the appropriateness of service delivery. These measures must include review of three key areas of life for people with disabilities: where they work, where and how they live, and where they may be receiving education (Berkowitz, 1987).

Quality assurance practices primarily reflect a single dimension of the interest of decision-makers: to determine the effects of services on the persons receiving them, and to protect these individuals from harm (Benshoff, 1990). Monitoring assists in identifying nonconformance to certain standards of safety and safeguarding the public's trust in government by assuring that tax dollars are used for the purposes for which they were intended. Periodic program evaluation is the strategy utilized most frequently to monitor quality of services. Virtually all purposes of monitoring in human services are related to stated interests in program improvement. However, caution must be exercised as monitoring tends to reinforce the notion of management by compliance and it fosters adherence to minimal standards and sometimes minimum services. Further, monitoring systems usually do not help to identify critical program activities that directly lead to improvements in performance outcomes.

The third theme that deserves consideration is changing the status of dependency that programs implicitly expect, if not openly demand, of the people receiving services. Clearly, an individual that is seen as dependent, or under the patronage of another, will be harder to evaluate in quantitative terms. The dependency role has many forms but perhaps the most familiar is through the application of the medical model to disability. People with disabilities are defined as sick and, therefore, are expected to behave like patients. Case managers define a client's needs according to what the formal system provides rather than what the individual wants. Professionals must be on guard against the dangers of social control and professional dominance that can trap people with disabilities. The myth that disability is a form of deviancy must be eradicated. In addition, while practitioners must respond to each individual situation differently, an individualistic approach to disability policy has ironically often "swallowed up" people with disabilities in a depersonalized system of large, bureaucratized, institutional structures. Community associations and networks of local consumers have organized to offset this negative approach and the resultant "loss of community" that frequently occurs. A cohesive attempt for unifying disability policy is to encourage both independence and integration and to discover some way of reaffirming the sense of belonging to a community that is both supportive and liberating (Berkowitz, 1987; Scotch, 1984; Scotch & Berkowitz, 1990).

Finally, professional rehabilitation counselors have an ethical obligation to remain knowledgeable of the laws pertinent and applicable to their practice. The areas of confidentiality and privilege, malpractice, and forensics clearly are in the forefront of importance. Nonetheless, they are not all-encompassing, and over the next decade they will be continually changing and expanding (Noble, 1985). Therefore, rehabilitation counselors are encouraged to remain abreast of all applicable laws. Rehabilitation counseling associations are urged to facilitate the availability of inservice training, continuing education, and pre-conference workshops for rehabilitation counselors which will focus on pertinent areas of existing, pending, and new laws. Likewise, pre-service rehabilitation counselor education programs are encouraged to develop and infuse into their curricula teaching modules with foci on law and legal issues applicable to the practice of rehabilitation counseling (Vallario & Emener, 1991).

## Conclusion

As new disability policies are proposed that affect professional practice, their importance and impact must be weighed against the goals that agencies promote. Policy must be examined in light of the need for early intervention programs in the schools that might assist special educators, high school counselors, and vocational educators (Borchen, 1989; Lombana, 1989). The use of computer technology and the advantages and curses expressed by practitioners must be rationally evaluated. Finally, the impact of policy decisions on special populations must be continually reviewed. Will there be a greater need for pre-service and post-service training in AIDS, chemical dependency and new emerging disabilities (i.e., traumatic brain injury, older workers)? Should PL 94-142, The Education for all Handicapped Children Act, and the Vocational Education Act be amended to call for expanded services to rehabilitation counselors on Individual Education Plans (IEPs) and in vocational planning with students experiencing disability (Fagan & Jenkins, 1989)?

In the 1990s it is virtually impossible for any one person to be current on all the disability service programs that exist, let alone the ways in which they interact. The pieces of disability policy should form a coherent whole, but people cannot agree on a common definition of disability and thus cannot create a disability policy that bridges the individual programs. Because these programs have been conceived and administered in isolation from one another, they are locked into an institutional structure that has proved resistant to change even though the programs have failed to serve those they were intended to help. The collection of incongruent programs should be replaced by a cohesive disability policy that reflects the aspirations and values that people with disabilities have for themselves.

It is clear that the list of possible agendas that could influence the professional practice of rehabilitation counseling in the '90s is comprehensive, possibly overwhelming, and thought provoking. All will not be addressed;

however, awareness of the possibilities and the challenges to seize the opportunities presented by some alternatives will hopefully be accepted by the profession. It is important to note that the definition of disability and the services which may result from potential eligibility are basically determined by public disability policy. To develop a viable, coherent national disability policy is a reachable goal. It is crucial that we provide support and rationale for a strong, advocacy-oriented articulation of clear disability policy and philosophy. It also reinforces the basic purpose of the rehabilitation process and reaffirms the inherent value and dignity of individuals who may be experiencing the limitations from disability.

# References

Atkins, B., Dew, D., Esser, C., Hansen, G., Mundt, P., Scalia, V., Thorton, L., & Wesolek, J. (1987). Continuing issues, suggestions and recommendations. In W. Emener (Ed.), *Public policy issues impacting the future of rehabilitation in America* (pp. 151–185). Stillwater, OK: National Clearing House of Rehabilitation Training Materials.

Beck, R. J. (1989). A survey of injured worker outcomes in Wisconsin. *Journal of Applied Rehabilitation Counseling, 20*(1), 20–24.

Benshoff, J. J. (1990). The role of rehabilitation and the issues of employment in the 1990s. In L. Perlman & C. Hansen (Eds.), *Employment and disability: Trends and issues for the 1990s* (p. 50–59). Alexandria, VA: National Rehabilitation Association.

Berkowitz, E. D. (1985). Social influences on rehabilitation: Introductory remarks. In L. Perlman & G. Austin (Eds.), *Social influences in rehabilitation planning: Blueprint for the 21st century* (pp. 11–18). Alexandria, VA: National Rehabilitation Association.

Berkowitz, E. D. (1987). *Disabled policy: America's programs for the Handicapped.* New York: Cambridge University Press.

Boschen, K. A. (1989). Early intervention in vocational rehabilitation. *Rehabilitation Counseling Bulletin, 32,* 254–265.

Bowe, F. (1978). *Handicapping America: Barriers to disabled people.* New York: Harper & Row.

Cohen, E. D. (1990). Confidentiality, counseling, and clients who have AIDS: Ethical foundations of a model rule. *Journal of Counseling and Development, 68,* 282–286.

DeJong, G. (1981). *Environmental accessibility and independent living outcomes: Directions for disability policy and research.* East Lansing: Michigan State University Center for International Rehabilitation.

DeJong, G., & Batavia, A. (1990). The Americans with Disabilities Act and the current state of U.S. disability policy. *Journal of Disability Policy Studies, I*(3), 65–75.

Fagan, T. K., & Jenkins, W. M. (1989). People with disabilities: An update. *Journal of Counseling & Development, 68,* 140–144.

Greenwood, R. (1990). Employment and disability: Emerging issues for the 1990s. In L. Perlman & C. Hansen, (Eds.), *Employment and disability: Trends and issues for the 1990s* (p. 9–16). Alexandria, VA: National Rehabilitation Association.

Habeck, R. V., Williams, C. L., Dugan, K. E., & Ewing, M. E. (1989). Balancing human and economic costs in disability management. *Journal of Rehabilitation, 55*(4), 16–19.

Haber, L. (1985). Trends and demographic studies on programs for disabled persons. In L. Perlman & G. Austin (Eds.), *Social influences in rehabilitation planning: Blueprint for the 21st century* (pp. 27–37). Alexandria, VA: National Rehabilitation Association.

Hahn, H. (1985). Changing perception of disability and the future of rehabilitation. In L. Perlman & G. Austin (Eds.), *Social influences in rehabilitation planning: Blueprint for the 21st century* (pp. 53–64). Alexandria, VA: National Rehabilitation Association.

Haveman, R. H., Halberstadt, V., & Burkhauser, R. V. (1984). *Public policy toward disabled workers.* Ithaca, NY: Cornell University Press.

Holmes, G. E., Hall, L., & Karst, R. H. (1989). Litigation avoidance through conflict resolution: Issues for state rehabilitation agencies. *American Rehabilitation, 15*(3), 12–15.

Kiernan, W., Sanchez, R., & Schalock, R. (1989). Economics, industry, and disability in the future. In W. Kiernan & R. Schalock (Eds.), *Economics, industry, and disability* (pp. 365–374). Baltimore, MD: Paul H. Brookes.

Lombana, J. H. (1989). Counseling persons with disabilities: Summary and projections. *Journal of Counseling and Development, 68*(2), 177–179.

McConnell, L. R. (1985). A response to the "Changing perception of disability and the future of rehabilitation" by Harlan Hahn. In L. Perlman & G. Austin (Eds.), *Social influences in rehabilitation planning: Blueprint for the 21st century* (pp. 92–93). Alexandria, VA: National Rehabilitation Association.

Nagi, S. Z. (1979). The concept and measurement of disability. In E. D. Berkowitz (Ed.), *Disability policies and government programs* (pp. 1–15). New York: Praeger.

National Council on the Handicapped. (1986). *Toward independence: An assessment of federal laws and programs affecting persons with disabilities—with legislative recommendations.* Washington DC: Author.

National Council on the Handicapped. (1988). *On the threshold of independence.* Washington, DC: Author.

Noble, J. H. (1985). Ethical considerations facing society in rehabilitating severely disabled persons. In L. Perlman & G. Austin (Eds.), *Social influences in rehabilitation planning: Blueprint for the 21st century* (pp. 71–79). Alexandria, VA: National Rehabilitation Association.

Nosek, M. A. (1985). Some thoughts on independence. In L. Perlman & G. Austin (Eds.), *Social influences in rehabilitation planning: Blueprint for the 21st century* (pp. 90–91). Alexandria, VA: National Rehabilitation Association.

Percy, S. L. (1989). *Disability, civil rights, and public policy: The politics of implementation.* Tuscaloosa: University of Alabama Press.

Roessler, R. T., & Schriner, K. F. (1991). The implications of selected employment concerns for disability policy and rehabilitation practice. *Rehabilitation Counseling Bulletin, 35*(1), 52–67.

Roth, W. (1985). The politics of disability: Future trends as shaped by current realities. In L. Perlman & G. Austin (Eds.), *Social influences in rehabilitation planning: Blueprint for the 21st century* (pp. 41–48). Alexandria, VA: National Rehabilitation Association.

Scotch, R. K. (1984). *From good will to civil rights: Transforming federal disability policy.* Philadelphia: Temple University Press.

Scotch, R. K., & Berkowitz, E. D. (1990). One comprehensive system? A historical perspective on federal disability policy. *Journal of Disability Policy Studies, 1*(4), 1–19.

Seventeenth Institute on Rehabilitation Issues. (1990). *Aging in America.* Menomonie, WI: University of Wisconsin–Stout, Stout Vocational Rehabilitation Institute, Research & Training Center.

Stone, D. A. (1984). *The disabled state.* Philadelphia: Temple University Press.

Vallario, J. P., & Emener, W. G. (1991). Rehabilitation counseling and the law: Critical considerations of confidentiality and privilege, malpractice, and forensics. *Journal of Applied Rehabilitation Counseling, 22*(2), 7–13.

Whitehead, C. (1989). Influencing employment through federal and state policy. In W. Kiernan & R. Schalock (Eds.), *Economics, industry, and disability* (pp. 27–36). Baltimore, MD: Paul H. Brookes.

Zola, I. K. (1989). Aging and disability: Toward a unified agenda. *Journal of Rehabilitation, 55*(4), 6–8.

# PART 3

## The Elderly Client

In Chapter 1 we presented data that document the aging of American society. Evidence was also presented in Chapters 1, 2, and 3 that suggests elders are at risk for psychological problems due to the losses that they often experience following retirement. However, despite their growing representation in the general population and the increasing risk for psychological problems with aging, there is substantial evidence that elders are underserved by counselors and psychologists (Gatz, Karel, & Wolkenstein, 1991). Some of the underservice can be attributed to unwillingness on the part of elders to seek mental health services. However, a great deal of the blame must rest on the counseling profession, which has failed to properly address the needs of the elderly.

In the chapters that follow in Part 3, the authors describe the experiences of the elderly and point up their counseling-related needs. They also discuss some specific counseling strategies that may be useful when working with elders. In Chapter 7, Clark provides an excellent overview of the issues that face older Americans. She gives special attention to the health policy debate on cost attainment, an issue that pits the needs of elders against those of younger generations. The need for financial planning for retirement and the need for some individuals to keep working beyond customary retirement age are discussed. Clark also points to life-style and psychological functioning as important issues for the elderly. She concludes by discussing assessment issues with which counselors should be familiar when counseling the elderly client.

In Chapter 8, Capuzzi and Friel provide a review of research on the effects of aging on sexual functioning. As suggested in Chapter 3, more myths about aging are associated with sexuality than with any other elder behavior. After reviewing the research on sexuality and aging and on medical conditions affecting the sexuality of older persons, Capuzzi and Friel examine some of the practical considerations that counselors should address when working with elders. These include improving overall physical and mental health to enhance sexual functioning and discussing physical limitations that may affect type of sexual activity. The authors also address the special needs of single older persons and those residing in an institutional setting that may restrict privacy.

In the final chapter in Part 3, Waters defines the life review process and provides a rationale for its use with elders. She suggests how counselors can conduct life reviews with both individuals and groups. Several examples of life reviews are presented.

## Reference

Gatz, M., Karel, M. J., & Wolkenstein, B. (1991). Survey of providers of psychological services to older adults. *Professional Psychology: Research and Practice, 22,* 413–415.

# 7

# Issues and Concerns of the Elderly: Implications for Counselors

*Lorraine H. Clark*

We were standing there at Alice's retirement reception/party, balancing a plate in one hand and a glass in the other, talking with Bob and Marie about their retirement life. Marie related their activities for the day: "We had an advisory board meeting at the community center at nine-thirty, and then we always play bridge at ten-thirty with this new group we formed there. So we played bridge until two-thirty, and now we're here at this party. Tonight we're supposed to go to an AARP chapter meeting.

"We really are too busy," she went on to say. "I wish they'd give Bob a smaller area to cover in his tax aide (volunteer) job. The whole top half of Texas is just too much territory!"

\*\*\*

Is this an unusual couple? Not necessarily. How individuals, and couples, use their time in retirement varies just as much as the retirees involved. Regardless of the life style they choose, many older people are very busy.

\*\*\*

George had been a patent lawyer for a petroleum company. Although he was a victim of early retirement incentives, he and his wife attend at least one Elderhostel program a year (usually in Australia, England, or other foreign country). They also go to Europe in the fall to take their annual wine tasting tour. George does some volunteer work, and golf and travel to visit children and grandchildren are important to both.

\*\*\*

Marge is a widow of limited means. She stays active doing volunteer work in the church, community, and aging organizations. She sews her own clothes, although she says she hates to sew. She also is an excellent cook, who ascribes her success to having friends with good recipes. She cannot afford to do much traveling, so she stays busy in her community.

\*\*\*

These retirees are typical of the elderly, when generalizing. Some are in better physical or economic or psychological condition than others are. The mode for most elderly, however, would place the example retirees in the normal range for almost all categories. Bob has heart disease. Marie has eye problems; she can't see out of her left eye. George has hypertension. Marge has skin problems. The wonder is that they cope with these problems rather than allow them to control their lives.

In short, these older persons have the qualities of life older persons need: independence, dignity, and purpose. What are the issues and concerns they have for themselves, for other older persons, and for their progeny?

## Introduction to Aging

Before any discussion of issues or concerns can proceed, counselors must understand, as best they can, what aging is all about. Many myths about aging must be put into context or deleted entirely.

First, to speak of "the elderly" or "the aged" as a group is difficult. Individuals within categories delineated by chronological years are the least homogeneous in grouping of all age-defined populations. The older one becomes, the more unlike everyone else one is. Cohort grouping may become the basis for certain historical similarities. For example, those who experienced the Depression of the 1930s, or veterans of wars, such as World War II, the Korean conflict, and so on, have some commonalities that separate them from the population that has not had similar experiences. This does not assume, however, that those experiences in common entitle those cohort groupings to be comparable in all aspects.

Dr. James MacKay, retired counselor/psychologist, has said that humans come into the world as helpless, totally dependent beings, and, if humans live long enough, they will depart this world as helpless, totally dependent beings. At this point in his life, at age 95+, perhaps he is discovering whether he is correct in his assumption. Certainly ethical issues of aging constitute one of the quandaries our country is facing—not only now but also in planning for the future, when the "baby boomers" will become the boomer majority.

The entire topic is changing rapidly. Already the baby boomers are into their 40s and have begun to challenge the contemporary scene of aging and becoming elderly. For example, the topic of health undoubtedly will change as this generation ages, because many of them have been more conscious of appropriate health measures necessary to function at or close to their peak. Consequently, as a group they will be healthier than the current generations of the elderly.

Gerontologists often challenge those who refer to the elderly as the entire population over age 65, countering with the question, "Would you put all humans from birth to age 30 or 40 in the same group and discuss human development in any category—chronological age, physiological age, psychological age, or social age?" We must remember that an elderly person of 65 is quite different from one aged 75 or 85 or 95! Another surprise may come if you ask a group of adults—almost any age, but especially those over 50: "How many of you are as old as you look in a mirror?" (Or ask yourself the same question!)

Delineating the elderly as being 65 and over is a purely arbitrary separation. It is a chronological age set for Social Security, a system put into law in the mid-1930s but still used today as the legal age for full participation in Social Security benefits. In the meantime, life expectancy has increased, and health care and technology have improved. The result, demographically, is that more—many more—people are living long, and our society/culture has no norms for them or for their caregivers. Resources, services, and public policy must plan how best to respond to new life stages for young and older adults alike.

## Areas of Concern

Areas of concern for the elderly, and for the remainder of society who must make decisions not only for the older generations but also for themselves, include:

- Health

- Finances

- Retirement/Employment

- Lifestyles/Housing

- Mental/Psychological functioning

- Counseling

### Health

According to Goldsmith (1986), one thing can be said confidently about the American health care system in the year 2000: Most of its ingredients—the patients, the professionals, technological development, and much of the capital—are already present. Payment for chronic health care presents our nation's most significant health planning and human challenge.

Arthur L. Caplan of the Hastings Center suggests that "the health issue of the future may not be so much whether the elderly are going to get a minimum, but whether they're going to take too much away from other age cohorts" (cited in Simmons, 1986, p. 3057). Daniel Callahan, director of the Hastings Center, has proposed age as a criterion in determining whether the elderly should be allowed to die and their diseases allowed to run their courses. In light of the recent Supreme Court decision regarding Mary Beth Cruzan, innumerable elderly people have completed living wills. Callahan (1990) pointed out two fears competing with each other among the elderly. The first is that they will be abandoned or neglected if they become critically ill or begin to die, and that few people will care about their fate. The second fear is that they will be kept alive and their lives extended when they have no hope for a quality life.

Health care systems are changing rapidly in America, principally because of the need to contain costs, which have escalated exponentially since passage of the 1965 law establishing Medicare as a health care package incorporated into the Social Security program, which offers a limited national health insurance. Since its passage, two major changes in health care have occurred:

1. Medicine is now more a business in the U.S. than it is elsewhere.
2. Patients are better informed, less submissive, and more open.

Even though more than 11.5% of our gross national product (GNP) is spent on today's better health care, adequate care for some population groups and in some areas is lacking. The Institute for the Future (Amara, 1988) has identified the driving forces to change health care:

- An aging population

- Sophisticated consumers

- Pressures from payers

- Pluralism and diversity

- Technological capability

- Health-care capacity

- Health-care growth

- Government as steering agent

In 1987 "A Debate: Medicare in 2020" was chaired by Senator Durenberger (R-MN), chairman of Americans for Generational Equity and ranking minority member of the Senate Subcommittee on Health. Panelists were the Honorable Richard D. Lamm, former governor of Colorado, and Dr. Robert Butler, first director of the National Institute on Aging. How will the total health care budget be confined and then distributed equitably? (Durenberger, Lamm, & Butler, 1988). Therein lies the debate for American society now, and for the aging of the baby boomers in the first half of the next century.

In a speech on "Equity and Resource Sharing," Daniel Callahan (1990) set forth six value changes he sees as necessary before Americans will accept health care reform:

1. Scale down aspirations for best care.
2. Remember that health and happiness do not necessarily go together. We can be happy and not healthy.
3. Shift the budget balance from individual care to the public good.

4. Give greater emphasis to care versus cure.
5. Do some rationing, using categorical states (e.g., age).
6. Change ideas about mortality; it's not just another disease to be cured.

Leading causes of death in people age 65+ (1989 estimates) are (National Pharmaceutical Council, 1990):

| | |
|---|---|
| Heart disease | 420,865 |
| Cancer | 327,635 |
| Stroke | 129,800 |

To date, a fountain of youth has not been discovered, but a number of factors may contribute to a better quality of life, if not to a longer life. Among these are proper nutrition (less fat/cholesterol, sugar, and salt, perhaps less food), exercise, stress management/rest and relaxation, cessation of smoking, and creative activities.

In the health policy debate on cost containment, two predominant views have emerged. The more popular paradigm generally assumes that the medical care system is overused because extensive health insurance coverage gives neither patients nor providers incentives to use the system efficiently. Proponents of this view believe that a great deal of care given is of little benefit. Hospitals and physicians are seen as overly cautious, ordering tests that may not be necessary, and encouraging excessive lengths-of-stay in hospitals.

In the second view of the cost containment problem, concern has been raised that as our society ages and as medical technology is increasingly applied to sustain life, the percentage of GNP attributable to medical care will greatly increase. Lamm (in Berk, Monheit, & Hagan, 1988) further argues that costs for the terminally ill limit our ability to finance both prenatal care and health services for the elderly. He states his concern over the choice between spending large amounts of money for medical treatments during the last year of life and spending the same amount of money for polio immunizations for school children.

The fastest growing age group in the nation is the same one on which the federal government spends the most money. The number of people age 80 and over is currently growing five times faster than the total population and is expected to double in size in 20 years. This means that many parents of baby boomers will be around as the boomers reach their 60s, and their parents' health may be a factor in determining their children's retirement/employment and financial decisions.

Usually family members provide most of the help older people need to continue living in their own homes and communities. The best way to begin planning is for family members to discuss frankly, before a crisis arises, issues that may be of concern. Concerns about health and financial issues are usually two of the major causes of anxiety for older people and those who care about them. The elderly paid substantially more out-of-pocket for health care than the national average—roughly twice the amount spent by younger families (National Center for Health Services Research and Health Care Technology Assessment, 1987).

Gerontologist Ken Dychtwald (Dychtwald & Floner, 1989) maintains that health care in America today is designed for the episodic, acute illnesses. As our population ages, however, health care emphasis must shift from acute to chronic illnesses. Long-term care is of special interest to women because long-term care is primarily needed by and provided by women. The proportion of women to men increases steadily with advancing age. In the 65–74 age group, 57% are women; in the 75–84 age group, 63% are women; for those age 85 and over, 70% are women. Because age and disability are highly correlated, the elderly experience the highest incidence of chronic and disabling conditions. In addition, older women are more likely than men to be widowed, living alone, and on fixed incomes. They also have greater needs for assistance with activities of daily living.

Overall, however, 99% of individuals below the age of 75 years are *not* in nursing homes, 80% of those over age 85, with an average age of nearly 89 years, are *not* in nursing homes. Many individuals in nursing homes are there because they have chronic conditions and need help with activities of daily living. Successful containment of health care costs will be related to our ability to prevent or cure age-dependent diseases and disorders that produce the greatest needs for long-term care.

## *Finances*

When people plan for retirement or old age, the three principal concerns are health, finances, and use of time. An old saw goes like this: "Tell me what my health will be and how much money I'll have, and I'll tell you what I plan to do in retirement." The three are interwoven. Yet, many people do not make financial plans for retirement in a timely and logical manner.

Lami Lucciano (1990) lists eight faulty beliefs about retirement:

- Most people need to save for no more than about 10 or 15 years of retirement.

- If you stay with one employer your entire career, you'll have a richer retirement than if you job hop to chase higher salaries.

- Preserving capital should be a retiree's main objective.

- You will pay a smaller fraction of your income in taxes.

- Your housing costs will go down.

- Your retirement nest will be empty.

- Your employer will provide good basic health insurance, and Medicare will cover the rest of your medical bills.

- Chances are good you will spend your last years in a nursing home, but long-term-care insurance can protect your wealth.

Whether one does or does not challenge these "faulty beliefs," people do need to plan financially for their later years of life.

Traditionally, financial plans for retirement years have related to a three-legged stool for sources of income: *pension* (if one works for an organization/company that provides a pension, or if one has arranged for that independently), *Social Security,* and *private assets and savings.* Within the last decade more and more interest has been shown in adding a fourth leg to income in retirement: *employment* or *work.*

In planning financially for retirement, one must look not only at sources of income but also at anticipated or desired lifestyle and expenditures. A proposed budget should be formulated and compared with anticipated income. If the budget exceeds the income, some adjustment must be made to the anticipated expenditures or the income must be increased. More and more "retirees" are returning to the workplace for additional income. Many times the site is different, and more often than not, the work pattern will be different, since companies are hiring part-time workers. Half-time, job sharing, and flexible hours and sites are becoming more common in job markets where entry-level workers no longer fill the vacancies.

Another important facet of financial planning, which continues throughout life and is particularly important to persons with fixed incomes, is that of coping with inflation. The value of fixed incomes declines with inflation, and some planning must be done to provide growth of income to match inflation so that buying power does not decline.

In focus groups related to retirement and work, AARP (1987) found that the baby boom generation does not plan to retire as their parents did. When asked why, the response was that they were living healthier longer and they would not be able to afford their desired lifestyle without working. Queried further about their career plans, there was almost consensus in the declaration that at about the age their parents retired, they intended to re-career and *do what they always had wanted to do!* Baby boomers may, indeed, change the world in the work arena. They obviously do not intend to take age discrimination without a good fight.

This brings us to the topic of Social Security. Confidence is eroding in this program as it is now and has been. When baby boomers reach retirement age, because of the "baby bust" in the generation following them, workers may be too few to finance their Social Security. Undoubtedly, Social Security as the elderly now experience it will change. A number of proposals for reorganization of Social Security have been made, but no definitive plan has been proposed upon which baby boomers may rely.

Maintaining sufficient security for the elderly will impact the whole of society. Fortunately, most older Americans are not poor; however, women and minorities are most likely to be the poorest.

## Retirement/Employment

As people become older, they customarily plan for retirement. This is a recent phenomenon in our society and, in fact, retirement as we now know it may be an historical event in the next century. Work can be essential for a number of reasons, two of which are income and status. In our society a question we usually ask is, "What do you do?" To say "I'm retired" is difficult for some. The implication is, "I do nothing; I do not contribute to my society; I do not earn money; therefore, I am worthless, or at least worth less."

Other reasons for working or continuing to work are the structure that regular working hours give to life, and an acceptable reason to be away from home with the "honey-do's" ("Honey, do this . . . Honey, do that") often extant there. And some people work because they like their work and can imagine no better way to fill their time.

Retirement means many things to different people. Over the years, retirement has meant fishing, traveling, and other leisure activities; or as a condition such as "refined poverty"; or *freedom!* Perhaps the concept of freedom to use time, formerly focused on work, as one wants to use it is most popular. Nowadays, the traditional meaning of retirement—no longer working for money—is changing to "another phase or stage of life," which may be of considerable length. Perhaps there is, or will be, another stage beyond retirement.

Working people may plan how they intend to use time in retirement. Women make "to do" lists; men plan to clean out the garage. When these activities, as well as Plans A, B, and C (ad infinitum) have been completed, and when people realize that they still may have 10, 15, 20, 25, or more years to live, they may redefine retirement. The honeymoon is over!

On the other hand, some find contentment in rocking and counting four-leaf clovers. Every person is indeed different from all others, and retirement has no rules.

One new phenomenon is becoming apparent. Employers are gradually becoming aware of the problems encountered by employees who are attempting to fulfill the obligations of a full-time job plus partial- to full-time care of a mate or relative. Among these companies are IBM, Travelers Insurance, Southwestern Bell Telephone, and many others.

Last but not least in this work/retirement issue is the changing concept of retirement. More and more employees are not retiring *from* something (a job with its "rat race" problems, perhaps) but, rather, *to* something—to another phase of life. Re-careering or second careers, standard for armed services retirees, are becoming more common for non-service employees. But finding a job with the same title (responsibility) and salary may be difficult. Even though mandatory retirement is now illegal (with a few exceptions), age discrimination may be encountered in recruiting, hiring, training, and managing older workers.

## Lifestyles/Housing

In a study to examine the relationship between perceived social competence, leisure participation, leisure satisfaction, and life satisfaction in middle-aged and older adults. Sneegas (1986) found that perceptions of social competence influenced levels of leisure participation and leisure satisfaction and, in turn, life satisfaction or quality of life. Age was not found to be a factor; however, health was found to influence perceptions of social competence or capacity to interact effectively.

In a program presented to an AAACE meeting, Burton and Doris Kreitlow (1988) advocated "retirement careers." They suggested that retirees break the links that have chained them to the past. After a short-term retirement (one to five years of basement workshop, travel, and sitting around) people still can have a 10- to 30-year retirement career . . . with new beginnings.

Emphasizing again the individuality of older persons, a recent news article described a 77-year-old retiree as an "activist extraordinaire" (Kelly, 1989). A typical day for this former public school administrator was described as "two-a-day meetings sandwiched between conferences, workshops and speaking engagements." The article went on to quote her: "The plow that rests rusts" and "I think leisure corrupts, and I think total leisure corrupts totally." Her lifestyle is devoted to making contributions to health care, homelessness, world peace, the environment, and education of young people.

In talking about leisure, one of the first psychologists to study life stages, Buhler (1966), said: "In our time even the aged and retired rarely wish to lead a life of contemplation. This may have to do with the fact that they have never been taught contemplation. Contemplation, which is neither just thinking nor reminiscing, is actually a very special type of mental activity that in our culture is hardly known and little practiced." She added that action ranks high in our cultural value systems, whereas passive activities are apt to be little appreciated.

Part of one's lifestyle is where (and perhaps when) one lives. Environment is becoming more and more an issue for the elderly. For the past few years the tendency has been to assume that elderly people want to remain in their homes and communities in preference to moving to senior, segregated housing, particularly in other states or countries. As Baldwin (1989) stated, however, "Until we understand and appreciate the diversity—the segmentation by age, economic status, cultural background, life goals, and psychological conditioning—of older persons, there really is no senior market and there really is no basis on which to plan for innovative housing" (p. 5).

Some community programs have been geared to keeping the present home in repair or modifying it to meet the needs of the elderly as they encounter differing health conditions. The Continuum of Care model for the elderly, which ranges from minimal help or assistance in current housing to full, 24-hour nursing care has been oriented to keeping elderly people in the community rather than institutionalizing them. Deciding whether to move or to institutionalize oneself or persons for whom one is responsible—especially parents or close relatives—is among the most difficult of decisions. Unless the elderly person understands the options and has good judgment and is able to make sound decisions, the issue for children or relatives is often divisive.

One also must not forget that many elderly people, particularly women, are single, whether widowed, divorced, or always single. Their independence may be by choice or by fate. At any rate, family members may not be as helpful as desired or they may be too involved. Unfortunately, many of the oldest women are also among the poorest of our population.

Sexuality and the elderly also is a fact of life. The expression of sexuality may be different, but acceptance by children and relatives is important for quality of life for the elderly. This is especially true in cases of late-life marriages and remarriages.

One other factor relating closely to the quality of life/lifestyle of the elderly is the possibility of criminal victimization, whether by mugging on the street or in the home; whether by strangers or by relatives, particularly caregivers who have burnt out. Mistreatment may occur in the form of physical abuse, psychological abuse, financial abuse or exploitation, abuse by spouse or children, or active neglect. Efforts should be made to prevent all abuse.

## Mental/Psychological Functioning

If one assumes that behavior is related to personality, do behavioral changes with age imply personality changes? Probably not! An old saw about the elderly and behavior says that as a person ages, he or she becomes more like himself or herself, personality-wise, but this does not hold true for behavior throughout aging. Many factors of physiology, psychology, and sociology (social relationships, finances, and environment) can affect behavior. Environment becomes especially important to persons as they become older. Whether restricted or expanded, changes in environmental factors affect behavior. Table 7.1 enumerates some factors affecting behavior of the elderly.

Over the years of life experiences, the self of the developing person has created behaviors to cope with change. Where coping behaviors have proved successful for the individual, they may have become habitual behaviors in terms of response to certain environmental or perceptual cues. When sensory losses or completely new environments are encountered or experienced, the "new" may be perceived incorrectly. An observer may judge the resultant behavior as inappropriate, even though the older person may be responding quite appropriately as he or she perceives the situation. Or the older person may fear the new or unknown because he or she has no repertoire of behaviors to cope with the new experience.

Locus of control also is quite important to the older person. If one assumes that every person, whether old or not, has needs for independence (financial and decision-making responsibility), dignity (worth), and purpose (to make life worthwhile), all aspects of the older person will be involved in behavior that responds to environmental cues and is self-directed toward meeting these needs.

# Table 7.1

**Perceptions of Environmental Factors Affecting Quality of Life, Behavior, and Locus of Control**

| Continuum of Care Environment | Human/Social Environment | Physical Environment |
| --- | --- | --- |
| Home furnishings | Family/spouse | Home |
| Pets | Close friends | Land |
| Community resources | Relatives | Neighborhood |
| Legal parameters (local) | Acquaintances | City/community |
| Political parameters (federal) | Community support | World extension, |
| Communication | system personnel | *via* travel, communication |
| Technology | Finances | Universe |
| | Health | |
| | Responsibilities | |
| | Use of time | |
| | Opportunity to work | |

Locus of control refers to a person's sense of being independent, or in control, which in turn involves an attitude or perception that he or she can make decisions regarding appropriate behavior and whether he or she has the physical ability to accomplish that behavior. This may be where personality plays an important part, because the older person's attitude is basic not only to behavior but also to the consequences of behavior on other aspects of his or her life.

If older people believe that external factors control their life, if others (health care professionals, adult children, governmental bureaucracy, etc.) are in charge of their life and behavior, they may rebel. If physical or mental abilities have declined so they cannot perform as they desire or need, frustration may cause depression or disruptive behavior. On the other hand, if they believe that they can do it—or at least try—their attitude may affect their behavior, and in trying, they may succeed or fail, yet be willing to forgive the failure because they know they tried. A positive attitude may lead to more satisfaction with life, whereas a negative attitude may result in depression or withdrawal physically from their environment. They may have difficulty accepting responsibility for self (personal) control of emotions and behaviors or for self-control of attitudes and responses to environmental changes if they have always had a behavioral response to environmental change that "blames" external factors for internal (self) response and attitude.

## Counseling the Elderly

Whether one defines aging or elderly as a measure of chronological years or of functional capabilities and abilities, this most heterogeneous group of society has been sadly neglected where services for mental health have been concerned. In writing of the mental health professionals, Barry Lebowitz (1988) named psychiatrists, psychologists, social workers, and psychiatric nurses. It is indeed a tragedy that counselors—those who work with the "normal" population and help them to continue their development and growth—were omitted from the very field where they are most able to help—mental health—particularly with the elderly. With a gerontological specialty, perhaps this omission will be remedied if the gerontological training of counselors is comprehensive. In addition to the concerns and issues of the elderly that have already been discussed, Miranda (1989) has identified the following factors that require attention from the mental health field:

- Alienation from significant societal responsibility

- Fragmented family support systems because of loss of spouse and mobility of children

- Declining physical health coupled with multiple health problems

- Demands of caregiving

- Depression

- Alcohol abuse

Lack of coordination of medications, especially prescriptions, and nutrition also might be added.

Unfortunately, to date, elderly people are reluctant to contact mental health professionals when they feel they need help. Perhaps this is a remembrance of the past, when mental illness was referred to as insanity and insane asylums were considered "snake pits." Stereotypes such as these may deter their seeking help.

Another deterrent may be the financing of mental health care, especially under Medicare. Perhaps the best hope for improvement in mental health coverage is found in a recent study that discovered that Medicaid patients who received mental health services in conjunction with health care cost less in the long run (Price, 1990).

## Medicare and Medicaid

At this point, perhaps the difference between Medicare and Medicaid should be explained, for those who have not had experience with either. Medicare (Title XVIII), enacted in 1965, provides health insurance coverage for people aged 65 and older, some disabled people under age 65, and those who have end-stage renal disease. The program consists of two parts: Part A, Hospital Insurance (HI); and Part B, Supplemental Medical Insurance (SMI). The program is administered by the Health Care Financing Administration (HCFA). Payment and reimbursement policies change from year to year; however, Medicare generally does not pay for out-of-hospital prescription drugs, eyeglasses, hearing aids, or immunization.

Medicaid, or Medical Assistance Program (Title XIX) provides medical assistance for certain low-income individuals and families. Generally, all who qualify for public assistance under federally funded categories (aged, blind, disabled, and families with dependent children) are eligible for Medicaid. Programs vary from state to state.

## Psychological Aging

Whereas counseling deals with the total person and all facets of life, it is imperative that the counselor understand psychological aging, insofar as it can be known at the present time. "The dignity or despair of older Americans rests largely in their capacity to provide for their basic needs—food, shelter, health care, safety, mobility—and to remain valued, productive, contributing members of their families and communities" (American Association of Retired Persons, 1988, p. 1).

When growth or progress is not possible, the counselor's task is still to help the individual cope, to uncover the strengths that remain and to help make decisions utilizing these strengths. When verbal communication is not possible, caring behavior such as feeding, touching, and singing or other music can communicate the message that the person is acknowledged as a human being who is alive and worth the caregiver's time and effort.

The counselor's job then, may be to enhance mental health and to treat or oversee (by referral, perhaps) treatment for mental problems in which the counselor has not had appropriate training and experience. Some illnesses, such as Alzheimer's may require helping caregivers to cope adequately.

Peer counseling has been found to be especially useful in cases of death, loss of job, illness, loneliness, and loss of self-esteem. A one-on-one relationship with someone who has coped successfully or progressed through similar life experiences provides an understanding confidante, a role model, and a supporter (permission giver) for resocialization activities.

*Hope* and *joy* are two words that are integral to life satisfaction. When these attitudes are lacking, life satisfaction or quality of life is lessened. Counseling the elderly may be much like coaching or cheerleading. As much as, or perhaps more than, other-aged persons, the elderly need positive reinforcement to create and maintain positive attitudes, behaviors, and continued growth in the later years. Indeed, *hopeless* and *unhappy* (*joyless*) are words often heard from depressed older people.

When counseling the elderly, we must remember that behavior is influenced by environment but also by individual physiological, psychological, and social factors. The problem presented to the counselor may be only the tip of an iceberg, and the gerontological counselor must have sufficient knowledge of the total person, the holistic person, to be able to provide help. To be able to respond appropriately to the needs of the individual, the gerontological counselor also should have sufficient knowledge of the continuum of counseling strategies.

## Assessment

Depending upon the degree of debilitation, the counselor must be able to assess the individual on at least four different scales or continua: (a) chronological (age), (b) physiological, (c) psychological, and (d) sociological. Many factors overlap or are interwoven, which make them difficult to delineate into neat entities. For example, legal aspects of aging are included in chronological; sensory acuity may affect physiological and psychological and sociological aspects. Psychological includes not only behavior but also cognition, personality, emotions (indeed, the cognitive, affective, and psychomotor domains). Sociological includes not only social relationships but economic factors as well. Somewhere in the overlap must be placed, for some, spiritual or philosophical issues. Undoubtedly, respect for older people as individuals, with all their complications, is a *must* for gerontological counselors.

Counseling assessment is best done informally rather than formally or in an "intake"—fill-out-the-form—manner. Rating might be done by placing the client on a continuum ranging from seriously ill to super healthy on the physiological dimension; from mentally ill to self-actualized or transpersonalized on the psychological; from dependent to interdependent on the social part of the sociological scale, and from dependent to independent on the economic part.

Chronological age is a puzzler. If MacKay (verbal communications, 1970–1985) is correct, perhaps the line should be circular rather than straight. In fact, perhaps all the lines should be circular and spiraling as Kegan (1982) has chosen to depict the "evolving self." At any rate, for one specific person or for one specific problem, straight-lined continua are used to demonstrate a method for assessing an elderly client.

## Holistic Counseling

Counseling the elderly requires a comprehensive, holistic look at the person. In addition to superior counseling skills, the counselor needs to create an empathic, basic understanding of the individual. The adult counseling paradigm in Table 7.2 provides an approach that will be helpful in providing care.

***

Mary Brown has been referred to you for help. When she comes to see you, you note that her clothes are too large for her and they are unkempt, with grease spots and wrinkles. Her flesh seems to hang loosely on her arms and hands. Her hair, pulled back from her face, appears to be unwashed and very thin. When you talk to her, she does not look you in the eyes, but keeps her eyes down, sometimes squinting. At times she does not seem to hear, and asks you to repeat the question or comment. She twists a handkerchief in her hands almost constantly.

Mary reveals to you that she was widowed 9 months ago after 48 years of marriage; that her only son died of a heart attack 5 years ago; and that she feels she has no one to help her. Her husband left a small insurance policy, but after funeral expenses she used what was left to pay doctors' bills. Her only income

# Table 7.2
## Adult Counseling Paradigm

### Physiological Status

| *Seriously Ill* | *Normal* | *Super-Healthy* |
|---|---|---|

If the individual is evaluated as being quite ill, the counselor must take immediate steps to get that person to proper health care professionals. This may require taking, or going with, the person, depending upon mobility. Finding a "super-healthy" older person will be a rare occasion, although that may change with the aging baby boomers! Most older persons have one or more chronic health conditions. Arthritis, diabetes, cardiovascular disorders, and respiratory problems are among the more common.

### Psychological Status

| *Mentally Ill* | *"Normal"* | *Self-Actualized* |
|---|---|---|

If the individual is evaluated as being quite mentally ill, or if dementia is suspected, specialized help must be sought and provided. Those within the "normal" range probably will be the ones that gerontological counselors see most often; however, elderly people who seem to be self-actualized or self-transcendent are not uncommon.

### Sociological Status

| *Economically Dependent* | *Normal* | *Independent* |
|---|---|---|
| *Socially Dependent* | | *Interdependent* |

The degree of economic dependence is a factor in determining what, if any, resources are available. The social relationships upon which the person can depend or utilize may be important. On the other hand, adult children may attempt to influence behaviors and decisions. In fact, the counselor may discover they are a major part of the client's problems.

### Counseling

| *Psychotherapy* | *Behavior Modification* | *Developmental, Guidance, Education* | *Non-directive* | *Existential Transpersonal* |
|---|---|---|---|---|

Between the poles of the continuum, between psychotherapy and existential/transpersonal counseling, the counselor may employ various counseling processes in working with the client. The type of counseling relates to the degree of illness or dependency, and the history of psychological counseling follows the same pattern: from psychotherapy to behaviorism to client-centered to transpersonal. The locus of control and the relationship of the client to the counselor changes from external to internal locus of control according to the type of counseling required and utilized.

Vertical lines drawn from the current rating of the client on any scale to the counseling continuum under it indicates the counseling technique required. Because most clients fall within or close to the normal range, most of the counseling required will be within the developmental categories.

comes from Social Security, amounting to $650 per month, but her apartment rent is $400 per month; medication for herself is $135 per month; supplemental insurance is $75 per month in addition to her Medicare. She thinks that her arthritis and cardiovascular condition plus her age preclude her getting a job or being able to work. She is 68 years old.

\*\*\*

How would you evaluate Mary's placement on each of the categories in Table 7.2? Why? How would you proceed to help her?

\*\*\*

## Conclusion

*Spring is gone*
*Summer is past*
*Winter is here*
*But the song,*
*The song I was meant to sing*
*Is still unsung.*
*For I have spent my days*
*stringing, unstringing, and*
*re-stringing my instrument.*

—Anonymous—

In counseling the elderly, counselors must customize their helping stance and methods to correspond with the physical, psychological, and social person that the elderly individual presents. Coping with a changing world is not easy for people of any age. It is even more difficult for the aging person, who must cope with internal changes as well as with the changes of the external world and universe. The challenge for counselors is to help the elderly to continue their development, to appreciate their quality of life, to achieve as much life satisfaction as possible, and to find a satisfactory closure to life—to sing the song they are meant to sing!

## References

Amara, R. (1988, November–December). Health care tomorrow. *The Futurist,* pp. 16–20.

American Association of Retired Persons. (1987). New Roles in Society, Focus Groups. Kansas City. October 5, 1987.

American Association of Retired Persons. (1988). *Aging in America—Dignity or despair* (issue guide).

American Association of Retired Persons. (1988). *Acronyms in aging.* Washington, DC: National Gerontology Resource Center.

American Association of Retired Persons. (1990, February). Issues in mental health care. *EBRI Issues Brief,* 99.

Baldwin, L. (1989). Accessing and understanding older consumers and their housing needs. *The Southwestern,* 5(2), 5–9.

Berk, M. L., Monheit, A. C., & Hagan, M. M. (1988, Fall). How the U.S. spent its health care dollar: 1929–1980. *Health Affairs,* pp. 45–60.

Buhler, C. (1966, No. 5). The theory of the leisure masses. *Kaiser Aluminum News,* p. 21.

Callahan, D. (1987, October/November). Terminating treatment: Age as a standard. *Hastings Center Report,* 21–25.

Callahan, D. (1990, April). *Equity and resource sharing.* Paper presented at American Society on Aging, San Francisco.

Doeringer, P. E. (Ed.). (1990). *Bridges to retirement.* Ithaca, NY: Cornell University.

Durenberger, D., Lamm, R. D., & Butler, R. (1988, April). A debate: Medicare in 2020. *Generational Journal,* pp. 64–76.

Dychtwald, K., & Floner, J. (1989). *Age wave.* Los Angeles: Tarcher.

Goldsmith, J. C. (1986). The U.S. health care system in the year 2000. *Journal of American Medical Association, 256*(24), 3371–3375.

Grau, L. (1989). The changing context of mental health care for the elderly. *Gerontology & Geriatrics Education, 9*(3), 7–15.

Kegan, R. (1982). *The evolving self.* Cambridge, MA: Harvard Press.

Kelly, F. (1989, August 12). Wheels of time haven't slowed fiery activist (Senior Diary). *Dallas Times Herald,* pp. E1–2.

Kreitlow, B., & Kreitlow, D. (1988, November 3). *Retirement careers.* Paper presented to AAACE meeting, Tulsa, OK.

Lebowitz, B. D. (1988, Spring). Mental health policy and aging. *Generations,* 53–56.

Lucciano, L. (1990, February). The eight myths of retirement. *Money Magazine,* pp. 111–116.

Miranda, M. F. (1989). Mental health services for the elderly. *Aging Network News. 5*(10), 6–7.

National Center for Health Services Research and Health Care Technology Assessment. (1987, September). Changes in health spending patterns found for poor and elderly. *Research Activities.*

National Pharmaceutical Council. (1990 Spring). *Medication trends for older adults,* p. 7.

Price, J. (1990, April 25). Mental therapy slashes Medicaid costs, study says. *Washington, D.C. Times.*

Simmons, K. (1986, June 13). Caring for elderly: Challenge for now and 21st-century medicine. *Journal of the American Medical Association, 225*(22), 3057–3058.

Sneegas, J. J. (1986). Components of life satisfaction in middle and later life adults: Perceived social competence, leisure participation, and leisure satisfaction. *Journal of Leisure Research, 18*(4), 248–258.

# Additional References

Boucouvalas, M. (1983). Social transformation, lifelong learning, and the fourth force—transpersonal psychology. *Lifelong Learning: The Adult Years, 9,* 609.

Bruce, P. (1983). Continuum of counseling goals: A framework for differentiating counseling strategies. *Personnel & Guidance Journal, 62,* 259–263.

*EBRI Issues Brief.* (1990, February). Issues in mental health care. 99. S.

Fries, J. F. The sunny side of aging. *Journal of American Medical Association, 263*(17), 2354–2355.

Gabor, D. (1972, November). Growth. *Intellectual Digest,* 65–72.

Hendricks, G., & Weinhold, B. (1982). *Transpersonal approaches to counseling and psychotherapy.* Denver: Love Publishing.

*Kaiser Aluminum News.* (1966). The theory of the leisure masses, p. 21.

LeShan, E. (1990, April). Aging gracefully requires passion for growing. *Senior Spotlight,* p. 16.

Longman, P. (1987). *Born to pay—the new politics of aging in America.* Boston: Houghton Mifflin.

Myers, J. (1989). *Adult children and aging parents.* Alexandria, VA: American Association for Counseling and Development.

National Center for Health Services Research and Health Care Technology Assessment. (1987, September). Changes in health spending patterns found for poor and elderly. *Research Activities.*

Santos, J. F., & Dawson, G. D. (1989). Interdisciplinary issues in mental health and aging. *Gerontology & Geriatrics Education, 9*(3), 1–6.

# 8

# Current Trends in Sexuality and Aging: An Update for Counselors

*Dave Capuzzi*
*Susan Eileen Friel*

Although there has been a substantial increase in the information available on, and attention given to, the topic of sexuality in the aging person in recent years, much of the published literature has been in the medical, social work, psychiatric, or professional gerontological journals (Berezin, 1969; Ludeman, 1981). Little emphasis has been placed in the counseling and mental health literature on this aspect of the aging process, although there have been some exceptions (Eidenberg, 1985; Weg, 1983). Mental health counselors working with older individuals need to have access to current information about both the physiological and the psychological components of aging and sexuality in order to be sensitive to the needs and concerns of their clients.

This article will summarize current information relating to the physical and emotional effects of aging on sexuality in both men and women and will briefly survey common medical problems in older people that can influence their sexuality. Finally, implications for mental health counselors and considerations for practical interventions will be discussed.

## Early Studies on Sexuality and Aging

Although the myth and stereotype of the older person as asexual or incapable of sexual activity persist (Gurian, 1986; Masters & Johnson, 1981; Rienzo, 1985; Rotberg, 1987; Steinke & Bergen, 1986), research data and clinical studies point to the fact that individuals continue to remain sexually active and responsive throughout the life span. Beginning with the reports of Kinsey and his team (Kinsey, Pomeroy, & Martin, 1948; Kinsey, Pomeroy, Martin, & Gebhard, 1953) and continuing with the work by Masters and Johnson (1966) and Rubin (1965), more accurate information on human sexuality and behavior was forthcoming and became available to counteract these cultural myths. Although these early studies included some relevant data on sexuality and the older person, this area of research was somewhat neglected because of such factors as lack of professional interest in the study of sexuality in older people, the reluctance of many older individuals to be open about their own sexuality, and the uncomfortableness of many family members with this topic (Bostwinick, 1978).

It was not until recent years that more extensive studies of the sexuality of older individuals were made. Rotberg (1987) cites several research projects, including the longitudinal studies conducted at Duke University's Center on Aging in 1954, 1968, and 1977, which collected data on the sexual activities of 254 men and women over a period of 20 years; the 1981 Starr-Weiner report, which was based on 800 volunteer responses gathered from members of senior citizen centers across the United States; and the Brecher Consumers Union Report of 1984, which was based on a survey of the sexual behavior and attitudes of over 4,000 individuals over the age of 50. Brecher (1984) published the results of this survey in his book *Love, Sex and Aging,* intended for a general readership. A consistent finding in the studies described above is that although there is some sexual decline with each decade of life, aging itself is not as significant a determining factor of older persons' sexual ability as their general physical health and their personal feelings about themselves and their sexuality. In general, individuals who have been sexually active throughout their life continue to retain their sexual interest and responsiveness as they age.

## Physiological Responses of Aging

In both men and women, the process of aging brings about certain physical changes that affect their sexual responses. In men, full penile erection takes longer, the erection may not be as full or as hard, and more direct partner involvement and stimulation is needed (Masters & Johnson, 1981; Rienzo, 1985). There is lessened skin sex flush, nipple erection, and perspiration during intercourse (Walbroehl, 1988). Vasocongestion of the scrotum is reduced, resulting is a lesser degree of elevation of the testicles (Steinke & Bergen, 1986). There is no sensation of the "ejaculatory inevitability" that occurs in younger men, and the process is one-stage, not two (Capuzzi, 1982; Masters & Johnson, 1981; Rienzo, 1985). The ejaculation itself is less forceful, the ejaculate is reduced in volume, and sperm count is reduced. Ejaculatory control increases, and orgasm takes longer to reach (Masters & Johnson, 1981; Rienzo, 1985; Thienhaus, 1988).

The aging male may experience a reduction in ejaculatory demand; perhaps one out of every three or four times he may not experience a specific demand for orgasm and ejaculatory release during intercourse (Masters & Johnson, 1981). This change in ejaculatory need may occur irregularly and without previous warning. If the man is not prepared with adequate knowledge of these normal responses, considerable anxiety may result (Masters & Johnson, 1981).

These changes in ejaculatory function also allow the aging male more control over ejaculation, may result in more erections, and can mean greater sexual satisfaction for some couples (Masters & Johnson, 1981; Rienzo, 1985; Thienhaus, 1988; Walbroehl, 1988).

Continued sexual activity may be helpful in maintaining adequate hormone levels for older men. Older men do show decreases in testosterone level, but the correlation between hormone levels and sexual activity is not clear (Walbroehl, 1988). Renshaw (1985) cites research from the National Gerontology Research Center in Baltimore that indicates that testosterone levels in older males may increase as a direct result of increased sexual activity.

It is important that older men have accurate information on the above-mentioned changes in their sexual functioning and understand that these changes are normal and natural consequences of their aging. Lack of information can lead to anxiety and psychological impotence in men who fear that these physiological changes are signs of their own sexual inadequacy, and such individuals may withdraw from sexual activity and intimacy with their partners altogether (Masters & Johnson, 1981).

In older women, certain changes result from the decline in estrogen production after menopause, including thinning and some atrophying of the vaginal wall, decreased vaginal lubrication, shortening of the vaginal width and length, and lessened elasticity of the vaginal wall (Masters & Johnson, 1981; Rienzo, 1985; Walbroehl, 1988). Orgasms may lessen in intensity and may take longer to reach, although a woman's capacity for multiple orgasms is not affected by age and, in contrast to the older male, her refractory period is not increased (Masters & Johnson, 1981; Rienzo, 1985). The excitement and plateau phases are increased in duration, with more time needed to achieve adequate vaginal lubrication (Rienzo, 1985). During orgasm, contractions are decreased by about one half, and the resolution phase occurs more quickly, the vagina returning more quickly to normal size (Capuzzi, 1981; Thienhaus, 1988).

Occasionally, the aging woman may experience spasmodic, painful involuntary contraction of the uterus as a result of orgasm, in which the usual regular contractions of the vagina and surrounding area become irregular and can be similar to the muscle spasms in the cramping of a major leg muscle. Estrogen supplementation may help to prevent these uterine spasms (Masters & Johnson, 1981; Rienzo, 1985).

Other possible consequences of aging in women are a greater risk of vaginal infections due to lessened acidic secretions in the vagina, urethral irritation resulting from intercourse, and possible urinary incontinence (Rienzo, 1985). Painful intercourse (dyspareunia) or involuntary constriction of the outer third of the vagina (vaginismus) may also occur (Masters & Johnson, 1981). Kegel exercises, involving alternately contracting and relaxing the pubococcygeal muscles, can help to restore tone to vaginal muscles and tissue and can also result in strengthened orgasmic contractions and maintenance of the shape of the vagina (Masters & Johnson, 1981; Rienzo, 1985).

Research has indicated that for many women, continued sexual activity on a regular basis through middle life can postpone or lessen the above-described physiological effects (Rienzo, 1985). In addition, many of these effects can be treated by such measures as use of topical lubrication, estrogen cream, or estrogen supplementation (Rienzo, 1985; Thienhaus, 1988). Older women should be encouraged to communicate closely with their physicians about such matters to ensure their maximum comfort and health. For many women, their emotional attitudes toward their own aging and personal sexuality are more of a determinant of their sexual responsiveness than the physiologically based reactions to lessened hormone levels (Fazio, 1987; Masters & Johnson, 1981; Rotberg, 1987).

For both older men and women, the changes in physical functioning do not necessarily result in any change in their subjective enjoyment and appreciation of sexual activity (Masters & Johnson, 1981). The mental health counselor can reassure older clients that maintaining sexual interest and responsiveness as they age is normal and appropriate and can provide accurate information on the aging process to help alleviate older clients' fears or anxieties. It may be necessary for the counselor to bring up the subject of sexual well-being with older clients gently by asking open-ended questions about their sexual health, such as "How do you handle your sexual feelings?" (Renshaw, 1985). Many older individuals may be hesitant to approach this subject with a counselor but may be relieved and open to communication once the topic is raised.

## Medical Conditions Affecting the Sexuality of Older Persons

Mental health counselors should familiarize themselves with the medical illnesses and conditions an older client may encounter that may affect his or her sexual functioning. Overviews of this topic are provided by Butler and Lewis (1976), Hogan (1980), Capuzzi (1982), Renshaw (1985), Scheingold and Wagner (1974), Thienhaus (1988), and Walbroehl (1988). Often clients will need counseling support in dealing with the emotional components of their medical conditions and in dealing with their own anxieties and insecurities regarding their sexual functioning. In particular, a mental health counselor should be sensitive to and aware of the psychological effects of any surgical procedures "down there" (Renshaw, 1985), such as hernia repair, hysterectomy, hemorrhoid removal, and prostate gland surgery. All of these may cause anxiety about sexual functioning.

The resulting negative emotions may lead to increased sexual problems if not dealt with in a constructive manner. Often, an older person may be hesitant to bring up questions about the sexual effects of an operation or medical illness with a physician, and the counselor may need to be both tactful and diplomatic in helping older clients deal with these concerns. Working closely with the physician and other medical personnel, when possible, can increase the mental health counselor's effectiveness in assisting older individuals with such matters.

Accurate information on the nature of the medical condition and the physiological effects may go a long way in alleviating an older person's anxiety. Older men who undergo a prostatectomy, for example, may be unaware that this procedure may lead to retrograde ejaculation into the bladder and may panic when ejaculation does not occur in the expected manner (Renshaw, 1985). Such anxiety can lead to further emotional complications and possible psychological impotence if the man is not offered an opportunity to discuss his concerns and obtain accurate information (Masters & Johnson, 1981).

Many medications that older persons may be taking can also affect their sexual functioning. For example, hypertensive medication may significantly lower sexual interest and responsiveness in some individuals (Walbroehl, 1988). Tricyclic antidepressants, as well as some antiparkinsonian and antipsychotic medications, may have side effects that impair erection (Thienhaus, 1988).

As medical procedures and interventions are constantly updated, mental health counselors should attempt to keep informed of current medical practices that may affect the physical and mental health of older clients. The counselor is referred to such periodicals as *Medical Aspects of Human Sexuality, Geriatrics,* and *Gerontological Nursing* to keep updated on current research and information regarding sexuality and aging.

## Practical Considerations and Interventions

A mental health counselor, by being alert to the issues and physical concerns discussed above, may be in a position to offer practical suggestions to clients who may be experiencing sexual difficulties either because of the normal aging process or as a result of an illness or disability. Harris (1988) discusses the positive benefits to older individuals of increasing exercises such as relaxation and gradual warm-up exercises, walking for short periods, and stretching and bending. All these may result in a greater sense of physical well-being for an older person and can be instrumental in improving the client's sexual interest and functioning. Often, doing gentle stretching and limbering exercises before engaging in sexual activity can increase the older individual's enjoyment and comfort during sex (Harris, 1988). Butler and Lewis (1976) provide holistic and practical guidelines for such items as nutrition, rest, exercise, and personal appearance that may provide positive suggestions to an older person in maintaining and maximizing sexual enjoyment and health. Such simple suggestions as adequate rest (7 to 10 hr of sleep a night), warm baths, a firm mattress, and back massage may help older individuals to improve their sexual desire and performance (Steinke & Bergen, 1986).

Suggestions for alternative coital positions can be provided to older clients, particularly for those who have had a coronary, stroke, or breast surgery or who suffer from an arthritic condition. In general, older individuals can benefit from learning at least one non-weight-bearing sexual position, such as a partially lateral position that allows both partners to recline (Renshaw, 1985). Other practical suggestions could include the use of skin lotion or baby oil, sharing a hot bath before intercourse, and emphasizing sensual, nongenital foreplay with the stress on providing pleasure and increasing intimacy with the sexual partner, and de-emphasizing any "achievement oriented" approaches to sexual activity (Thienhaus, 1988). Although older clients with extensive or prolonged sexual difficulties should be referred to appropriate specialists, the use of Helen Singer Kaplan's (1974) sexual therapy techniques of a gentle, graduated, and nondemanding approach to increasing intimacy between partners may benefit older clients who are troubled by minor sexual dysfunction (Thienhaus, 1988).

Bibliotherapy may be an appropriate intervention in educating older clients about the topic of aging and sexuality. . . . Two books intended for a general readership that a mental health counselor could recommend to an older individual are Brecher's (1984) *Love, Sex and Aging* and *Sex After Sixty* by Butler and Lewis (1976). Numerous advice books for the older person have been published in recent years, and in general these books take a positive approach toward the topic of sexuality and aging (Arluke, Levin, & Suchwalko, 1984).

Mental health counselors may wish to be especially alert to complaints of depression from older clients, as depression can both decrease sexual responsiveness and result from problems with sexual functioning. If reduced sexual desire is caused by depression, the client should experience alleviation of this lessened sexual responsiveness within approximately 4 weeks of receiving appropriate antidepressant medication (Renshaw, 1985). However, older clients may suffer from depression as a direct result of their sexual frustrations (Lemkau, 1985).

## Single Older People: Special Needs

Some groups of older people may have special concerns relating to their sexual functioning and health. Masters and Johnson (1981) coined the terms *widow's syndrome* and *widower's syndrome* to refer to the special sexual problems faced by older men and women who experience a period of either voluntary or involuntary sexual abstinence of a year or more because of the death or disability of their spouse. Such individuals may need to deal with specific physiological responses when they do resume a sexual relationship after such a period of inactivity.

For the aging man, there may be an inability to maintain a functional erection, even if there has been no previous difficulty in this area. Such an event can have a major impact on the sexual confidence of the man, who may develop high anxiety related to his sexual performance unless adequate counseling and information are provided to him. For older women, the widow's syndrome expresses itself in comparable ways in the female physiology. There may be some atrophying of the vaginal walls, constriction of the vaginal barrel, and thinning of the major and minor labia as a result of an extensive period of sexual inactivity (Masters & Johnson, 1981). When sex is resumed, there may be a significantly lessened production of vaginal lubrication in response to sexual stimulation. These changes in the older woman, though related to the physiological changes due to the aging process and decreased hormonal levels discussed above, are intensified by prolonged sexual inactivity. For both older men and women, accurate information on the processes involved and a sympathetic and understanding sexual partner can do much to counteract the effects of this process (Masters & Johnson, 1981).

For older single individuals, other, more psychosocial problems may present themselves. Significant social disapproval is still often attached in our culture to older people, especially widows or widowers, who resume dating and sexual relationships. For many older individuals, the relationships they have with their children may be a source of strength and may help to meet the single older person's need for intimacy. However, conflict with children often develops when the older person attempts to marry again or form a new sexual relationship (Rotberg, 1987). These social and familial sanctions and pressures can make it even more difficult for an older person to cope adequately and responsibly with his or her sexual needs.

Women form a larger percentage of the elderly single population. Rotberg (1987) cites statistics showing that approximately two thirds of the older people in America are female and that 85% of surviving spouses are women. The single older woman may experience special challenges in meeting needs for emotional support and sexual contact. For many women, the need for an intimate relationship may be met by an attachment to and/or living arrangement with another older woman. Though not sexual, such relationships can do much to provide older women with support and a means of meeting needs for emotional intimacy. Malatesta, Chambles, Pollack, and Cantor (1988) report that for some older women such activities as wearing lingerie, having their hair done, and wearing attractive clothing, as well as other indirect means of expressing personal intimacy, such as being with children and grandchildren and attending religious activities, were helpful in meeting their affectional and sexual needs.

For many older men and women, masturbation may be the only form of sexual release available, but personal attitudes and moral beliefs may cause guilt or anxiety over this activity. A mental health counselor sensitive to this issue can help by comfortably and matter-of-factly pointing out to such older individuals that sexual feelings and self-release are normal and acceptable (Renshaw, 1985; Walbroehl, 1988).

# Institutionalized Older Persons

The question of sexual activity and behavior in older men and women may be complicated by the realities of an institutional setting. In many such institutions, sexual contact and behavior among the residents are actively discouraged, so that considerable barriers may be created to the ability of an older person to find a suitable sexual outlet. Glass, Mustian, and Carter (1986) studied the attitudes of health care providers toward sexual activity in institutionalized older people and found that such care providers generally held highly restrictive attitudes toward such sexual behavior. Szasz (1983) cites further data indicating that sexual behavior among nursing home residents was viewed by staff as constituting negative behavioral problems. Masturbatory activities were viewed in conflicting ways by various staff persons, some acknowledging this as acceptable behavior when done in private and others expressing more restrictive attitudes.

The significance of the attitudes and beliefs of staff in determining the opportunity for sexual involvement among institutionalized men and women is underscored by McCartney, Izeman, Rogers, and Cohen (1987). This study cites several case examples of how institutional staff could approach the situation of a romantic attachment between residents, ranging from the restrictive reactions discussed above to a more open environment. In one case, that of "Mr. M," a 72-year-old man, the nursing home staff were supportive of his romantic attachment with a woman resident of the nursing home who was 8 years older than he and provided a "Do Not Disturb" sign and the use of a private and comfortable lounge area to the couple when needed. The couple eventually married. In this case, an important consideration for the staff was the fact that both individuals were mentally alert and did not suffer from dementia and thus were able to make responsible choices regarding their sexual behavior (McCartney et al., 1987). Renshaw (1984) reinforces the suggestion of a small recreation room within the nursing home that could be made available to older couples wishing privacy but points up the alternative need for staff to provide protection to residents from dominant or aggressive individuals who might force their sexual attention on vulnerable others.

# Conclusion

Older individuals in our society need the freedom to express their sexual needs without the negative interference of sexual stereotypes and prejudices. For all individuals, and particularly for older men and women, intimacy, affection, and sexuality are intertwined (Rice & Kelly, 1987). Viewing sexuality in older people from a holistic and developmental framework, in which sexual expression is seen as normal and natural over the life span and an integral part of an individual's involvement with life, can provide a counterpart to these prejudices and offer a framework for the positive acceptance of sexuality in the aging person. Steinke and Bergen (1986) suggest the application of Maslow's self-actualization model to the concept of continual personal growth and expression throughout the life span, in which the sexual expressiveness of older people is seen not in terms of how it relates to "what they could do" when they were younger but as a potential area for growth of intimacy and affection.

Older individuals can be shown that their mature responses to an open and expressive sensual involvement with their partner as opposed to a more performance and genital orientation to sexual activity, provide an opportunity for increased intimacy and emotional closeness among older couples (Datan & Rodeheaver, 1983). Mental health counselors approaching clients with such an attitude of respect and openness toward the sexual potential of older people can be highly effective in assisting such individuals to perceive their own sexuality in a positive and constructive light.

# References

Arluke, A., Levin, J., & Suchwalko, J. (1984). Sexuality and romance in advice books for the elderly. *Gerontologist, 24,* 415–418.

Berezin, M. A. (1969). Sex and old age: A review of the literature. *Journal of Geriatric Psychiatry, 2*(2), 131–149.

Bostwinick, J. (1978). *Aging and behavior.* New York: Springer.

Brecher, E. (1984). *Love, sex and aging.* Boston: Little, Brown.

Butler, R. N., & Lewis, M. I. (1976). *Sex after sixty: A guide for men and women for their later years.* New York: Harper & Row.

Capuzzi, D. (1982). Sexuality and aging: An overview for counselors. *Personnel and Guidance Journal, 61,* 31–34.

Datan, N., & Rodeheaver, D. (1983). Beyond generativity: Toward a sensuality of later life. In R. B. Weg (Ed.), *Sexuality in the later years: Roles and behavior.* Orlando, FL: Academic Press.

Eidenberg, M. A. (1985). *Mental health practice with the elderly.* Englewood Cliffs, NJ: Prentice-Hall.

Fazio, L. (1987). Sexuality and aging: A community wellness program. *Physical and Occupational Therapy in Geriatrics, 6*(1), 59–69.

Glass, J., Mustian, R., & Carter, L. (1986). Knowledge and attitudes of health-care providers toward sexuality in the institutionalized elderly. *Educational Gerontology, 12*(5), 465–475.

Gurian, B. S. (1986). The myth of the aged as asexual: Countertransference issues in therapy. *Hospital and Community Psychiatry, 37*(4), 345–346.

Harris, R. (1988). Exercise and sex in the aging patient. *Medical Aspects of Human Sexuality, 22*(1), 148–159.

Hogan, R. (1980). *Human sexuality: A nursing perspective.* East Norwalk, CT: Appleton-Century Crofts.

Kaplan, H. S. (1974). *The new sex therapy.* New York: Brunner/Mazel.

Kinsey, A. C., Pomeroy, W. B., & Martin, C. E. (1948). *Sexual behavior in the human male.* Philadelphia: W. B. Saunders.

Kinsey, A. C., Pomeroy, W. B., Martin, C. E., & Gebhard, P. H. (1953). *Sexual behavior in the human female.* Philadelphia: W. B. Saunders.

Lemkau, J. P. (1985). Sex as a pivotal issue in the psychotherapy of a depressed elderly physician. *Clinical Gerontologist, 4*(2), 46–48.

Ludeman, K. (1981). The sexuality of the older person: Review of the literature. *Gerontologist, 21,* 203–208.

Malatesta, V., Chambles, D., Pollack, M., & Cantor, A. (1988). Widowhood, sexuality and aging: A life span analysis. *Journal of Sex and Marital Therapy, 14*(1), 49–63.

Masters, W. H., & Johnson, V. E. (1966). *Human sexual response.* Boston: Little, Brown.

Masters, W. H., & Johnson, V. E. (1981). Sex and the aging process. *Journal of the American Geriatrics Society, 29*(9), 385–390.

McCartney, J., Izeman, H., Rogers, D., & Cohen, N. (1987). Sexuality and the institutionalized elderly. *Journal of the American Geriatrics Society, 35*(4), 331–333.

Renshaw, D. C. (1984). Geriatric sex problems. *Journal of Geriatric Psychiatry, 17,* 123–138.

Renshaw, D. C. (1985). Sex, age and values. *Journal of the American Geriatrics Society, 33*(9), 635–643.

Rice, S., & Kelly, J. J. (1987). Love and intimacy needs of the elderly: Some philosophical and intervention issues. *Journal of Social Work and Human Sexuality, 5*(2), 89–96.

Rienzo, B. (1985). The impact of aging on human sexuality. *Journal of School Health, 55*(2), 66–68.

Rotberg, A. (1987). An introduction to the study of women, aging, and sexuality. *Physical and Occupational Therapy in Geriatrics, 5*(3), 3–12.

Rubin, I. (1965). *Sexual life after sixty.* New York: Basic Books.

Scheingold, L. D., & Wagner, N. N. (1974). *Sound sex and the aging heart.* New York: Human Sciences Press.

Steinke, E., & Bergen, M. (1986). Sexuality and aging. *Gerontological Nursing, 12*(6), 6–10.

Szasz, G. (1983). Sexual incidents in an extended care unit for aged men. *Journal of the American Geriatrics Society, 31,* 407–411.

Thienhaus, O. J. (1988). Practical overview of sexual function and advancing age. *Geriatrics, 43*(8), 63–67.

Walbroehl, G. (1988). Effects of medical problems on sexuality in the elderly. *Medical Aspects of Human Sexuality, 22,*(10), 56–66.

Weg, R. B. (1983). Concepts of sexuality in the later years: The physiological perspective. In R. B. Weg (Ed.), *Sexuality in the later years: Roles and behavior.* Orlando, FL: Academic Press.

# 9

# The Life Review:
# Strategies for Working with
# Individuals and Groups

*Elinor B. Waters*

In a room on the oncology floor of a large hospital, a woman talks quietly with the staff counselor about her days as a young mother. At a nearby senior center, a group of men and women, mostly immigrants from Eastern Europe, are having a spirited discussion about the amazing difficulties they weathered in coming to this country. And a few blocks away, a 75-year-old man is telling a high school history class about his days as a union organizer. All are engaged in some form of life review.

For over 25 years, since Robert Butler first articulated the concept, gerontologists have touted the use of life review techniques with older adults. This article will discuss the rationale for the technique, consider its advantages and limitations, and then present a variety of approaches to "doing" a life review. It combines a presentation of the theory of life review with some practical strategies designed to add new tools to the repertoire of mental health counselors.

## What Do We Mean by Life Review?

In his seminal article, Butler (1963) described life review as "a naturally occurring, universal mental process characterized by the progressive return to consciousness of past experiences, and, particularly, the resurgence of unresolved conflicts" (p. 66). Butler saw this process as being triggered by the realization of approaching death and therefore as more common among older people. As they undertake such a review, people examine their lives with such existential questions as Who am I?, Who have I been?, or How did I live my life? Putting it all together and taking stock, they may be asking, "All things considered, how did I do?" When the answer to this question is generally

Reprinted from *Journal of Mental Health Counseling, 12,* 270–278, 1990. © ACA. Reprinted with permission. No further reproduction authorized without written permission of American Counseling Association.

positive, people are likely to experience satisfaction and self-acceptance (Butler & Lewis, 1982). A negative answer, however, may lead to self-criticism and depression. Stated differently, the outcome of a life review may determine whether an older adult achieves integrity, the developmental task of old age identified by Erikson (1963). Thus, from the vantage point of mental health counselors, the major goal of a life review is to help clients reach a sense of acceptance or integrity. Given this broad goal, counselors and others in the field of aging have found many different ways to facilitate the life review process. Major questions to be raised are why the concept is so widespread and how it has worked as a counseling technique over the years.

To mark the 25th anniversary of Butler's article, the *Journal of Gerontological Social Work* published a special issue that discusses theoretical and practical considerations of the life review. In that volume, Moody (1988) talks of why this concept has captured the interest of gerontologists and the lay public alike and suggests that "there is something to this idea of reminiscence and life review that is compelling, something which is very far from being merely a form of group-work or a technique of therapy. The idea of life review is, finally, more akin to a wish, a hope, an act of the imagination itself" (p. 8). In this sense the impact of a life review cannot be evaluated solely in terms of its clinical impact.

Moody's article discusses the uses of life review for oral history research and transmission of culture across the generations, as well as for therapeutic interventions in behalf of the mental health of older persons. On one hand, he lauds the well-established place in the theory and practice of gerontology that life review techniques have achieved. On the other hand, he warns that "the practice of life review is in danger of becoming a kind of ersatz religion into which we unwittingly project conflicting hopes and wishes about the end of life" (p. 12).

Disch (1988) also comments on the popularity of the life review and warns that it is in danger of becoming a fad. The danger, in his view, is that, in the desire to jump on the bandwagon and use life review techniques, counselors and other service providers may field poorly designed and executed programs. His "warning" is included here not to deter mental health counselors from conducting life reviews with their clients or from initiating good programs, but as a reminder of the importance of quality control. Readers should keep that caution in mind as we move to the section on implementation.

## How Do Mental Health Counselors Facilitate Life Reviews?

Life reviews can be done with individuals, families, or groups of unrelated people. This section first considers techniques for conducting life reviews with individuals and then moves to a discussion of group approaches to life review.

## Working with Individuals

In guiding individuals through a life review, mental health counselors can use imagery, or make various requests for recollections. Regardless of the technique used, the goal is to help clients recall past events and relationships, consider their meaning, and, ideally, develop a sense of pride in their accomplishments. The focus on the past, which is basic to a life review, may require some adaptations on the part of mental health counselors who are committed to a "here and now" approach. However, past, present, and future often come together. According to Butler (1975),

> A major goal of a life review is to deal with the resurgence of unresolved conflicts which can now be surveyed and reintegrated. The old are not only taking stock of themselves as they review their lives, they are trying to think and feel through what they will do with the time that is left and with whatever emotional and material legacies they have to give to others. (p. 412)

This stock-taking and decision-making process affords counselors many opportunities to help clients resolve past conflicts or complete "unfinished business." As mental health counselors hear about strained relations among members of clients' families, perhaps dating back to childhood, they may be able to help them put these old grievances in perspective. Sometimes clients may want an opportunity to express anger over treatment they received from parents or other family members, without being judged for criticizing people who are dead. In other cases they may come to see that the harm was not intentional and realize that their parents (or other "offending" persons) may have done the best they knew how to do at the time. Sometimes the unfinished business focuses more on concerns about the clients' own role as parent, spouse, or friend. In such cases, mental health counselors may be able to assist clients in forgiving themselves.

With appropriate support, clients may be able to contact relatives and friends to express appreciation, to apologize for past transgressions, or to seek to "bury the hatchet." For example, they may be encouraged to tell a sibling, "You really helped me survive when our parents were going through their divorce" or "I guess it's time to stop holding it against you that Mother always loved you most." Alternatively, clients may need help in reframing their present situation or their views of their past. Older persons who express regrets about their roles as parents, citizens, or friends may be helped to see that they did the best they could with the emotional and financial resources they had. Sometimes, in working with people who express regrets or "if only"s, it is helpful to ask them to develop a "ledger" that has "credits" consisting of the things they are glad they did, to balance the "debits" or things they wish they had done.

Despite efforts to help clients gain a sense of perspective about their past lives, we may discover that the major causes of pain lie in the present. Butler (1975, p. 413) warns us that, in doing a life review, we may encounter people who feel powerless "because their fate depends upon so many elements over which they have little control." A major task for mental health counselors, in such cases, is to help their clients to think about what areas of their lives they can control and to accept those that they cannot. Community-living older people in good health have a great many choices about how they spend their time, energy, and money. Sometimes life reviews can help them recall earlier interests and abilities that can be rekindled. Even frail older people may be empowered if they realize they have choices about where to sit or whom they prefer to have as a visitor on a given day. However, such frail older people seldom contact a counselor directly.

Often counselors are approached not by older people themselves but by their adult children. In such cases, the request is typically for a consultation on "what to do about Mother," and mental health counselors will want to respond at a very practical level by providing information about community resources and linkages with the aging network. Such a consultation may also provide a good opportunity to talk about family relationships and communications and to explain the importance of life reviews. Mental health counselors can encourage family members to look for signs, such as increased reminiscence, that the older person is beginning the life review process. When family members are involved in the process, greater intimacy can result as people learn new things about each other. As Myers (1989, p. 175) puts it, "The normal process of life review offers a unique opportunity for adult children to interact with aging parents and learn about their own family history while assisting aging parents to achieve ego integrity."

Although life reviews typically lead to positive feelings, this is not always true, and mental health counselors need to be aware of limitations to the technique. In an interesting article on late-life divorce and the life review, Weingarten (1988) cautions that life reviews may improve mental health and life satisfaction for some people and have the opposite effect for others. She urges counselors to exercise clinical judgment "as they balance self criticism about the past with demands of living in the present" (p. 95). In a similar vein, Edinberg (1985) notes that in reviewing their lives most people will encounter some memories that trigger feelings of guilt, anger, despair, regret, or sadness. Mental health practitioners must decide whether to comfort the person, encourage further expression of feelings, or move the client away from the subject. The decision will undoubtedly be based on a number of factors, such as the degree of trust that has been established and the counselor's view of the client's resiliency and the support available, as well as logistical questions such as how much time the counselor will have to help the client work through feelings. Similar questions should be asked when considering the use of life reviews in a group.

## Group Approaches to Life Review

When a life review is done in a group, it clearly has the added dimension of providing an opportunity for participants to discuss their recollections with others. In the process, group members are likely to discover a number of common experiences or identify shared feelings. As in any group counseling experience, such a discovery of commonalities may be relieving to people who thought, "I'm the only one who thinks that way."

In leading a group life review, mental health counselors must plan carefully so that all members get to tell their stories. As each member reports on personal recollections, the leader and other group members can help that person identify themes that run through his or her life and strengths and coping techniques he or she has developed and can continue to use. The continuity in people's lives was illustrated in one group that I facilitated. One group member repeatedly remembered and tracked the statements of other members from one session to the next. In doing a life review, she described her childhood role as that of family historian. She was delighted when we pointed out the similarities between her early behavior and her behavior in the group 60 years later.

The group in which the "family historian" was a member was made up of intact, community-living older people. Life review groups have also been conducted in institutional settings, where the self-esteem of members is apt to be more precarious. Kiernat (1984) reported on a pilot project conducted with confused residents of a nursing home. She found that "conversation can be stimulated, interest can be sparked, and attention span can be increased through the recall and review of past life experiences" (p. 305).

When working with groups, mental health counselors may wish to use a variety of stimuli to trigger the life review process. Edinberg (1985) identifies a number of such triggers, including (a) *music* in the form of old records or a sing-along, (b) *scents* such as spices or foods, flowers or perfumes, (c) *imaging* based on affect or social interactions (group members may be asked to remember a particular time when they were happy, sad, or scared or to recall a particular holiday or historic event), and (d) *memorabilia,* such as old photographs, school yearbooks, newspapers, greeting cards, election buttons, old household appliances, or favorite knickknacks. These techniques can also be used with individuals, as noted in the following examples.

## Examples of Life Review

A few examples of how life review techniques have been used in counseling may bring the foregoing discussion to life. McCloskey (1990) writes poignantly of how she uses music as an adjunct to her counseling activities. She states that "through familiar music an unfamiliar environment can be made to feel safe and secure, so that conversation and interaction are less threatening and more easily initiated." To illustrate her point, she tells the following story:

I was working with a small group of older adults, all with some degree of dementia. We started reminiscing about autumn, school days, and changes that occur with the seasons. I sang some familiar songs such as "Try to Remember," "September Song," "School Days," and others. When I had finished, each person responded verbally . . . [with] thoughts [which] suggested that the speakers were coming to terms with what those memories represented.

McCloskey's approach, though extremely powerful, is more effective when used by people with musical talent as well as counseling skills. Two simpler life review activities are described below, which encourage people to look back over their lives and to use these recollections in future planning. Both activities have been used in group counseling programs offered by the Oakland University Continuum Center and are described more fully in Waters and Goodman (in press).

## Learning from Your Past

This approach to life review, which is appropriate for community-living older people, can be particularly helpful in life-planning activities, including pre- or postretirement planning programs. The mental health counselor asks participants to fill in a worksheet that has four columns headed (a) past activities (educational, vocational, or leisure), (b) what you liked about this activity, (c) what you disliked, and (d) what skills you developed as part of this activity and what values they represent. The counselor gives a personal example of how past activities may relate to future choices and asks individuals or group members to fill in the worksheet and then discuss it with the counselor or in their group. Our experience indicates that sharing recollections is both intrinsically pleasurable and suggestive of new possibilities. People who recall past school successes may decide to seek new opportunities for learning, while those who remember their pride in making furniture may look into new handicraft projects. In many career and retirement programs, we have observed that when people recall past accomplishments, they are better able to identify transferable skills that they can use in new paid or unpaid endeavors.

## Personal Sharing: A Guided Life Review

This activity uses imagery to encourage clients to do a very brief life review and then to discuss their recollections in small groups. The mental health counselor tells the group that they will have an opportunity to think back through their lives about the people and experiences that have been most significant and then encourages members to get comfortable and close their eyes. When members seem to be comfortable, the leader begins the journey back with instructions to "picture yourself as a child. Where are you? Is anyone with you? What sights and smells are you aware of? What are you thinking about? How are you feeling?" After allowing people time to think, the mental health counselor asks people to picture themselves as young adults and poses similar questions. The activity continues through various life stages, ending with the present. When people seem ready, the counselor asks group members to open their eyes and leads a discussion of each person's recollections. I have found that the discussions that ensue typically lead to feelings of pride on the part of the individuals and closeness among the group. And those are indeed among the major reasons for conducting life reviews.

## Conclusions

Since 1963, when Robert Butler first wrote about the life review, mental health practitioners have been using this technique to help older adults achieve a sense of integrity in the Eriksonian sense. Indeed, life reviews can help many older adults develop an appreciation for the way they have coped with their lives, resolve past conflicts, or finish "unfinished business." However, life reviews may trigger sadness and depression for people who feel extreme dissatisfaction with their lives. Suggestions were made concerning how life reviews can be conducted with individuals, families, and groups in order to maximize the positive impact of the experience.

## References

Butler, R. N. (1963). The life review: An interpretation of reminiscence in the aged. *Psychiatry, 26,* 65–76.

Butler, R. N. (1975). *Why survive? Being old in America.* New York: Harper & Row.

Butler, R. N., & Lewis, M. I. (1982). *Aging and mental health: Positive psychosocial and biomedical approaches.* St. Louis: Mosby.

Disch, R. (Ed.). (1988). *Twenty-five years of the life review: Theoretical and practical considerations.* New York: Haworth Press.

Edinberg, M. A. (1985). *Mental health practice with the elderly.* Englewood Cliffs, NJ: Prentice-Hall.

Erikson, E. H. (1963). *Childhood and society* (2nd ed.). New York: Norton.

Kiernat, J. M. (1984). The use of life review activity. In I. M. Burnside (Ed.), *Working with the elderly: Group process and techniques* (pp. 298–307). Pacific Grove, CA: Brooks/Cole.

McCloskey, L. (1990). The silent heart sings: Reminiscence and life review through music. *Generations, 14,* 63–65.

Moody, H. R. (1988). Twenty-five years of the life review: Where did we come from? Where are we going? In R. Disch (Ed.), *Twenty-five years of the life review: Theoretical and practical considerations* (pp. 7–24). New York: Haworth Press.

Myers, J. E. (1989). *Adult children & aging parents.* Alexandria, VA: American Association for Counseling and Development.

Waters, E. B., & Goodman, J. (in press). *Counseling older adults: Practical strategies for counselors.* San Francisco: Jossey-Bass.

Weingarten, H. R. (1988). Late life divorce and the life review. In R. Disch (Ed.). *Twenty-five years of the life review: Theoretical and practical considerations* (pp. 83–100). New York: Haworth Press.

# PART 4

## The Female Client

$P$sychology's treatment of women has been marred by sexism and discrimination in the past, and that legacy continues to influence the field to some extent. Nevertheless, over the past two decades there has been an explosion of research on the psychology of women, with consequent advances in the counseling and psychotherapy literature (Worell & Remer, 1992). Our knowledge of the psychology of gender and gender issues in counseling has progressed markedly (Betz & Fitzgerald, 1993). Unfortunately, many counselors remain uninformed about women's issues, gender influences on psychological distress, and the special techniques necessary for ethical and effective counseling with female clients.

In the late 1970s, Division 17, the Division of Counseling Psychology of the American Psychological Association, passed a set of guidelines for counseling women. Fitzgerald and Nutt (1986) expand on these principles, clarify their rationale, present extensive documentation in support of each principle from the literature on the psychology of women, and provide guidance for their implementation in counseling. These principles represent the essential minimal competencies for counseling women.

Beginning with a solid grounding in the literature on the psychology of women, counselors must then go on to develop a thorough understanding of the impact of gender on psychological theory and practice, the needs of special subgroups of women, the effects of sexism on women's and men's lives, and the influence of gender on the counseling process (Fitzgerald & Nutt, 1986). The counselor's gender-related attitudes and biases must continually be examined and confronted; sexism can easily creep into counseling, to the detriment of the client. Only after working on their attitudes and acquiring the requisite knowledge can counselors effectively employ some of the singular skills useful in counseling women (Fitzgerald & Nutt, 1986).

Implicit within the principles for counseling women is the assumption that counselors must, at the very least, adopt a nonsexist approach with their female clients. Many counselors believe that counseling should be neutral or value-free, and that avoiding explicitly sexist attitudes, remarks, and behavior results in nonsexist counseling. However, attempts to adopt a "neutral" stance very often result in inadvertent sexism. The next two articles cover two approaches to feminist counseling. The term "feminist" simply refers to an advocate of equality between the sexes, but feminist therapy has been concerned primarily with women's issues (Worell & Remer, 1992).

Good, Gilbert, and Scher (1990) move beyond the principles outlined by Fitzgerald and Nutt (1986), arguing that counselors must be actively feminist in their work, and that feminist approaches, informed by the psychology of gender, are equally important for male and female clients. Good et al. (1990) coined the term "Gender Aware Therapy" to describe their approach. They articulate five core aspects of gender aware therapy: considering gender as central to counseling; viewing problems in their societal context, actively addressing gender injustices; developing a collaborative relationship with clients; and respecting the client's right to choose (Good, et al., 1990). Good et al. (1990) then provide illustrations of how gender aware therapy can be implemented.

Finally, McNamara and Rickard (1989) explore another dimension of feminist counseling, that is, adapting one's counseling approach to the stage of feminist identity development of the client. Feminist identity development refers to the process of coming to terms with sexism and gender-related influences on women's lives. Female clients vary considerably in their views of the world, their awareness of sexism, and their perspectives on the issues that bring them to counseling. McNamara and Rickard (1989) describe an existing model of feminist identity development, discuss how this model can be an aid to the counselor in understanding the client, suggest how the feminist counselor may respond differently to clients at different stages of awareness, and provide some suggestions for future research on the topic. Throughout their article, McNamara and Rickard (1989) emphasize ways in which the counselor may effectively address gender issues in a manner respectful of the client's beliefs and needs.

## References

Fitzgerald, L. F., & Nutt, R. (1986). The Division 17 principles concerning the counseling/psychotherapy of women: Rationale and implementation. *The Counseling Psychologist, 14,* 180–216.

Good, G. E., Gilbert, L. A., & Scher, M. (1990). Gender aware therapy: A synthesis of feminist therapy and knowledge about gender. *Journal of Counseling and Development, 68,* 376–380.

McNamara, K., & Rickard, K. M. (1989). Feminist identity development: Implications for feminist therapy with women. *Journal of Counseling and Development, 68,* 184–189.

Worell, J., & Remer, P. (1992). *Feminist perspectives in therapy: An empowerment model for women.* New York: Wiley.

# 10

# The Division 17 Principles Concerning the Counseling/Psychotherapy of Women: Rationale and Implementation

*Louise F. Fitzgerald*
*University of California, Santa Barbara*
*Roberta Nutt*
*Texas Women's University*
*Principal Authors*

In 1978 the Division of Counseling Psychology of the American Psychological Association (APA) approved the *Principles Concerning the Counseling and Psychotherapy of Women* as an official policy statement for the Division. These Principles, subsequently endorsed by Divisions 16, 29, and 35, have also served as a general resource document for the APA, and are cited as a resource in the *Guidelines for the Provision of Counseling Psychological Services* (APA, 1983).

Almost from the inception of the *Principles,* the Division 17 Committee on Women, which authored them, had anticipated the need for an extensive exposition of each principle, to guide psychologists seeking to implement both their spirit and their content. Thus, the present document, which presents the background and rationale for each principle as well as suggestions for implementation, was born. The result of over 5 years of work, the document has been extensively reviewed, revised, and again reviewed—not only by the committee and its various resource and support persons but also by psychologists from all across the country, both within and without Division 17. The process of cooperation, incorporation, and revision has been both frustrating and inspiring, as

From L. F. Fitzgerald and R. Nutt, "The Division 17 Principles Concerning the Counseling/ Psychotherapy of Women: Rationale and Implementation" in *The Counseling Psychologist, 14,* 180–216, 1986. Copyright © 1986. Reprinted by permission of Sage Publications, Inc., Newbury Park, CA.

we worked to produce a document that could stand as a guide to our science and our profession for at least a decade. The final version was approved by the Division 17 Executive Committee at its 1984 midyear meeting.

This document is the product of literally hundreds of women (and men) who have contributed time, thought, and effort over nearly half a decade to bring this project to fruition, and thus, to contribute to the welfare of women everywhere. Although it bears our names, we are intensely aware that it is truly a cooperative product of the committee, the division, and ultimately, our profession as a whole.

## PRINCIPLE I. Counselors/therapists should be knowledgeable about women, particularly with regard to biological, psychological, and social issues which have impact on women in general or on particular groups of women in our society.

Historically, the discipline of psychology has been male-defined and male-oriented (Unger & Denmark, 1975). O'Leary (1977) notes that theories of human behavior were advanced mostly by male psychologists, who investigated and attempted to verify their formulations through empirical investigations of male subjects (Carlson & Carlson, 1961; Dan & Beekman, 1972; Weisstein, 1971). She points out that female subjects were excluded from research on a variety of grounds, including the greater variability of female response, the practical difficulties involved in obtaining sufficient numbers of subjects for analysis of sex differences, and the researchers' lack of interest in such differences in areas in which they had been demonstrated to exist (Prescott & Foster, 1974). The most dramatic example of such male bias in psychology is that of achievement motivation research, in which the existence of sex differences has long been recognized (McClelland, Atkinson, Clark, & Lowell, 1953) but ignored. Only recently have (female) researchers begun to explore such differences (Farmer, 1976; Helmreich & Spence, 1978; Mednick, Tangri, Hoffman, 1975). Tellingly, O'Leary writes, "As a traditionally trained social psychologist, I was taught to view sex differences as a nuisance variable to be controlled, not investigated" (p. 3).

Although there are, no doubt, many psychologists who still subscribe to this position, believing the study of women to be of only peripheral interest, knowledge about, and interest in, women has virtually exploded in the last decade. The study of women has attained scientific respectability, as formally recognized by the American Psychological Association's (APA) formation of a Division of the Psychology of Women. Despite such advances, many counselors/therapists have little or no knowledge of the various biological, psychological, and social issues that have such great impact on their women clients. Counselors sampled by Bingham and House (1973) were misinformed on over 50% of the material presented them concerning women and work, and a recent replication (Pope, 1982) showed only minimal change. In this same vein, Birk and Fitzgerald's (1979) survey of APA-approved counseling psychology training programs indicated that only 56% of the respondents offered a course in the psychology of women on an annual basis.

It is difficult to conceive of a counselor/therapist functioning effectively with women clients unless that counselor or therapist has been, in some fashion, trained in the psychology, biology, and sociology of women. Although few of us would still subscribe to the psychoanalytical dictum that biology is destiny, few would deny that biology is basic—that it exerts an enormous effect on women's lives, both as an organismic variable and as a stimulus variable (Unger, 1979). Not only does the natural functioning of biological processes, such as menstruation, pregnancy, parturition, and menopause, affect the experience of every woman; but disruptions in these processes, such as premenstrual syndrome, infertility, miscarriage, and stillbirth, have tremendous physiological, psychological, and social impact. Familiarity with this body of knowledge is prerequisite for therapeutic work with women. The counselor/therapist must also be prepared with knowledge concerning the determinants of sexual differentiation, both genetic and hormonal. Because of the widespread misconceptions concerning the link between hormones and behavior, it is vital that the professional be familiar with research in this area. Similarly, Money and Ehrhardt (1972) provide data helpful to the understanding of the acquisition of gender identity. And, the therapist should understand the menstrual cycle and the climacterium. Finally, it should be noted that natural processes, such as aging and illness, as well as conditions of physiological and emotional disability have particular impact on women in a society that values them most highly for their conformity to a youthful, physically perfect, and sexually appealing stereotype. Knowledge of the physiological and psychological correlates of disability is essential to working with handicapped women (Dailey, 1979, 1982).

Maccoby and Jacklin (1974) review the literature on psychological sex differences and note four such differences that appear to be reliable— differences in verbal ability, visual-spatial ability, mathematical performance, and aggression. Work in this area of differential psychology is proceeding very rapidly, requiring that counselors and therapists stay abreast of current research. Other psychological factors—such as possible differences in achievement motivation (Helmreich & Spence, 1978), sex-role bias in various theories of personality development (Williams, 1977), and the emerging career psychology of women (Fitzgerald & Betz, 1983; Fitzgerald & Crites, 1980; Hansen & Rapoza, 1978)—are an indispensable component of the knowledge base for counseling women. Similarly, Gilligan (1982), in a landmark volume, demonstrates that previous theories of moral development, based exclusively on studies of male subjects, have resulted in formulations in which women are usually characterized as morally unevolved, and their thinking as an irrational, illogical, and underdeveloped form of thought. Her work forms the basis for a new formulation concerning the dimensions of moral thought that appears to characterize more accurately and completely the development of women.

Familiarity with these and similar findings provides a richer and more balanced context within which counselors and therapists may comprehend more accurately the experience of their women clients.

Sociological issues are also of great importance here. Even if some underlying biological predisposition for sex-typed behavior were to be established, the role of socialization and role prescription would retain its enormous significance in women's lives. Familiarity with the work of sociologists (Skolnick & Skolnick, 1971) and social psychologists (O'Leary, 1977) is necessary for an understanding of the social context of women's behavior.

Finally, it should be pointed out that, above all, counselors and therapists deal with problems—emotional, psychological, and social problems—as well as with the developmental issues of everyday living. Whatever the final biological and/or environmental underpinnings of such problems may turn out to be, it is clear that certain of them are more common to the experience of women (e.g., eating disorders, depression, agoraphobia). Similarly, women more often experience certain "shaping" conditions (e.g., incest) that may predispose them to certain kinds of psychological vulnerability. It is critical for counselors/therapists to know these pathologic/pathogenic areas, as well as the normal areas of differences, if they are to function effectively with female clients.

Principle I requires that counselors/therapists be knowledgeable about women, particularly in the biological, psychological, and social areas outlined above. Such knowledge presupposes, at a minimum, formal coursework in these areas, preferably supplemented by advanced seminars, continuing education courses, and so forth. Further, training programs are encouraged to include modules in core courses (e.g., developmental psychology, personality theory, career psychology) relating their content to women's issues.

**PRINCIPLE II. Counselors/therapists are aware that the assumptions and precepts of theories relevant to their practice may apply differently to men and women. Counselors/therapists are aware of those theories and models that prescribe or limit the potential of women clients, as well as those that may have particular usefulness for women clients.**

Psychological theory, developed and investigated largely through the study of men, has often had little to offer that is useful for predicting and explaining the behavior of women. One of the major reasons for this has been the assumption, largely implicit, of an androcentric (male-centered) model of behavior (Rawlings & Carter, 1977). That is, theories have been constructed that have attempted to explain human behavior largely in terms of masculine behavior. Female behavior patterns have been (1) assumed to be similar; (2) assumed to be the opposite (Broverman, Broverman, Clarkson, Rosenkrantz, & Vogel, 1970); or (3) more generally, simply ignored.

Fitzgerald and Crites (1980) note that it has become commonplace among career psychologists to suggest that current theories of career choice cannot adequately explain the vocational behavior of women. Osipow (1975) suggested that career development theory is based on several implicit assumptions (e.g., a choice supply, motivation to choose) that women, as a group, often cannot meet. Thus is the explanatory power of the theories attenuated for women. For example,

> the developmental stages of exploration and specification postulated by Super (Super, Starishevsky, Matlin, & Jordaan, 1963) may not accurately describe women's development, suggesting that female adolescent exploration may well be pseudo-exploration pending marriage plans . . . more significant exploration may actually occur later, when the major duties of child rearing have been completed. Thus, the establishment and maintenance stages are correspondingly delayed. (Fitzgerald & Crites, 1980, p. 46)

Osipow (1975) further points out that the concept of occupational environments is problematic for predicting women's behavior, as the Realistic environment of Holland's (1973) classification has been essentially closed to them. And, the idea of personality types is similarly problematic, as sex-role prescriptions inhibit the implementation of a full range of role types of women. Thus, the assumptions and precepts of these theories clearly apply differently to men and women.

In addition, it is obvious that some theories and models have a clearly limiting effect on women's options. "Shields (1975) and other historians have suggested that psychology and science in general have replaced religion as the justifier of women's inferior position in society" (Grady, 1979, p. 172). She notes that the most damaging assertions are in the area of personality: "It is in the field of personality that women are labeled 'field dependent' or [as] having an 'external locus of control' and the inferior position of women is subtly supported" (Grady, 1979, p. 176). In general, however, feminist psychologists agree that it is classical psychoanalytic personality theory and some of its offshoots (e.g., Deutsch, 1944, 1945; Erikson, 1964, 1975) that have been most damaging to women. With its strong androcentric bias and focus on biological determinism, this model has become a symbol of everything women have found wrong with psychology—as well as of everything that psychology has found wrong with women.

Vaughter (1976) suggests that our theoretical models be analyzed from a social-political perspective and notes certain theoretical positions that may be helpful in explaining women's behavior.

> Though the inadequacies of naive behaviorism are apparent (Sutherland, 1974), behavioristic models do encourage us to assume that woman is sane, not crazy; that she is bright and reasonable, not hysterical; and that ill-advised behavior patterns may not be ill advised at all, given the nature of the environment in which her behaviors take place. (p. 132)

Vaughter continues her analysis by suggesting that ethological approaches can enhance our understanding of the development of women's behavior patterns. In this vein, probably the most obvious example is that provided by the experiences of battered women. Whereas traditional models address the (to some) inexplicable behavior of such women (self-reproach, assumption of responsibility for the battering, and staying in the battering relationship) in terms of the women's personality dynamics (e.g., masochism), an ethological analysis outlines the *context* of the behavior, both proximate and in the larger society, and comes to entirely different conclusions.

Theories based on biological determinism have been criticized repeatedly by feminist and nonfeminist writers alike. In this context, it seems important to point out the subtle, but critical, distinction between those formulations dictating that behavior is biologically *determined* and those suggesting that it may be biologically *influenced.* The ways in which biology influences women's behavior are extensively discussed under Principle I; review of this material suggests that it would be naive to state that biology has no impact on women's lives. There is, however, a great difference between suggesting that biology *influences* women's behavior and stating that it *determines* such behavior.

Additionally, although there is obviously nothing inherently negative or repressive in the suggestion of a partial biological basis for behavior, such notions can certainly be used inappropriately and have often been applied unthinkingly. It seems reasonable to suggest that, rather than shy away from such theories, effort be put into accurately elaborating their applicability to women.

In addition to social learning theory, ethological analysis, and recapitulation of biological approaches, script analysis (Steiner, 1972; Wyckoff, 1977)—which has developed out of the radical psychiatry movement—also provides a helpful framework for describing, predicting, and altering what Vaughter labeled "ill-advised behavior patterns." Finally, feminist analysis and therapy (Brodsky, 1977; Brodsky & Hare-Mustin, 1980; Gilbert, 1980; Rawlings & Carter, 1977) is the example of *par excellence* of a psychological model that has particular usefulness for women clients.

Specific suggestions for implementation of Principle II are difficult to formulate; compliance with its spirit requires an awareness that is difficult to operationalize. Until research provides us with a firmer base, counselors/therapists are reminded

> 1. The great body of psychological theory is constructed on an androcentric model, with a concomitant masculine bias. This is particularly true of personality theory. It is necessary to examine continually our theoretical bases to identify androcentric assumptions that are, at best, unhelpful, and more usually, damaging.
>
> 2. Certain theoretical models are, by their nature, facilitative of women's growth. In general, those models that emphasize the influence of social learning are to be preferred to those that are committed to biological determinism. However,

Principle II encourages, above all, critical thinking and attempts at understanding the meaning of all existing theories for women, including those that have not dealt with women in full or helpful ways in the past.

## PRINCIPLE III. After formal training, counselors/therapists continue to explore and learn of issues related to women, including the special problems of female subgroups, throughout their professional careers.

Research has thoroughly documented the role that counselors/therapists have played in the imposition and perpetuation of sex-role stereotypes (Abramowitz, Abramowitz, Jackson, & Gomes, 1973; Broverman et al., 1970; Chesler, 1972; Fabrikant, 1974; Maslin & Davis, 1975; Neulinger, 1968; Steinmann, 1975). Arguably, much, if not most, of this research has investigated the attitudes and behavior of counselors/therapists trained before the advent of the women's movement. Thus, their training and professional socialization were not informed by recent developments in the psychology of women, nor did they (and their clients) benefit from the more liberal attitudes stimulated by these developments. Such an argument would suggest that therapeutic repression of women is a phenomenon of the past, not to be found among younger practitioners.

It is true that the classic studies of counselor bias investigated, for the most part, a population trained before the advent of modern psychology of women, although it should be pointed out that the research of Maslin and Davis (1975)—among others—studied counselors who were in training in the mid-1970s. Still, it is likely that current graduate students in counseling and clinical psychology are receiving better training for working with women than did their predecessors. Although Birk and Fitzgerald (1979) found that only 56% of those responding to their informal survey of APA-approved counseling psychology training programs were offering a yearly course in the psychology of women in 1979, it seems reasonable to assume that this represents an almost 100% increase over, say, 1969.

However, given that current students are indeed receiving better training in this area than before, at least two issues remain to be addressed: First, what is the responsibility of professionals who completed their training without exposure to current theory and research in the psychology and counseling/psychotherapy of women; and second, what is the responsibility of any professional—whenever and however trained—for incorporating the almost explosive expansion of knowledge currently taking place in this area?

It seems almost unnecessary to observe that the more senior counselors/therapists have the same responsibility for equipping themselves with basic theory, knowledge, and skills for working with women as do current trainees. To do otherwise would appear to be in violation of ethical codes and licensing laws that require that one not practice outside one's area of competence. Postgraduate courses in the psychology and counseling of women, seminars, and continuing education workshops are currently widely available. Division 35 of the APA and the journal, *Psychology of Women Quarterly,* are completely devoted to the study and counseling of women, as is the Association of Women in Psychology (AWP) and its annual conference. The Committee on Women of the Division of Counseling Psychology is actively developing training guidelines, synthesizing various knowledge bases, and creating and documenting resource materials for counseling women. Other APA and AACD (American Association for Counseling and Development) divisions have also developed similar groups concerned with these issues. For example, Division 12 (Clinical Psychology) of the APA has a Committee on Equal Opportunity and Affirmative Action, as well as a section on Clinical Psychology of Women; and Division 29 (Psychotherapy) has developed a Committee on Women. Thus, senior counselors and therapists should have little difficulty meeting their training needs in this area.

In a similar vein, it is incumbent upon all mental health professionals to keep abreast of the rapidly expanding knowledge concerning women. Recent research concerning sex differences, brain lateralization, female occupational stress, and sex restrictiveness in interest inventories are only some of the more obvious examples. In particular, work concerning the special needs and problems of diverse subgroups of the female population is proceeding quite rapidly. For example, knowledge concerning gay women (Escamilla-Mandanaro, 1977), female prison inmates (Giallombardo, 1966; Heffernan, 1972), and female members of racial minorities (Helms, 1979; Lerner, 1973) is becoming increasingly available. Again, there is no lack of training and resource materials for the counselor who wishes to stay abreast of current developments affecting his or her practice with women. Counselors and therapists can grow in understanding of self and others through facilitating or participating in sex-role awareness groups or specific program groups (e.g. returning women's groups) and so forth.

In summary, review of the above discussion suggests the following guidelines for complying with Principle III:

> 1. Counselors/therapists whose training did not include basic material concerning women (outlined in Principle I) should equip themselves appropriately for working with women through postgraduate study, continuing education courses and workshops, and acquaintance with the various professional groups and materials devoted to the psychology and counseling of women.
>
> 2. Similarly, all counselors/therapists should continue to keep abreast of developments in this rapidly expanding area of knowledge. Effective practice with female clients requires continuing education for all practitioners.

**PRINCIPLE IV. Counselors/therapists recognize and are aware of all forms of oppression and how these interact with sexism.**

Prejudice has been defined as

> an antipathy based upon a faulty and inflexible generalization. It may be felt or expressed. It may be directed toward a group as a whole, or toward an individual because he [sic] is a member of that group. . . . The net effect of prejudice, thus defined, is to place the object of prejudice at some disadvantage not merited by his own misconduct. (Allport, 1954)

Various forms of prejudice, with their consequent oppression, operate more or less openly in Western society, and in fact, have been—at least until quite recently—institutionalized in many of the legal statutes of this country. Probably the most obvious example is that of racial prejudice; however, prejudice against the so-called lower classes, the elderly, and homosexual persons is also widespread.

Race and social class intertwine with sex to form an interlocking structure that is particularly oppressive to minority group women. Socialized from birth into a society that devalues females and severely limits their choice of roles and rewards, no woman remains untouched by sexism. However, the oppression experienced by Third World (i.e., minority) women and lower-class women is compounded by the force of racism and classism. The life experiences of minority women and poor women have largely been omitted from formulations of the psychology of women, as well as from traditional psychology (Griscom, 1979). The theories that are only now being constructed about female psychology are often, ironically, as irrelevant to the description and explanation of the experience and behavior of black, Chicano, poor, elderly, and gay women as were the androcentric formulations of mainstream psychology to the behavior of white, middle-class women a decade ago. Frieze, Parsons, Johnson, Ruble, and Zellman (1978) point out the differences between the black and white female experience. They note that the women's liberation movement has been largely a white, middle-class phenomenon and that black women have generally not played a prominent role. Suggesting that black women may feel that they must take a supportive role vis-à-vis black men who have been psychologically scarred by racism (Hare & Hare, 1970), they indicate that the whole issue of differential treatment on the basis of sex may be of less concern to black women. Some data suggest that black women may not be as discriminated against on the basis of sex as are white women, that they are less likely to derogate other women, and are more self-confident than their white counterparts (Frieze et al., 1978). Ironically, however, black women suffer more economically from a system that incorporates both sexism and racism. And, in fact, they earn, on the average, less than any other group with the same education. It would appear that work with black women, and other Third World female clients, requires different knowledge, skills, and abilities than does work with female clients in general. For example, counselors/therapists would need familiarity with the ways in which racial attitudes and political or institutional policies have restricted the lives of minority persons; an awareness of myths and stereotypes of Third World women to understand their harmful impact on clients; sensitivity to and acceptance of nontraditional (and possibly nonfeminist) cultural values; special knowledge of subgroups (e.g., the high rate of suicide among black female adolescents); a willingness to examine their own racial attitudes; and finally, flexible basic counseling skills that are sensitive to individual differences while taking into account discrimination based on group membership (Helms, 1979; McDavis, 1978). Additionally, it is important to recognize the strengths of minority women (e.g., self-reliance and independence) that can be utilized effectively in counseling (Ford, 1978).

Lower-class women, like minority women, traditionally have been thought neither to need nor to be able to profit from counseling and psychotherapy. Untrained to address the unique needs of the lower classes, mental health professionals have often abandoned poor women to the least trained professionals, frequently substituting medication for psychotherapy. Poverty narrows not only the realistic choices available to many women, but also limits their sense of control over their lives; insensitivity to a woman's struggle to manage multiple life stresses related to insufficient resources can reduce the effectiveness of therapeutic interventions. Still, it is important to remember that although economic and social problems may be a priority for lower-income women, mental health problems, for which counseling or psychotherapy *is* appropriate, afflict poor no less than middle-class women (Siassi, 1974).

Prejudice against lesbian women has been particularly virulent, possibly because it is these women who are seen as being the most deviant in terms of traditional female role prescriptions. Lesbian mothers have repeatedly had to defend their fitness for motherhood. In Seattle, one lesbian couple won custody of their children, but were forced to establish separate residences; whereas in Santa Cruz, a lesbian mother maintained custody of her children only under the condition that she live separately from her lover (Rawlings & Carter, 1977). In addition, lesbian women have unique problems relating to the lack of sufficient support systems. Fear of being labeled "gay," and the resulting social ostracism, operates to isolate lesbian women from one another. Further, such social isolation often results in the continuation of incompatible or destructive relationships, because of fear of loneliness, lack of comfort and support (Zaller, 1982). Although there is a rapidly growing network of gay counselors/therapists, which is becoming increasingly active in professional organizations and affairs, and whose members possess the particular skills and expertise to work with lesbian women, it is incumbent upon all counselors/therapists who work with female clients to acquaint themselves with this most critical area.

Finally, Frieze et al. (1978) point out that "statistics on psychological disorders consistently show that women over 40 have a higher incidence of disorders than men of the same age or younger women. Among the many possible reasons for this disparity, two seem crucial: loss of self-esteem due to the physical effects of aging, and role loss associated with children's departure from the home" (p. 268). These authors suggest resources and strategies for counselors/therapists who work with women facing the aging process in our youth-oriented society. For example, many writers have suggested that the negative consequences of children leaving home have been overemphasized, pointing out that this can be a time of freedom, relief, peace, and a time to do things for oneself.

In reviewing the discussion above, it would appear that the prerequisites for effective counseling with women are complicated almost to the point of being unmanageable. However, the complexity of the issue must not be taken as grounds for avoiding it. As a beginning, it is important to note that no one person, obviously, can be expert in all areas. Rather, compliance with this Principle requires an acquaintance with and sensitivity to the various issues raised, and a willingness to refer appropriately to those with special expertise in the appropriate area.

### PRINCIPLE V. Counselors/therapists are knowledgeable and aware of verbal and nonverbal process variables (particularly with regard to power in the relationship) as these affect women in counseling/therapy so that the counselor/therapist interactions are not adversely affected. The need for shared responsibility between clients and counselors/therapists is acknowledged and implemented.

Counseling/psychotherapy traditionally has implied an unequal power relationship between the therapist and the client. Although the degree of this power differential varies, depending on the theoretical orientation of the counselor, only feminist therapy (Rawlings & Carter, 1977) and radical psychiatry approaches (Steiner, 1972; Wyckoff, 1977) specifically abjure this differential as being destructive to the client.

The unequal distribution of power in the counseling relationship has been recognized and discussed by many writers, many of whom see such a distribution as inherent in the process, and not necessarily unfortunate. Strong (1968), for example, sees counseling as a process of interpersonal influence and discusses the three counselor power bases of expertness, attractiveness, and trustworthiness that facilitate counselor influence attempts. The APA explicitly recognizes the client-counselor power inequality when it states in its ethical code, "Psychologists are continually cognizant of their own needs and of *their inherently powerful position vis-à-vis clients* [emphasis added] in order to avoid exploiting their trust and dependency" (APA, 1981). Halleck (1971), in his analysis of the politics of psychotherapy, discussed the significance of power in the therapeutic relationship, particularly with respect to symptomatology, therapeutic intervention, and societal focus.

It is probably true that all therapeutic encounters are inherently and unavoidably characterized by the power inequality described above. The counselor/therapist in his or her role as expert caregiver can probably not avoid being seen by the client—who has come to the encounter because of a perceived need for assistance—as a potent, powerful individual. Even feminist and radical therapists, with their explicit disclaimer of the power role, and a strong commitment to joint client-counselor responsibility, can probably not avoid such client perceptions, at least in the early stages of the process. Thus, sensitivity to the issue and use of power and influence variables is necessary for the counselor who does not wish to exploit client trust.

This issue is all the more salient for women clients. Chesler (1972) has stated, "For women, the psychotherapeutic encounter is just one more instance of an unequal relationship, just one more opportunity to be rewarded for expressing distress and to be helped by being expertly dominated" (p. 373). Symonds (1973) discusses the psychology of submission, which affects women's sense of adequacy and immobilizes them. The typical patriarchal model encourages women to be helpless and dependent; counselors/therapists must ensure that they do not reinforce and perpetuate such dynamics through their interventions.

This is particularly true when the counselor/therapist is a male. The power differential between counselor and client is paralleled by the corresponding male/female power differential. When both sets of dynamics are operative, as they are when a woman is being seen by a male counselor/therapist, the power inequality is exacerbated.

Frieze et al. (1978) discuss how dominance and status are communicated nonverbally. They note that nonverbal channels of communication are of major importance for perceiving emotion (Auger, 1969), and conclude that the two major types of nonverbal messages are those indicating dominance or status, and those communicating warmth and expressiveness. They state that men are generally more dominant and display higher status on a nonverbal level, whereas women show more liking and warmth. They then proceed to discuss the role of such indicators as dress, use of space, body position and gesture, touching, eye contact, and smiling in sending dominance messages. Even a cursory reading of their analysis leads to the conclusion that many of the nonverbal variables that characterize male dominance behaviors also characterize therapist status behaviors.

Although it is difficult, and some would say undesirable, to eliminate all power differential in the counseling relationship, counselors/therapists can and should ensure that their power is used in therapeutic ways for their clients' benefit, and not to maintain stereotypic dependency behaviors. A good beginning for ensuring shared responsibility between counselors/therapists and clients can be found in Rawlings and Carter (1977). In discussing client safeguards against the misuse of influence by therapists, they note the parallels between feminist therapy and Argyris's (1975) model of reciprocal influence. Such strategies as contract setting, explication of counselor values, encouraging autonomy, nonuse of diagnostic labels, and cautious use of diagnostic testing are not unique to feminist therapy; however, they take on a powerful role in equalizing the power differential when used in this context, whereas the use of videotape emerges as a powerful training tool for assisting counselors and therapists to identify and modify nonverbal behaviors. Counselors/therapists are referred to Rawlings and Carter (1977) for a complete discussion of these and other strategies for ensuring joint counselor/client responsibility for change.

Finally, it is important to educate the client concerning her rights and responsibilities in the therapy relationship, either through discussion or the use of written materials. The Association for Women in Psychology and Division 35 of the APA have developed a booklet that provides an excellent example of such material.

**PRINCIPLE VI. Counselors/therapists have the capability of utilizing skills that are particularly facilitative to women in general and to particular subgroups of women.**

Given that the nature of women's existential position leads to the exacerbation and complication of the wide range of concerns brought to the counseling process, as well as to many problems unique to their sex, it seems reasonable to propose that counselors/therapists need to review and add to their skills in order to better facilitate the growth of their women clients. Although it is probably true that there are few, if any, skills and techniques that are *uniquely* necessary for working with women, it is also true that there *are* specific techniques that have been developed in response to women's problems, and that are critically necessary and particularly facilitative for such work.

One of the most well-known of these techniques is assertion training. Although criticized by some as a focus on technique rather than on attitude change (Collier, 1982), assertiveness training has emerged as a preeminent method for assisting women to deal with a wide variety of life problems. In the context of his theory of learned helplessness, Seligman (1973) draws a connection between lack of assertiveness and women's depression. He suggests that because women are socialized to be more passive and dependent than are men, they are more likely to learn to depend on others to take care of them, and therefore, do not acquire a wide repertoire of coping skills. According to Seligman's theory, this would explain why women are more likely than men to become depressed. It also suggests that assertion training would be a powerful treatment for the depression, as well as a preventative of depression (Jakubowski-Spector, 1973). Case studies have been reported that provide suggestive evidence that assertion training can be helpful in treating depression (Bean, 1970; Cameron, 1951; Fensterheim, 1972; Katz, 1971; Lazarus & Serber, 1968; Stevenson & Wolpe, 1960). In addition, it is reasonable to suggest that such training would produce positive effects in treatment of role conflict, dual-career problems, and issues of discrimination, sexual harassment, and response to similar sexist behaviors of others.

A second technique that seems quite promising is the sex-role analysis (Brodsky, 1977). This technique consists of a structured comparison of the positive and negative consequences of traditional and nontraditional sex-role behaviors. It can be used with groups as well as with individual clients, and can be made as individualized or generic as the situation calls for. Such analysis can identify (unconscious) sex-role expectations, bringing these expectations into awareness for client exploration. As women clients become aware of sex-role constrictions in their behavior, they discover strengths in themselves that had previously been unknown, or regarded negatively. Rawlings and Carter (1977) also suggest that this technique can lessen the feelings of discouragement and depression that are sometimes experienced in the initial stages of therapy through inducing a change of frame in which responsibility for the woman's failure to act in desired ways is partially shifted to societal conditions, thus allowing her a rationale that does not threaten self-esteem. In addition, sex-role analysis explores the consequences of nontraditional behavior and explains why it is sometimes unacceptable to others.

A third technique that has had promising results with women is the use of consciousness-raising groups (Brodsky, 1977). Although traditionally leaderless groups, and thus not amenable to counselor/therapist facilitation, these groups constitute powerful referral resources and therapeutic adjuncts. They are particularly suited to the exploration of personal identity issues and the heightening of self-awareness that results from the comparing of personal experiences. Consciousness-raising groups help to develop awareness of shared frustrations, anger, and self-doubt, and the structure of the group provides peer support for the process of growth. The process of modeling (Bandura, 1965, 1969) assists group members to learn new roles and behaviors from other members.

There are many other techniques and processes particularly suited to working with women clients. Wyckoff (1977) describes the application of script analysis to solving women's problems; Zaller (1982) suggests the unique suitability of Gestalt techniques for women. Dewey (1974) proposes the Nonsexist Vocational Card Sort as an alternative to traditional interest inventories; whereas Fitzgerald and Crites (1980) and Harmon (1977) point to the positive benefits of career counseling for women. And, these are only a few.

## PRINCIPLE VII. Counselors/therapists ascribe no preconceived limitations on the direction or nature of potential changes or goals in counseling/therapy for women.

Role possibilities for women traditionally have been defined in terms of what is considered appropriate for a female. In effect, choices in life-styles and career opportunities have been constrained, because the only acceptable female roles were those of wife and mother (Weisstein, 1977). Psychological theories that have formed the base for counseling and psychotherapy have incorporated and institutionalized such role definitions and set them as the criteria against which female mental health was evaluated, as well as postulating them as the (only) desirable outcomes of the counseling process. Classical psychoanalytic theory is the most obvious example, but there are others. For example, Bettleheim (1965) proposed that, other considerations aside, women "want first and foremost to be womanly companions of men and to be mothers," whereas neo-Freudian psychologist Erik Erikson (1964, 1975), in discussing women's "inner space," stated that women had a biological, psychological, and ethical commitment to take care of human infancy. Erikson (1981) has recently softened this position somewhat, noting that issues of identity are affected by changing cultural norms and that women have a "right to postpone both marriage and motherhood and first care for things men have traditionally cared for—productivity in business, and creativity, from art to politics" (p. 255). This statement, however, still carries the notion of the eventual inevitability of the traditional role functions. Thus does the sociological status quo become reified into the psychological ideal.

During the last two decades, critics of the mental health professions began to suggest that these professions were functioning as agents of social control by relying on an adjustment model of mental health that requires acceptance of biologically based traditional roles and behaviors as the criterion for psychological and emotional well-being. Evidence began to accumulate indicating strongly that when traditional role behavior was used as a *predictor* of mental health, rather than as a *criterion* of mental health, the correlation was strongly and consistently negative. Such data as Rice and Rice's (1973) finding that femininity in females is associated with poor adjustment and Bernard's (1971) famous study of marriage, which found married women to be less well-adjusted than single women on a variety of indicators, suggested that female clients might be well served by counselors/therapists who assist them to exercise more freedom in choosing satisfying roles. Yet, studies—such as those by Broverman et al. (1970), Maslin and Davis (1975), and others—indicate that therapists have often demonstrated a "double standard" of mental health, which operates to stigmatize women who deviate from the feminine stereotype.

Similarly, the literature in career psychology has consistently shown that when women do work outside the home (and most of them do, or will, at some point), they are overwhelmingly overrepresented in the lower-level "traditionally female" occupations, in which the job duties and tasks parallel the helping, nurturing, and serving aspects of the traditional female sex role (Fitzgerald & Betz, 1983; Fitzgerald & Crites, 1980). Moreover, it has been demonstrated repeatedly that career counselors encourage and approve such gender-appropriate occupational involvement and negatively evaluate clients who wish to pursue nontraditional occupations (Bingham & House, 1973; Fitzgerald & Cherpas, 1985; Pope, 1982; Thomas & Stewart, 1971) despite a veritable explosion of materials designed to educate counselors concerning vocational counseling for women (e.g., Farmer & Backer, 1977; Hansen & Rapoza, 1978). Such data suggest that counselors/therapists have often set preconceived limits on the direction or nature of therapeutic and counseling goals for women, such limits being defined by the traditional dimensions of the female gender role. It is to such a priori limitations that this principle speaks.

It is important to note that counselors'/therapists' insistence on *nontraditional* goals or changes for all women clients is equally in violation of this principle. For example, Harmon (1977) notes that, traditionally, career counseling has dealt mainly with the gratification of higher-level psychological needs of the individual, and that many women may not be prepared for such career counseling. Counselor insistence on career goals that hold the promise of self-actualization may be very threatening to traditional women who have yet to meet their lower-order needs for safety and self-esteem (Maslow, 1970) or to work through adequately the conflict posed by combining work and family roles. Clearly, "no preconceived limitations" means just that and is applicable whether those limitations are conservative or radical in nature. The critical consideration is acknowledgement of a respect for individual differences and client responsibility for choice. In that spirit, counselors/therapists are reminded:

1. Marriage, singleness, parenting, or choosing to remain child free, and/or gay relationships are all viable life choices. They are each capable of being healthy and growth-producing conditions, or being damaging and exploitative, depending on the characteristics and dynamics of each situation. Counselors/therapists encourage their clients to explore themselves, their values, and their options.

2. Realistic career choice consists of obtaining the best possible match between a woman's abilities, interests, and values, and those which are required and rewarded by the occupation. Many women require a great deal of encouragement and permission to explore beyond the traditional boundaries, even when interest and aptitude data indicate that this is appropriate.

3. Differential psychology, as one of the traditional foundations of counseling psychology, carries a philosophical commitment to the value of individual differences, on which Principle VII is based.

### PRINCIPLE VIII. Counselors/therapists are sensitive to circumstances where it is more desirable for a woman client to be seen by a female or male counselor/therapist.

Many writers have suggested that it is advisable for women clients to be seen, not by the traditionally male counselor or therapist, but rather by a female who presumably possesses heightened sensitivity to a woman's experiences (Chesler, 1972; Rice & Rice, 1973). For example, Radov et al. (1977) write that in the current climate of social change, "it is especially necessary for women to have therapists who are sensitive to issues highlighted by the women's liberation movement" (p. 508). Rice and Rice (1973) note

Advantages of pairing a female therapist with a female patient struggling with conflictual role demands in a changing society include a greater sensitivity to issues and an ability to empathize with feelings; the provision of a role identification model; and the offer of potentially important solutions that may stem from the therapists's own personal experience. (p. 195)

Thomas (1982) indicates that women are more likely to seek female therapists during crises such as rape, pregnancy, or domestic violence.

These prescriptions of female counselors for female clients contain two assumptions: first, that female counselors are likely to be more effective with female clients, presumably because they will be more sympathetic to women's concerns; and second, that female clients *prefer* female counselors, which preference is further assumed to have impact on the progress of the subsequent therapeutic relationship. These assumptions have gone largely unexamined and, despite their logical appeal, may not be completely well founded. Orlinsky and Howard (1966, 1980) in a reanalysis of their original process study (Howard, Orlinsky, & Hill, 1970) found that female therapists were, overall, more effective with female clients than were male therapists, particularly with schizophrenic women or women with an anxiety reaction. Female therapists were also found to be more effective with every type of woman client (e.g., single, married, mothers) except one—the male therapists were more effective with female single parents. However, when therapist experience was examined, highly experienced male therapists were as effective as the female therapists, demonstrating that male therapists can learn to work effectively with women. Therefore, the general assumption that a female counselor is de facto more effective with women clients than is her male colleague is not always justified. In particular, research concerning sex bias in psychotherapy suggests that at least some female therapists share with their male colleagues a separate standard of mental health for female clients (Abramowitz et al., 1973; Broverman et al., 1970). Likewise, bias in career counseling has been demonstrated in female as well as male counselors (Scholssberg & Pietrofessa, 1973; Thomas & Stewart, 1971). Such studies present strong evidence against equating "female" with "feminist" or even "nonsexist," despite the commonsense appeal of such an equation. Frieze (1975) has pointed out, in another context, that women are often mistakenly treated as a homogeneous group. This process is probably responsible for the fallacy inherent in the present case. It should, however, be obvious that femaleness is neither a necessary nor a sufficient qualification for feminism.

Research on female client preference for male and female counselors is sparse and inconclusive (Tanney & Birk, 1973). Although some studies have found that women prefer same-sex therapists (Howard et al., 1970; Koile & Bird, 1956), others have reported that women prefer male counselors (Fuller, 1964; Mezzans, 1971), whereas still others report no gender effect (Heppner & Pew, 1977). Other variables, such as type of problems, counselor age, race, and level of experience, no doubt overdetermine or interact with counselor gender in studies of counselor preference. For example, Fuller (1964) found that female college clients with personal-social problems expressed a preference for female counselors. Similarly, Brodsky (1977) writes that retrospective reports indicate that there are two answers to the question, "Should women clients see male therapists?"

> 1. "No," for young, single women, uncertain as to their direction in life, or in their relationships with men, or both; and
>
> 2. "Yes," if the client is older or married. *We do not, however, know what other factors, yet to be studied, may also have a bearing on the answer.* (p. 335; emphasis added)

These prescriptions receive support from Orlinsky and Howard (1980), who write, "Those women who most clearly benefited from having a female therapist were the single women and the young, single women" (p. 27).

It appears that at the present time, research is not completely adequate as a base for recommendations concerning the advisability of women clients seeing male or female therapists. Yet, such recommendations must be made, and indeed, are being made every day. On what basis, then, should this be done?

Principle VIII requires that counselors/therapists be sensitive to circumstances in which it is more desirable for a woman client to be seen by a female or male counselor/therapist. As a beginning, it seems reasonable to suspect that the sex of the therapist may take on added salience in working with special subgroups of female clients. For instance, the victims of rape, incest, and domestic violence may respond in a more trusting and open manner to women therapists than to males. Similarly, women with sexual concerns and those seeking abortion counseling may feel more comfortable working with female counselors.

Highly vulnerable in the one-down power relationship between the sexes that is exemplified by the traditional male therapist-female client dyad, submissive female clients may benefit greatly from working with a woman therapist who effectively models assertiveness and appropriately shares responsibility for the counseling process with the client. The use of a male cotherapist in marital counseling may be effective in modeling an egalitarian male-female relationship for the couple and a wide range of affect for both partners. Finally, it is likely that issues of job discrimination and sexual harassment would warrant working with a female therapist.

Until research provides the basis for formulating more than the most tentative of guidelines, counselors and therapists are reminded

> 1. There appears to be no firm basis for assuming a priori that all female counselors/therapists are more effective and less sex-biased than their male counterparts when working with female clients.
>
> 2. The research on client preference for a same- or opposite-sex counselor is inconclusive. Open discussion with the client regarding her preferences, combined with professional judgement, appears to be the most appropriate course at present.

3. It is assumed that the sex of the counselor becomes particularly salient in certain situations. Rape, incest, abortion counseling, domestic violence, and other, mostly sexual, concerns are assumed, at present, to be more appropriately assigned to a female therapist. Similarly, young, single women are likely to benefit most from treatment by a female counselor.

## PRINCIPLE IX. Counselors/therapists use nonsexist language in counseling/therapy, supervision, teaching, and journal publication.

Contemporary linguistic theory points out that the language one speaks not only *reflects* one's view of the world, but also *determines* one's view of it (Bolinger, 1968). As Cormican (1977) states

> Whatever a particular culture considers to be the "real world" is really constructed, unconsciously for the most part, by the language spoken in that culture (Barnouw, 1963). The language one speaks, then, will both inculcate and reflect the cultural belief about, among other things, women and men. (p. 1)

Feminists have asserted that the use of male terms as generic or gender neutral reflects bias against women. In the last century, Elizabeth Cady Stanton (1895) recognized the relationship between language and sexism and criticized the use of *he, his,* and *man* in the Bible. More recently, Christ (1980) notes that although sophisticated religious thinkers "would deny that they think of God as an old white man in the sky, the unconscious association of deity with maleness is perpetuated by language and symbol" (p. 117). In an empirical investigation of the hypothesis that the generic masculine is gender neutral, Moulton, Robinson, and Elias (1978) demonstrated that the use of male terms in a generic sense induces people to think of males, even in contexts that are specifically gender neutral. In other words, when the generic masculine was used, Moulton et al.'s subjects thought of males. Persons who are unimpressed by the logic or evidence in this argument, who maintain that attention to language is a trivial matter and that the generic use of masculine terminology is indeed gender neutral, are invited to test this hypothesis by suggesting that the use of the generic *feminine* is equally gender neutral.

The *Publication Manual of the American Psychological Association* (1974) first addressed this issue in its second edition by suggesting that journal authors "be aware of the current move to avoid generic use of male nouns and pronouns when content refers to both sexes" (p. 28). This position was strengthened and elaborated in 1977 through the publication of "Guidelines for Nonsexist Language in APA Journals" (APA, 1977) and again in 1983 with the third edition of the *Publication Manual of the American Psychological Association* (APA, 1983), which require that authors exercise care in choosing nouns, pronouns, and adjectives that minimize or eliminate ambiguity in sex role or sex identity and that writing be free of implied or irrelevant evaluation of the sexes.

Commitment to nonsexist language, however, requires more than the elimination of generic masculine forms. This usage, which Graham (1975) labels as *exclusion,* has been merely the most obvious form of linguistic sexism, not the only one. In an extensive analysis of this phenomenon, Graham identifies a number of socialization mechanisms that operate to linguistically distort gender-specific words:

> 1. Labeling the supposed "exception to the rule" (e.g., woman doctor, male nurse, lady lawyer). Unger (1979) notes that the term "feminine logic" is a particularly sexist example of this usage.
>
> 2. Trivializing female gender forms (e.g., poetess, suffragette, and—lately— libber).

Unger (1979) points out that terminology referring to women resembles that referring to children to a surprising extent. For example,

> excluding any negative connotations, words like doll, honey, pussycat, and baby can apply equally well to women or children (particularly girl children). Our language, like our culture, equates adulthood with manhood (Graham, 1975). There is a clear demarcation between the words boy and man that does not exist between girl and woman. (Unger, 1979, p. 41)

Greer (1970) has noted a parallel similarity between the terminology referring to women and that referring to food, suggesting that the use of words such as honey, tomato, sugar, cupcake, and so forth perpetuate the stereotyping of women as consumable objects.

The third form of sexist language to which this principle calls attention is that often found in the resource materials related to counseling women. In particular, career information is often not sex-fair, perpetuating through exclusion and other stereotyping mechanisms the notions that some careers are, or are not, appropriate for women (Fitzgerald & Crites, 1980). Although some progress is being made in this area, much remains to be done. Counselors/ therapists are referred to the *Guidelines for the Preparation and Evaluation of Non-print Career Media* recently published by the National Vocational Guidance Association (National Vocational Guidance Association, 1977) and, more generally, to the list of sources on nondiscriminatory language (particularly Bass, 1979) in the APA *Publication Manual* (American Psychological Association, 1983) and similar documents.

Finally, a related issue is that of the desirability of sensitivity to all generic labels of women, including *blind, deaf, epileptic,* and so forth. Such labels focus attention on the disability as the defining aspect of the woman's existence and encourage stereotyping of the most undesirable sort. The use of descriptive phrases (e.g., women with visual handicaps, women with hearing problems) is much preferred to the more generic adjectives.

In summary, this principle requires

1. Counselors/therapists avoid the use of the generic masculine form in all professional activities (counseling/therapy, supervision, teaching, and journal publications).

2. Counselors/therapists avoid other forms of sexist language (e.g., trivializing, labeling "exceptions") in all professional activities.

3. Counselors/therapists ensure that resource materials related to counseling women are adequate, complete, and sex-fair. If sex-stereotypic career information is retained because it is otherwise accurate and the best available, it should be clearly labeled with the caution that it is, indeed, sex-stereotypic.

4. Counselors/therapists avoid the use of generic adjectives describing women with handicaps, in order to avoid excessive focus on the disability.

## PRINCIPLE X. Counselors/therapists do not engage in sexual activity with their women clients under any circumstances.

One of the most basic issues that arises concerning women is that of actual emotional, physical, and/or sexual exploitation. For many years, professionals and laypeople alike have heard "horror stories" of women who sought psychological assistance, but were sexually and emotionally exploited by their counselor/therapist. Evidence provided by Holroyd and Brodsky (1977) indicates that such stories have a foundation in fact. Surveying licensed Ph.D. psychologists, they found that 5.5% of male and 0.6% of female respondents reported having had sexual intercourse with clients. Bouhoutsos, Holroyd, Lerman, Forer, and Greenberg (1983) report similar figures (4.8% and 0.8% for males and females, respectively).

Although sexual activity with either male or female clients is clearly unethical under any circumstances, it is emphasized here as a particular problem for female clients. Karasu (1980) has argued that the dyadic relationship in traditional counseling/psychotherapy replicates the "one-down" position in which women are frequently placed.

> This may encourage the fantasy that an idealized relationship with a powerful other is a more desirable solution to life's problems than taking autonomous action. Such a posture, in fact, may set the stage for the kind of sexual exploitation that occurs in instances of therapist-patient sex. (Karasu, 1980, p. 1510)

It should be pointed out that these comments are equally applicable to homosexual, as well as to heterosexual liaisons, although there is currently little, if any, data on this phenomenon in gay therapy. Bouhoutsos et al. (1983) state that, in their study of 559 patients who were sexually intimate with their therapists, the overwhelming majority of the cases (92%) occurred between female clients and male therapists. Interestingly, the majority of sexual relationships with male clients (58%) also involved male therapists.

The American Psychological Association Task Force on Sex Bias and Psychotherapy describes three ways in which sexual relations between client and counselor/therapist reflect sex bias:

1. nearly all complaints are from women patients regarding male therapists;

2. stereotypic feminine qualities, especially passive dependence, are exploited; and

3. the male therapist has considerably more power in the therapy situation than the female patient, a classic situation for the operation of sexual politics. (APA, 1975, p. 1170)

It should be gratuitous to point out that erotic contact with clients is based on the counselor/therapist's need for power, reassurance, or sexual gratification and is not an activity that is engaged in for the benefit of the client. Holroyd and Brodsky (1977) discuss the results of Butler's (1975) study in which psychologists and psychiatrists who had had sexual relations with clients were interviewed. Of this sample 90% of the therapists said they were vulnerable, needy, or lonely when the relationship began; 55% admitted they were frightened of intimacy; 70% said they maintained a dominant position in the relationship; and 60% saw themselves in a fatherly role with the client.

Bouhoutsos et al. (1983) present powerful evidence that such conduct is not only self-serving and unethical but results in damage to the client. In their sample, ill effects included depression, loss of motivation, impaired social or marital adjustment, significant emotional disturbance, suicidal feelings or behavior, and increased drug and alcohol use. Of those surveyed, 48% had difficulty recommencing therapy, and 64% experienced ill effects on their personal adjustment; overall, 90% of the clients suffered negative effects. These authors suggest that their data provide a rationale for enacting legislation proscribing sexual conduct between therapist and patient. Such prohibitions against client-counselor sexual relationships are consistent with the ethical formulations of all traditional mental health professions (American Psychiatric Association, 1973; American Psychological Association, 1981; National Association of Social Workers, 1980). In this context, the Ethical Standards of the American Psychological Association state:

Psychologists are continually cognizant of their own needs and of their potentially influential position vis-à-vis persons such as clients, students, and subordinates. They avoid exploiting the trust and dependency of such persons. Psychologists make every effort to avoid dual relationships that could impair their professional judgment or increase the risk of exploitation. . . . Sexual intimacies with clients are unethical. (APA, 1981, p. 636)

**PRINCIPLE XI. Counselors/therapists are aware of and continually review their own values and biases and the effects of these on their women clients. Counselors/therapists understand the effects of sex-role**

**socialization upon their own development and functioning and the consequent values and attitudes they hold for themselves and others. They recognize that behaviors and roles need not be sex-based.**

Frieze et al. (1978) have written, "Most types of psychotherapy rely upon a fairly long-term relationship between the therapist and the client, during which the client's actions, feelings, and attitudes are discussed and interpreted *according to the training and biases of the therapist*" (p. 274; emphasis added). Bart (1971) states directly that value-free counseling/psychotherapy is a myth, whereas Halleck (1971) maintains that all systems of psychotherapy contain implicit value systems, and Strong (1968) describes counseling as a process of interpersonal influence. According to Rawlings and Carter (1977), "In deciding who to treat, what diagnostic categories to assign, which treatment goals to set, and which techniques or strategies to employ, therapists are exercising value judgments" (p. 5).

Agreement on the point is widespread (London, 1964; Pepinsky & Karst, 1964; Rosenthal, 1955). Although some writers demur (e.g., Harkness, 1976; Kremer, 1973), most counselors/therapists have accepted the evidence that indicates that it is not possible for the counselor to be value-free during the therapeutic interaction. Rosenthal (1955), for example, has demonstrated that it was the clients who modified their values to resemble more clearly those of their therapists who were judged to be most improved in therapy.

Given that counselors'/therapists' values powerfully influence both process and outcome, it becomes important to examine those values and the implications they have for women clients. Rawlings and Carter (1977) agree with Halleck (1971), who suggests that psychotherapy ordinarily operates "to conceal the existence of social conflict and to preserve the *status quo*" (Halleck, 1971, p. 30). Thus, women, who constitute the majority of clients (Chesler, 1972), are the largest consumers of a service that may work against their best interests.

Rawlings and Carter (1977) discuss the personal sources of therapist/counselor values that work against women clients' interests, such as personality traits of dogmatism and authoritarianism, as well as stereotypic views of masculinity and femininity. They further note three *professional* sources of counselor/therapist values about women: first, the personality theories they adopt, which shape their view of human nature; second, their models of psychopathology, which determine which problems get treated; and third, their models of mental health, which determine the goals of treatment. As has been pointed out in earlier sections of these guidelines (see, for example, Principle II), models of both personality and psychopathology that are guided by the principles of biological determinism tend to be both limiting and damaging to women clients, whereas models emphasizing cultural determinism and social learning help women to locate the causes of their problems *outside of themselves* and to suggest corrective actions.

Rawlings and Carter (1977) identify three models of mental health that shape the goals of treatment: the *normative* model, which prescribes conformity to sex-stereotypic patterns of behavior; the *androcentric* model, which values male-associated characteristics and behaviors for *both* sexes; and the *androgynous* model, which emphasizes a blend or balance of both male-associated and female-associated behaviors for both sexes. Rawlings and Carter (1977) cite extensive evidence of benefits to be derived from the androgynous model, including higher levels of moral judgment (Block, 1973); ego maturity (Block, 1973); cognitive functioning (Maccoby, 1966); creativity (Hammer, 1964; Helson, 1966); and sex-role adaptability (Bem, 1975).

Review of the foregoing discussion gives rise to two conclusions, on which Principle XI is based: first, the counselor/therapist's value system plays an important role in the therapeutic process; and second, some value systems, as guided by various theoretical models of personality, psychopathology, and mental health, are limiting and damaging to women clients, whereas others are facilitative. In complying with Principle XI, counselors/therapists are reminded:

1. We are all products of our culture, and therefore, subject to the influences of sex-role socialization. We, like other people, have been taught the "normative model" of sex-role behavior and must work to develop unbiased attitudes and values so that clients are neither covertly nor overtly forced into sex-based behaviors or roles (Nutt, 1979). Suggested methods of self-examination and development include personal counseling/therapy, independent study, workshop attendance, and experiments in personal life styles.

2. Samler (1960) has written, "Drawing upon models of the healthy personality, it should be possible to develop testable hypotheses relative to the values to be supported (in counseling)" (p. 37). The evidence at present suggest adherence to personality models which emphasize cultural determinism and the influence of social learning, as well as acceptance of psychological androgyny as a viable model of mental health.

3. Self-disclosure by the counselor/therapist of relevant personal values is not only appropriate for a relationship for which the counselor and client are mutually responsible, but may facilitate therapeutic change.

**PRINCIPLE XII. Counselors/therapists are aware of how their personal functioning may influence their effectiveness in counseling/therapy with women clients. They monitor their functioning through consultation, supervision, or therapy so that it does not adversely affect their work with women clients.**

It is imperative for counselors/therapists to be aware of their own psychological functioning so that it does not interfere with their work with clients. Corey (1977) states that it is the therapists' responsibility to themselves and to their clients to work actively toward expanding their own areas of distortion, bias, prejudices, and vulnerability.

Counselors whose personal needs are not being met outside of the counseling relationship may possibly set a course of work that is more appropriate to their own needs than to those of their clients. Butler's (1975) investigation of therapists who had engaged in sexual relations with clients indicated that these psychologists and psychiatrists reported themselves as vulnerable, needy, or lonely when the relationship began.

Other research points to a relationship between counselor needs and client treatment. For example, therapist scores on the Machiavellianism Scale, which measures willingness to manipulate others, appears related to attitudes about clients and therapy (Maracek, 1975). In a small sample of clinicians who were members of the American Psychological Association (N = 55; 43 males and 12 females), Machiavellianism in male therapists was linked to a preference for treating women clients. This relationship was not found for female therapists, but this may be due to the extremely small sample size. Machiavellian therapists of both sexes were more likely to favor the use of placebo drug treatments and the coercion of individuals into treatment, as well as to place importance on control over their clients. Those therapists with a strong control orientation were more likely to feel that sex was permitted in therapy in more circumstances than therapists who were less concerned about control. Unger (1979) interprets Maracek's data to mean that some power-oriented therapists may seek female clients and may respond to them in a not altogether therapeutic way.

Issues in counselors'/therapists' personal lives may have great impact on their work. For example, Aslin (1978) points out, with reference to working with divorced women, that the counseling psychologist's attitudes are particularly important in dealing with women who have lost the wife role. A therapist who supports the normative expectation that a female be primarily wife and mother will at least subtly communicate this attitude to her. Thus, the therapist may reinforce the client's sense of failure and lost identity and even encourage her to desperately find another mate rather than to be assertive and develop herself socially and intellectually. Although Aslin does not point it out, this may also be true for a counselor who is herself in the process of giving up the wife role. The point here is that personal issues often become therapeutic issues—our own, not our clients'. In the event that the counselor/therapist feels that his or her effectiveness is threatened in establishing or maintaining a healthy therapeutic relationship, he or she is reminded of the ethical guideline of the American Psychological Association that states:

> Psychologists recognize that personal problems and conflicts may interfere with professional effectiveness. Accordingly, they refrain from undertaking any activity in which their personal problems are likely to lead to inadequate performance or harm to a client, colleague, student, or research participant. If engaged in such activity when they become aware of their personal problems,

they seek competent professional assistance to determine whether they should suspend, terminate, or limit the scope of their professional and/or scientific activities. (APA, 1981, p. 634)

In addition, this principle addresses the need for adequate consultation and supervision, a need often neglected once the neophyte counselor/therapist attains full professional status. In addition to the formal consultation suggested by the APA guidelines, the formation of ongoing peer supervision groups is encouraged, to assist in increasing early awareness of issues that may have a damaging effect on therapeutic effectiveness and client welfare.

## PRINCIPLE XIII. Counselors/therapists support the elimination of sex bias within institutions and individuals.

According to Rice and Rice (1973), the increasing efforts of women to reexamine their personal, social and sexual roles have had important implications for many social institutions, such as work, marriage, religion, and education. Because it is the nature of institutions to resist change, great tension often exists, not only in the relationship between individual women and such societal institutions but also in the relationship of counselors and therapists to the institutions in which they live and work. Thus, it is not unusual to find mental health professionals who are committed to eliminating sexist treatment of women employed by institutions and surrounded by colleagues who perpetuate such treatment. Similarly, many find themselves in institutions or situations in which sexist treatment of individual clients, or students, would not be tolerated; and yet paternalistic, stereotyped, and often, degrading treatment of *groups* of women, or women as a group, is the warp and woof of everyday life.

The issue implicit in this situation can be framed as follows: Is it sufficient for counselors/therapists to attempt to change the behavior of individuals (e.g., clients, students) or does nonsexist treatment of women imply the necessity of working for institutional and social change? And, if so, how?

For many feminist counselors/therapists, the choice is clear. Agel (1971) writes, "Feminist therapy is opposed to personal adjustment to social conditions. The goal is social and political change." Similarly, Rice and Rice (1973) tell us:

> Aiding a handful of individuals to paths of greater self esteem and personal fulfillment within one's lifetime can, of course, be personally rewarding and meaningful, but if our goal is to achieve a truly egalitarian society, we must do more. The provision of community, consultative, and political experience for trainees is one solution. (p. 193)

It seems reasonable to suggest that it is difficult for the counselor who maintains a placid view regarding social and political change to encourage action in his or her client—or, to serve as a role model for his or her students and trainees. It seems even more difficult to attempt to change the behavior of large numbers of people without changing the organizations and institutions that influence the behaviors of those people.

Despite such considerations, many counselors/therapists have adopted a passive stance towards individual and institutional practices that have a detrimental effect on women, although such practices may be inimical to their own personal value system. Gluckstern (1977) has suggested that this passivity may result partially from the nature of counselor training that militates against being effective activists in the social arena. Noting that "our training encourages us to look for and focus on factors *within* the individual which restrict growth" (p. 443), she suggests that the person-centered explanations of problem behavior learned in training inhibit the search for structural change. Gluckstern presents a model for personal and institutional change interaction that demonstrates that involvement in the process of institutional change produces therapeutic personal change.

Rawlings and Carter (1977) suggest further ways that counselors/therapists can become involved in social action, either personally or through encouraging client activism. They note the training of paraprofessionals, both as clinicians (Sobey, 1969) and as client advocates (Felton, Wallach, & Gallo, 1974) and the sharing of expert knowledge that allows the development of what Iscoe (1974) has called a *competent community;* and they remind us that the 1973 Vail Conference (Ivey & Leptaluoto, 1975) of professional psychology clearly supported the advocacy of social change as an appropriate and necessary professional responsibility.

The notion of working for social change, or intervening at levels beyond the individual, is a difficult one for many professionals. Some are clearly uninterested, according to Halpern (cited in Roe, 1959), whereas others fear a backlash effect, either for themselves or for women in general. In this context, it is helpful to review Freeman's (1975) concept of the "null environment." Speaking specifically to academic environments, but with implications for all institutions, Freeman notes that a null environment (i.e., one lacking in support and encouragement) has effects on women similar to those of overt discrimination, due to the nature of previous socialization and experience. She argues that unless we make special efforts to create institutional support for women, we are—by accepting the status quo—continuing to place women at a disadvantage.

Obviously, there are as many methods and levels of involvement as there are persons; each must determine the nature of his or her own commitment. What is required by Principle XIII is that individuals not *ignore* sex bias, sex discrimination, and the like, on the part of individuals and institutions with whom we work. Samler wrote, almost 20 years ago,

> It is important that we do not be above it all, that we not be dispassionate and neutral. Apart from the abnegation of moral responsibility, if we are so impossibly dispassionate, time and events will shunt us aside. Let us decide that we will be part of the events that move and determine our collective fate. We are each part of one another, and we must act so. (1969, p. 22)

It is difficult to offer practical guidelines for counselors/therapists supporting the elimination of sex bias within institutions and individuals. Each situation is unique and requires its own response. At the very least, it would seem necessary that we avoid working in and for organizations that discriminate against women, either formally or informally. When this is not possible, this principle suggests the necessity of using all feasible means to confront such discrimination and to ensure its elimination. As Vetter (1973) has written,

> Counselors must not continue to perpetuate such a situation. . . . It seems time for counseling psychology to pick up the challenge, rather hesitantly offered by Samler (1964) to become involved in social action; to make it a definite part of our professional task to set out to affect the status quo. (p. 64)

# References

Abramowitz, S. I., Abramowitz, C. V., Jackson, C., & Gomes, B. (1973). The politics of clinical judgment: What nonliberal examiners infer about women who don't stifle themselves. *Journal of Consulting and Clinical Psychology, 41,* 385–391.

Agel, J. (Ed.) (1971). *The radical therapist.* New York: Ballantine Books.

Allport, G. W. (1954). *The nature of prejudice.* Cambridge, MA: Addison-Wesley.

American Psychiatric Association. (1973). The principles of medical ethics with annotations especially applicable to psychiatry. *American Journal of Psychiatry, 130,* 1057–1064.

American Psychological Association. (1974). *Publication manual* (2nd ed.). Washington, DC: Author.

American Psychological Association. (1975). Report of the task force on sex bias and sex-role stereotyping in psychotherapeutic practice. *American Psychologist, 30,* 1170–1178.

American Psychological Association. (1981). Ethical principles of psychologists. *American Psychologist, 36,* 633–638.

American Psychological Association. (1983). *Publication manual* (3rd ed.). Washington, DC: Author.

American Psychological Association Publication Manual Task Force. (1977). Guidelines for nonsexist language in APA journals: Publication manual change sheet 2. *American Psychologist, 32,* 487–494.

Argyris, C. (1975). Dangers in applying results from experimental social psychology. *American Psychologist, 30,* 469–475.

Aslin, A. L. (1978). Counseling "single-again" (divorced and widowed) women. In L. W. Harmon, J. M Birk, & M. F. Tanney (Eds.), *Counseling women.* Monterey, CA: Brooks/Cole.

Auger, E. R. (1969). *Nonverbal communication of normal individuals and schizophrenic patients in the psychology interview.* Unpublished doctoral dissertation, University of California, Los Angeles.

Bandura, A. (1965). Influence of models' reinforcement contingencies on the acquisition of imitative responses. *Journal of Personality and Social Psychology, I,* 589–595.

Bandura, A. (1969). Social learning theory of identification processes. In D. A. Goslin (Ed.), *Handbook of socialization theory and research.* Chicago: Rand McNally.

Barnouw, V. (1963). *Culture and personality.* Homewood, IL: Dorsey Press.

Bart, P. (1971). Depression in middle-aged women. In V. Gornick & B. K. Moran (Eds.), *Women in sexist society.* New York: Basic Books.

Bass, B. M. (1979). Confessions of a former male chauvinist. *American Psychologist, 34,* 194–195.

Bean, K. (1970). Desensitization, behavior rehearsal, then reality: A preliminary report on a new procedure. *Behavior Therapy, I,* 542.

Bem, S. L. (1975). Sex-role adaptability: One consequence of psychological androgyny. *Journal of Personality and Social Psychology, 31,* 634–643.

Bernard, J. (1971). The paradox of the happy marriage. In V. Gornick & B. K. Moran (Eds.), *Women in sexist society*. New York: Basic Books.

Bettleheim, B. (1965). The commitment required of a woman entering a scientific profession in present-day American society. In J. A. Mattfield & C. G. Van Aken (Eds.), *Women and the scientific professions*. Cambridge, MA: MIT Press.

Bingham, W. C., & House, E. W. (1973). Counselors' attitudes toward women and work. *Vocational Guidance Quarterly, 22,* 16–32.

Birk, J., & Fitzgerald, L. F. (1979). Survey of APA-approved counseling psychology training programs concerning preparation for counseling women. Unpublished survey.

Block, J. H. (1973). Conceptions of sex-role: Some cross-cultural and longitudinal perspectives. *American Psychologist, 28,* 512–526.

Bolinger, D. (1968). *Aspects of languages*. New York: Harcourt Brace Jovanovich.

Bouhoutsos, J., Holroyd, J., Lerman, H., Forer, B. R., & Greenberg, M. (1983). Sexual intimacy between psychotherapists and patients. *Professional Psychology: Research and Practice, 14,* 185–196.

Brodsky, A. M. (1975, March). *Is there feminist therapy?* Paper presented at the Southeastern Psychological Association Symposium, Atlanta.

Brodsky, A. M. (1977). Therapeutic aspects of consciousness-raising groups. In E. I. Rawlings & D. K. Carter (Eds.), *Psychotherapy for women: Treatment toward equality*. Springfield, IL: Charles C Thomas.

Brodsky, A. M., & Hare-Mustin, R. T. (1980). *Women and psychotherapy*. New York: The Guilford Press.

Broverman, I. K., Broverman, D. M., Clarkson, F. E., Rosenkrantz, P. S., & Vogel, S. R. (1970). Sex-role stereotypes and clinical judgments of mental health. *Journal of Consulting and Clinical Psychology, 34,* 1–7.

Butler, S. (1975). *Sexual contact between therapists and patients*. Unpublished doctoral dissertation, California School of Professional Psychology, Los Angeles.

Cameron, D. E. (1951). The conversion of passivity into normal self-assertion. *American Journal of Psychiatry, 98.*

Carlson, E. R., & Carlson, R. (1961). Male and female subjects in personality research. *Journal of Abnormal and Social Psychology, 61,* 482–483.

Chesler, P. (1972). *Women and madness*. Garden City, NY: Doubleday.

Christ, C. (1980). *Diving deep and surfacing*. Boston: Beacon Press.

Collier, H. (1982). *Counseling women: A guide for therapists*. New York: Free Press.

Corey, G. (1977). *Theory and practice of counseling and psychotherapy*. Monterey, CA: Brooks/Cole.

Cormican, J. D. (1977). *How the English language distorts the psychology of women*. Unpublished manuscript, Syracuse University, Syracuse, NY.

Dailey, A. I. (1979). Physically handicapped women. *The Counseling Psychologist, 8,* 41–42.

Dailey, A. L. (1982). Sexuality in spinal cord injured high school students. *The School Counselor, 29,* 213–219.

Dan, A. J., & Beekman, S. (1972). Male versus female representation in psychological research. *American Psychologist, 27,* 1078.

Deutsch, H. (1944). *The psychology of women* (Vol. 1). New York: Grune & Stratton.

Deutsch, H. (1945). *The psychology of women* (Vol. 2). New York: Grune & Stratton.

Dewey, C. R. (1974). Exploring interests: A nonsexist method. *Personnel and Guidance Journal, 52,* 311–315.

Erikson, E. (1968). *Identity: Youth and crisis*. New York: Norton.

Erikson, E. H. (1964). The inner and outer space: Reflections on womanhood. *Daedalus, 92,* 582–606.

Erikson, E. H. (1975). Once more the inner space. In *Life and history and the historical moment*. New York: Norton.

Escamilla-Mondanaro, J. (1977). Lesbians and therapy. In E. I. Rawlings & D. K. Carter (Eds.), *Psychotherapy for women: Treatment toward equality*. Springfield, IL: Charles C Thomas.

Fabrikant, B. (1974). The psychotherapist and the female patient: Perceptions, misperceptions and change. In V. Franks and V. Burtle (Eds.), *Women and therapy*. New York: Bruner/Mazel.

Farmer, H S. (1976). What inhibits achievement and career motivation in women? *The Counseling Psychologist, 6,* 12–14.

Farmer, H., & Backer, T. (1977). *New career options for women: A counselor's sourcebook.* New York: Human Science Press.

Felton, G. S., Wallach, H. F., & Gallo, C. L. (1974). Training mental health workers to better meet patient needs. *Hospital and Community Psychiatry, 25,* 299–302.

Fensterheim, H. (1972). Assertive methods and marital problems. In Ruben, R. D., Kinsterheim, H., Henderson, G. D., & Ullman, L. P. (Eds.). *Advances in behavior therapy.* New York: Academic Press.

Fitzgerald, L. F., & Betz, N. E. (1983). Issues in the vocational psychology of women. In W. B. Walsh & S. H. Osipow (Eds.), *Handbook of vocational psychology* (Vol. 1). Hillsdale, NJ: Lawrence Erlbaum.

Fitzgerald, L. F., & Cherpas, C. (1985). On the reciprocal relationship between gender and occupation: Rethinking the assumptions concerning masculine career development. *Journal of Vocational Behavior, 27,* 109–122.

Fitzgerald, L. F., & Crites, J. O. (1980). Toward a career psychology of women: What do we know? What do we need to know? *Journal of Counseling Psychology, 27,* 44–62.

Ford, D. J. (1978). Counseling for the strengths of the black woman. In L. W. Harmon, J. M. Birk, & M. F. Tanney (Eds.), *Counseling women.* Monterey, CA: Brooks/Cole.

Freeman, J. (1975). *Women: A feminist perspective.* Palo Alto, CA: Mayfield.

Frieze, I. H. (1975). Women's expectations for and causal attributions of success and failure. In M. T. S. Mednick, S. S. Tangri, & L. W. Hoffman (Eds.), *Women and achievement.* New York: John Wiley.

Frieze, I. H., Parsons, J. E., Johnson, P. B., Ruble, D. N., & Zellman, T. L. (1978). *Women and sex roles: A social psychological perspective.* New York: W. W. Norton.

Fuller, F. F. (1964). Preference for female and male counselors. *Personnel and Guidance Journal, 42,* 463–467.

Giallombardo, R. (1966). *Society of women: A study of a women's prison.* New York: John Wiley.

Gilbert, L. A. (1980). Feminist therapy. In A. M. Brodsky & R. T. Hare-Mustin (Eds.), *Women and psychotherapy.* New York: The Guilford Press.

Gilligan, C. (1982). *In a different voice.* Cambridge, MA: Harvard University Press.

Gluckstern, N. B. (1977). Beyond therapy: Personal and institutional change. In E. Rawlings & D. Carter (Eds.), *Psychotherapy for women: Treatment toward equality.* Springfield, IL: Charles C Thomas.

Grady, K. E. (1979). Androgyny reconsidered. In J. H. Williams (Ed.), *Psychology of women: Selected readings.* New York: W. W. Norton.

Graham, A. (1975). The making of a nonsexist dictionary. In B. Thorne & N. Henley (Eds.), *Language and sex: Difference and dominance.* Rowley, MA: Newbury House.

Greer, G. (1970). *The female eunuch.* London: Paladin.

Griscom, J. L. (1979). Sex, race, and class: Three dimensions of women's experience. *The Counseling Psychologist, 9,* 10–11.

Halleck, S. L. (1971). *The politics of therapy.* New York: Science House.

Hammer, E. (1964). Creativity and feminine ingredients in young male artists. *Perceptual and Motor Skills, 19,* 414.

Hansen, L. S., & Rapoza, R. S. (Eds.). (1978). *Career development and counseling of women.* Springfield, IL: Charles C Thomas.

Hare, N., & Hare, J. (1970). Black women 1970. *Transaction, 8,* 65–68.

Harkness, C. C. (1976). Career counseling: Dreams and reality. Springfield, IL: Charles C Thomas.

Harmon, L. W. (1977). Career counseling for women. In E. I. Rawlings & D. K. Carter (Eds.), *Psychotherapy for women.* Springfield, IL: Charles C Thomas.

Heffernan, E. (1972). *Making it in prison: The square, the cool, and the life.* New York: John Wiley.

Helmreich, R., & Spence, J. T. (1978). The Work and Family Orientation Questionnaire: An objective instrument to assess components of achievement motivation and attitudes toward family and career (Ms. No. 1677). *JSAS Catalog of Selected Documents in Psychology, 8,* 35.

Helms, J. E. (1979). Black women. *The Counseling Psychologist, 8,* 40–41.

Helson, R. (1966). Personality of women with imaginative and artistic interests: The role of masculinity, originality, and other characteristics in their creativity. *Journal of Personality, 34,* 1–25.

Heppner, P. P., & Pew, B. (1977). Effects of diplomas, awards, and counselor sex on perceived expertness. *Journal of Counseling Psychology, 24,* 147–149.

Holland, J. L. (1973). *Making vocational choices: A theory of careers.* Englewood Cliffs, NJ: Prentice-Hall.

Holroyd, J. C., & Brodsky, A. M. (1977). Psychologists' attitudes and practices regarding erotic and non-erotic physical contact with patients. *American Psychologist, 32,* 843–849.

Horner, M. S. (1968). *Sex differences in achievement motivation and performance in competitive and noncompetitive situations.* Unpublished doctoral dissertation, University of Michigan, Ann Arbor.

Horner, M. S. (1972). The motive to avoid success and changing aspirations of women. In J. M. Bardwick (Ed.), *Readings on the psychology of women.* New York: Harper & Row.

Howard, K. I., Orlinsky, D. E., & Hill, J. A. (1970). Patients' satisfaction in psychotherapy as a function of patient-therapist pairing. *Psychotherapy: Theory, Research and Practice, 7,* 130–134.

Iscoe, I. (1974). Is clinical child psychology obsolete? Some observations on the current scene. In G. J. Williams & S. Gordon (Eds.), *Clinical child psychology: Current practices and future perspectives.* New York: Behavioral Publications.

Ivey, A. E., & Leptaluoto, J. R. (1975). Changes ahead: Implications of the Vail Conference. *Personnel and Guidance Journal, 53,* 747–752.

Jakubowski-Spector, P. (1973). Facilitating the growth of women through assertiveness training. *The Counseling Psychologist, 4,* 75.

Karasu, T. B. (1980). The ethics of psychotherapy. *American Journal of Psychiatry, 137,* 1510.

Katz, R. (1971). Case conference: Rapid development of activity in a case of chronic passivity. *Journal of Behavior Therapy and Experimental Psychiatry, 2,* 187–193.

Koile, E. A., & Bird, D. J. (1956). Preferences for counselor help on freshman problems. *Journal of Counseling Psychology, 3,* 97–106.

Kremer, B. J. (1973). What the hell are counselors for? Literary perceptions. *Personnel and Guidance Journal, 51,* 706–710.

Lazarus, A. A., & Serber, M. (1968). Is systematic desensitization being misapplied? *Psychological Reports, 23,* 215–218.

Lerner, G. (1973). *Black women in white America: A documentary history.* New York: Vintage Books.

London, P. (1964). *The models and morals of psychotherapy.* New York: Holt, Rinehart & Winston.

Maccoby, E. E. (1966). Sex differences in intellectual functioning. In E. E. Maccoby (Ed.), *The development of sex differences.* Stanford, CA: Stanford University Press.

Maccoby, E. M., & Jacklin, C. N. (1974). *The psychology of sex differences.* Stanford, CA: Stanford University Press.

Maracek, J. (1975, April). *Power and women's psychological disorders: Preliminary observations.* Paper presented at the meeting of the Eastern Psychological Association, New York.

Maslin, A., & Davis, J. L. (1975). Sex-role stereotyping as a factor in mental health standards among counselors-in-training. *Journal of Counseling Psychology, 22,* 87–91.

Maslow, A. (1970). Motivation and personality (2nd ed.). New York: Harper & Row.

McClelland, D. C., Atkinson, J. W., Clark, R. A., & Lowell, E. L. (1953). *The achievement motive.* New York: Appleton-Century-Crofts.

McDavis, R. J. (1978). Counseling Black clients effectively: The eclectic approach. *Journal of Non-White Concerns in Personnel and Guidance, 7,* 41–47.

Mednick, M. T. S., Tangri, S. S., & Hoffman, L. W. (Eds.). (1975). *Women and achievement.* New York: John Wiley.

Mezzans, J. (1971). Concerns of students and preference for male and female counselors. *Vocational Guidance Quarterly, 20,* 42–47.

Money, J., & Ehrhardt, A. A. (1972). *Man and woman, boy and girl: Differentiation and dimorphism of gender identity.* Baltimore: Johns Hopkins University Press.

Moulton, J., Robinson, G. M., & Elias, C. (1975). Sex bias in language use: Neutral pronouns that aren't. *American Psychologist, 33,* 1032–1036.

National Association of Social Workers. (1980). *Code of ethics.* Washington, DC: Author.

National Vocational Guidance Association. (1977). *Guidelines for the preparation and evaluation of nonprint career media.* Author.

Neulinger, J. (1968). Perceptions of the optimally integrated person: A redefinition of mental health. *Proceedings of the 76th Annual Convention of the American Psychological Association, 3,* 553–554.

Nutt, R. L. (1979). Review and preview of attitudes and values of counselors of women. *The Counseling Psychologist, 8,* 18–20.

O'Leary, V. E. (1977). *Toward understanding women.* Monterey, CA: Brooks/Cole.

Orlinsky, D. E., & Howard, K. I. (1976). The affect of sex of therapist on the therapeutic experiences of women. *Psychotherapy: Theory, Research and Practice, 13,* 82–88.

Orlinsky, D. E., & Howard, K. I. (1980). Gender and psychotherapeutic outcome. In A. M. Brodsky & R. T. Hare-Mustin (Eds.), *Women and psychotherapy.* New York: The Guilford Press.

Osipow, S. H. (1975). The relevance of theories of career development to special groups: Problems, needed data, and implications. In S. Picou & R. Campbell (Eds.), *Career behavior of special groups.* Columbus, OH: Charles E. Merrill.

Pepinsky, H. H., & Karst, T. O. (1964). Convergence: A phenomenon in counseling and in psychotherapy. *American Psychologist, 19,* 333–338.

Pope, D. J. (1982). *Women and work: A comparison of graduate students in counseling and business on attitudes, factual knowledge, and androgyny.* Unpublished doctoral dissertation, Kent State University, Kent, OH.

Prescott, S., & Foster, K. (1974, September). *Why researchers don't study women: The responses of 67 researchers.* Paper presented at the annual convention of the American Psychological Association, New Orleans.

Radov, C. G., Masnick, B. B., & Hauser, B. B. (1977). Issues in feminist therapy: The work of a women's study group. *Social Work, 22,* 507–509.

Rawlings, E., & Carter, D. (Eds.). (1977). *Psychotherapy for women: Treatment toward equality.* Springfield, IL: Charles C Thomas.

Rice, J. K., & Rice, D. G. (1973). Implications of the women's liberation movement for psychotherapy. *American Journal of Psychiatry, 30,* 191–196.

Roe, A. (1956). *The psychology of occupation.* New York: John Wiley.

Rosenthal, D. (1955). Changes in some moral values following psychotherapy. *Journal of Consulting Psychology, 19,* 431–436.

Samler, J. (1960). Change in values: A goal in counseling. *Journal of Counseling Psychology, 7,* 32–39.

Samler, J. (1969). The vocational counselor and social action. Washington, DC: National Vocational Guidance Association.

Schlossberg, N. K., & Pietrofessa, J. J. (1973). Perspectives on counseling bias: Implications for counselor education. *The Counseling Psychologist, 4,* 44–54.

Seligman, M. E. P. (1973). Fall into helplessness. *Psychology Today, 6,* 43.

Shields, S. A. (1975). Functionalism, Darwinism, and the psychology of women: A study in social myth. *American Psychologist, 30,* 739–754.

Siassi, I. (1974). Psychotherapy with women and men of lower classes. In V. Franks & V. Burtle (Eds.), *Women in therapy.* New York: Bruner/Mazel.

Skolnick, A. S., & Skolnick, J. H. (Eds.). (1971). *Family in transition: Rethinking marriage, sexuality, childrearing, and family organization.* Boston: Little, Brown.

Sobey, F. (1969). Volunteer services in mental health: An annotated bibliography 1955–1969. *National Clearing House for Mental Health Information,* p. 1002.

Stanton, E. C. (1895). *The woman's Bible.* New York: European.

Steiner, C. (1972). *Scripts people live.* New York: Grove Press.

Steinmann, A. (1975, September) *Male-female concepts of sex roles: Twenty years of cross-cultural research.* Paper presented at the annual convention of the American Psychological Association, Chicago.

Stevenson, I., & Wolpe, J. (1960). Recovery from sexual deviation through overcoming non-sexual neurotic responses. *American Journal of Psychology, 116,* 737–742.

Strong, S. R. (1968). Counseling: An interpersonal influence process. *Journal of Counseling Psychology, 15,* 215–224.

Super, D. E., Stariskevsky, R., Matlin, N., Jordaan, J. P. (1963). *Career development: Self-concept theory.* Princeton, NJ: College Entrance Exam Board.

Sutherland, J. W. (1974). Beyond behaviorism and determinism. *Fields within fields, Winter,* 32–46.

Symonds, A. (1973, October). *The liberated woman: Healthy and neurotic.* Paper presented at the meeting of the Association for the Advancement of Psychoanalysis.

Tanney, M. F., & Birk, J. M. (1973). Women counselors for women clients? A review of the research. In L. W. Harmon, J. M. Birk, L. E. Fitzgerald, & M. F. Tanney (Eds.), *Counseling women.* Monterey, CA: Brooks/Cole.

Thomas, A. H., & Stewart, N. R. (1971). Counselor response to female clients with deviate and conforming career goals. *Journal of Counseling Psychology, 18,* 352–357.

Thomas, B. (1982). Unpublished paper, Kent State University, Kent, OH.

Unger, R. K. (1979). *Female and male: Psychological perspectives.* New York: Harper & Row.

Unger, R. K., & Denmark, F. L. (Eds.). (1975). *Woman: Dependent or independent variable?* New York: Psychological Dimensions.

Vaughter, R. M. (1976). Review essay: Psychology. *Signs, 2,*120–146.

Vetter, L. (1973). Career counseling for women. *The Counseling Psychologist, 4,* 54–66.

Weisstein, N. (1971). Psychology constructs the female, or the fantasy life of the male psychologist. In M. H. Garskof (Ed.), *Roles women play: Readings toward women's liberation* (pp. 68–83). Monterey, CA: Brooks/Cole.

Williams, J. H. (1977). *The psychology of women: Behavior in a biosocial context.* New York: W. W. Norton.

Wyckoff, H. (1977). *Solving women's problems.* New York: Grove Press.

Zaller, S. (1982). Unpublished paper, Kent State University, Kent, OH.

# 11

# Gender Aware Therapy: A Synthesis of Feminist Therapy and Knowledge about Gender

*Glenn E. Good, Lucia A. Gilbert, and Murray Scher*

The time has come to integrate feminist therapy and knowledge of gender into principles of counseling for both women and men. Gender Aware Therapy (GAT) is such a synthesis. GAT encourages counselors to facilitate the development of women and men through exploration of their unique gender-related experiences. The foundations, principles, stages, and applications of GAT are described.

The development of feminist therapy has created an evolution in the ways in which psychotherapy is practiced. At the time feminist therapy evolved, one purpose was to promote the understanding of women's experiences within their societal context and to construct nonsexist theories of female development. Since feminist therapy initially focused on the needs of women, and because the root of feminism is *femina* (woman), many people have viewed feminist therapy as not applicable to male clients. While there has been no theory developed for men that parallels feminist theory, in recent years research on conceptions of the male gender and its detrimental consequences has been undertaken. (*Note to the reader:* The term *gender* acknowledges the broader meaning that has become associated with biological sex and thus refers to the psychological, social, and cultural features and characteristics frequently associated with the biological categories of male and female.) The new knowledge yielded about gender has not yet been adequately incorporated into therapeutic models and practice. Hence, the purpose of this article is to integrate the principles of feminist therapy with recent knowledge of both female and male gender from theories and research and then to suggest a new means for conceptualizing therapy, which is called Gender Aware Therapy (GAT). This article examines the roots of GAT in greater detail and then discusses its principles. The stages of GAT are described next, followed by specific problems for which GAT is recommended. Finally, some cautions regarding this new model of counseling are noted.

## Roots of Gender Aware Therapy

Sexist notions frequently have been applied to women seeking therapy, usually with deleterious consequences for them. Four general areas of bias identified by a task force of the American Psychological Association were: 1) fostering traditional sex roles, 2) bias in expectations and devaluation of women, 3) sexist use of psychoanalytic concepts, and 4) responding to women as sex objects, including seduction of female clients (APA, 1975). Similarly, in early writings on feminist therapy, the power which counselors, predominantly male at the time, had over their clients, most of whom were female, was noted. This unquestioned power of men over women paralleled the social order in which men defined women's needs and characteristics, and on this basis passed judgments about women's optimal functioning. In response, writers on feminist therapy proposed key concepts to correct this situation. Some of these concepts included recognizing that the personal is political, encouraging women's anger, viewing the therapist-client relationship as egalitarian, advocating female therapists for women, and challenging sexist aspects of psychodynamic theories (Gilbert, 1980).

The women's movement made it apparent that women in our society had not had the full range of options open to them. With regard to the mental health profession, both female clients and helping professionals were cautioned about sexism in the profession. More specifically, women seeking mental health services were encouraged to confront traditional gender roles (APA, 1975), and practitioners were warned that psychotherapy can no longer tolerate sexism in the diagnosis or treatment of female clients, or in the training of practitioners (Marecek & Hare-Mustin, 1987).

As was the case with women prior to the women's movement and the advent of feminist therapy, the current goal of most therapies is to restore troubled men to their traditional gender role model of mental health (i.e., to be strong, assertive, and independent). Yet recently, concern has been focused on the detrimental aspects of the traditional male gender role socialization on the psychological development and adjustment of men (Scher, Stevens, Good, & Eichenfield, 1987). Extant beliefs that men have few problems because of their more privileged position in our society have hindered attempts to understand the male gender role and its effects both on subgroups of men and on individual men (Pleck, 1985).

Fortunately, in our speedily evolving society, conceptions of optimal mental health have also been rapidly changing. The "adjustment" or "restoration" of clients' mental health—men's or women's—to conform with traditional conceptions of gender is no longer a necessarily desirable outcome (cf. Cook, 1985).

# Principles of Gender Aware Therapy

There are many competing and overlapping schools of therapy, including the various humanistic, cognitive, behavioral, psychodynamic, and familial therapies. We argue that the following principles of GAT warrant incorporation within all these approaches.

## 1. Regard Conceptions of Gender as Integral Aspects of Counseling and Mental Health

It is all too easy for counselors to assume that gender plays no part in their clients' lives and in the therapeutic process, despite vast evidence to the contrary. To date, the resistance has been strong and the negative consequences in the form of harm to clients have been unfortunately large (APA Task Force, 1975; Hare-Mustin, 1983; Marecek & Hare-Mustin, 1987). Jacklin (1989) recently concluded that: "The times are changing. Change may be occurring too quickly for some, but change is not occurring quickly enough for many girls and boys [and women and men] limited by their gender roles to less than full lives" (p. 132).

Counselors must not only be nonsexist in their work with clients, but they must also understand clients' difficulties within a gender perspective. Nonsexist counseling and therapy refer to equal treatments for women and men. Although GAT embraces the need for nonsexist treatment, it also incorporates an understanding of gender effects and sexism in its therapeutic strategies and goals. A case in point is an adult client with a 6-month-old child, who is seeking assistance with his or her conflict in combining occupational and family roles. Nonsexist therapy would prescribe that the same issues be raised for both a male or female client. Yet the issues involved in combing work and family often differ remarkably for women and men due to gender role socialization. These differences must be considered and discussed for counseling to be effective.

## 2. Consider Problems Within Their Societal Context

The personal and the political cannot be separated for women or men in society. Thus, the availability of quality child care or an employer's policy with regard to paternity or maternity leave would need to be considered in understanding the experience of personal stresses and conflicts. It may also be noted that this principle is based on the feminist therapy principle that the personal is political (Gilbert, 1980; Rawlings & Carter, 1977).

## 3. Actively Seek to Change Gender Injustices Experienced by Women and Men

Although counseling is primarily a means of individual change, not broad social change, an awareness of gender issues and sexism can shape and direct the purpose of counseling such that individual issues can be understood within the context of a patriarchy that has denied, and to a large degree continues to deny, women and men equal access to social, political, and economic resources.

Of particular relevance here is an extension of Freeman's (1975) null environment hypothesis. More specifically, counselors who fail to actively examine gender stereotypes with their clients may inadvertently support traditional conceptions of gender. This occurs because such counselors fail to actively counteract the otherwise pervasive gender biases experienced by our clients within this society. Thus, in the earlier example of a dual-career couple, a counselor who neglects to actively explore both the benefits and liabilities of a woman in a dual-career relationship who sacrifices her career to assume child care responsibilities is likely to be abandoning the client to the pervasive societal pressures urging her to leave her career. The GAT counselor would encourage the client to also carefully explore other viable options for which there may be less external support, such as having her partner take a leave from his employment or some arrangement requiring mutual accommodation. Likewise, the counselor should not assume that a man in a dual-career relationship would not want to consider being the primary caretaker of children.

## 4. Emphasize Development of Collaborative Therapeutic Relationships

Given its foundation in feminist therapy, GAT presumes that competent counselors are knowledgeable about how gender constructs affect not only women's and men's lives, but also therapeutic interventions and models of mental health. Furthermore, like feminist therapy, GAT seeks to deemphasize the expert role of the counselor: A collaborative and egalitarian relationship is sought (Gilbert, 1980). This is done to empower women and to short-circuit the competitive urge/drive in men. The collaborative and egalitarian therapeutic relationship may also allow clients to experience, recognize, and "own" their tendency to form "socially acceptable" dependent relationships with the other sex.

The therapeutic process becomes one of helping clients discover the optimal solutions for themselves. This process provides the possibility for a freer less stereotyped relationship. Clients frequently have not had such an opportunity up until this point, and the effect of such a relationship may be very powerful.

### 5. Respect Clients' Freedom to Choose

Choice is no less complex and intriguing an issue today than it was a thousand years ago. GAT values the rights of people to select views, behaviors, and feelings that are most congruent for them, despite the gender scripts they may have previously learned, currently experience, or fear in the future. This freedom to choose involves having awareness of the messages one has experienced, is currently experiencing, or may experience in the future from others, as well as a sense of what is right for oneself. GAT recognizes, for example, that both rigid traditional and nontraditional gender roles can be equally confining. Individuals are urged to choose that which is right for them, despite dogma: GAT eschews notions of political correctness. For instance, people may choose to generally follow a gender role yet realize that aspects of that role are not for them. An ardent feminist may choose to have a beautiful marriage ceremony, a man who prides himself on his physical strength may find carrying a purse convenient, a man who loves cooking and caring for the house may also enjoy watching football with the boys, and a soft-spoken woman may be enraged about sexism in the workplace. In summary, GAT supports the notion that particular behaviors, preferences, and attributes need not be categorized as falling into the domain of traditional or nontraditional, male or female, gender roles. Rather, what GAT advocates is simply choice, despite gender conceptions or political correctness.

## Stages of Gender Aware Therapy

GAT principles are germane to all therapies and warrant incorporation into counselors' approaches to the therapeutic situation. They represent a basic approach to and principles about counseling. Most approaches to therapy share similar stages in terms of how therapy is to be conducted. GAT focuses on the contribution of social forms, customs, and structures to individuals' development as a woman or man throughout these stages of counseling.

While brief therapy methods are frequently employed, an exploration in some depth of clients' difficulties is a valuable component of GAT when circumstances allow. The contribution of gender to the development of personality and behavior is generally quite significant and begins so early that a deep exploration may be required in order to understand, and if one so chooses, to change, its effects.

### Problem Conceptualization

In the initial assessment phase of counseling, the conceptualization phase—an understanding of the client's perception of the problem—is obtained. Counselors using GAT seek to understand which aspects of gender socialization may have played a part in their clients' concerns. In the case of sexual molestation where the victim is a male, for example, it is important for the client to know that extant views of maleness stress being in control and hence often keep the boy from telling because of his shame at having allowed himself to be overpowered. Conversely, the shame typically causing a female victim not to reveal sexual molestation may in part come from the stereotypic view of women as seductresses and hence blameworthy for whatever happened.

## Therapeutic Interventions

During the course of counseling clients may be introduced to emerging views of gender and socialization, as well as to how their own development has been affected. The range of interventions employed in GAT encompass all of those of counseling, including direct discussion, support, clarification, interpretation, confrontation, information offering, guided fantasy, experimentation, modeling, self-disclosure, bibliotherapy, and support groups. In the examples of sexual molestation discussed previously, GAT counselors would work with the client to facilitate the client's understanding of how he or she may have internalized stereotypic views of maleness and femaleness and then help him or her to realize that as a child one could not possibly be responsible either for causing the act or for preventing it.

In addition to gaining new knowledge and perspectives, clients will generally benefit from the opportunity to apply and rehearse new skills and behaviors in the session so that they may use them effectively in life. The application of these newly acquired skills necessitates determination on the part of the client and support from the counselor. During this stage GAT recognizes that these changes may have a profound impact on clients and the people in their lives. Hence, clients are encouraged to explore the implications of changes that they are considering, to anticipate potential difficulties, and to develop the skills necessary to successfully implement the changes that they desire. For example, a woman who gave up her artistic career goals after marriage may become depressed and enter therapy. Through counseling, she may begin to recognize her wants and then take actions to meet her needs. However, the people in her life have not necessarily also been simultaneously changing in counseling. Hence, they may unconsciously attempt to maintain the homeostasis by stifling or punishing her efforts. Likewise, a man who has been restricting his awareness and expression of affect may decide in the course of counseling that he desires to start sharing more of his feelings. However, the people in his life may be quite uncomfortable with such unusual male behaviors as his stating that he sometimes feels frightened, unsure, or vulnerable. The counselor employing GAT would assist the client in anticipating the likely reactions she or he may receive to the changes that are considered. The GAT counselor likewise would both support and assist the client in developing effective methods to cope with the barriers to and consequences of desired goals.

## Termination

The gender aware therapist recognizes the liabilities associated with traditional conceptions of gender and assists the client in learning from the opportunities that termination offers. For example, a male client during the course of therapy may learn to allow both the experiences of deeply caring for someone and feeling deeply cared for. Through the process of termination, he may learn to acknowledge feelings of sadness, vulnerability, and the pain of good-byes. Conversely, a female client who has been developing a sense of personal self-efficacy during therapy may find termination an opportunity to further increase her sense of self-reliance and self-direction.

# Problems for which GAT is Recommended

The following is but a brief summary of some problems that have been identified as associated with gender socialization. As such, these problems would be especially appropriate for treatment with GAT. It is important to note, however, that all problems bringing people to therapy are anchored in some way in their view of the world, which is in part determined by the dimensions of their gender roles and how these roles have been inculcated in their particular case.

## For Women

GAT is especially salient for the career development of women. Numerous obstacles typically prevent women from equal access to higher paying careers. One particularly problematic filter for women is the lack of sufficient support for persistence in mathematics, science, and computer courses that are prerequisites for entrance into many of the best career opportunities in society (Betz & Fitzgerald, 1987). Another barrier for women seeking to enter higher education, business, and industrial settings is the lack of adequate mentors and role models (Douvan, 1976). Women also frequently face extreme conflicts between establishing career priorities and attending to family responsibilities, as well as encountering unrealistic societal and personal expectations for being superwomen (Betz & Fitzgerald, 1987).

Another area that has earned increased attention recently is eating disorders and body image disturbances. Women are urged to conform to unrealistically thin weight expectations, which precipitate unhealthy attempts to control weight. Furthermore, the more women adhere to socio-cultural mores about thinness and attractiveness, the more likely they are to engage in disordered eating to achieve these unrealistic expectations (Mintz & Betz, 1988). Hence, GAT would present a highly effective approach to the treatment of these concerns.

Moreover, we live in a society that sexually oppresses women. The statistics for women who survive incest, sexual abuse, sexual harassment, and rape are staggering, and women's experiences horrendous (cf. Brownmiller, 1977; Courtois, 1988). In addition to a great deal of therapeutic skill, the effective GAT counselor possesses and conveys a deep, empathic understanding of the survivor's experience and facilitates appropriate attribution of causality.

## For Men

Men ascribing to the traditional views of maleness are generally reluctant to ask for help of any kind, even to the point of not asking for directions when lost. Adherence to this traditional role has been found to be associated with men's reluctance to seek assistance for psychosocial concerns (Good, Dell, & Mintz, 1989; Robertson & Fitzgerald, 1989; Werrbach, 1989). Men are prohibited from "giving voice" to that which is perceived as "unmasculine," such as fears, vulnerabilities, and insecurities. Thus, for many men, normal life reactions are denied expression and perhaps eventually even blocked from self-awareness. Hence, at the very thought of seeking counseling, conceptions of gender may have a notable impact.

The traditional male gender role has also been linked to a variety of problems (Harrison, 1978). These problems are hypothesized to include a prohibition against experiencing depression (Warren, 1983). Yet adherence to aspects of the male gender role have been found to be associated with an increased likelihood of depression (Good & Mintz, in press). Sexual dysfunction is another problem often related to traditional conceptions of maleness, whereby a mistaken emphasis on control and performance interfere with normal functioning (Fracher & Kimmel, 1987; Zilbergeld, 1978). Additionally, substance abuse is another area likely to contain a significant gender component, as men seek to cope with restricted feelings, unacceptable thoughts, and prohibited behaviors through the use of alcohol and/or drugs (Diamond, 1987). Increasing attention is also being focused on the detrimental side of extreme independence. Traditional conceptions of the male gender promote interpersonal isolation, as emotional intimacy is associated with vulnerability. Hence, interpersonal intimacy (relationship) and intrapersonal intimacy (self-awareness) become confused with loss of invulnerability, autonomy, and instrumentality. Clearly, men have much to learn about the ethics of care and the notions of interdependence (cf. Belenky, Clinchy, Goldberger, & Tarule, 1986; Gilligan, 1982).

## For Couples and Families

Gender also needs to be examined for its impact on relationships, marriages, and families. As noted by Carter (1989), "For us to ignore the relevance of gender at every level of the system, or to ignore the enormous differences in male and female value systems, or to ignore the ways in which gender organizes our functioning as therapists is to truly blind ourselves" (p. 60). Communication patterns, marital dissatisfaction, domestic violence, financial concerns, childrearing, substance abuse, and sexual dysfunction are all concerns that are likely to have roots in gender scripting. For example, a couple involved in repeated domestic violence is highly likely to have gender issues as central to their difficulties (Long, 1987; Scher & Stevens, 1987; Walker, 1979). While couple, marital, and family problems are complex, an awareness of gender socialization by the therapist and the use of GAT principles are likely to contribute to the effectiveness of treatment.

## Cautions

GAT is a potentially powerful approach to the amelioration of psychological difficulties. This manner of viewing clients and their gender in their societal contexts is likely to change how they progress in dealing with their lives. However, counselors must also use care due to the social, political, as well as personal, implications of this approach. Changing rights, roles, and privileges are political acts, and the repercussions for individuals and society are significant (Scher, 1984). In short, GAT is not a philosophical position to be taken lightly.

Due to the nascent nature of gender theory and research, coupled with recognition of the salience of gender issues in the lives of clients, counselors must often work beyond the current bounds of empirically validated knowledge of gender. This is a necessary but not ideal state of affairs. At this time the challenge for counselors is to integrate gender theories, case reports, and empirical research and then to apply this knowledge of gender to the idiosyncratic needs of their individual clients. Thus, counselors seeking to address the gender issues of their clients face significant challenges in their efforts to develop and facilitate healing interventions. The possibility of change in such a core concept as one's gender role is often surprising and disorienting; most people are raised believing that gender qualities are "givens" rather than characteristics that are learned. Even when interventions are wisely chosen, many clients are implicitly or explicitly resistant to changing elements of their conceptions about gender.

Clearly, it is not desirable to indiscriminately force clients in a nontraditional direction. Counselors need to be cognizant of their values and careful not to devalue clients with differing views. Furthermore, GAT should also not be applied indiscriminately across different ethnic groups. More research, writing, and dialogue are necessary to investigate the application of GAT across different ethnic, socioeconomic, and life stage groups.

# Conclusion

It is time to end the era of sexism and obliviousness to gender by the mental health profession. GAT advocates that counselors need to possess the knowledge, attitudes, and skills necessary to assist women and men in leading lives free from oppressive societal and personal stereotypes of gender. To help accomplish this, GAT proposes guiding principles, which include 1) regarding conceptions of gender as integral to counseling, 2) considering problems within their societal context, 3) actively seeking to change gender injustices, 4) emphasizing development of a collaborative therapeutic relationship, and 5) respecting clients' freedom to choose. As our society continues to change rapidly and increase in complexity, the ability to be situationally flexible appears desirable. GAT encourages clients to gain an understanding of societal conceptions of gender and how they limit the feelings, thoughts, and behaviors of men and women. An important goal of GAT is to help clients learn to act in new ways that will allow them to develop healthier and more fulfilling lives.

# References

American Psychological Association. (1975). Report of the task force on sex bias and sex-role stereotyping in psychotherapeutic practice. *American Psychologist, 30,* 1170–1178.

Belenky, M. F., Clinchy, B. M., Goldberger, N. R., & Tarule, J. M. (1986). *Women's ways of knowing: The development of self, voice, and mind.* New York: Basic Books.

Betz, N. E., & Fitzgerald, L. F. (Eds.). (1987). *The career psychology of women.* Orlando, FL: Academic Press.

Brownmiller, S. (1977). *Against our will.* New York: Simon & Schuster.

Carter, B. (1989). Gender sensitive therapy: Moving from theory to practice. *Family Therapy Networker, 13,* 57–60.

Cook, E. P. (1985). Androgyny: A goal for counseling? *Journal of Counseling and Development, 63,* 567–571.

Courtois, C. A. (1988). *Healing the incest wound: Adult survivors in therapy.* New York: Norton.

Diamond, J. (1987). Counseling male substance abusers. In M. Scher, S. Stevens, G. Good, & G. Eichenfield (Eds), *The handbook of counseling and psychotherapy with men* (pp. 332–342). Newbury Park, CA: Sage.

Douvan, E. (1976). The role models in women's professional development. *Psychology of Women Quarterly, 1,* 5–20.

Fracher, J. C., & Kimmel, M. S. (1987). Hard issues and soft spots: Counseling men about sexuality. In M. Scher, S. Stevens, G. Good, & G. Eichenfield (Eds.), *The handbook of counseling and psychotherapy with men* (pp. 83–96). Newbury Park, CA: Sage.

Freeman, J. (1975). How to discriminate against women without really trying. In J. Freeman (Ed.), *Women: A feminist perspective* (pp. 194–208). Palo Alto, CA: Mayfield.

Gilbert, L. A. (1980). Feminist therapy. In A. N. Brodsky & R. T. Hare-Mustin (Eds.), *Women and psychotherapy: An assessment of research and practice.* New York: Guilford.

Gilligan, C. (1982). *In a different voice: Psychological theory and women's development.* Cambridge, MA: Harvard University Press.

Good, G. E., Dell, D. M., & Mintz, L. M. (1989). The male role and gender role conflict: Relationships to help-seeking. *Journal of Counseling Psychology, 36,* 295–300.

Good, G. E., & Mintz, L. M. (in press). Depression and the male gender role: Evidence of compounded risk. *Journal of Counseling & Development.*

Hare-Mustin, R. T. (1983). An appraisal of the relationship between women and psychotherapy: Eighty years after the case of Dora. *American Psychologist, 38,* 593–601.

Harrison, J. (1978). Warning: The male sex role may be dangerous to your health. *Journal of Social Issues, 34,* 65–86.

Jacklin, C. N. (1989). Female and male: Issues of gender. *American Psychologist, 44,* 127–133.

Long, D. (1987). Working with men who batter. In M. Scher, S. Stevens, G. Good, & G. Eichenfield (Eds.), *The handbook of counseling and psychotherapy with men* (pp. 305–320). Newbury Park, CA: Sage.

Marecek, J., & Hare-Mustin, R. T. (1987, March). *Feminism and therapy: Can this relationship be saved?* Paper presented at the meeting of the American Orthopsychiatric Association, Washington, DC.

Mintz, L. M., & Betz, N. E. (1988). Prevalence and correlates of eating disordered behaviors among undergraduate women. *Journal of Counseling Psychology, 35,* 463–471.

Pleck, J. (1985). *Working wives/working husbands.* Newbury Park, CA: Sage.

Rawlings, E. I., & Carter, D. K. (Eds.). (1977). *Psychotherapy for women: Treatment toward equality.* Springfield, IL: Charles C Thomas.

Robertson, J., & Fitzgerald, L. (1989, August). *Men who avoid counseling: Correlates and preferences for assistance alternatives.* In G. E. Good (Chair), Male gender roles and psychological services: Examination of issues. 97th Annual Convention of the American Psychological Association, New Orleans.

Scher, M. (1984). Men in therapy: Commonalities and politics. *Voices, 20,* 41–45.

Scher, M., & Stevens, M. (1987). Men and violence. *Journal of Counseling and Development, 65,* 351–355.

Scher, M., Stevens, M., Good, G. E., & Eichenfield, G. (1987). *The handbook of counseling and psychotherapy with men.* Newbury Park, CA: Sage.

Walker, L. (1979). *The battered woman.* New York: Harper & Row.

Warren, L. W. (1983). Male intolerance of depression: A review with implications for psychotherapy. *Clinical Psychology Review, 3,* 147–156.

Werrbach, J. (1989). *Psychologists perceptions of the male gender role and its influence in the psychotherapeutic process with men.* Unpublished doctoral dissertation, University of Texas at Austin.

Zilbergeld, B. (1978). *Male sexuality.* New York: Bantam.

# 12

# Feminist Identity Development: Implications for Feminist Therapy with Women

*Kathleen McNamara and Kathryn M. Rickard*

This article discusses the implications of the Downing and Roush (1985) model of feminist identity development for feminist therapy with women. Following a summary of the model, the potential pitfalls of feminist therapy with the passive-acceptant client are described, as well as potential issues at subsequent stages of the client's identity development. Suggestions are made regarding how to facilitate clients' movement to higher levels of development. Finally, a research agenda is proposed that suggests hypotheses to be tested that arise from applying this model to conducting therapy with women.

Downing and Roush (1985) proposed a model of feminist identity development based, in part, on Cross's (1971) model of Black identity development. The model provides a framework for understanding the developmental process women go through in confronting sexism in contemporary society and coming to terms with the personal meaning sexism has in their lives. The model proposes a five-stage theory: (1) passive-acceptance, (2) revelation, (3) embeddedness-emanation, (4) synthesis, and (5) active commitment.

The Downing and Roush (1985) model has significant implications for feminist psychotherapy with women. Feminist therapists come from diverse schools of psychotherapy; however, there are certain inherent values and beliefs that distinguish feminist therapy from other brands of psychotherapy (Rawlings & Carter, 1977). In feminist therapy, the sociopolitical roots of women's problems are emphasized in conceptualizing the etiology and maintenance of clinical problems. There is a fundamental assumption that women have less political and economic power than men do and that the patriarchal structure of

Reprinted from *Journal of Counseling & Development, 68,* 184–189, 1989. © ACA. Reprinted with permission. No further reproduction authorized without written permission of American Counseling Association.

society is detrimental to women's mental health. Feminist therapy involves a process of helping the woman explore the extent to which her difficulties may be social (external) in origin. The presenting clinical problem itself may be depression, anxiety, an eating disorder, or a relationship issue. However, rather than focusing predominantly on psychodynamics or behavioral contingencies, as the psychoanalyst or behavior therapist might do, the feminist therapist focuses on how being female in a patriarchal society contributes to the development and maintenance of the problem. Although feminist therapists use a variety of therapeutic techniques, there is a common emphasis placed on assisting clients in developing their autonomy, their self-sufficiency, and ultimately effecting sociopolitical change to benefit women. *Nonsexist therapy* is distinguished from *feminist therapy* in that it typically functions from a humanistic-egalitarian model and does not emphasize sociopolitical explanations of mental health problems among women (Rawlings & Carter, 1977).

The Downing and Roush (1985) model of feminist identity development offers a framework for viewing the developmental process that is likely to take place in successful feminist therapy. Furthermore, the model provides insight into the potential issues that are likely to emerge as women go through the therapeutic change process. Finally, it can be logically inferred from the model what the pitfalls of feminist psychotherapy might be if the client's developmental level is not considered.

Following a summary of the model, this article will explore the process of feminist psychotherapy at each stage of a client's feminist identity development. The potential pitfalls of feminist therapy, particularly with the passive-acceptant woman, are discussed and suggestions are made regarding how to facilitate the client's movement to higher levels of development. These suggestions are based on the work of Greenspan (1983), who has outlined a unified feminist approach to therapy with women that integrates the useful aspects of the traditional therapies with the tenets of feminism.

A second purpose of this article is to offer hypotheses for future research into the issues raised by the model. Although there has been some research conducted to validate the Downing and Roush model (Rickard, 1988a; Rickard, 1988b), the usefulness of applying the model to an understanding of the therapeutic change process, as described here, remains to be tested.

## The Downing and Roush Model

In Stage 1, *passive-acceptance,* the woman accepts traditional sex roles, seeing them as advantageous to her, and she considers men to be superior to women. She is either unaware of or denies prejudice and discrimination against women, and she unquestioningly accepts the "white male system" (Schaef, 1985). She carefully selects her peers in order to maintain her equilibrium.

In Stage 2, *revelation,* a crisis, or series of crises or contradictions occur that cannot be ignored or denied. These experiences might include participation in a consciousness-raising group, discrimination against female children, divorce, denial of credit or job application, and so forth. For a woman in this stage, anger, and secondarily, guilt, are intensely felt over oppression experienced in the past and her participation in that oppression. Intense self-examination and questioning of previous roles occur. This stage is also characterized by dualistic thinking regarding male-female relationships, where all men are seen as negative and all women as positive.

In Stage 3, *embeddedness-emanation,* a woman develops close emotional connections with other similar women, which provides her with the opportunity to discharge her anger in a supportive environment. Carefully chosen other women also provide affirmation and strength in her new identity. Much like the immersion of Blacks in the "Black is Beautiful" culture, women become embedded in a "Sisterhood is Beautiful" culture during Stage 3. Emanation occurs as more relativistic thinking replaces dualism, and men are interacted with cautiously.

Stage 4, *synthesis,* is characterized by the development of a positive feminist identity, where both oppression-related explanations for events and other causal factors can be considered in making attributions. No longer does the woman see sexism as the cause for all social and personal ills. She is able to take a stand that may separate her from many other feminists and yet still maintain her identity as a feminist. There is an integration of personal and feminist values that result in an authentic feminist identity.

Stage 5, *active commitment,* is characterized by translation of the consolidated feminist identity of stage four into meaningful and effective action. Women in this stage set personal priorities, based on their unique talents, for effecting societal change.

Recently, data were reported that provide empirical support for the validity of the Downing and Roush (1985) model. Rickard (1987) developed an inventory (Feminist Identity Scale, FIS) to measure level of feminist identity. A factor analysis of that measure supported the stages as proposed. A significant positive relationship was found between self-esteem and level of identity development, indicating that the higher the level of feminist identity development, the higher the self-esteem score. Ascending positive correlations between stage of feminist identity and positive attitudes toward working women were also found. Individuals categorized as highly passive-acceptant had significantly lower androgyny scores than low passive-acceptant individuals and high synthesis level individuals. Groups hypothesized to score higher on passive-acceptance (Right to Life, College Textiles & Clothing organizations) had significantly higher passive-acceptance scores and lower revelation, embeddedness, and synthesis scores than did groups expected to score low on passive-acceptance (Gay/Lesbian Alliance, NOW organization) (Rickard, 1987). Dating behaviors displayed by women at different FIS levels were consistent with differing sex role behaviors hypothesized to accompany feminist identity development (Rickard, in review). Finally, quality ratings of slides attributed to either a male or female artist were significantly different for women in varying levels of feminist identity development. Passive-acceptance level women valued the work of male artists more than identical work attributed to a female artist. The effect was reversed for revelation level women, and synthesis level women did not preferentially rate the work of one gender over that of another (Rickard, in press).

The Downing and Roush (1985) model probably relates to women's cognitive-developmental levels. Specifically, Perry's (1970) theory of intellectual-ethical development, and the ego and moral developmental theories of Kohlberg (1981), Loevinger and Wessler (1970), and Gilligan (1982) are relevant to this model. An individual's experiences, and his or her cognitive-developmental understanding of those experiences, interact in a reciprocally facilitative manner, and behaviors are reorganized at successive developmental stages. It is believed that identity is one central schema through which experience is approached and integrated. Although not all women use feminist identity as a developmental blueprint, the model is useful for those women who do.

## Feminist Therapy and the Stage 1 Client

Typically, feminist therapists begin their work with clients by attempting to establish an equal relationship and demystifying the therapeutic process (Rawlings & Carter, 1977). This might be done by encouraging the client to ask the therapist questions, not for diagnostic reasons, but to encourage the client to raise legitimate concerns about the therapist and the therapeutic process. Demystifying the therapeutic process also usually involves assisting the client in naming a therapeutic goal in concrete terms and deciding together what the "treatment plan" will be. Questioning the therapist and setting clear goals are designed to encourage the client to take responsibility for the selection of her therapist and for evaluating the progress of her own therapy (Greenspan, 1983).

Early on in feminist therapy the therapist often encourages the client to trust herself as a person who is knowledgeable and powerful in her own right, and the feminist therapist resists forming roles of "expert" and "subordinate." The feminist therapist attempts to uncover the social etiology of her client's problems and uses her own personal experience as a woman in a male-dominated culture to identify with the client. Identification with the client and self-disclosure are strategies commonly employed by feminist therapists (Greenspan, 1983) and are designed to help convey to the client the common social condition that women share. These strategies are also designed to achieve one of the primary goals of feminist therapy: to help a woman see how her power as an individual is inextricably bound to the collective power of women as a group (Greenspan, 1983).

This seemingly positive and egalitarian approach to working therapeutically with women may be experienced adversely by the passive-acceptant woman entering therapy. According to the model, the passive-acceptant woman accepts the patriarchal structure of society without question or scrutiny and sees her role in society as advantageous. Given her worldview, she is likely to be searching for an expert who will tell her what to do and she is likely to be uncomfortable with the feminist therapist's attempt to equalize the relationship. She is likely to see herself as the "patient" or "victim" and see the therapist as "the doctor" or "rescuer" who will have solutions to her problems.

Naming a therapeutic goal may be exceedingly difficult for the Stage 1 woman. Her goal may be "to be happier," "not to nag her husband so much," or "not to be so needy." Turning these global concerns into concrete goals can be difficult. The woman in passive-acceptance tends to rely on the therapist to tell her what to do to feel better rather than explore the source of her difficulties.

As the feminist therapist conveys the idea that the client's problems may stem from social roots, the client may feel misunderstood and may lose confidence in her therapist's ability to help her. The Stage 1 client is likely to believe the problem is her problem, not due to the social conditions women face. For example, a Stage 1 woman who is attempting to work full time and simultaneously fulfill the traditional role of wife and mother may come to therapy with the goal of being less irritable, more easygoing, and less "stressed-out." The Stage 1 client is likely to see her situation as a personal one and have difficulty viewing her situation as part of a larger dilemma that women face in this culture. If the therapist self-discloses in order to convey the commonalities that women share, the client may wonder how the therapist can help if she too struggles with similar issues.

These possible reactions to and experiences of feminist therapy stem, in part, from the Stage 1 client's view of herself as a subordinate to the therapist, and her passive acceptance of the patriarchal structure of society as the way it is and the way it should be. However, these possible reactions may also occur when the feminist therapist fails to consider the developmental aspects of feminist identity and the world and self view of the Stage 1 client.

## Avoiding the Pitfalls

There are some key issues that might be addressed, and a process that might take place in Stage 1, that would help the client remain in therapy and move past the first stage in her feminist identity development.

First, it would seem to be important to be explicit with the client about the attempts that are made to equalize the relationship and demystify the process. The therapist might elicit the client's feelings about efforts made to engage in a therapeutic relationship that is nonhierarchical. Responding to the client's fears and skepticism about the process and emphasizing the benefits the therapist believes she stands to gain are more direct ways of meeting the client at her developmental level. Greenspan (1983) emphasizes the importance of avoiding heavy social interpretations of client problems, and instead, asking the right questions and empathetically listening to what the client says. It would seem to be crucial with the Stage 1 client to move at the client's pace in order to help her discover for herself the role sexism plays in her problems.

With respect to therapist self-disclosures, it would seem especially important at Stage 1 to check out how the client feels when the therapist discloses. It is important not to assume that the client feels warmly toward the therapist just because she acts warmly in response to self-disclosures. The Stage 1 woman has likely been conditioned to respond this way, and her actual feelings may or may not be congruent with her behavior.

A discussion of how she feels about therapist disclosures may provide the inroad for discussing the "rescue fantasy" that Greenspan (1983) has noted is common in many female clients. This fantasy involves the woman viewing herself as a victim and the therapist as a rescuer. A discussion of this possible fantasy can lead into a discussion of her historic reliance on a male provider for sustenance and status. Movement might then take place into an analysis of the benefits that are derived from maintaining her worldview: factors such as economic security and less pressure to achieve. A key question might be: *What does your reliance on a male provider cost you?* These costs may include her tentative self-esteem, lack of autonomy, lack of skills and training, and lack of self-sufficiency.

Focusing on these kinds of issues and using this kind of process are potential ways of avoiding the pitfalls of feminist therapy with the Stage 1 woman and facilitating her movement to Stage 2, revelation.

## Feminist Therapy and the Stage 2 Client

Several therapeutic issues might be considered when working with the Stage 2 client, whether she has entered the revelation stage as part of the therapeutic process or entered therapy as a result of a revelation experience in her life. There is likely to be a shift in terms of the client-therapist dependency issue. The client may be less likely to depend on the therapist to give her solutions but instead depend on her to affirm her anger and dualistic thinking about male-female relationships. Anger is a key characteristic of this stage, as is dualistic thinking, and the client may openly question herself and her roles. She may be more open to the change process at this point, given the flux she is likely to be experiencing.

At this point in therapy, the dependency between the client and therapist can be viewed as a "legitimate dependency," in that her need for affirmation and the therapist's willingness to provide it may facilitate her movement on to Stage 3, embeddedness. At this stage of development, the client is likely to be ready to be mobilized. Additionally, feminist therapists are noted for being particularly effective at legitimizing and validating angry feelings and using anger to combat feelings of helplessness, powerlessness, and low self-esteem (Rawlings & Carter, 1977). Due to the openness to change at this stage, clients would likely be receptive to interventions aimed at helping them to use straight communication and possibly dropping covert, manipulative behaviors. While it may be difficult to point out contradictions between the client's newly formed ideas about herself and her behaviors (because she wants affirmation), clients are likely to be energized at this stage to try new behaviors (e.g., assertion skills) that enable them to test their autonomy and independence.

Stage 2 would seem to be the ideal time to encourage the client to participate in some form of group work. During Stage 1, individual psychotherapy can be more efficient in helping the client move past passive-acceptance, because the therapist can focus exclusively on the woman's own sex-role history and help her examine the price she pays for remaining passive. However, in Stage 2, the client most likely needs to begin to form connections with other women, besides the therapist, in order to move on to Stage 3. The therapist may wish to make referrals to existing community groups or she may be able to refer to her own ongoing women's group.

The goal of therapy during Stage 2 is to "use" the anger and "work" the client's self-questioning to encourage identification with other women. This would seem to be crucial to her continued movement. If the connection with other women is not achieved, Stage 3 is not possible.

## Feminist Therapy and the Stage 3 Client

Stage 3 involves an embeddedness in the female culture and valuing what is uniquely female. Connection with other women provides a safe environment to discharge anger and receive affirmation of one's new identity. However, a barrier to Stage 3 may be feelings of fear and competition with other women. For clients who experience these feelings, it would seem important to explore how these feelings may stem from a view of women as "products" to be either selected or rejected by men. If the client gives up this view of herself as an object or product, she is likely to shift to a view that women must bind together against messages that perpetuate this view of women.

A client may become "embedded" in feminism as she matures through the developmental process in therapy or she may enter therapy at this point in her feminist identity development. Typically, women in this stage of development will want to remain in the "safety" of an all-female culture and may shy away from or be hostile toward men. There is a dualistic mode of thinking that views males as "bad" and females as "good." Women at this stage will tend to be hypervigilant of sexism in their lives and view all problems in their lives as stemming from sexism. Relationships with male superiors, co-workers, spouses, and even acquaintances may become strained.

In therapy, the affirmation a client receives from her therapist and other women in her therapy group may serve to reinforce her anger, and if the client's relationships with men are not examined, she may become stuck at this stage of her development, remain angry, and have difficulty reaching synthesis. In order to move on to synthesis, the client must begin to separate her anger toward a male system that perpetuates discrimination against women from her anger against individual men in her life.

Although the men in her life are indeed part of the system she rejects, and may in fact benefit from it, the individual male is not the system itself. The process of combining and separating causal attributions for events in her life is necessary for her to make accurate attributions and take personal responsibility for her part in the conflict and problems in her life. For example, a woman struggling with an eating disorder and low body esteem might benefit from acknowledging the research that has revealed that women are more critical of their bodies and desire lower body weights than men expect or desire for women (Fallon & Rozin, 1985). These are attitudes some women have internalized from a system that objectifies women's bodies but which individual men do not by and large support.

As the client begins to view men more as individuals with their own problems and issues, "emanation" occurs and the client can move on to the next stage.

## Feminist Therapy and Stages 4 and 5

The next step, labeled *synthesis* in the model, is really a process of differentiating the self from the feminist "party line" in which she is embedded. Again, the dependency issues may emerge in the form of questions regarding how her feminist friends will view her if she decides she does not fully adhere to the typical feminist perspective on a particular issue. For example, the client may be opposed to abortion but feels this is not "the feminist" perspective. The client is faced with the task of integrating her personal beliefs with her feminist convictions. Here the struggle is to be authentic within her feminist identity and break out of playing a role that is not truly genuine or carefully self-examined.

It would seem that the therapist needs to validate the feelings of confusion and questioning and facilitate the differentiation process that allows synthesis to occur. In addition, the therapist might want to guard against viewing the client as backsliding or regressing if she struggles with traditional versus "liberated" attitudes. Allowing the client to fully explore her genuine beliefs and opinions is necessary for her to achieve an authentic feminist identity.

From this process it would seem that Stage 5 would naturally follow; here the process reaches a culmination in active commitment. At this stage the therapist would facilitate the prioritizing and decision-making process. The client is now faced with how she will implement her feminist identity via commitment to carefully selected personal and political goals. Her goal may be to strive toward an egalitarian marriage or raise her children as freely as possible from sex-role constraints. She may choose to commit to local political action on behalf of women or to promote feminism in her line of work. She may initially wrestle with what the "correct" feminist commitments might be— signs that she is still struggling at Stage 4, but as she lets go of an externally defined identity and truly makes a personal commitment, she will begin functioning at Stage 5.

## Therapist Level of Feminist Identity

The model, as proposed by Downing and Roush (1985), is considered to be recyclical in nature. Therefore, therapists themselves may be at different points in their development on different issues in their lives and thus able to help some clients better than others. For example, a therapist who has cycled through the stages regarding career/professional issues, but finds she is recycling again as she re-experiences revelation (Stage 2) regarding issues in her marriage, may work very effectively with a woman dealing with discrimination on the job but not so effectively with a woman going through a divorce. It would seem important for feminist therapists to be vigilant of their own process with respect to their feminist identities and clarify for themselves how their own developmental level of functioning may help or hinder their work with clients at any given time. Seeking supervision from a colleague on such cases where the therapist's developmental process may interfere with the facilitation of the client's growth would certainly be a responsible way of dealing with these kinds of client-therapist developmental interactions. In addition to supervision and case consultation for feminist therapists working through their own "stuck points" as they relate to their clinical work, training programs on developmental theory for feminist therapists-in-training would promote self-examination and self-monitoring of new therapists.

## Future Research

Rationally and experientially, we have found the model to have significant implications for understanding the developmental issues of some female clients. However, research has not directly addressed the application of the model to the therapy process. Therefore, the purpose of this section is to briefly delineate research hypotheses derived directly from the model, from previous writings on feminist therapy, and from our work with clients. The research hypotheses will be presented in three sections:

1. hypotheses relating to client developmental level
2. hypotheses involving therapist factors that may impinge on therapy
3. the issues posed by the interaction of clients and therapists of differing feminist identity levels

It would be expected that clients at varying feminist identity levels would differ in their ability to label emotional states and to link them to specific environmental antecedents. For instance, passive-acceptant level women should experience more global, undifferentiated emotional responses, such as depression, shame, or diffuse anxiety, than women at subsequent levels. They might present to the therapist more frequently with vague complaints of feeling down, tired, or nervous, or with frequent headaches. Since negative affect is not viewed as appropriate female behavior, it may be internalized or somaticized. It is believed that women who have managed to work through to subsequent feminist identity level 5 would have recognized and legitimized such anger and fear. They should be acutely aware of examples of the series of losses often involved in relinquishing past ways of coping and giving up illusions of safety and certainty. Therefore, more specific labeling of emotional responses (sadness and pain, loss, resentment) and greater facility in linking affect to environmental antecedents would be expected.

It would also be hypothesized that clients at synthesis and active commitment levels would have higher self-esteem and experience greater personal responsibility for therapy gains (perhaps exhibited through self-efficacy measures). The synthesis level woman's broader understanding of the societal forces from which she has struggled to be free would suggest a greater ability to integrate personal problems within a societal context and more appropriate selection of internal or external attributions for her difficulties. She would not be expected to view the self-focus often required to work through issues as "selfish," but to view it as necessary to her ability to fully function with others.

It would be anticipated that clients at differing levels would vary in their willingness to join support groups, with embeddedness level women being most responsive to these alternatives. Embeddedness level women would be expected to respond less positively to bibliotherapy than clients at other levels for the same reasons. Passive-acceptant level clients would be most likely to request concrete, specific interventions for targeted behaviors, since they often view the therapist as "the doctor."

Therapist variables center on the therapist's ability to understand these clients, and, therefore, their ability to facilitate growth. It is hypothesized that therapists at passive-acceptance and revelation levels would experience stronger countertransference issues yet be less aware of their potential influence on the client. Anger and urgency often felt by revelation level women might cause these therapists to be most directive and least tolerant with their clients' issues. It would be expected that revelation level therapists as a group would be least interested in, and less effective with, clients desiring to resolve heterosexual relationship problems or clients experiencing difficult authority-individuation issues.

The manner in which therapists conceptualize presenting problems should reflect their level of feminist identity development. The degree to which therapists view issues within a societal context should influence their assessments and interventions with clients. Systems assessments would be expected in therapists at higher feminist identity levels. Therapists at embeddedness, synthesis, and active commitment levels would be expected to value and utilize available resources outside of therapy, to encourage feminist support groups when appropriate, and to be most aware of available community resources.

Mismatches in the client-therapist dyad may lead to clients dropping out of therapy. It would be hypothesized that passive-acceptance level clients would be more likely to drop out of therapy with a revelation level therapist than with synthesis or active commitment level therapists. The passive-acceptant therapist might mislabel the revelation level client's anger, perhaps as hostility, with clients at higher developmental levels eventually dropping out of therapy. Clients at synthesis or active commitment levels would be unlikely to remain in therapy with therapists in earlier identity levels. Generally, it would be anticipated that synthesis or active commitment level therapists would be most prepared to understand the developmental issues, the affect, and the fear regarding developmental progression in clients at all feminist identity levels, and to validate and assist the client in working through the process.

Finally, one note on therapist-client gender match seems relevant. When Cross's (1971) developmental racial identity model was tested on Black college students seeking therapy (Parham & Helms, 1981) a significant preference for Black versus White counselors was found. Specifically, pro-White, anti-Black therapist preference was found for individuals in Stage 1. During Stages 2 and 3 (resembling revelation and embeddedness level feminist development), pro-Black, anti-White counselor preferences emerged. Finally, latter stage attitudes were not associated with preference for either Black or White counselors. The authors concluded that increasing comfort with one's own racial identity facilitated comfort with therapists regardless of race. This conceptualization and the findings of Parham and Helms (1981) parallel that expected to account for differences in therapist preference by feminist identity level. Passive-acceptance women would be expected to prefer male therapists, while revelation and embeddedness women should prefer female therapists. Synthesis level and active commitment level women would not be expected to prefer therapists of one gender over another.

Recent research has suggested that, under certain circumstances, female clients benefit from female therapists more than male therapists (Howard & Orlensky, 1979; Kaplan, 1979; Kirshner, Genak, & Hauser, 1978; Mogul, 1982), particularly with less experienced therapists. The authors suggest that the positive quality of the relational bond between female therapists and clients, the female therapist's sensitivity to inherent power differences, and the willingness of women to use themselves as vehicles for reaching empathic understanding may account for these effects. Within this developmental model, it would be predicted that women entering therapy in revelation and embeddedness, particularly, might experience greater satisfaction and a more positive therapeutic outcome when working with female therapists rather than male therapists.

# References

Cross, W. E. (1971). Negro-to-Black conversion experience: Toward a psychology of black liberation. *Black World, 20*(9), 13–27.

Downing, N. E., & Roush, K. L. (1985). From passive-acceptance to active commitment: A model of feminist identity development for women. *The Counseling Psychologist, 13*(4), 695–709.

Fallon, A. E., & Rozin, P. (1985). Sex differences in perceptions of desirable body shape. *Journal of Abnormal Psychology, 94,* 102–105.

Gilligan, C. (1982). *In a different voice.* Cambridge, MA: Harvard University Press.

Greenspan, M. (1983). *A new approach to women and therapy.* New York: McGraw-Hill.

Howard, K. I., & Orlinsky, P. E. (1979). *What effect does therapist gender have on outcome for women in psychotherapy?* Paper presented at The American Psychological Association, New York.

Kaplan, A. G. (1979). Toward an analysis of sex-role related issues in the therapeutic relationship. *Psychiatry, 42,* 112–120.

Kirshner, L. A., Genak, A., & Hauser, S. T. (1978). Effects of gender on short-term psychotherapy. *Psychotherapy: Theory, Research, and Practice, 15,* 158–167.

Kohlberg, L. (1981). *The philosophy of moral development.* San Francisco: Harper & Row.

Loevinger, S., & Wessler, R. (1970). *Measuring ego development.* San Francisco: Jossey-Bass.

Mogul, K. M. (1982). Overview: The sex of the therapist. *American Journal of Psychiatry, 139,* 1–11.

Parham, T. A., & Helms, J. E. (1981). The influence of Black students' racial identity on preferences for counselor race. *Journal of Counseling Psychology, 82,* 250–257.

Perry, W. (1970). *Forms of ethical and intellectual development in the college years.* New York: Holt, Rinehart and Winston.

Rawlings, E. I., & Carter, D. K. (1977). *Psychotherapy for women.* Springfield, IL: Charles C Thomas.

Rickard, K. (1987, March). *A model of feminist identity development.* Paper presented at the annual meeting of the Association for Women in Psychology, Denver, Colorado.

Rickard, K. (in review). The effect of feminist identity level on gender prejudice toward artists' illustrations. Manuscript submitted for publication.

Rickard, K. (in press). The relationship of self-monitored dating behaviors to level of feminist identity on the FIS. Manuscript submitted for publication. *Sex Roles.*

Schaef, A. W. (1985). *Women's realities: An emerging female system in a white male society.* New York: Winston Press.

# PART 5

## The Gay Client

**A**lthough the psychological literature on gays has moved from a focus on pathology to an emphasis on diversity and affirmation, practicing counselors and therapists have not necessarily changed their views to the same extent (Dworkin & Gutierrez, 1992). As we saw in Chapter 3, many counselors and therapists remain misinformed and continue to hold negative attitudes about gays (Betz & Fitzgerald, 1993). Despite ethical guidelines mandating egalitarian treatment of gay men and lesbian women, not all counselors have taken the necessary steps to address their homophobic attitudes and increase their knowledge and awareness of lesbian women and gay men. Further, although gay men and lesbian women have many concerns in common, there are unique issues faced by each group (Dworkin & Gutierrez, 1992). In the first two chapters in this section, essential attitudes, knowledge, and skills necessary for gay-affirmative counseling are explored in some depth, while the third chapter covers the literature on counselors' attitudes toward gays.

Browning, Reynolds, and Dworkin (1991) address a range of issues and concerns confronting lesbian women, with special attention to those that may arise in counseling. Important aspects of the lesbian experience, all of which counselors must understand in order to work effectively with lesbian clients, are discussed: the coming out process, career development, aging, the problems and prospects of lesbian couples, and lesbian parenting. The special issues related to counseling concerns of lesbians are also covered, e.g., substance abuse, domestic violence, and sexual abuse. Some attention is devoted to the concerns of lesbian women of color. The article ends with a series of recommendations for counseling, including a discussion of the need for feminist counseling with lesbian clients.

In their article "Affirmative Psychotherapy for Gay Men," Shannon and Wood (1991) cover some of the same issues, e.g., the coming out process, career issues, aging, gay couples and gay parenting, and cultural influences, describing some of the unique ways in which these issues are played out in the experiences of gay men in our society. Shannon and Wood (1991) also address concerns of particular importance to gay men, e.g., antigay violence and AIDS. This article, too, ends with a series of recommendations for counselors.

Finally, Rudolph (1988) presents an overview of counselors' attitudes toward homosexuality. His review of the literature documents the continuing problem of counselor bias toward gay people and highlights the ways in which counselors' negative attitudes have been detrimental to gay clients. One of the most intriguing aspects of the article is the exploration of the ambivalent and even contradictory attitudes of mental health practitioners toward gay people. His analysis underscores how imperative it is that counselors and therapists honestly explore and confront their own biases; knowledge alone will not serve either counselors or gay clients well.

# References

Betz, N. E., & Fitzgerald, L. F. (1993). Individuality and diversity: Theory and research in counseling psychology. *Annual Review of Psychology, 44,* 343–381.

Browning, C., Reynolds, A. L., & Dworkin, S. H. (1991). Affirmative psychotherapy for lesbian women. *The Counseling Psychologist, 19,* 197–215.

Dworkin, S. H., & Gutierrez, F. J. (Eds.). (1992). *Counseling gay men and lesbians: Journey to the end of the rainbow.* Alexandria, VA: American Association for Counseling and Development.

Rudolph, J. (1988). Counselors' attitudes toward homosexuality: A selective review of the literature. *Journal of Counseling and Development, 67,* 165–168.

Shannon, J. W., & Woods, W. J. (1991). Affirmative psychotherapy for gay men. *The Counseling Psychologist, 19,* 197–215.

# 13

# Affirmative Psychotherapy
# for Lesbian Women

*Christine Browning*
*University of California, Irvine*
*Amy L. Reynolds*
*University of Iowa*
*Sari H. Dworkin*
*California State University, Fresno*

This article explores the unique issues and concerns facing lesbian women in our culture. Theoretical issues and effective therapeutic interventions in counseling lesbians are examined. Specific content areas highlighted include lesbian identity development and management, interpersonal and couple issues, and specific problems such as substance abuse, domestic violence, and sexual abuse. The article concludes with recommendations for treatment and suggestions for research.

There is a full range of psychological issues within the lesbian community, as in all communities, which may be addressed within a therapeutic context. Lesbians struggle with the same intra- and interpersonal issues that nongays experience. Yet lesbians also experience concerns that are uniquely related to surviving in a world that is heterosexist and homophobic.

As psychologists, we must be willing and able to offer affirmative psychotherapy for lesbian women and work to educate the nongay community to accept and celebrate lesbian relationships and communities. We must seek out information and experiences that will educate us about the unique concerns that lesbian women face, and we must learn about the theories and therapeutic strategies necessary for effective therapy with lesbian clients.

From C. Browning, A. L. Reynolds, and S. H. Dworkin, "Affirmative Psychotherapy for Lesbian Women" in *The Counseling Psychologist, 19,* 177–196, 1991. Copyright © 1991. Reprinted by permission of Sage Publications, Inc., Newbury Park, CA.

This article presents a theoretical overview of issues in counseling lesbian women, as well as offering suggestions for effective therapeutic interventions with lesbian clients. Sections of this article include identity development, identity management, interpersonal issues, and special issues germane to counseling lesbians such as substance abuse, domestic violence, and sexual abuse. We conclude with recommendations for treatment and suggestions for research.

## Identity Development

In the broadest sense, "coming out" as a lesbian is "adopting a nontraditional identity [and] involves restructuring one's self-concept, reorganizing one's personal sense of history, and altering one's relations with others and with society" (DeMonteflores & Schultz, 1978, p. 61). Many psychological models of identity formation have examined how lesbian women and gay men experience the lifelong process of coming out to themselves and others (Fassinger, this issue). Here we highlight those aspects of the identity development process unique to lesbians.

The issues affecting lesbians can be best understood by examining the situation of many women in U.S. culture. Growing up in a sexist culture creates a double bind for women and, therefore, lesbians (Vargo, 1987). If women fulfill their traditional socialized roles and behaviors (e.g., caregiver, dependent), then they are seen as unhealthy. Yet if women step outside their prescribed gender-role expectations and take on behaviors and roles ascribed to men (e.g., provider, instrumentality), they are often seen as inappropriate (Vargo, 1987). By choosing to be woman-identified, lesbians construct their self-image differently from heterosexual women (Vargo, 1987). Research suggests that some lesbians may reject a stereotypic female role early in their development (Groves, 1985); however, even lesbians characterized by the stereotypic female role will encounter homophobia in their daily lives.

The lesbian community provides a social context in which a woman can define herself as lesbian (Groves, 1985) and has helped women to develop an awareness of the dynamics of being female and lesbian. Because the boundaries of acceptable role behavior are often different within the lesbian community, lesbians may find support there for aspects of their identity as women that are not traditionally accepted by the nongay community (Moses & Hawkins, 1982). According to DeMonteflores and Schultz (1978), feminism and the women's movement facilitated the coming-out process for many lesbians by providing a sense of solidarity, community, and positive role models, which are vital to the formation of a positive lesbian identity (Sophie, 1988). Despite homophobia within the feminist community, many lesbians have felt safer coming out within the women's movement rather than in the male-dominated gay movement (Clinton, 1989).

Women may also develop their lesbian identity by a different route than gay men, because of the influence of feminist culture. Faderman (1984) identifies three phases of self-definition for lesbians, which she believes may be reversed for gay men: (a) critical evaluation of dominant social norms, (b) encounters with stigma and internalized homophobia, and (c) sexual experiences. Faderman's work, though controversial, suggests that for at least some lesbians, the feminist community provides a facilitative sociopolitical context for the development of erotic preferences. Therapists can help clients in all phases of the identity development process to participate in lesbian or feminist communities, thereby using the potentially facilitative environment for the development of a positive lesbian identity.

# Identity Management

The process of identity management is an ongoing, ever-changing process through which one defines and redefines what it means to be lesbian or gay (Cass, 1979). As has been suggested, increased contact with the lesbian community, as well as a broadening definition of what it means to be a lesbian, creates an opportunity for a positive identity even within a homophobic culture.

## *Coming Out to Others*

Coming out to friends and family is an important step in the process of claiming a positive and integrated identity and is crucial for self-acceptance and self-esteem (Murphy, 1989). Unlike nongays or members of particular racial groups, lesbian women are usually part of a culture to which their parents do not belong (Zitter, 1987). Lesbians may come out to family or friends in order to decrease feelings of isolation and to maintain a sense of personal integrity. As women, lesbians are often relationship-oriented; as a result, coming out to others may be especially stressful (Zitter, 1987).

Regardless of preparation, a family's response to self-disclosure often is unpredictable (Griffin, Wirth, & Wirth, 1986). Families may need time to unlearn negative messages about lesbians and to grieve the loss of expectations and hopes. Families may respond in many ways. They may be immediately accepting, they may try to ignore or deny the new information, or they may reject the family member temporarily or permanently. The process of coming out to one's family is also affected by long-standing family patterns and dysfunctions. Old family wounds, such as alcoholism and sexual abuse, may be reopened while the family is in conflict, which further complicates this process and creates additional pain, vulnerability, and confusion (Brown, 1988).

Nongay friends may have less difficulty accepting a friend's self-disclosure because they have less at stake in her identity and less involvement in her future life (Moses & Hawkins, 1982). Both families and close friends have their own coming out to do and may also become targets of homophobia and discrimination. In fact, families often have limited support systems, and this isolation makes their process of acceptance more difficult (Brown, 1988). Thus the adjustment and acceptance of families is often determined by the availability of resources and social support (Neisen, 1988).

Therapists can aid a lesbian woman in her decision-making process about how to come out and with whom to share her identity. By examining her motivations, goals, and the potential costs and benefits of sharing her lesbian identity with others, she will be able to make the most positive decision. Therapists must help ensure that alternative social supports are available and that different methods (by letter, in person) have been explored (see Berzon [1988] for a thorough discussion of coming out issues).

## Occupational/Career Issues

Coming out as a lesbian has implications for choosing a career and managing one's identity within a career. A lesbian woman may realize at an early age that she will never depend on a man's salary (Hetherington & Orzek, 1989) and may, therefore, choose a male-dominated occupation in order to maximize her earning potential. Because women, however, are still not widely supported in pursuing nontraditional occupations (Wilcox-Matthew & Minor, 1989), lesbians who have chosen these occupations may experience discrimination and other difficulties. A lesbian will need to decide if she wants to work in an occupation in which her sexual orientation need not be hidden, because self-disclosure in many occupations will result in overt or covert discrimination (Hetherington & Orzek, 1989). For example, many lesbians in such fields as teaching, child care, and child psychology remain "closeted" because of the myth that they recruit children to the gay life-style. A lesbian woman may choose to live in a large city or become involved in national gay/lesbian professional organizations in order to decrease feelings of isolation.

The interdependence of careers and relationships is also important for many lesbians (Berzon, 1988). Lesbian couples face the same dual-career issues as nongay couples, but because their relationship is not validated by society, they usually cannot get support or assistance in dealing with these issues (Hetherington & Orzek, 1989). Therapists can help clients explore occupational options and distinguish between realistic and unrealistic fears; they can also provide information and support, as the following case example illustrates:

> Kay is a 22-year-old confident, assertive lesbian woman. She enjoys working outdoors with her hands and wants to earn a good salary, so she decided to become a construction worker. She recently enrolled in a local community college's 2-year program. Kay decided to see a counselor when the sexist remarks of the male students and teachers began affecting her self-esteem. Kay was one of only two women in the program. Some of the male students frequently alluded to the fact that women do not belong in the construction trades and that any woman who is interested in this field must be "queer." Kay was terrified that they would discover that she was a lesbian.

When Kay entered therapy she was depressed, and not eating or sleeping well. She did not want to give up the program and yet was unsure if she could continue to handle the hostile climate. Kay was very involved in the lesbian community and had a good support system. Her friends supported her interest in construction, which increased Kay's concern that she might betray the community if she left the program. Therapy consisted of providing a safe environment to express her anger and frustration, cognitive disputations of irrational beliefs, role-playing ways to approach male instructors and students, assertiveness training to express discomfort with community expectations for her, and rehearsal of behavioral responses to potential problems.

## Race, Ethnicity, Class, Locale

The development of a lesbian identity does not occur in a vacuum. Intrapsychic dimensions play a part in identity development, as well as factors such as race, ethnicity, class, and locale. For women of some racial and ethnic groups, acceptance of a lesbian identity means violating the role expectations of the culture (Chan, 1989; Espin, 1987; Loiacano, 1989). Women of such groups are polycultural and multiply oppressed (Espin, 1987), identified as a woman in patriarchal culture, as a minority in a culture that is racist and anti-Semitic, and as a lesbian in a homophobic culture.

Lesbian women who are members of certain racial and ethnic groups need to balance their identities within the lesbian/gay culture and within their racial/ethnic communities. The limited research available suggests that developing a lesbian identity may be the more salient process (Chan, 1989; Espin, 1987; Loiacano, 1989). Research suggests (e.g., Chan, 1989) that more social interaction as an ethnic woman or woman of color takes place within the lesbian community than interaction as a lesbian within her racial/ethnic communities. This often creates problems because the lesbian community itself is permeated by racism (Chan, 1989; Espin, 1987) and anti-Semitism (Beck, 1982). Because coming out to families within racial/ethnic communities often means rejection and loss of support, survival in a racist culture becomes more difficult. Larger urban areas may offer opportunities for women to more effectively integrate both aspects of their identity because of the availability of a wider variety of racial/ethnic lesbian organizations.

There has been little research on rural lesbian women or research examining the impact of class or socioeconomic status on the development of a lesbian identity. Many authors believe that the isolation of rural lesbians, the lack of information about lesbians, the lack of role models, and the homophobia present in rural communities affect the coming-out process (D'Augelli, 1989; Moses & Buckner, 1986). The key to managing a lesbian identity in rural areas is discretion (D'Augelli, 1989); thus a major challenge for the rural lesbian is meeting other lesbians. Sometimes the anxiety over being discovered is so severe that rural lesbians isolate themselves from most social situations (Moses & Buckner, 1986). Isolated from other lesbians and in need of social support, rural lesbians are less likely to self-disclose to their families because they fear the loss of family contact. One major consequence of isolation is the difficulty in meeting potential partners; thus rural lesbians often resign themselves to being single and lonely, or they may stay in long-term relationships that are dysfunctional (Moses & Buckner, 1986). The difficulties of rural life for lesbians often lead to low self-esteem and offer a special challenge to therapists working in these geographical areas.

## Age-Related Issues

There are two areas on the aging continuum which are frequently neglected in research on lesbian lives: the young and the old. Each has unique needs and issues which are not always captured by our current generic models of lesbian identity development. Coming out for the adolescent lesbian is generally more difficult than for the adult lesbian (Schneider, 1989). The adolescent generally is more dependent (economically and emotionally) on her family, which intensifies her fear of parental rejection. She also has more restricted access to the lesbian/gay community for support and guidance. The young lesbian does not typically have adult lesbian role models available to help her develop a positive lesbian identity. Because most lesbians are raised in nongay households, they do not learn how to cope with societal discrimination. Lesbians of some racial/ethnic groups may learn from parents how to deal with racism, but they will not learn coping strategies to deal with the heterosexism and homophobia within their own culture as well as the dominant culture.

There are two major areas in which lesbian adolescents may need assistance: (a) making decisions about coming out to family, and (b) developing a social support network. If a lesbian adolescent chooses to come out to her parents, the therapist can identify resources to help parents (e.g., Griffin et al., 1986). Frequently the young lesbian feels as though she is the "only one." Gibson (1988) found that of suicide attempts among adolescents, approximately one third are thought to be related to concerns about sexual orientation. Therapists should help young lesbians identify resources that will reduce isolation and facilitate the development of a social support network (see Gerstel, Feraiso, & Herdt, 1989, for a description of a lesbian and gay youth program in a lesbian/gay community). Books, newsletters, films, and lesbian and woman-identified music may help the young lesbian feel connected to the larger lesbian and gay community.

At the other end of the age continuum are older lesbians. Most of the research on the aged ignores issues of sexual orientation or focuses on relationship issues within traditional heterosexual marriages (Fassinger & Schlossberg, in press). In addition to the era and chronological age at which a woman came out, other variables such as ethnicity/race, health status, economic resources, and strength of her social support system must also be considered. As lesbians age, they become aware of the potential need to interact with professional caregivers. However, in her study on midlife (over 50) lesbian women, Tully (1989) found reluctance to be completely open about sexual orientation with caregivers and unwillingness to trust caregiving systems and the legal system. Kehoe (1988), in her study of 100 lesbians over 60, found that the most serious problems expressed by old lesbian women were loneliness and economic worries. As therapists, we must be sensitive to the needs of the older lesbian by recognizing the impact on identity of coming out during an era when lesbians were viewed as sick or sinful. Health-care institutions, as well as senior-services centers, must be monitored for systematic discrimination or ignorance of the needs of the older lesbian, and advocacy interventions must be implemented as needed.

## Interpersonal Issues

No matter how well integrated into the nongay culture or how supported one feels by a lesbian community, being a lesbian creates a feeling of alienation and marginality. Even in supportive settings, there is always the experience of being "other" (Brown, 1989), which affects one's identity and self-esteem, as well as having pervasive impact on interpersonal relationships.

### Lesbian Couples

All romantic relationships have certain qualities in common, yet lesbian couples can never be viewed separate from their socialization as women or their experience of living and loving in a homophobic culture. Because the heterosexual world does not honor lesbian relationships and offers little institutional or personal support for them, lesbians often see their relationships as temporary or unimportant (Pharr, 1988). Few role models exist for lesbians to learn how to maintain long-term relationships. Public affection, relationship rituals (such as weddings and bridal showers), and legal benefits represent several examples of social support to which most lesbian couples do not have access. Berzon (1988) outlines three factors that block long-term lesbian relationships: (a) expectation of failure, (b) lack of legal and social supports, and (c) invisibility of long-term relationships. These factors exacerbate many of the conflict areas experienced by lesbian couples, such as power, autonomy and intimacy, sex, monogamy versus nonmonogamy, stages in the coming-out process, role-playing, differences of race and culture, political and class differences, and money and family conflicts (Berzon, 1988; Clunis & Green, 1988). Many of these issues are common in nongay relationships as well, but several deserve discussion, as they affect lesbian couples in unique ways.

Nonmonogamy is a major area of ongoing attention within the lesbian community. Often monogamy is seen as a patriarchal value (Toder, 1979), and nonmonogamy is seen as a political statement about disclaiming ownership of one's partner. Lesbian nonmonogamy is often open and consciously planned and consists of ongoing, rather than casual, sexual affairs (Kassoff, 1989). Lesbians also express a strong desire for equality and shared power within relationships (Peplau, Cochran, Rook, & Padesky, 1978), and often dislike conventional relational roles (Clunis & Green, 1988). Although these relationship values may be strongly espoused by some lesbian couples, there are often many differences in each partner's expectations, confounded by the reality of trying to maintain a relationship within a nonsupportive context.

When a couple's differences threaten the relationship, therapists can help partners learn to negotiate. The female socialization process may create a tendency in lesbians to listen to each other intensely but to have difficulty in asserting their own needs, thereby blocking the resolution of issues (Roth, 1989). Traditional female gender-role socialization also has encouraged women to value a high degree of emotional intimacy in relationships. As a result, when two women form a relationship, there is a tremendous potential for emotional closeness between partners (McCandlish, 1982). In addition, there are elements of lesbian relationships that support the value of women's individual independence. When individuals are able to achieve a balance between the need for autonomy and the need for intimacy, the relationship will frequently be perceived as satisfying. When this balance is not present, couples frequently experience conflicts over power, dependency, and nurturing within the relationship (Burch, 1987).

Many authors have discussed the issue of fusion in lesbian relationships, that is, the difficulty of maintaining separate identities within the relationship, and a tendency for merging in thoughts, actions, or feelings (Burch, 1982; Kresten & Bepko, 1980; Pearlman, 1989). For some, this merger or fusion is a more pervasive state, in which excessive dependency leads to tension and anxiety when there is emotional and/or physical distance between partners. Sometimes couples find themselves merged when there is a perceived threat to either the relationship or a member of the couple; given societal homophobia and heterosexism, there is always an underlying threat to lesbian couples, and additional energy must be put into defining and affirming relationship boundaries. For example, during holiday times, the parents of a lesbian woman may ignore her relationship by expecting their daughter to come home without her partner, forcing the daughter to assert more adamantly her commitment to her partner, or to capitulate to family demands and later make up for the denial by increased attention to her partner and by self-imposed social isolation. Hence societal homophobia reinforces a propensity for merging.

Helping couples achieve balance between intimacy and autonomy requires that therapists not impose their own ideas of appropriate balance (McCandlish, 1982), and couples groups may be especially helpful to lesbian couples for support in maintaining healthy relationships. Therapists can also facilitate an understanding of the role that heterosexist culture plays in creating relationship stress, which can result in either emotional distance or enmeshment.

Because lesbian communities are often small, interracial couples are fairly common and the impact of racial/cultural differences must be addressed because each partner will experience the relationship differently based on her race (Garcia, Kennedy, Pearlman, & Perez, 1987). A Caucasian woman, for example, may experience extreme guilt and pain when she hurts her partner in an intended or unintended way; her partner, on the other hand, may experience pain, hurt, and rage when the woman closest to her appears to be "the enemy" (Garcia et al., 1987). Many women of color or ethnic women have experienced multiple interracial friendships or relationships, whereas Caucasian women often have little history of significant interracial relationships. Interracial relationships create risks for both women, including loss of support from family or racial/ethnic community, daily stresses of dealing with racism as a couple, and misunderstanding and miscommunication, as the following case example illustrates:

> When Toni and Megan entered therapy, they had been in a relationship for 2 years. Toni was a 32-year-old African-American woman who worked as an attorney for a local firm. Megan was a 29-year-old Caucasian woman who was completing a doctorate in women's studies and sociology. Megan was very active and "out" in the women's community and had an open relationship with her family while Toni was more cautious with whom she disclosed their relationship. Megan resented how Toni's decision to be closeted was beginning to affect their relationship and their social support networks. Toni was angered by Megan's inability to understand the complexities of being an African-American lesbian.
>
> Couples therapy began with an emphasis on listening to and expressing feelings, and discussing the dynamics of being an interracial couple. Their social group was mostly Caucasian women, which made Toni feel like an outsider. Megan began to realize that she had never examined her privilege as a Caucasian woman and how those dynamics affected their relationship. Using a conflict resolution and negotiation model allowed each woman to express her feelings and feel heard. Therapy created more empathy in their relationship and improved their communication skills, especially with angry feelings. They made some agreements about changes they both wanted in the relationship including broadening their social group, making initial introductions between Megan and Toni's family, and deciding to join an interracial couples' support group.

Sexual issues are another area of potential difficulty in lesbian relationships. Loulan (1984) describes lesbian sex as "anything that two lesbians do together," implying that lesbian sexuality and its importance to individual women cannot be described simply. Not all lesbians engage in all forms of sexual behaviors, and there are very few studies that have examined what actually constitutes sex for lesbians (Loulan, 1987). The definition of lesbian sex is important primarily in its meaning for the couple; thus the focus should be on the individual's and couple's perceptions of what constitutes sex rather than societal or therapists' definitions. According to Berzon (1988), women are programmed to prefer a loving context for their sexual expression, and the type of sexual contact commonly expressed by lesbian couples may emphasize cuddling or passionate kissing, in addition to genital contact (Clunis & Green, 1988).

Discrepancy in sexual desire and absence of sexual desire are the most frequent problems reported by lesbian couples (Hall, 1987). Blumstein and Schwartz (1983) report that the decrease in sexual frequency sometimes experienced by lesbian couples is related to lack of time, lack of physical energy, and becoming accustomed to one's partner. Hall (1987) suggests that although the initial merging between partners is experienced as highly erotic, after time it becomes necessary for individuality to emerge in order to reactivate erotic interest. Therapists can help clients negotiate intimacy and autonomy as a way to increase sexual satisfaction.

Absence of sexual desire may be related to the mixed messages about sexuality given to women in our culture (see Loulan, 1984). These messages about female sexuality are combined with negative messages about lesbians and can be powerful inhibitors toward the positive expression of lesbian sexuality (Loulan, 1987). When these negative messages are internalized, they may become manifested in shame, anxiety, guilt, or avoidance of sex. Also the process of recovery influences lesbian sexuality, whether the recovery is from chemical dependency, eating disorders, emotional/physical illness, or sexual abuse (discussed later in this article). It should be noted that although lesbian women are in the lowest risk category for the transmission of sexually transmitted diseases (STDs) and AIDS, they should give full consideration to the precautions for safer sex (Loulan, 1987); also, lesbians who are seeking to become pregnant through insemination may be at risk for AIDS if the donor has engaged in high-risk behavior, and appropriate caution should be exercised.

Increasing numbers of lesbians are choosing to parent (see Fassinger, this issue). There have always been lesbian mothers and families; in the past, however, most children of lesbian families were conceived in the context of a nongay relationship and later the mother came out as a lesbian. Today many lesbian women are choosing to have children, either within a relationship or as single parents (Clunis & Green, 1988).

There are several excellent resource books available for lesbians contemplating parenthood (Alpert, 1988; Pies, 1985). Deciding to become a lesbian mother requires a great deal of planning and decision making, with attention to issues such as deciding how to get pregnant or adopt a child; coming out (to children, child-care and school personnel); the role of the nonbiological mother and the impact of having two mothers; and concerns about the child's reactions and welfare in a context of societal prejudice. Where children are already present, the loss of custody becomes an important issue because the legal system rests on homophobic and sexist assumptions that question the fitness of a lesbian mother. Despite prejudice, studies that have examined these issues have not found any deleterious effects on children raised by lesbian mothers (Falk, 1989).

A final parenting issue to consider is the impact of children on the couple's relationship. One major stress for lesbian couples is the invisibility of the nonbiological parent and the lack of legal rights for the nonbiological parent in the event of the mother's death or the dissolution of the relationship. When a couple decides to have children or begin a relationship in which there are already children, there may also be changes in the couple's support system. These reactions are important because for many lesbians, friendships serve as alternative families. Lesbian mothers need to learn how to renegotiate their relationships with friends and/or develop new support groups that provide such opportunities.

Despite the large number of enduring lesbian relationships, many relationships between women end, whether by choice, illness, death, or other means. The lack of legal and social support can contribute to the dissolution of the relationship, and it also makes the parting more difficult (Becker, 1988). Engelhardt and Triantafillou (1987) discuss the viability of a lesbian/feminist mediation process as a method for dealing with both legal and emotional ramifications created by the ending of relationships. Lesbians ending relationships may need to come out publicly in order to receive the support they need. Also, because many lesbians come out in the context of a relationship, the loss of that relationship may threaten their lesbian identity. However, Becker (1988) has pointed out that because women have traditionally been socialized to put others' needs first, the end of a relationship can be an opportunity to redefine priorities that reflect her emerging needs.

Research indicates that most lesbians report friends as their primary source of support during a relationship termination (Becker, 1988). However, lesbian couples need to negotiate how to communicate with friends and establish separate spaces for themselves with friends within the context of small communities and overlapping social networks. In fact, one of the unique elements of lesbian relationships is that many ex-lovers continue to be friends and maintain close ties with each other (Becker, 1988). Thus the need to negotiate the ex-lover relationship may reflect not only the previous level of emotional bonding between partners, but also the reality of lesbian communities, where women may continue to socialize, attend cultural events, and work on political activities together. Therapists can help their lesbian clients by identifying strategies to facilitate the transition between ending a partner relationship and developing a friendship relationship with an ex-lover.

# Special Issues in Counseling Lesbians

## Substance Abuse

An issue of special concern to the lesbian community is substance abuse. Research indicates that the rates of substance abuse are higher for lesbians than for nongay women and that lesbians are more likely to be children of an alcoholic parent (Glaus, 1989). As members of an oppressed group, lesbians experience ongoing discrimination, and some authors point to a connection between oppression and addiction (Nicoloff & Stiglitz, 1987). A confounding factor is that, historically, bars were often the only place where lesbian women could meet one another. Even today, for many lesbians, the bar continues to be the first place to explore one's sexual identity. In order to access alternatives to the bar culture, a lesbian must be at the point in her identity development where she is comfortable enough to participate in community-oriented groups and activities that may require a greater degree of self-disclosure and identity acceptance (Glaus, 1989).

Internalized homophobia is thought by some authors to influence the use of drugs and alcohol (Glaus, 1989). In the early stages of the coming-out process, a woman may experience conflict between the emerging awareness of her lesbian sexual orientation and the social prejudices she has internalized. Using drugs/alcohol may be an attempt to numb herself to her emotions and to avoid accepting herself as a lesbian. Glaus (1989) notes that the chemically dependent lesbian may also use denial to protect herself from an unsupportive social environment.

Unique factors experienced by lesbians must be incorporated within treatment approaches. Some of these issues involve whether or not to come out to staff while in treatment; the involvement of the lesbian's partner and friendship network in her recovery; and the difficulty some lesbian clients have with the Alcoholic Anonymous (AA) model, as well as group members who might express homophobic and sexist attitudes. Lesbians who are involved with recovering substance abusers or who grew up in alcoholic homes may utilize the resources of Al-Anon or Adult Children of Alcoholics (ACOA) groups, with attention to the issues already noted. The therapist who is knowledgeable about lesbian and gay community resources that address chemical dependency will be better able to assist her/his client in achieving and maintaining sobriety in the context of an affirming social environment.

### Domestic Violence

Since the early 1980s, domestic-violence service providers have been witnessing physical abuse within lesbian relationships and describing intervention strategies for both mental health providers and the lesbian community (e.g., Hart, 1986). Despite the minimal empirical data regarding the frequency of abuse in lesbian couples, abusive relationships occur across all socioeconomic classes, ages, and ethnicities/races (Hart, 1986). There is a myth that lesbians, because of their socialization as women and commitment to egalitarian relationships, do not encounter domestic violence. Lesbians, however, do engage in physical abuse and the reasons are similar to those of male abusers: the belief that others exist for the abuser's well-being, possessiveness, the need to dominate, and often abuse of alcohol and drugs (Hart, 1986). It is important for therapists to recognize, however, that although chemical abuse may be a factor, women may remain abusive even after recovery from their addiction (Morrow & Hawkhurst, 1989).

There are some significant issues about lesbian violence that are critical for understanding the lesbian survivor's experience. These issues relate to (a) the denial of the existence of lesbian violence within the lesbian community; (b) the victim's difficulty in identifying the abuse (often because the victim has exercised self-defense); (c) the lack of adequately trained service providers; and (d) the difficulties domestic violence shelters experience in providing services to lesbians because of the fear that funding sources will be cut. Effective intervention strategies must focus not only on individual treatment for the victim and abuser but also on education about domestic violence within the lesbian community.

## Sexual Abuse

A survey by Loulan (1987) found that 38% of lesbians had experienced sexual abuse from a family member or stranger before the age of 18, which is similar to the proportion of nongay women who have experienced abuse. The high proportion of women who have experienced sexual abuse suggests that there is a high probability in lesbian couples that one or both of the partners will be survivors of abuse. This poses some unique challenges for the lesbian couple because they may be at different stages of the recovery process or have different needs. Frequently a survivor may experience flashbacks of the abuse during sex or be unable to engage in sex, which may anger, frustrate, or even trigger a flashback for the partner.

In addition, clients may believe that their lesbian identity results from prior sexual abuse. Information about the prevalence of abuse among nongay women, with an emphasis on sexual orientation as an attraction to women rather than a rejection of men, may help clients separate feelings about sexual abuse from concerns about sexual orientation. Many communities have incest/sexual abuse groups and services for survivors and their partners; these groups, however, are not always inclusive of lesbians or their partners, or designed to meet their unique needs, and therapists may be needed to advocate for such services. The following case example illustrates some of the issues related to sexual abuse:

> Terry, a 45-year-old, Caucasian lesbian, sought therapy after the ending of her 2-year relationship. This had been her first long-term relationship and was the first time Terry had experienced any sadness when a relationship had ended. The relationship ended in a familiar way when Terry initiated an affair with a mutual friend. Terry grew up in a chaotic family system. Her alcoholic father spent time in prison and her mother was chronically ill and died when Terry was a young teenager. When Terry was 10 and her parents were unavailable, she was molested daily by her uncle. She reported that this was the only time she remembered feeling loved.
>
> As an adult she always conveyed a strong, independent image to others while feeling very vulnerable and scared. Terry coped with these feelings by frequent casual sex, binge eating, and compulsive shopping. She had previously abused

drugs and alcohol but had been sober for 5 years prior to beginning therapy. Insight-oriented therapy focused on increasing Terry's self-esteem by developing self-nurturing behaviors and restructuring self-perceptions. Terry gained insight regarding how she had connected sex with affection and attention. She also recognized how her mistrust of women and difficulty in establishing nonsexual friendships was related to her experiences of sexual abuse and inadequate parenting. The breakup had given her "permission" to grieve for years of unmet emotional needs and begin to change her pattern of controlling her level of emotional involvement in relationships. In therapy she was able to begin to develop stronger personal boundaries and relate more honestly with others.

## Spiritual and Existential Issues

Rainone (1987) defines spirituality as compassion for self and for others. Prior to the women's movement, the lesbian social scene consisted of bars, softball, and secret organizations (DeCrescenzo & Fifield, 1979). Although these outlets still exist, the feminist movement gave rise to a politically active community that created a political analysis of the oppression of lesbians (Pearlman, 1987). Lesbians may create meaning in their lives by working to end oppression while at the same time developing friendship networks and creating alternative families.

Traditionally, people have met their spiritual needs through caring for others and through religion. The Western Judeo-Christian tradition has not been kind to lesbian women, with scriptural interpretations, customs, and religious doctrine used to create shame (Ritter & O'Neill, 1989). Thus many lesbians have left the church and others have joined groups such as Metropolitan Community Church and gay/lesbian synagogues within the Reform Jewish Movement in order to meet spiritual needs within an accepting context (Ritter & O'Neill, 1989). Still others have recreated witchcraft or the goddess movement, where women and those who are not bound by rigid gender roles are esteemed and valued (Adler, 1986).

Therapists can help lesbians recognize and validate needs for spiritual community and discover how to fulfill them. Awareness of gay/lesbian organizations within existing religions and alternatives to traditional religion will help therapists provide these resources for clients seeking to meet their spiritual needs.

## Conclusions and Recommendations

In this article, we have provided a broad overview of many of the issues that challenge lesbians in contemporary living, including some suggestions for therapeutic interventions. The other articles in this issue articulate many of the specific guidelines critical in working effectively with lesbian and gay clients (i.e., confidentiality, therapist attitudes incorporating diversity, and the impact of societal oppression on identity). The following are recommendations that we would like to add, pertaining to therapeutic and research work with lesbian women:

1. *Feminist therapy.* The recognition that the personal is political is a basic tenet of feminist therapy. Working with lesbian clients requires that the therapist acknowledge the influence that heterosexism and sexism have on lesbian women and the concerns that they bring to therapy. Feminist therapy incorporates the reality of societal oppression into the therapeutic work, recognizes the role of power differences within the therapist/client relationship, and recognizes the impact that gender, ethnicity/race, and sexual orientation have on the experience of both the client and therapist.

   Therapists can help empower the lesbian client by acknowledging that she is the expert about her life, by demystifying the process of therapy, by making relevant self-disclosures to facilitate client growth, and by collaboratively negotiating the goals of therapy. Therapists must ensure that they are aware of any biases that might impair their ability to respect the lesbian client's life experience.

2. *Advocacy.* As Fassinger (this issue) notes, the field of psychology does not have a long history of providing affirmative psychotherapy to lesbian and gay people and has been used as an instrument of social control to label difference as deviance. As gay and lesbian people assert their right to exist and to access the rights and privileges accorded to nongay people, there are growing efforts to criminalize and label lesbians and gays as mentally ill. The current resurgence, for example, of the "reparative therapies" to "convert" lesbians and gays to heterosexuality is one area in which psychology is again being used as an agent of social control (Welch, 1990). Although the American Psychological Association (APA) has made several policy statements that a person's sexual orientation is not indicative of psychological impairment, psychologists must do more. Psychologists (including nongay psychologists) can be in very powerful positions to serve as advocates for lesbian and gay people, and they have the expertise and credibility to educate society about these issues. With specific training, as described in more detail by Buhrke and Douce (this issue), psychologists can serve as expert witnesses in child-custody cases; help to organize services in communities where none exist; and provide sensitivity training in hospitals, police departments, community agencies, schools, churches, and mental-health training programs.

3. *Research implications.* The literature that has been published on lesbian women has primarily presented survey research, theoretical articles, and clinical observations. More empirical research needs to be done in a number of areas that involve the daily life challenges faced by lesbians and ways to change social attitudes to eliminate homophobia and heterosexism. The following are areas in which research is critically needed:

1. The coming-out process for lesbians and how the process is affected by variables of race/ethnicity, age, physical ability, and sociopolitical climate.

2. The effect of gender, race, and sexual orientation on career decisions and employment discrimination.

3. The emergence of the lesbian "baby boom" and the definition of family, as well as longitudinal studies on the experiences of the children of lesbians.

4. Process and outcome studies on effective psychotherapy for lesbians, particularly in areas such as sexual abuse, substance abuse, and domestic violence.

5. How AIDS is affecting lesbians in their roles as caregivers to persons with AIDS, and other health-care issues for lesbians (including AIDS).

6. Process and outcome studies on the influence of training in lesbian/gay psychology for providers of mental health services.

These recommendations represent a first step toward developing a professional response to the needs of lesbians. Historically, women, and lesbians in particular, have been ignored in the historical and psychological literature. As we enter the 1990s, we have a great deal of work to do to make psychology reflective of and responsive to the needs of diverse human populations. In our roles as educators, investigators, healers, and advocates, psychologists can influence society to become a more supportive environment for lesbian women to grow and develop to their full capacities.

# References

Adler, M. (1986). *Drawing down the moon.* Boston, MA: Beacon.

Alpert, H. (Ed.). (1988). *We are everywhere: Writings by and about lesbian parents.* Freedom, CA: Crossing Press.

Beck, E. T. (Ed.). (1982). *Nice Jewish girls: A lesbian anthology.* Watertown, MA: Persephone.

Becker, C. S. (1988). *Unbroken ties: Lesbian ex-lovers.* Boston: Alyson.

Berzon, B. (1988). *Permanent partners.* New York: Dutton.

Blumstein, P., & Schwartz, P. (1983). *American couples.* New York: Morrow.

Brown, L. S. (1988). Lesbians, gay men and their families: Common clinical issues. *Journal of Gay and Lesbian Psychotherapy, 1,* 65–78.

Brown, L. (1989). New voices, new visions: Toward a lesbian/gay paradigm for psychology. *Psychology of Women Quarterly, 13,* 445–458.

Burch, B. (1982). Psychological merger in lesbian couples: A joint psychology and systems approach. *Family Therapy, 9* (3), 201–208.

Burch, B. (1987). Barriers to intimacy: Conflicts over power, dependency, and nurturing in lesbian relationships. In Boston Lesbian Psychologies Collective (Eds.), *Lesbian psychologies* (pp. 126–141). Chicago: University of Illinois Press.

Cass, V. C. (1979). Homosexual identity formation: A theoretical model. *Journal of Homosexuality, 4,* 219–235.

Chan, C. S. (1989). Issues of identity development among Asian-American lesbians and gay men. *Journal of Counseling and Development, 68,* 16–20.

Clinton, K. (1989, June 25). Kate Clinton: The gay '90s. *San Francisco Examiner,* p. 63.

Clunis, D. M., & Green, G. D. (1988). *Lesbian couples.* Seattle: Seal Press.

D'Augelli, A. R. (1989). Lesbian women in a rural helping network: Exploring informal helping resources. *Women and Therapy, 8,* 119–130.

DeCrescenzo, T., & Fifield, L. (1979). The changing lesbian social scene. In B. Berzon (Ed.), *Positively gay* (pp. 15–23). Los Angeles: Mediamix.

DeMonteflores, C., & Schultz, S. (1978). Coming out: Similarities and differences for lesbians and gay men. *Journal of Social Issues, 34,* 59–72.

Engelhardt, B. J., & Triantafillou, K. (1987). Mediation for lesbians. In Boston Lesbian Psychologies Collective (Ed.), *Lesbian psychologies* (pp. 327–343). Chicago: University of Illinois Press.

Espin, O. (1987). Latina lesbian women. In Boston Lesbian Psychologies Collective (Ed.), *Lesbian psychologies* (pp. 35–55). Chicago: University of Illinois Press.

Faderman, L. (1984). The "new gay" lesbians. *Journal of Homosexuality, 10,* 85–95.

Falk, P. J. (1989). Lesbian mothers: Psychosocial assumptions in family law. *American Psychologist, 44,* 941–947.

Fassinger, R. E., & Schlossberg, N. K. (in press). Understanding the adult years: Theoretical advances in lifespan development. In S. Brown & R. Lent (Eds.), *Handbook of counseling psychology* (2nd ed.). New York: Wiley.

Garcia, N., Kennedy, C., Pearlman, S., & Perez, J. (1987). The impact of race and cultural differences: Challenges to intimacy in lesbian relationships. In Boston Lesbian Psychologies Collective (Eds.), *Lesbian psychologies* (pp. 142–160). Chicago: University of Illinois Press.

Gerstel, C. J., Feraiso, A. J., & Herdt, G. (1989). Widening circles: An ethnographic profile of a youth group. *Journal of Homosexuality, 17,* 75–92.

Gibson, P. (1988, August). Gay male and lesbian youth suicide. In *Report of the secretary's [Department of Health and Human Services] tack force on youth suicide* (pp. 3–110 to 3–142). Washington, DC: U.S. Government Printing Office.

Glaus, K. O. (1989). Alcoholism, chemical dependency and the lesbian client. *Women and Therapy, 8,* 131–144.

Griffin, C. W., Wirth, M. J., & Wirth, A. G. (1986). *Beyond acceptance: Parents of lesbians and gays talk about their experience.* Englewood Cliffs, NJ: Prentice-Hall.

Groves, P. (1985). Coming out: Issues for the therapist working with women in the process of lesbian identity formation. *Women and Therapy, 4,* 17–22.

Hall, M. (1987). Sex therapy with lesbian couples: A four-stage approach. *Journal of Homosexuality, 14,* 137–156.

Hart, B. (1986). Lesbian battering: An examination. In K. Loebel (Ed.), *Naming the violence: Speaking out about lesbian battering* (pp. 173–189). Seattle: Seal Press.

Hetherington, C., & Orzek, A. (1989). Career counseling and life planning with lesbian women. *Journal of Counseling and Development, 68,* 52–57.

Kassoff, E. (1989). Nonmonogamy in the lesbian community. *Women and Therapy, 8,* 167–182.

Kehoe, M. (1988). The present: Growing old (1950–1980). *Journal of Homosexuality, 16,* 53–62.

Kresten, J. A., & Bepko, C. S. (1980). The problem of fusion in the lesbian relationship. *Family Process, 19,* 277–289.

Loiacano, D. K. (1989). Gay identity issues among Black Americans: Racism, homophobia, and the need for validation. *Journal of Counseling and Development, 68,* 21–25.

Loulan, J. (1984). *Lesbian sex.* San Francisco: Spinsters Ink.

Loulan, J. (1987). *Lesbian passion: Loving ourselves and each other.* San Francisco: Spinsters/Aunt Lute.

McCandlish, B. (1982). Therapeutic issues with lesbian clients. *Journal of Homosexuality, 7,* 71–78.

Morrow, S. L., & Hawkhurst, D. M. (1989). Lesbian partner abuse: Implications for therapists. *Journal of Counseling and Development, 68,* 58–62.

Moses, A. E., & Buckner, J. A. (1986). The special problems of rural gay clients. In A. E. Moses & R. O. Hawkins (Eds.), *Counseling lesbian women and gay men: A life issues approach* (pp. 173–180). St. Louis, MO: C. V. Mosby.

Moses, A. E., & Hawkins, R. O. (1982). *Counseling lesbian women and gay men: A life issues approach.* St. Louis, MO: C. V. Mosby.

Murphy, B. C. (1989). Lesbian couples and their parents: The effects of perceived parental attitudes on the couple. *Journal of Counseling and Development, 68,* 46–51.

Neisen, J. (1988). Resources for families with a gay/lesbian member. In E. Coleman (Ed.), *Integrated identity for gay men and lesbians: Psychotherapeutic approaches for emotional well-being* (pp. 239–251). New York: Harrington Park.

Nicoloff, L. K., & Stiglitz, E. A. (1987). Lesbian alcoholism: Etiology, treatment and recovery. In Boston Lesbian Psychologies Collective (Ed.), *Lesbian psychologies* (pp. 283–293). Chicago: University of Illinois Press.

Pearlman, S. F. (1987). The saga of the continuing clash in the lesbian community, or will an army of ex-lovers fail? In Boston Lesbian Psychologies Collective (Eds.), *Lesbian psychologies* (pp. 313–326). Chicago: University of Illinois Press.

Pearlman, S. F. (1989). Distancing and connectedness: Impact on couple formation in lesbian relationships. *Women and Therapy, 8,* 77–88.

Peplau, L. A., Cochran, S., Rook, K., & Padesky, C. (1978). Loving women: Attachment and autonomy in lesbian relationships. *Journal of Social Issues, 34,* 7–27.

Pharr, S. (1988). *Homophobia—A weapon of sexism.* Little Rock, AR: Chardon.

Pies, C. (1985). *Considering parenthood: A workbook for lesbians.* San Francisco: Spinsters Ink.

Rainone, F. L. (1987). Beyond community: Politics and spirituality. In Boston Lesbian Psychologies Collective (Ed.), *Lesbian psychologies* (pp. 344-353). Chicago: University of Illinois Press.

Ritter, K. Y., & O'Neill, C. W. (1989). Moving through loss: The spiritual journey of gay men and lesbian women. *Journal of Counseling and Development, 68,* 9–15.

Roth, S. (1989). Psychotherapy with lesbian couples: Individual issues, female socialization and the social context. In M. McGoldrick, C. M. Anderson, & F. Walsh (Eds.), *Women in families* (pp. 286–307). New York: Norton.

Schneider, M. (1989). Sappho was a right-on adolescent: Growing up lesbian. *Journal of Homosexuality, 17,* 111–130.

Sophie, J. (1988). Internalized homophobia and lesbian identity. In E. Coleman (Ed.), *Integrated identity for gay men and lesbians: Psychotherapeutic approaches for emotional well-being* (pp. 53–66). New York: Harrington Park.

Toder, N. (1979). Lesbian couples: Special issues. In B. Berzon & R. Leighton (Eds.), *Positively gay* (pp. 41–55). Los Angeles: Mediamix.

Tully, C. T. (1989). Caregiving: What do midlife lesbians view as important? *Journal of Gay and Lesbian Psychotherapy, 1,* 87–104.

Vargo, S. (1987). The effects of women's socialization on lesbian couples. In Boston Lesbian Psychologies Collective (Eds.), *Lesbian psychologies* (pp. 161–174). Chicago: University of Illinois Press.

Welch, B. L. (1990, January). Statement made at a press conference on reparative therapies. (Available from the American Psychological Association, 1200 Seventeenth St., NW, Washington, DC 20036)

Wilcox-Matthew, L., & Minor, C. W. (1989). The dual career couples: Concerns, benefits, and counseling implications. *Journal of Counseling and Development, 68,* 194–198.

Zitter, S. (1987). Coming out to mom: Theoretical aspects of the mother–daughter process. In Boston Lesbian Psychologies Collective (Eds.), *Lesbian psychologies* (pp. 177–194). Chicago: University of Illinois Press.

# 14

# Affirmative Psychotherapy for Gay Men

*Joseph W. Shannon*
*Shannon & Associates*
*William J. Woods*
*University of California, San Francisco*

This article explores unique issues that confront gay male clients. These issues include identity development and management, interpersonal issues, and special issues, such as the impact of aging, antigay violence, and acquired immune deficiency syndrome (AIDS). Diversity within the male gay community is also addressed throughout the article, and case examples are used to illustrate issues more fully. The article concludes with recommendations for treatment and research.

Gay men struggle with many of the same issues that confront other clients, but they also have to learn how to cope with problems that are unique to their lifestyles and sexual orientation. Moreover, as Tievsky (1988) notes, gays must often come to terms with their concerns in the context of a "largely fearful and rejecting society." As counseling psychologists, we must be sensitive to the special issues gays will bring to therapy. We also need to avail ourselves of training in the theories, strategies, and techniques of effective psychotherapy with gay clients.

The purpose of this article is to present an overview of basic issues in counseling gay men. Our discussion will include sections on identity development, identity management, interpersonal issues, and special issues germane to counseling gay men, including the impact of aging, antigay violence, and acquired immune deficiency syndrome (AIDS). We will conclude with recommendations for treatment and research. Diversity within the male gay community will be addressed throughout the article, and case examples will be presented to illustrate more fully the issues being discussed.

From J. W. Shannon and W. J. Woods, "Affirmative Psychotherapy for Gay Men" in *The Counseling Psychologist, 19,* 197–215, 1991. Copyright © 1991. Reprinted by permission of Sage Publications, Inc., Newbury Park, CA.

# Identity Development in Gay Men

Colgon (1987) defines identity as a "personal construct of self worth." Many current theorists (e.g., Colgon & Riebel, 1981; Isay, 1989; Johnson, 1985) suggest that optimal identity formation and development represents an ongoing dialogue between one's personal construct of self-worth and the responses of significant people (most notably parental figures) in the individual's life. If the responses are consistently negative, the individual's capacity for self-valuing is diminished markedly. Identity development then becomes interrupted or disordered. An identity disorder will have a profoundly negative impact on the adult, especially with regard to self-esteem and the ability to develop satisfying interpersonal relationships. Conversely, if responses from others are largely positive or affirming, the individual will come to see himself as having positive self-worth. Ideally, as the individual grows and matures, he will rely more on his internalized sense of self and less on the reactions of others to determine self-perceptions and courses of action.

Although many gay clients do not present serious identity issues, it is important for the therapist to have a conceptual framework for understanding normal gay identity development so that he/she can assess how healthy the individual is. The therapist can calibrate the client's level of identity development by addressing a number of critical areas early in treatment, including (a) early relationships with parents (especially the father), siblings, and other significant caretakers; (b) ways in which tenderness/affection was or was not expressed in the family; (c) how conflict was handled within the family; (d) at what age he knew he was "different" from other boys and his understanding of this difference; (e) his first awareness of sexual/affectual feelings for other males; (f) a careful description of his process of "coming out"; (g) a history of significant romantic relationships (i.e., dating, boyfriends, and lover relationships); (h) a thorough sexual history, including a frank discussion of sexual fantasies and sexual preferences; and (i) gender-role conformity/nonconformity and the impact this had/has on the individual's process of coming out.

The importance of establishing a positive gay identity cannot be overstated. As Colgon (1987) notes, positive identity and intimacy interact to reinforce each other. Thus gay men with identity disorders will have significant difficulty in establishing and maintaining healthy relationships, romantic and otherwise, with others.

Colgon (1987) and others (e.g., Beattie, 1989) describe two specific intimacy issues that are directly related to poor identity development. Counterdependence (overseparation) involves forming and maintaining one's identity at the expense of emotionally satisfying relationships. The counterdependent person tends to repress or deny his emotional needs, has difficulty discriminating/labeling and expressing feelings, especially vulnerable feelings, and tends to create psychological distance by relating to others in an unemotional, detached, or superficial manner.

By contrast, the codependent (overattached) individual tends to feel insecure and anxious unless he is attached to others. He will have difficulty choosing healthy partners and will often tolerate extremely inappropriate and even abusive behavior from significant others. Like the counterdependent person, the codependent individual has difficulty attending to his feelings; however, he is usually inordinately attentive to the feelings of others. Codependent individuals invariably look to others for something that must ultimately come from within—self-validation (Beattie, 1989; Black, 1989).

Both the counterdependent and codependent client share characteristics of excessive needs for personal and interpersonal affect regulation (Colgon, 1987). In each case, control is exercised to prevent or create emotional involvement and thus reduce unmanageable anxiety. Both conditions are shame-based (Black, 1989) in that the counter- or codependent client feels that he is fundamentally flawed. These feelings result from lack of emotional support/affirmation early in life, which is later exacerbated by the shame of being different (i.e., homosexual) in a rejecting social context. It should also be noted that counter- and codependent clients may have other difficulties besides problems with interpersonal relationships per se. Compulsive (and addictive) patterns such as compulsive overeating, dieting, spending, sex, and drinking are often part of the symptom picture. All of these conditions have their origins in a shame-based upbringing, in which the gay child/adolescent is given a clear message from parents, siblings, peers, or others that he is somehow defective. The compulsive behaviors are developed to ward off feelings of anxiety and shame, to gain control of the environment, and to nurture the wounded self. Some of these behaviors may initially serve as a replacement for parental love and affirmation and later replace self-validation. This partially explains why a number of male gay clients will initially present with problems related to alcohol abuse or other compulsive behaviors (Fifield, 1975).

The case of Tim illustrates the phenomenon of identity disorder:

> Tim is a 34-year-old computer programmer with 12 months of sobriety after a 20-year battle with alcohol. Despite regular attendance at Alcoholics Anonymous (AA) meetings and diligent efforts at 12-step work, Tim continued to feel depressed and anxious. Tim also reported frustration over his inability to develop a satisfying romantic relationship. From addressing the aforementioned critical areas in Tim's background, it became very apparent that he was suffering from a disorder of identity. Tim grew up in an extremely dysfunctional (shame-based) family. He also had difficulty making friends in the neighborhood and in school because he was very quiet and shy. Tim avoided competitive games and sports (non-gender-role conforming) and was quickly labeled a "sissy" by his peers. This label and others like it followed Tim throughout his primary and secondary education. He began drinking in high school, shortly after his first sexual encounter with another boy. Tim had always known he was different but had

hoped he would change and be more like the other boys. As Tim's despair increased, so did his drinking. By the age of 24 he was a full-blown alcoholic. Sex by this time had also become compulsive. During his 20s and early 30s, Tim had a series of short-lived sexual relationships. In most cases, Tim found himself uncomfortable being with other men sexually (or otherwise) unless he was attending to their needs (codependency). With sexual encounters Tim would seldom allow his partner to reciprocate but would masturbate later when he was alone (counterdependent). Tim knew that he was oftentimes looking for affirmation from another person because he had no clear sense of who he was or of his inherent value as a human being. Before Tim could begin to develop healthier relationships, he clearly needed to address his lack of a positive identity as a gay male. Identity development thus became the primary focus of treatment.

# Identity Management

## Obstacles and Opportunities

As McDonald (1982) and Berube (1990) point out, gay men live in an antagonistic society, which can be experienced on many levels. Initial identity affirmation brings with it a certain peace of mind, even bliss, but ongoing confrontation with homophobia and heterosexist social policies, laws, institutions and organizations quickly challenges the individual's view of himself and the world and throws his sexual orientation into sharp relief. As the gay male client comes to grips with society's reaction to him, the therapist needs to assist him in identifying those issues that he feels compelled to fight and to support him in that fight, as well as to teach coping skills to deal with the issues that must be left for another time or for others to confront. These obstacles often present opportunities for gay men to develop further their positive gay identity and to integrate that identity within the larger context of their social/professional/familial lives. Therapists may work with gay men at any stage of development confronting these issues. As with similar issues among nongay clients, their task is to assist these men toward positive resolution of the conflict.

## Coming Out

One very important step in identity development that fosters integration is coming out to family and friends. When gay men choose to come out, especially the first few times, caution and planning are worthwhile (Borhek, 1983). Therapists can assist clients to be sensitive to timing, needs, circumstances, and the identity of the recipient (e.g., fundamentalist Christian) first. Many recipients of the information will, in fact, experience initial grief at the loss of the person they thought they knew. Gay men should be aware of this possible reaction and be prepared to deal appropriately with it. Initial reactions, especially unfavorable ones, can change with some time and effort, and positive, stable relationships may flourish again.

Sometimes coming out ends a relationship with a friend or family member. In such cases, the gay man needs love and support as he (knowingly or unknowingly) passes through the various stages of grief and loss. Understandably, he may feel intense anger toward the rejecting friend or relative, or he may attempt to bargain with that person in a number of ways. He may also introject the anger and experience depression, despair, and even suicidal thoughts and feelings (Babuscio, 1976; Berzon, 1979c; Jay & Young, 1977; McDonald, 1982). Of course, the duration and intensity of these emotions depends on the significance of the relationship and the emotional maturity and ego strength of the gay man, as well as, to some degree, the kinds of ways that he was dependent on the rejecting person.

The case of Jim clarifies a number of the issues related to coming out:

> Jim is a 33-year-old White male. He lives in an urban area with his lover of 5 years. Jim feels relatively comfortable with his gay identity, having been aware of his sexuality since his early teens, and out to his parents since his late teens. He came to therapy presenting concerns about his isolation and depression and his deteriorating relationship with his family. Jim came out to his parents in a fit of teenage anger. He needed something to hurt them and used his sexuality. His parents had always identified with their fundamentalist Christian church, and Jim's revelation, and the manner in which he revealed it, put additional stress on their already strained relationship.
>
> In therapy, Jim began to consider the double standard he set for his family. He was strongly gay-identified and could not believe the teachings of his parents' church. Yet he expected them to deny their identity with that church and accept his sexuality fully. He realized that compromise was necessary. He had to allow his family their religious beliefs, but could ask them not to preach to him or to attempt to change him.
>
> By the end of therapy, Jim had had a number of very positive experiences with several family members. Although tension with his family occurred from time to time, he saw these tensions as part of his family learning how to be with him as an adult, not as their rejecting him and his sexuality.

Gay men do, of course, come out to others besides friends and family. They can have similar experiences with colleagues at work or school, employers, clients, religious leaders, roommates, neighbors, and others with whom they have social and occupational associations. Depending on the state or city, one may have legal recourse to negative reactions (such as loss of job or housing), and the therapist can help the client in deciding whether and when to engage in such battles. The bottom line is that coming out is a matter of personal choice, and it will involve a certain degree of risk for most individuals. Clients must carefully prepare for the possible consequences of their choice to share or withhold information about their sexual orientation. Although sharing may result in some painful rejections, it may also lead to a deepening of relationships, less isolation, and a more integrated life-style.

## Occupational/Career Issues

Given that the choice to live out an openly gay life-style may well lead to discrimination, ostracism, and even violence, career counseling and life-style planning represent special challenges to therapists working with gay individuals. Careful vocational/life-style planning might include, for example, preparing while still young for an occupation or profession in which there is a maximum of freedom from constraints imposed by other people. Or it might involve restructuring one's income-producing activity later in life to enable such freedom (Berzon, 1979b). Life-style planning might mean coming out to family and friends early in life so that deception does not have to become a painful habit to be broken later. Shifting one's values may also be necessary so that projects and goals would yield greater personal affirmation and freedom (versus material reward, for example). For clients who are exploring career/job choice per se, therapists need to be aware of special resources available to gays (Schmitz, 1988). These would include gay professional networks (e.g., National Lawyers Guild Gay Caucus, Association of Gay Social Workers, Gay Airline Pilots Association, and gay business and professional organizations in major cities); viable corporate climates (i.e., organizations recognized as possessing nondiscriminatory policies toward gays: see National Gay Task Force for listing); legal codes and statutes that protect the rights of gays in the job setting (i.e., legislation which prohibits discriminating practices based on sexual orientation); and printed materials that provide information relevant to the job search (e.g., *Gayellow Pages,* which provides an annual listing of gay networks, professional associations, and businesses, and can be purchased at gay bookstores). Therapists also need to educate their gay clients about careers that continue to discriminate based on sexual orientation (e.g., many federal government positions requiring a security clearance are not open to gays; Herek, 1990).

## Race, Ethnicity, Class, Locale

We have described the general development and management of a gay male identity in the face of a homophobic and heterosexist society. For the most part, what has been studied and written about is based on a White male experience in a White, male-dominated culture. Obviously, men of other racial/ethnic groups are likely to have a different experience and to live within a subculture that has its own attitudes and beliefs about homosexuality (Moses & Hawkins, 1982). Therapists need to be aware of their own racism and prevailing cultural attitudes toward sexual and racial differences. Moreover, clients experiencing the "double whammy" of homophobia and racism will need special encouragement and support.

Class distinctions are also important. Across various racial and ethnic groups there can be more within-class similarity than within-race similarity in terms of how sexual diversity is viewed/tolerated (Atkinson & Hackett, 1988).

It is clearly necessary to draw out a man's values and beliefs as related to his perceived social class and to assess how these may affect his identity as a gay man.

Finally, there are differences in locale. Regional differences across the country influence mores within the gay subcultures and the individuals who participate or choose not to participate in those subcultures (Clark, 1987). Within regions, there are also differences between rural and urban areas (Moses & Buckner, 1982). These differences include values and goals as well as resources and needs. Therapists need to be sensitive to the influence of locale on the developing gay identity. Generally speaking, the individual will fare better if he has the opportunity to develop in an urban, more psychologically sophisticated, and more tolerant setting. This is why so many gays emigrate to large urban settings that typically have large gay subcommunities. In these settings, the gay individual has greater opportunity to develop a network of supportive friends and an open life-style that will enhance his emerging identity.

# Interpersonal Issues
## Isolation, Marginality

Despite coming to terms with his sexuality and his own homophobia, each gay man will continue to live in a world of covert and obvious oppression. The temptation to isolate oneself will be constant, especially as one confronts new or renewed homophobia internally or in others. Sometimes isolation is complete aloneness in the comfort of one's closet; other times it manifests itself in token participation in relationships in which parts of oneself are continually and purposely hidden for fear of rejection. The isolation can also generalize beyond the gay issues and become part of a more general way of interacting with others (Clark, 1987).

Part of any successful therapy will be the enabling of fully interpersonal relationships with gay and nongay friends and relatives (Berzon, 1979b; Clark, 1987; McDonald, 1982). It will also entail encouraging the client to participate in the larger community. This may include gay and nongay interactions with social, political, religious, or other groups.

## Gay Male Couples

There is very little descriptive or empirical research on gays seeking couples therapy. However, most writers (e.g., Berzon, 1988) point out that gay couples struggle with many of the same types of conflict and stress that nongay couples present in treatment; this conflict/stress may be exacerbated by living with oppression and the effects of same-sex socialization. Common issues include communication problems; sexual issues; money problems; intimacy issues with each other (e.g., the danger of fusion) and with others (e.g., the importance of developing supportive relationships outside the primary relationship); parenting issues, for a number of gay men do have at least partial custody of biological children from previous heterosexual unions and are choosing to parent (Cramer, 1986); and how to deal with differences (e.g., differences in background, values, and goals).

Clearly, as George and Behrendt (1987) note, all couples in a healthy relationship, whether gay or nongay, have similar characteristics: Partners are committed to each other, share feelings, respect each other, are intimate, and have the capacity to resolve conflicts. We would add to this list for male couples the following:

1. *Each partner is able to accept (and value) his homosexuality.* This acceptance is necessary for positive self-esteem and vital to the acceptance of the sexuality of one's partner. Significant stress may occur in a gay relationship when there is a discrepancy between the two partners with regard to level of "outness." For example, one partner may be more closeted than the other. The less closeted person's openness about his sexuality will be potentially threatening to his partner, and conflict and stress could ensue. Therapists need to assess degree of outness with each partner in a male couple and determine whether there is a major discrepancy and how the latter may be affecting the relationship.

2. *Each partner has relinquished rigid male stereotypic roles.* The stereotypic male role in our culture is to be aggressive, competitive, unemotional, in control, always strong/competent, and independent. The problems that result are probably obvious: How do two men, behaving according to the rigid male stereotypic role, communicate (especially feelings of vulnerability) to each other? What kind of intimate, loving relationship can develop if both partners are constantly competing with each other? Therapists must assess the degree to which stereotypic male roles may be contributing to the couple's presenting problems and assist parties in expanding their behavioral and attitudinal repertoires.

3. *Each partner has relinquished stereotypic sexual roles.* As Zilbergeld (1978) notes, men are supposed to be sexually active, experienced, ready and able to perform at any time and under any circumstance. The gay male's self-esteem may be too dependent on his partner's perception of him as being masculine and as a good sex partner. The belief that he must always be desirous and capable of having sex may create considerable stress (George & Behrendt, 1987). There is also the danger of equating specific sex acts with masculinity and femininity. Most gay men prefer a variety of sexual positions and activities. Problems will occur when partners get locked into a specific sexual act because of a role that is being played. This limits the quality of sexual interactions and creates stressful expectations for both partners. Finally, the need to be always competent at sex, with the focus being on mutual orgasm and ejaculation (versus

communion, intimacy, and playfulness), adds additional stress. This could ultimately result in sexual dysfunction for either partner.

4. *Each partner is committed to not abusing mood-altering chemicals or each other.* Although substance abuse and partner abuse are by no means unique to gay couples, they are clearly common issues in treatment. Both issues typically go hand in hand, in that it is rare to treat a case of partner abuse where neither partner has a serious problem with chemical abuse or dependency (Beattie, 1989). Moreover, a number of writers (e.g., Fifield, 1975) have suggested that substance abuse (particularly alcohol abuse or dependency) is a much more pervasive phenomenon in the gay community than in the general population. This is understandable in light of the previous discussion about the relationship between low self-esteem and addictive behaviors. Also, gay bars continue to be the primary (and, in some settings, the only) social outlet for gay men. Therapists working with gay individuals or couples should have a solid foundation in assessment and treatment of chemical dependency, and the impact of chemical abuse/dependency on the individual and his partner should be assessed and addressed before other issues are dealt with in treatment, including partner abuse. With regard to the latter, firm guidelines regarding fair fighting (e.g., no physical violence, use of win-win conflict resolution model, "time-out") should be presented to the couple. Therapy would then involve helping the couple learn how to use a conflict resolution model to resolve sources of difficulty without resorting to physical or verbal abuse. A number of therapists (e.g., Berzon, 1979a, 1988) also recommend using a fair-fighting, conflict-resolution model to develop a relationship contract that clearly specifies boundaries, expectations, and values for the couple. If conflict cannot be resolved, or if abusive patterns persist, termination of the relationship will need to be presented as a viable option.

To illustrate some of the issues and interventions relevant to couples therapy, we will briefly discuss the case of Joe and Terry:

> Joe is a 43-year-old florist who originally presented symptoms of a chronic, low-grade depression and alcohol dependence. Joe had also expressed concern about maintaining the stability of his 16-year relationship with Terry, a 36-year-old accountant. Joe completed an inpatient detox program, began a 12-step recovery program, was placed on an appropriate anti-depressant medication, and was seen for individual treatment for approximately 3 months before Terry was asked to come in for couples therapy. Many of the issues that Joe presented in his individual therapy were later discovered to have had a negative impact on his relationship with Terry. These included low self-esteem (to the extent that self-worth was equated with achievement), the need to be in control, a difficulty in accepting and sharing vulnerable feelings, a tendency to fear and avoid conflict with a corresponding tendency to internalize anger or express anger passive-aggressively, and intense performance anxiety during sexual encounters with Terry, which occasionally resulted in sexual dysfunction. Terry's level of

self-esteem was significantly higher than Joe's, but he too was very fearful and avoidant of conflict. The initial task for the therapist was to help each party identify how they were contributing to the stress in the relationship. Once issues were identified, a constructive fighting model was presented to help Joe and Terry work through sources of distress as well as eliminate their fear of dealing with conflict directly. The process of conflict resolution enhanced intimacy for Joe and Terry and made it easier for them to approach and resolve future problems. Eventually, Terry was able to see how he had enabled Joe's drinking and reinforced Joe's unrealistic expectations about performance. Terry began attending Al-Anon meetings while Joe continued with AA. Both grew closer and reinforced each other's recovery and growth. Therapy had served as an effective catalyst for both individual and systemic change.

# Special Issues

## *Impact of Aging*

There has been little research done on older homosexual adults. The available research is primarily descriptive in nature and based on small samples of subjects. Much of this research has attempted to explore the validity of certain myths and stereotypes regarding the process of aging for homosexual persons (e.g., Almvig, 1982; Berger, 1980; Kimmel, 1977, 1978). This research would seem to suggest that older (i.e., age 55 and older) gay people have many of the assets and liabilities of older people in general. Aging is often seen as an equalizer of differences, in terms of social class, educational background, race, sex, and sexual orientation. The dominant issue for the aged person regardless of these variables is health status. Thus, as with nongays, older gays are concerned about maintaining good health and access to high quality medical care.

However, older gay men do have some unique issues. Being gay subjects one to special threats of exposure, loss of job (if still working), social stigma, arrest, or physical violence. Whether these threats are reality-based or not, they may exist in the mind of the older gay man because today's older gay men grew up in a more sexually repressive period; the fear of, and sense of vulnerability to, social oppression is often much stronger among older gays than among younger gays (Kimmel, 1977, 1978).

Older gay men are more likely to be angry at years of oppression. Generally, this anger may have been dealt with constructively via hard work in an occupation, developing a strong network of friends, and/or political activism. For others, anger was largely introjected, resulting in anxiety, depression, and self-esteem problems related to internalized homophobia.

Getting sexual/affectual needs met without being perceived as a "dirty old man" is another common issue. This may have less to do with being gay and more to do with society's negative views regarding sex among the elderly (one type of ageism). Also, as Kimmel (1977) notes, for many older gay men, the conquest-oriented, competitive, orgasm-focused emphasis of sex in youth often gives way during the second half of life to more concern with communion, companionship, and mutual sexual enjoyment.

Although all older individuals deal with issues of loss, older gays may receive less sympathy and attention when dealing with the loss of a long-term lover or close companions and friends. Legal issues, problems with family members, the reactions of health-care professionals, and the (oftentimes grossly) insensitive reactions of the bereaved's family can also complicate the grieving process (Kimmel, 1977).

Kimmel (1977, 1978) and others (e.g., Friend, 1987) have also elucidated some of the advantages of aging among gays, namely, that gays may be more prepared to live independently in older age, in that they do not have unrealistic expectations of relying on children or family to care for them as they grow older. There may also be greater continuity of life for gay men, who have not had to deal with children leaving home, who have not confined themselves to rigid male roles in the necessary tasks of living, and who may have already lived alone as adults. Gay men as a group are also more likely to develop a strong network of supportive friends apart from their primary relationships. Thus, as the gay man grows older, and as significant others die, he is less likely to feel completely isolated and lonely, unless he has led an extremely closeted existence.

Although the research discussed above may be helpful in understanding the issues of the older gay client, there is clearly a need for more extensive research (perhaps longitudinal studies of large samples) that would clarify the normal psychological changes and challenges that occur as gays grow older.

One related topic that has received virtually no attention in empirical research is the impact of AIDS on the generational structure of the gay male community. Thousands of gay men are dying or have died in their prime because of AIDS. How will this affect those who live? For example, how will gay men turning 55 in the next 20 years deal with the significant lack of men their age? Peers who die prematurely of AIDS in their 30s and 40s will not be there to provide support and continuity, nor will they be there to provide healthy role models for our gay youth. Our hope is that this and other topics related to aging will receive the attention they deserve in future research.

## Antigay Violence

Antigay hate crimes can be defined as any action that is intended to harm or intimidate individuals who are gay or lesbian (Herek, 1989). Actions can include anything from slurs yelled by a passing motorist to torture and murder. Though prevalent throughout history (see Fassinger, this issue), antigay hate crimes are beginning to receive more attention, especially in the gay community. Some of this attention has been aimed at identifying the prevalence and severity of the problem. Despite the methodological flaws inherent in doing formal research on this issue (see Herek, 1989), several studies have clarified the epidemic proportions of hate crimes directed at gays. Because the problem of antigay violence occurs so frequently and is experienced by so many gay men, it is imperative that therapists be aware of the problem and assist their clients in confronting the reality of the hate crimes they experience. Obviously, these crimes can have insidious effects on self-esteem (Bohn, 1984), resulting in feelings of guilt, shame, depression, and isolation. Rage and anger toward society and the gay community can also ensue (Anderson, 1982). To the extent these crimes go largely unacknowledged by the criminal justice system and society, it is also likely that the victims of such crimes will give them inadequate attention, despite the long-term aversive effects (Finn & McNeil, 1987).

Therapists can play several vital roles in addressing antigay abuse. In treatment, the therapist can help the client acknowledge the problem and explore the potentially serious impact on the individual's sense of security and self-esteem. Helping the client to identify feelings about the experience and directing those feelings in positive channels facilitates a healthy recuperation from the encounter. As an advocate, the therapist can assist the client in identifying resources, such as legal and medical, for dealing with consequences of the crime. Furthermore, therapists can watch for suicidal ideation, particularly with rape-trauma victims. With the latter group, crisis intervention, advocacy, follow-up counseling, self-defense training, and community interventions (such as community education programs) could be legitimate functions of the therapist (Anderson, 1982; Herek, 1989; Miller & Humphreys, 1980).

## AIDS

AIDS, though not a gay disease, is completely entwined with the gay experience in America, and perhaps throughout the world (Kübler-Ross, 1987). Even if a gay man has never known anyone who has had AIDS, he must still question any potential partner about previous sexual partners and experiences. Young gay men must face the issue in their already difficult struggle in coming to terms with their sexuality; not surprisingly, they wonder if a gay life-style is viable for them, given the potential consequences. Older gay men have had to accommodate major changes in their sexual practices, as well as confront the loss of friends and lovers. Grieving and death became a commonplace experience for many gay men of all ages during the 1980s and will increase in the 1990s. The other problems of gay men and the gay rights agenda have suffered serious setbacks as a result of a change of emphasis to the epidemic, draining the community of talent and resources.

The epidemic presents many areas of intervention for therapists. Most of these interventions have to do with coping with changes and making decisions. The spread of the virus compels all gay men to make changes in how they find partners and how they engage in sex with their partners (Silven & Caldarola,

1989). These changes require learning new behaviors, like how to use a condom, how to ask about previous partners, and how to insist on safe sex in highly charged sexual encounters. They also require examining values, such as monogamy and fidelity, and determining what kinds of risks one will take and not take, such as deep kissing (Stall, Coates, & Hoff, 1988). Gay men must accept that the old ways of being sexual are gone. Friends will die and the individual himself may get sick and progress through a series of stages of losing more and more physical independence. All these changes require letting go and coping with the losses.

Decisions are multiple for gay men in the era of AIDS. Many, if not most, gay men have reason to at least raise the question of whether they should take the HIV antibody test. This decision is extremely important and should never be minimized or taken lightly; the information obtained from testing can be psychologically devastating (Marks & Goldblum, 1989). One should take the test with an awareness of the consequences and some firm ideas about the direction to take if the results are positive (i.e., indicate that the individual is infected). Therapists can be very helpful in preparing an individual to make this decision and then to follow through and implement it. Obviously, this process requires directive and educational interventions, as well as support (Moskowitz, 1989). Other decisions include the degree to which the individual may want to take an aggressive approach to fighting the illness, and when such an approach might commence (Woods, 1989). These decisions will involve finding appropriate medical support (i.e., physicians who are willing to be as aggressive as the patient) and treatment information about alternative, nonmedical treatments. Other medical and legal decisions must be made, such as when life-sustaining efforts should be withheld and designating power of attorney.

The complexity of decisions and issues that arise in working with AIDS is evident in the case of Jack:

> Jack is a 50-year-old Black male who had recently stopped his successful career due to an AIDS diagnosis. Jack began therapy because of depression, loneliness, and isolation related to his illness and the recent loss of his lover, Tom. Apart from participating in therapy, Jack joined a support group and an activist group, the latter leading to several important relationships. He also took advantage of practical support services in the community. However, despite the success at breaking down the isolation, much of the loneliness and depression continued. Tom's death was not the only important loss in Jack's life. He had also lost many friends during the 1980s to the epidemic. The grieving process for one loss overlapped with that of so many others, to the point where Jack often felt completely overwhelmed with sadness and depression. Kaposi's sarcoma began to limit his mobility, and he soon noticed lesions growing on his face, a particularly scary and difficult development. Physicians had been treating the lesions topically, but a decision needed to be made concerning treating the lesions systemically, and by what means. The process of coming to terms with the decisions was agonizing for Jack. As with most things, there were no guarantees, and he was already feeling such loss and fear that decision making grew more and

more difficult. The possible decision to stop fighting and let the disease take its course also existed. Jack continues to struggle with that question, as well as suicidal ideation that has plagued him since the loss of his lover. After all, for Jack, as for many persons living with AIDS (PLWAs), "death" holds promise and relief; it is the loss of bodily control and independence, the long-suffered pain before death, in a word, the "dying," that he fears.

Working with a client who has already been diagnosed with AIDS or an AIDS-related illness typically involves coordinating treatment with other professionals who are treating the client as well. For example, it is important for the therapist to maintain ongoing contact with the client's primary-care physician in order to ensure an integrated, holistic approach and to provide continuity of care. Therapists may find themselves acting as an advocate for the client, assisting him with obtaining vital resources (e.g., disability income, health insurance, hospice care) from public and private agencies. There may also be professional involvement with the client's significant others, for example, providing supportive counseling to the client's lover or family members as they struggle with issues of loss and grief. Finally, therapists who work with advanced cases of AIDS may find themselves providing increasing care and advocacy for the dying client as he finds it more difficult to interact directly with others providing care. Needless to say, working with clients diagnosed with AIDS is very demanding and draining. It is absolutely essential that the therapist examine his/her own issues about death and dying, explore his/her feelings of frustration and helplessness, and obtain emotional support from other colleagues and friends.

## Spiritual/Existential Issues

Psychotherapy that does not address the existential/spiritual dimension is seriously lacking (Fortunato, 1982). Although many clients struggle with "meaning of life" questions, it is important for therapists to be sensitive to the existential issues commonly presented by gay clients. Many men, particularly in the early stages of coming out, struggle with the question of why they are gay. Some attempt to change their gayness in order to fit into the nongay world; the shame of being fundamentally different or flawed and the resulting fear of being despised, abused, and ultimately rejected by others make it difficult for gay men to see the positive meaning in their gayness.

One's confusion and internalized homophobia can be exacerbated further by religious teachings (McNaught, 1979; Nelson, 1982). Clients often have a difficult time reconciling their sexuality with the views of their religion and may detach completely from the organized religion. This can lead to feelings of isolation and alienation, or clients may repress their sexuality or live a double life in order to maintain ties with a religious institution that essentially does not support or affirm them (Nelson, 1982).

Therapists working with gay clients need to help them distinguish between spirituality and religiosity. One can believe in a deity or "higher power" or otherwise find meaning in life without participating in an organized religion that is antithetical to the individual's personhood. For those clients who wish to be involved with an organized religion, there are interdenominational groups (e.g., Metropolitan Community Church, Unity) that offer structure, community, and a gay-affirming theology. As McNaught (1979) notes, the spiritual search for meaning is ultimately a search for truth; the living of one's own truth can contribute to a sense of inner joy and wholeness.

## Conclusions and Recommendations

Although therapeutic strategies have been discussed throughout this article, it is helpful to conclude with some general guidelines for treatment:

1. Therapists working with gay male clients need to adopt a nonhomophobic stance. In terms of practice, this translates into the therapist's being open to hear the client's story rather than jumping to conclusions about the client based on stereotyped pathological assumptions (Dillon, 1986).

2. Therapists working with gay male clients need to have a firm foundation of training and experience in conceptualizing and treating addictive disorders, including alcoholism and other substance abuse, sexual compulsiveness, and eating disorders. Although none of these disorders are unique to gay men, a number of gay clients will present symptoms of these disorders in treatment. Because of the painful process of coming to terms with one's homosexuality, there is a greater potential for narcissistic injury; this, in turn, fuels the development of compulsive coping responses.

3. Therapists providing couples therapy to gay clients need to educate themselves about issues unique to male couples (e.g., stereotypic male roles, stereotypic sexual roles) and how these may relate to the problems presented in treatment. It is often helpful for the therapist to teach the couple a win-win conflict resolution model so that they have a tool they can use to address issues as they arise. This facilitates problem resolution as well as enhancing the level of intimacy between the two partners.

4. Group therapy can often be a helpful adjunct to individual and couples treatment. Participants can address issues within a supportive, empathic environment, as well as learn vital information and interpersonal skills.

5. The smallness of gay communities sets the stage for unique ethical problems for gay psychologists. Even in large cities, the gay community is usually relatively small, or at least small enough that therapists and clients can find themselves interrelated through friendships, lovers, organizations, and social functions. Some gay therapists solve this problem by cutting themselves off from all but a small part of the community; others set limited boundaries between themselves and the community, whereas some, unfortunately, set no boundaries at all (the most extreme example, of course, would be therapists

who engage in emotionally intimate or sexual relationships with their clients). These problems are not often addressed by gay-identified counselors and require more attention, discussion, and research.

6. Finally, it should be noted that, regardless of a therapist's theoretical orientation, there is a strong ethical obligation to inform gay men of safe-sex guidelines. It is especially urgent in this time of epidemic that we respond to the ignorance and denial of our clients. Although we must not promote sensationalism or a hysterical response, we also must not sit back and listen passively to material that includes the individual putting himself or others at risk for the transmission of HIV. A careful but direct, nonjudgmental inquiry into a client's knowledge, attitudes, and behaviors regarding safe sex is the best approach. Accurate information should also be given in a nonjudgmental manner. Also, therapists should keep in mind that behavior change is not rapid or easy and that clients need much reinforcement for their successes.

The demands of working with gay men can be a challenge to both gay and nongay therapists. Without question we must confront and work through our own homophobia and the many myths and stereotypes about gays. We also need to continue to educate ourselves about gay identity development and management, therapy issues unique to male gay clients, gay resources, and affirmative counseling models.

For those who conduct research in the area of counseling and development, there clearly needs to be continued effort at identifying "normal" developmental issues and tasks for the gay client, as well as special challenges he may face throughout his life span. Unique issues related to identity development and maintenance, career development, race/ethnicity/social class, coping with antigay violence, AIDS, same-sex coupling, and parenting also need further clarification and validation via longitudinal studies of large samples of subjects. Apart from further identification of these issues, challenges, and tasks, research must ultimately elucidate effective adaptive strategies. As counseling psychologists, we value preventive as well as ameliorative intervention efforts. For this reason, we must provide our gay clients with the necessary tools to cope with their special problems and concerns as well as with guidelines for developing a happy, healthy, and integrated life-style.

# References

Almvig, C. (1982). *The invisible minority: Aging and lesbianism.* New York: Utica College of Syracuse University Press.

Anderson, C. L. (1982). Males as sexual assault victims: Multiple levels of trauma. *Journal of Homosexuality, 7,* 145–162.

Atkinson, D. R., & Hackett, G. (1988). *Counseling non-ethnic American minorities.* Springfield, IL: Charles C Thomas.

Babuscio, J. (1976). *We speak for ourselves.* Philadelphia: Fortress.

Beattie, M. (1989). *Beyond co-dependency.* New York: Harper/Hazelden.

Berger, R. M. (1980). Psychological adaptation of the older homosexual male. *Journal of Homosexuality, 5,* 161–175.

Berube, A. (1990). *Coming out under fire: The history of gay men and women in WW II.* New York: Free Press.

Berzon, B. (1979a). Achieving success as a gay couple. In B. Berzon (Ed.), *Positively gay: New approaches in gay and lesbian life* (pp. 30–40). Los Angeles: Mediamix.

Berzon, B. (1979b). Developing a positive gay identity. In B. Berzon (Ed.), *Positively gay: New approaches in gay and lesbian life* (pp. 1–14). Los Angeles: Mediamix.

Berzon, B. (1979c). Telling the family you're gay. In B. Berzon (Ed.), *Positively gay: New approaches in gay and lesbian life* (pp. 88–100). Los Angeles: Mediamix.

Berzon, B. (1988). *Permanent partners: Building gay and lesbian relationships that last.* New York: Dutton.

Black, C. (1989). *Shame* (Videocassette). Denver: MAC Publishing.

Bohn, T. R. (1984). Homophobic violence: Implications for social work practice. In R. Schoenberg & R. S. Goldberg (Eds.), *With compassion toward some: Homosexuality and social work in America* (pp. 91–112). New York: Harrington Park.

Borhek, M. V. (1983). *Coming out to parents: A two-way survival guide for lesbians and gay men and their parents.* New York: Pilgrim.

Clark, D. (1987). *The new loving someone gay.* Berkeley, CA: Celestial Arts.

Colgon, P. (1987). Treatment of identity and intimacy issues in gay males. *Journal of Homosexuality, 14,* 101–123.

Colgon, P., & Riebel, J. (1981). *Sexuality education for foster parents.* Minneapolis: University of Minnesota.

Cramer, D. (1986). Gay parents and their children: A review of research and practical implications. *Journal of Counseling and Development, 64,* 605–607.

Dillon, C. (1986). Preparing college health professionals to deliver gay-affirmative services. *Journal of American College Health, 34*(1), 36–40.

Fifield, L. (1975). *On my way to nowhere: Alienated, isolated, drunk.* Los Angeles: Gay Community Services Center and Department of Health Services.

Finn, P., & McNeil, T. (1987, October 7). *The response of the criminal justice system to bias crime: An exploratory review.* Washington, DC: U.S. Department of Justice, National Institute of Justice.

Fortunato, J. E. (1982). *Embracing the exile: Healing journeys for gay Christians.* New York: Harper & Row.

Friend, R. A. (1987). The individual and social psychology of aging: Clinical implications for lesbians and gay men. *Journal of Homosexuality, 14,* 307–331.

George, K. D., & Behrendt, A. E. (1987). Therapy for male couples experiencing relationship problems and sexual problems. *Journal of Homosexuality, 14,* 77–89.

Herek, G. M. (1989). Hate crimes against lesbians and gay men: Issues for research and policy. *American Psychologist, 44,* 948–955.

Herek, G. M. (1990). Gay people and government security clearances. *American Psychologist, 45,* 1035–1042.

Isay, R. A. (1989). *Being homosexual: Gay men and their development.* New York: Giroux.

Jay, K., & Young, A. (1977). *The gay report: Lesbians and gay men speak out about sexual experiences and lifestyles.* New York: Summit.

Johnson, S. (1985). *Characterological transformation: The hard work miracle.* New York: Norton.

Kimmel, D. C. (1977). Psychotherapy and the older gay male. *Psychotherapy: Theory, research and practice, 14,* 386–393.

Kimmel, D. C. (1978). Adult development and aging: A gay perspective. *Journal of Social Issues, 34,* 113–130.

Kübler-Ross, E. (1987). *AIDS: The ultimate challenge.* New York: Macmillan.

Marks, R., & Goldblum, P. B. (1989). The decision to test: A personal choice. In J. W. Dilley, C. Pies, & M. Helquist (Eds.), *Face to face: A guide to AIDS counseling* (pp. 49–58). San Francisco: University of California.

McDonald, G. J. (1982). Individual differences in the coming out process for gay men: Implications for theoretical models. *Journal of Homosexuality, 8,* 47–60.

McNaught, B. (1979). Gay and Catholic. In B. Berzon (Ed.), *Positively gay: New approaches to gay and lesbian life* (pp. 56–64). Los Angeles: Mediamix.

Miller, B., & Humphreys, L. (1980). Lifestyles and violence: Homosexual victims of assault and murder. *Qualitative Sociology, 3*(3), 169–185.

Moses, A. E., & Buckner, J. A. (1982). The special problems of rural gay clients. In A. E. Moses & R. O. Hawkins (Eds.), *Counseling lesbian women and gay men: A life-issues approach* (pp. 173–180). St. Louis: C. V. Mosby.

Moses, A. E., & Hawkins, R. O. (Eds.). (1982). *Counseling lesbian women and gay men: A life-issues approach.* St. Louis: C. V. Mosby.

Moskowitz, R. D. (1989). Being seronegative in a seropositive world: A personal perspective. In J. W. Dilley, C. Pies, & M. Helquist (Eds.), *Face to face: A guide to AIDS counseling* (pp. 102–106). San Francisco: University of California.

Nelson, J. B. (1982). Religious and moral issues in working with homosexual clients. *Journal of Homosexuality, 7,* 163–176.

Raphael, S. M., & Robinson, M. K. (1980). The older lesbian. *Alternative Lifestyles, 3,* 207–229.

Schmitz, T. J. (1988). Career counseling implications with the gay and lesbian population. *Journal of Employment Counseling, 25,* 51–56.

Silven, D., & Caldarola, T. J. (1989). The HIV-positive client. In J. W. Dilley, C. Pies, & M. Helquist (Eds.), *Face to face: A guide to AIDS counseling* (pp. 307–310). San Francisco: University of California.

Stall, R., Coates, T., & Hoff, C. (1988). Behavioral risk reduction for HIV infection among gay and bisexual men: A review of results from the United States. *American Psychologist, 43,* 878–885.

Tievsky, D. L. (1988). Homosexual clients and homophobic social workers. *Journal of Independent Social Work, 2,* 51–62.

Woods, W. J. (1989). Experimental treatments and counseling issues. In J. W. Dilley, C. Pies, & M. Helquist (Eds.), *Face to face: A guide to AIDS counseling* (pp. 59–66). San Francisco: University of California.

Zilbergeld, B. (1978). *Male sexuality.* Boston: Little, Brown.

# 15

# Counselors' Attitudes toward Homosexuality: A Selective Review of the Literature

*James Rudolph*

A selective review of counselors' and psychotherapists' attitudes toward homosexuality is presented. Analysis of the patterns emerging from published survey literature reveals considerable division and contradiction in the attitudes reported. The author proposes the source of such inconsistency to be the mixed messages mental health personnel receive from their professional organizations, which affirm gay self-determination, and society-at-large, which is generally gay-negating. Recommendations are offered for practitioners working with homosexual clients.

Estimates of the percentage of gay persons who seek counseling or psychotherapy range from approximately 25% to 65%, rates two to four times higher than those for heterosexuals (Bell & Weinberg, 1978; Jay & Young, 1979; May, 1974; Saghir, Robins, Walbran, & Gentry, 1970a, 1970b). Such percentages are not surprising given that homosexuals experience higher rates of depression, anxiety, suicidal ideation and gesturing, and other psychological distress in comparison with heterosexuals (e.g., Bell & Weinberg, 1978; Nurius, 1983).

Survey and anecdotal literature reveal that there is often little satisfaction or therapeutic success for the gay client in counseling. The source of such dissatisfaction centers on counselors' negative, prejudicial attitudes toward, and lack of understanding of, homosexuality (e.g., Abbott & Love, 1972; Adair & Adair, 1978; Bell & Weinberg, 1978; Saghir & Robins, 1973; Woodman & Lenna, 1982). The dissatisfaction rates of homosexual clients drop dramatically when they are treated by gay therapists (Jay & Young, 1979), and gay clients more frequently cite counselors' "professional manner" as a source of dissatisfaction with their counseling experiences than do heterosexuals (Bell & Weinberg, 1978). Up to 50% of gay clients have reported discontent with their professional counseling experiences, with an average rate of dissatisfaction of approximately 40%, a rate exceeding that usually reported by heterosexual clients (Bell & Weinberg, 1978; Jay & Young, 1979; May, 1974; Saghir & Robins, 1973).

Given that homosexual persons seek professional counseling services in great numbers, and that a significant portion leave such experiences dissatisfied because of the antigay sentiment reportedly encountered from counselors, steps must be taken to correct counselors' negative attitudes. Developing solutions requires knowledge of specific attitudinal problems of counselors toward homosexuality, knowledge that can in part be obtained from a review of the survey literature.

One such problem could involve counselors' inconsistency of opinion about the acceptability of homosexuality, if this is conveyed to gay clients. Such inconsistency may, in turn, reflect the mixed messages counselors receive about the nature of homosexuality. On the one hand, since the watershed statement of the American Psychiatric Association depathologizing homosexuality per se in 1973 (to be shortly followed by similar gay affirmative statements from the allied human service professions), it has become expected, even somewhat fashionable, for "enlightened" professionals to support gay self-determination. On the other hand, counselors and other helping professionals live in a society that historically has been, and remains, predominantly antigay in sentiment (e.g., Bayer, 1981; Rudolph, in press). A counselor is as much a member of the society in which he or she is enculturated as any other person, and thus is as vulnerable to its social and political influences (e.g., Sundberg, 1981).

This review of the literature is designed to examine whether attitudes of counselors toward homosexuality are inconsistent, both within the ranks of the profession (i.e., opinion is divided) and within individual practitioners (i.e., opinion is self-contradictory). It is not the divergence of opinion per se that is especially noteworthy, because a certain amount of divergence is to be expected on any issue. Rather, it is the negative impact such division and contradiction of opinion have on in-session interaction (i.e., through the sending and receiving of mixed messages) that is of central concern.

This review includes, first, only those studies using a survey format to assess counselors' attitudes toward homosexuality (see Casas, Brady, & Ponterotto, 1983, and Garfinkel & Morin, 1978, for examples of nonsurvey methods of assessing counselors' attitudes), and second, only those studies using respondents whose practice of counseling or psychotherapy is their principal professional activity. Of course, counseling is also conducted by allied human service personnel such as members of the clergy, teaching, and nonpsychiatric medical professions. Because these individuals do not counsel as their primary professional activity, however, their attitudes toward homosexuality are only briefly and collectively noted. In addition, all the surveys are post-1970 in date of origin. This is relevant insofar as the gay liberation movement burst into prominence in 1969 with the Stonewall riots in New York City, and with it the public consciousness of homosexual oppression was raised. Had surveys been available before 1970, they might have told a very different story. Finally, only those attitudes toward homosexuality that contained a strongly evaluative (i.e., moral or political) valence were chosen for this review, as it is this realm of personal judgment or sentiment that seems most directly implicated in gay clients' discontent with counselors' attitudes toward homosexuality.

# Review of Survey Research

## Inconsistencies among Counselors and Therapists: Professional Ambivalence

In late 1973, the Board of Directors of the American Psychiatric Association formally depathologized homosexuality per se, stating that it implied "no impairment in judgment, stability, reliability, or general social or vocational capabilities" (American Psychiatric Association, 1974, p. 497). A substantial portion of the Association's rank and file members, however, did not endorse the action of the board, and a plebiscite on the issue was forced. Although more than one-half (58%) of the membership supported the board's decision, more than one-third (37%) opposed it (Bayer, 1981).

This split of opinion by psychiatrists has been replayed in various forms in surveys of counselors and psychotherapists. Barr and Catts (1974) reported on a random sample of 87 psychiatrists and 69 psychiatric trainees in Australia. The results revealed that 35% of the psychiatrists and 19% of the trainees believed homosexuality to be a developmental anomaly not necessarily or commonly associated with neurotic symptoms. Gartrell, Kraemer, and Brodie (1974) surveyed the predominantly male Northern California Psychiatric Association. The survey revealed that two-thirds of the psychiatrists endorsed, and one-third failed to endorse, two statements pertaining to female homosexuality. The first statement was "I oppose the use of psychiatric labels as a way of categorizing female sexual behavior"; the second was "Female homosexuality can no longer be equated only with sickness or inadequacy, but may properly be considered as a preference, orientation, or propensity for certain kinds of life-styles."

In a third survey of psychiatrists, Lief (1977) reported that of the 2,500 respondents polled for the publication *Medical Aspects of Human Sexuality,* 69% agreed that homosexuality is a pathological adaptation. Also, 60% stated that homosexual men and 55% stated that homosexual women are less capable than heterosexuals of mature, loving relationships. Furthermore, 70% of the psychiatrists believed that homosexual problems in living are the result of personal conflicts more than stigmatization. Roman, Charles, and Karasu

(1978), reporting on a sample of 124 predominantly male psychiatric residents and fellows, social service staff, psychologists, and attending psychiatrists, supervisors, and other medical staff in a department of psychiatry at a large urban hospital, revealed that two-thirds agreed and one-third did not agree that "homosexual experience is acceptable for others."

A similar divergence of opinion has been seen among therapists other than psychiatrists. Using a population of 64 male and female master's and doctoral level counseling students, Thompson and Fisburn (1977) reported that 53% agreed, 27% disagreed, and 20% were neutral, or had no opinion, that a person's sexual orientation is an irrelevant point on which to judge that person's ability to function in any given situation. It should be noted "neutral" and "no opinion" do not necessarily hold the same meaning for everyone. For example, whereas "neutral" may reflect ambivalence in one person, it may reflect indifference in another—two very different feelings. Thus, one-fifth of this particular sample may have experienced anything from intense confusion to simple ignorance about the issue. Such ambiguities in wording are always a problem in interpreting results from attitude surveys.

Clark (1979) assessed the homophobia of 29 master's level counseling practicum students and reported that almost equal numbers of the students endorsed and failed to endorse the statement, "I find the thought of homosexual acts disgusting." Furthermore, approximately one-third of the respondents stated they did not believe a homosexual could be a good president of the United States, and almost one-fourth stated they would be afraid for their child to have a homosexual teacher. Finally, Rudolph (1988a) surveyed the attitudes toward homosexuality of 52 master's and doctoral level clinicians and clinicians-in-training. Questionnaire items were clustered into six categories, and participants' collective positive and negative responses to each category were reported: eroticized interaction between same-sex persons (positive, 33%; negative, 67%); noneroticized interaction between same-sex persons (75%, 25%); civil liberties/legality of homosexuality (67%, 33%); psychological character of homosexuals (86%, 14%); morality of homosexual behavior (77%, 33%); and the placement of homosexuals in sensitive professional positions (33%, 67%).

In a brief summary of these studies, it can be seen that counseling professionals hold divergent opinions regarding the acceptability of homosexuality, with as many as one-third in many samples expressing negative attitudes. The reports described below demonstrate that counselors often have contradictory attitudes about homosexuality, as well.

## Inconsistencies Within Counselors and Therapists: Contradictory Attitudes

Fort, Steiner, and Conrad (1971) reported the attitudes toward homosexuality of 129 private practice psychotherapists in the San Francisco Bay area. On the one hand, 97% stated they would work with a therapy goal other than to change the sexual orientation of the client, and 98% believed it was possible for homosexuals to function effectively. Also, 99% opposed laws treating private homosexual acts between consenting adults as criminal, 64% did not consider homosexuality to be an illness or disease, and only 8% believed that homosexuality should disqualify an individual from teaching, 27% from security-sensitive federal employment, and 12% from the armed services. On the other hand, 73% labeled homosexuality a "personality disorder," and 83% labeled it a "sexual deviation."

Davison and Wilson (1973) reported that 91% of 86 randomly chosen behavior therapists stated they believed it possible for a homosexual to be happy and well-adjusted, 87% denied homosexuality is prima facie evidence of psychopathology, and 87% supported a gay client's self-acceptance of his or her homosexuality by choosing as a therapy goal helping the client be more at ease as a homosexual. Yet, on a semantic differential scale, the same therapists consistently rated homosexuals as less desirable than heterosexuals on all dimensions employed, such as bad versus good, immoral versus moral, and shallow versus deep.

The samples of psychiatrists displayed contradictory opinions as well. Gartrell et al. (1974) reported that 87% of their participants stated that their concept of mental health includes the possibility of a well-adjusted homosexual woman, and 84% stated that a search for love and affection is the central theme in female homosexuality. In addition, 99% urged the repeal of criminal laws that proscribe sexual behavior between consenting adults. A total of 84%, however, also agreed that homosexual women usually have as background a history of disturbed relationships with both parents, particularly in the areas that affect normal sexual maturation. Barr and Catts (1974) reported that although more than one-half of both their psychiatrists and psychiatric trainees endorsed the statement that homosexuality is a developmental anomaly not necessarily or commonly associated with neurotic symptoms, only 13% of the psychiatrists and 21% of the trainees believed that homosexuality is a normal variant of sexual expression. Also, in a third survey, Roman et al. (1978) reported that two-thirds of their 124 psychiatrists and social service personnel agreed that homosexual experience is "acceptable for others," but only 4% chose the response "acceptable for yourself." (Again, interpretation of these responses is hindered by the several possible meanings of the survey statements.)

In Thompson and Fishburn's (1977) study of the attitudes toward homosexuality of 64 graduate counseling students, more than three-fourths endorsed the statement that there is no evidence to indicate that homosexuals should be barred from such "sensitive" professions as teaching, social work, and the ministry, yet only slightly more than one-half were able to state unequivocally that a person's sexual orientation is irrelevant to his or her ability to function in a general sense. Clark (1979) reported that only 7% of 29 graduate counseling students stated they would be upset to find out they were alone with a homosexual, 3% would get nervous if a homosexual sat next to them on a bus, and 10% would not want to be a member of an organization that had any homosexuals in its membership, yet almost one-half found the thought of homosexual acts disgusting. Finally, Rudolph (1988a) reported that although two-thirds of 52 clinicians and clinical trainees disagreed with the statement "Homosexuals are sick," only slightly more than two-fifths supported the statement "Just as in other species, homosexuality in humans is a natural expression of sexuality."

Briefly summarizing, it can be seen that therapists are often of two minds when it comes to evaluating the acceptability of homosexuality. The ambivalence of individual practitioners seems to parallel ambivalence in the profession more generally. In only two areas did participants, from survey to survey, respond consistently with a substantial majority of opinion. First, a noncriminal (but *not* nonpathological) perception of homosexuality was supported. Second, clients' self-acceptance of their homosexuality was affirmed, but counselors' acceptance of homosexual experience for themselves was not. The same checkered pattern of attitudes toward homosexuality can be observed in the results of investigations of clergy, teaching, and nonpsychiatric medical personnel (see Anderson, 1981; Bohne, 1986; Douglas, Kalman, & Kalman, 1985; Fischer, 1982; McCann-Winter, 1983; Morris, 1973; Pauly & Goldstein, 1970).

## Discussion

The evaluative attitudes of counseling professionals toward homosexuality are both divided and contradictory. Counselors, psychologists, and psychiatrists seem to believe at one and the same time, for example, in the psychological health *and* potential pathology of homosexuality. They believe in the ability of gay persons to fully function in any situation, and yet to be hampered in their performance in certain positions by the very fact of their sexual orientation. Also, they believe the locus of homosexuals' problems to be both internal *and* societal.

The counselor is torn. He or she is formally told one thing about homosexuality from the profession (i.e., "homosexuality is okay"), and more informally, but no less persuasive, quite another from society-at-large ("homosexuality is not okay"). Support for this contention is provided by data indicating attitudes toward homosexuality in the adult population to be generally more consistently (albeit not exclusively) antigay in nature than is true of the attitudes of human service personnel (e.g., Gallup, 1977, 1982, 1983; Leo, 1986; National Opinion Research Center, 1985). Unlike human service professionals, those in the general population are not in the untenable position of having to serve two masters.

The resulting lack of resolve and residual gay negating sentiment harbored by counseling personnel can only exert a counterproductive influence on the quality of the therapeutic experiences of gay clients. Recall that approximately one-half of gay clients express dissatisfaction with counseling, with the data suggesting such discontent to center on client-perceived antigay prejudice in counselors. Although the admittedly homophobic or heterosexist counselor can clearly be harmful to a gay client, a greater risk of danger may lie with the homophobic or heterosexist counselor who is not aware of his or her prejudicial sentiment. In the former instance, the cards, such as they are, are all on the table to be played accordingly. In the latter scenario, however, gay negation (and thus gay client negation) is a subtler, more potentially corrosive process, and therefore the extent of the harm to the client's well-being may not be fully known until much later, when such damage may be appreciable and irreparable. (See Rudolph, in press, for development of the thesis of unconscious counselor undermining of gay psychotherapy, and Riddle & Sang, 1978, for examples of particular gay-undermining counselor behavior.)

It is important that counselors who wish to work with homosexual clients be cognizant (i.e., vigorously self-conscious) of their attitudes toward homosexuality, homosexual behavior, and homosexual persons. Counselors should not choose to treat gay clients by simple whim or default, complacent in the deceptive reassurance that they are "relatively tolerant" or "basically open minded" about an issue decidedly more complicated and elusive than is immediately apparent. Counselors must become more fully aware of gay issues and concerns. This process can be facilitated by counselor educators offering course work or workshops on homosexuality and gay psychotherapy (see Rudolph, 1988b, for an example).

Although survey research on attitudes is helpful, it is also limited. What is assessed in attitude surveys is what respondents say they believe, and this may or may not reflect their actual behavior. What is needed is further research assessing counselors' *in-session* behavior with gay clients. Under such conditions, the complex factors constituting the therapeutic interaction in toto could be considered (e.g., body language, paralinguistics, immediacy of response), and thus a finer, more accurate picture of counselors' attitudes toward homosexuality could be determined. Given a sociopolitical climate that is strongly, perhaps increasingly antigay (e.g., Clark, 1985; Morrow, 1985), along with the life-threatening crisis of AIDS, greater numbers of homosexual persons than ever before can be anticipated to seek psychotherapeutic support. Now is surely not the time to fail this beleaguered and needy population.

# References

Abbott, S., & Love, B. (1972). *Sappho was a right-on woman.* New York: Stein & Day.

Adair, N., & Adair, C. (1978). *Word is out: Stories of some of our lives.* New York: Dell.

American Psychiatric Association. (1974). Position statement on homosexuality and civil rights. *American Journal of Psychiatry, 131,* 497.

Anderson, C. L. (1981). The effects of a workshop on attitudes of female nursing students toward male homosexuality. *Journal of Homosexuality, 7,* 57–69.

Barr, R. F., & Catts, S. V. (1974). Psychiatric opinion and homosexuality: A short report. *Journal of Homosexuality, 1,* 213–215.

Bayer, R. (1981). *Homosexuality and American psychiatry.* New York: Basic Books.

Bell, A. P., & Weinberg, M. S. (1978). *Homosexualities: A study of diversity among men and women.* New York: Simon & Schuster.

Bohne, J. (1986). AIDS: Ministry issues for chaplains. *Pastoral Psychology, 34,* 173–192.

Casas, J. M., Brady, S., & Ponterotto, J. G. (1983). Sexual preference biases in counseling: An information processing approach. *Journal of Counseling Psychology, 30,* 139–145.

Clark, G. (1985, August 12). In the middle of a war. *Time,* p. 46.

Clark, M. F. (1979). Attitudes, information and behavior of counselors toward homosexual clients (Doctoral dissertation, Wayne State University, 1979). *Dissertation Abstracts International, 40,* 5729A.

Davison, G. C., & Wilson, G. T. (1973) Attitudes of behavior therapists toward homosexuality. *Behavior Therapy, 4,* 686–696.

Douglas, C. J., Kalman, C. M., & Kalman, T. P. (1985). Homophobia among physicians and nurses: An empirical study. *Hospital and Community Psychiatry, 36,* 1309–1311.

Fischer, T. R. (1982). A study of educators' attitudes toward homosexuality. *Dissertation Abstracts International, 43,* 3294A.

Fort, J., Steiner, C. M., & Conrad, F. (1971). Attitudes of mental health professionals toward homosexuality and its treatment. *Psychological Reports, 29,* 347–350.

Gallup, G. (1982). *The Gallup opinion index* (Report No. 205). Princeton, NJ: The American Institute of Public Opinion.

Gallup, G. (1983). *The Gallup opinion index* (Report No. 216). Princeton, NJ: The American Institute of Public Opinion.

Garfinkle, E. M., & Morin, S. F. (1978). Psychologists' attitudes toward homosexual psychotherapy clients. *Journal of Social Issues, 34*(3), 101–112.

Gartrell, N., Kraemer, H., & Brodie, H. K. H. (1974). Psychiatrists' attitudes toward female homosexuality. *The Journal of Nervous and Mental Disease, 159,* 141–144.

Jay, K., & Young, A. (1979). *The gay report.* New York: Summit.

Leo, J. (1986, November 24). Sex and schools. *Time,* pp. 54–63.

Lief, H. I. (1977). Sexual survey No. 4: Current thinking on homosexuality. *Medical Aspects of Human Sexuality, 11,* 110–111.

McCann-Winter, E. J. S. (1983). Clergy education about homosexuality: An outcomes analysis of knowledge, attitudes, and counseling behavior (Doctoral dissertation, University of Pennsylvania, 1983). *Dissertation Abstracts International, 44,* 675A.

May, E. P. (1974). Counselors', psychologists', and homosexuals' philosophies of human nature and attitudes toward homosexual behavior. *The Homosexual Counseling Journal, 1,* 3–25.

Morris, P. A. (1973). Doctors' attitudes to homosexuality. *British Journal of Psychiatry, 122,* 434–436.

Morrow, L. (1985, September 23). The start of a plague mentality. *Time,* p. 92.

National Opinion Research Center. (1985). *General social survey, 1972–1985: Cumulative codebook.* Chicago: University of Chicago Press.

Nurius, P. S. (1983). Mental health implications of sexual orientation. *Journal of Sex Research, 19,* 119–136.

Pauly, I. B., & Goldstein, S. B. (1970). Physicians' attitudes in treating male homosexuals. *Medical Aspects of Human Sexuality, 4*(12), 26–45.

Riddle, D. I., & Sang, B. (1978). Psychotherapy with lesbians. *Journal of Social Issues, 34,* 71–85.

Roman, M., Charles, E., & Karasu, T. B. (1978). The value systems of psychotherapists and changing mores. *Psychotherapy: Theory, Research, and Practice, 15,* 409–415.

Rudolph, J. (in press). The impact of contemporary ideology and AIDS upon the counseling of gay clients. *Counseling and Values.*

Rudolph, J. (1988a). *Attitudes toward homosexuality in the era of AIDS: A brief report.* Manuscript submitted for publication.

Rudolph, J. (1988b). *The effects of a multimodal seminar on mental health practitioners' attitudes toward homosexuality, authoritarianism, and counseling effectiveness.* Unpublished doctoral dissertation, Lehigh University, Bethlehem, PA.

Saghir, M., & Robins, E. (1973). *Male and female homosexuality: A comprehensive investigation.* Baltimore: Williams & Wilkins.

Saghir, M. T., Robins, E., Walbran, B., & Gentry, K. A. (1970a). Psychiatric disorders and disability in the male homosexual. *American Journal of Psychiatry, 126,* 1079–1086.

Saghir, M. T., Robins, E., Walbran, B., & Gentry, K. A. (1970b). Psychiatric disorders and disability in the female homosexual. *American Journal of Psychiatry, 127,* 147–154.

Sundberg, N. D. (1981). Cross-cultural counseling and psychotherapy: A research overview. In A. J. Marsella & P. B. Pedersen (Eds.), *Cross-cultural counseling and psychotherapy* (pp. 28–62). New York: Pergamon.

Thompson, G. J., & Fishburn, W. R. (1977). Attitudes toward homosexuality among graduate counseling students. *Counselor Education and Supervision, 17,* 121–130.

Woodman, N. J., & Lenna, H. R. (1982). *Counseling with gay men and women.* San Francisco: Jossey-Bass.

# PART 6
## Implications

# 16

# Diversity Imperatives for Counseling Practice, Counselor Training, and Counseling Research

In Chapter 1 we developed a rationale for viewing selected nonethnic groups as minorities, and we presented profiles of persons with disabilities, elders, women, and gay people. In Chapter 2 the treatment of these four groups by society and psychology was placed in a historical perspective, and in Chapter 3 their treatment in contemporary society was examined. Chapters 4–15 focused on both the experiences and counseling-related needs of individuals in each group. Chapters 4–15 also provided suggestions for counseling persons with disabilities, elders, women, and gay people from a human rights perspective as well as a traditional counseling perspective. In this chapter we highlight several aspects of counseling practice that we feel need special attention, and we discuss changes that are needed in counselor-training programs in order to adequately prepare counselors to work with nonethnic minorities and in counseling research in order to reduce research bias against nonethnic minorities.

## Counseling Practice

In addition to the counseling practices specifically directed toward the four nonethnic minorities discussed in Chapters 4–15, we feel it is important to draw attention to three practice topics that are relevant to all four groups. These topics are language, ethics, and advocacy.

### Language

Professional counselors often unintentionally use imprecise and demeaning language that serves to reinforce stereotypes of people with disabilities, elders, women, and gay people. Practicing counselors can help reduce discrimination against these groups and take a major step toward increasing their credibility and effectiveness with nonethnic minority clients by eliminating imprecise and demeaning language from their vocabulary, and by sensitively and knowledgeably using the terminology employed by their clients. In the following sections we examine language used with each of the four nonethnic minority groups.

## Persons with Disabilities

Perhaps no group has more demeaning terms directed toward them unintentionally than do people with disabilities. Concern over the widespread use of inappropriate language in reference to persons with disabilities has been a theme in the rehabilitation counseling literature since 1980. Hadley and Brodwin (1988) reviewed the rehabilitation literature and developed four simple principles that they recommended counselors follow when discussing persons with disabilities:

1. *Precision:* Language should convey a speaker's or writer's intended meanings exactly and unambiguously.
2. *Objectivity:* One should avoid language that (a) implicitly expresses biases or unwanted surplus meanings or (b) treats opinions, interpretations, or impressions as facts.
3. *Perspective:* When one communicates about a person, the language chosen should emphasize the person and represent any disability in its proper perspective among his or her many other characteristics. This perspective is governed by the issues at hand; if disability is totally irrelevant to these issues, it may be omitted entirely.
4. *Portrayal:* People with disabilities should be portrayed as actively going about the business of living as other people do, *not* as passive victims, tragic figures, or super-heroes. (p. 147)

Hadley and Brodwin (1988) point out that all professional counselors, not just rehabilitation counselors, should be concerned about the use of language since people with disabilities often seek out counselors in other specialties to discuss problems with living that are unrelated to their disability. They go on to make several concrete suggestions about the use of language, although they qualify their suggestions by pointing out that the most appropriate use of language is often situation specific:

1. A form of the verb *to have* is usually the most effective way to express the link between a person and a disability.

   a. A person "has arthritis," *not* "is an arthritic"; "has diabetes" is preferable to "is a diabetic."
   b. One should scrupulously avoid words such as "victim" or "afflicted" to express this link. These words carry surplus emotional meaning.
   c. The word "patient" correctly expresses a relationship with a medical service provider such as a physician or a hospital; it is a poor word choice for other uses. "Is a lupus patient" is an *imprecise* substitute for "has lupus."

d. To have a disability is not necessarily to "suffer from" it. Such gratuitous use of "suffer" conveys a stereotypical attitude. . . . If one wants to say a particular person is suffering, this point should be developed explicitly.

2. A disability should never be represented as causing (a) an individual's emotional or behavioral reactions to it or (b) sequelae to these reactions. We prefer to represent people as the causes of their own feelings and behavior, although disability often serves as a cue. For example:

   a. It is neither precise nor objective to say that a disability or any other circumstance "makes" a person feel any particular way. "She feels depressed about her hearing loss" is better than "her hearing loss is making her depressed."
   b. Neither blindness nor paraplegia has ever caused alcoholism. People have reacted to these conditions, however, with patterns of drinking that caused alcoholism.

3. A disability should not be represented, either explicitly or implicitly, as the sole cause of circumstances resulting from social reactions to it. For example, a person should not be described as unemployed because he or she has impaired vision, if the reason is employers' discriminatory hiring.

4. Wheelchairs, prostheses, and other assistive devices are tools that people use in their various activities; word choices should represent this fact. For example:

   a. A client with paralyzed legs *uses* a wheelchair. The common expression, "confined to a wheelchair," is obviously imprecise and carries many of the same surplus meanings as "wheelchair-bound." Although "is in a wheelchair" is somewhat less offensive, . . . this expression . . . portrays the person as "passive."
   b. It is preferable to say a person "walks with" crutches rather than "has to use" or "is on" crutches. (Hadley & Brodwin, 1988, pp. 148–149).

Similarly, Byrd, Crews, and Ebener (1991) identified the following points that should be taken into consideration when making written or verbal reference to persons with disabilities:

1. only make reference to a person's disability when it is important to the context;
2. avoid using adjectives as nouns;
3. place persons or individuals before the disability;
4. avoid value laden descriptions;
5. do not sensationalize the effects of disability;
6. avoid statements that qualify the person with a disability (e.g., he uses a wheelchair, but is very bright);
7. avoid implying sickness when discussing disability conditions. (p. 40).

# Elders

Cohen (1990) reviewed 60 issues of the *Gerontologist,* 30 issues of *Generations,* and a number of miscellaneous articles and monographs published by the federal government and reported having turned up:

> . . . an array of negative terms applied to or describing the elderly. . . . The following is a partial list of words and phrases that reinforce the elderly mystique from a variety of literatures, learned, policy, and legal. Elderly-at-risk, frail elderly, impaired elderly, institutionalized elderly, homebound elderly, chairbound elderly, bedridden elderly, wheelchairbound elderly, vulnerable elderly, dependent elderly, patient (rather than consumer), and "the Alzheimer" (referring to the person who has the disease). (p. 14)

Schaie (1993) has pointed out that ageist attitudes and language permeate both empirical research and psychological practice. With regard to research, he identified a number of language problems related to the description of the research topic, language used in describing study designs, descriptions of methodology and choice of participants, and language used in the analysis and interpretation of research findings. These problems and Schaie's (1993) recommendations for avoiding them are as follows:

I. *Description of Research Topic*
   A. *Problems:*
      1. Focus of description of research topic on delineating a "problem of aging" rather than on building or extending an explanatory model.
      2. Reliance on biological models of decrement or decline.
      3. Neglect of research participants' health status.
      4. Age assumed to be the cause of differences or changes in behavior with little consideration of alternative explanations.
      5. Undue focus on elders as care needing, instead of care providing; the emphasis is often on dependent aspects, ignoring sustaining aspects.
   B. *Recommendations*
      1. Recognize that older persons constitute a diverse population. Heterogeneity should be stressed and gender should always be considered.
      2. Recognize that ageism can apply to individuals at any age, not only to those who are old.
      3. Consider a life span context in formulating the research topic.
      4. Carefully reference existing literature on older persons, and in reviewing previous studies evaluate their possible age bias.
      5. Consider the impact of possible findings on public policy.
II. *Design of the Study*
   A. *Problems*
      1. Failure to distinguish between normal age changes and disease.

2. Reliance on chronological age.
3. Lack of attention to age-sex-culture interaction; failure to describe other relevant demographic dimensions in which age groups in the population may differ, for example, culture/ethnicity, sexual orientation.
B. *Recommendations*
1. Examine the choice and definition of hypotheses. Is there a causal inference that involves age or aging? Is it influenced by age bias?
2. Consider whether chronological age is the most relevant variable. Would classification by other variables, such as educational level, income, duration of marriage, retirement, duration of retirement, or generational membership, be more appropriate?
3. Document that the constructs used in a study retain the same meaning at different ages. . . . Acknowledge that use of measures of such constructs developed for younger adults may introduce bias into a study of elders.
III. *Methods*
A. *Problems*
1. Inadequate operational definition of the age variable.
2. Inappropriate or offensive research instruments.
B. *Recommendations*
1. Instruments should be evaluated to ensure that they do not contain explicit or implicit age bias.
2. Avoid uncalled-for assumptions.
3. Beware of experimenter bias about how questions are asked of various age groups.
4. Check measures for inappropriate questions.
5. Consider use of alternative definitions for chronological age, such as subjective age or functional age.
IV. *Description of Data Analysis and Interpretation*
A. *Problems*
1. Confusing age differences with age changes.
2. Overlooking individual differences.
3. Ignoring the magnitude of age change.
4. Not reporting the absence of difference relevant to ageist stereotypes.
5. Reporting age differences found accidentally (where age is included as a variable in the analysis without a clear rationale) as "findings."
B. *Recommendations*
1. Age-group differences should be characterized as such and not be labeled as *decline*. Often the term *age/cohort differences* is to be preferred.

2. Age differences often can be explained by other variables and interactive effects; these should be discussed and ruled out before age is assumed to be the cause of differences in the dependent variable.
3. In some instances it would be more desirable to use age as the dependent variable.
4. Consider the practical significance of an age difference, especially when the data are relevant to public policy or might result in recommendations leading to important changes in an individual's life situation.
5. Consider the impact of ageist assumptions and models applied to data analysis and interpretation. Formulate competing models that test for alternate interpretations.
6. Use caution in generalizing results.
7. Beware of interpreting trends or marginally significant findings, especially when they either fit or contradict social stereotypes about aging and older persons.
8. Avoid value-laden language that implies negative characteristics for all study participants. (p. 49–51)

## Women

Psychologists are also guilty of reinforcing sexism though the use of imprecise and derogatory language. The *Publication Manual of the American Psychological Association* first addressed this issue in 1974 in its second edition by suggesting that journal authors "be aware of the current move to avoid generic use of male nouns and pronouns when content refers to both sexes." This position was strengthened and elaborated on in 1977 when the APA published the "Guidelines for Nonsexist Language in APA Journals" in the *American Psychologist.* In 1982, the APA Publications and Communications Board adopted a formal policy that requires authors who are submitting manuscripts to APA journals to use nonsexist language.

The *Publication Manual of the American Psychological Association* (1983) describes two types of problems with respect to sexist language: problems of designation and problems of evaluation. These categories can be in turn divided into two subcategories: ambiguity of referent and stereotyping. The most common problem of designation involves ambiguity of referent. This occurs when an author uses "man" as a generic noun, creating ambiguity as to the sex of the referent. Another problem of designation involves the use of stereotyping terms or phrases. For example, referring to the professional role of doctor as "the doctor . . . he" stereotypes all doctors (a respected profession in our society) as men. Adding a gender designation ("woman doctor") to an occupational or other role is inappropriate, as it only reinforces the notion of woman as "other" (i.e., men are doctors).

Ambiguity of referent can also create a problem of evaluation. It is common practice in the professional literature to cite authors in the text by their last name or by their first and last name. Referring to an author as Mrs. John Doe instead of Jane Doe implies an evaluation has been placed on the author because she is a woman and creates an ambiguity since she is not clearly identified by her given name. Problems of evaluation can also result from the use of stereotypic language. For example, nonparallel terms like "men and girls" (instead of "men and women") when both groups are adults stereotypes women as more child-like than men. As mentioned in Chapter 1, counselors and researchers should be careful to distinguish between sex and gender and use other important terms such as gender-role, masculinity, and femininity precisely.

Eichler (1988) suggests five questions to ask to ensure nonsexist language; a *yes* to any indicates the need for modifications:

1. Are any male (or female) terms used for generic purposes? [e.g., referring to all clients as "she"]

2. Are any generic terms employed when, in fact, the author(s) is (are) speaking about only one sex?

3. Are females and males in parallel situations described by nonparallel terms? [e.g., man and wife]

4. When both sexes are mentioned together in particular phrases, does one sex consistently precede the other? [e.g., "men and women"]

5. Are the two sexes consistently discussed in different grammatical modes? [e.g., using the passive voice when referring to women, but the active voice when referring to men] (p. 137)

## Gay People

Issues of appropriate language usage are more complicated with gay men and lesbian women than with the other three groups. Obviously, attention to the language issues raised in Chapter 1 is a starting point. The terms *gay men* and *lesbian women* are preferable to "homosexual" to distinguish gay identity from sexual behavior. The term *sexual orientation* rather than sexual preference reminds us that gay people do not choose their sexual orientation any more than nongays choose to be heterosexual. It is also extremely important that counselors not confuse sexual orientation with other descriptors such as gender role, gender identity, transvestism, or transsexuality. And, of course, counselors should not only refrain from using any of the vast array of derogatory labels for gay people in their professional roles, but must also extend this behavior to their personal lives, as such usage only serves to perpetuate the homophobia that is the primary source of oppression for gays. Beyond these basics, however, the issues become muddier.

When counseling gay men and lesbian women, it is incumbent upon the counselor to understand the client's preferences for self-labels. There is often a considerable time gap (sometimes years) between a gay individual's first

awareness of feelings for the same sex and their full acceptance of their gay identity (Dworkin & Gutierrez, 1992). In the earliest stages of the coming out process clients may not accept that they are gay, and the counselor must consequently be careful in attaching labels to clients; however, neither should the counselor assume that homoerotic feelings are "just a phase."
Understanding the coming out process is vital to gay affirmative counseling (Garnets, Hancock, Cochran, Goodchilds, & Peplau, 1991). Even clients who are fairly comfortable with being gay may prefer one self-descriptor over others, e.g., a woman who prefers to call herself gay rather than lesbian. Counselors must always recall that gay clients are no more immune from the effects of homophobia than nongay clients. Finally, some gay men and lesbian women have reclaimed some of society's derogatory labels, e.g., queer or dyke, using them in a gay-affirmative manner. It is usually wise for the nongay counselor to refrain from such usage because of possible misinterpretations.

In all aspects of practice, counselors must scrupulously avoid heterosexist assumptions and language reflecting those assumptions. As we previously discussed, *heterosexist bias* is defined as "conceptualizing human experience in strictly heterosexual terms and consequently ignoring, invalidating, or derogating homosexual behaviors and sexual orientation, and lesbian, gay, and bisexual relationships and lifestyles" (Herek, Kimmel, Amaro, & Melton, 1991, p. 958). Even with nongay clients (or clients who are presumed to be nongay) counselors must take care to examine the ways in which the assumption that everyone is heterosexual can influence practice. A common example is assuming the sex of a client's significant other or partner (e.g., with a male client, assuming that the partner is female).

APA's Committee on Gay and Lesbian Concerns (1991) summarized the goals for reducing heterosexual bias in language, to be included in the next edition of the APA *Publication Manual,* as follows:

1. *Reducing heterosexual bias and increasing visibility of lesbians, gay men, and bisexual persons.* Unless an author is referring specifically to heterosexual people, writing should be free of heterosexual bias. Ways to increase the visibility of lesbians, gay men, and bisexual persons include the following:
   a. Using examples of lesbians, gay men, and bisexual persons when referring to activities (e.g., parenting, athletic ability) that are erroneously associated only with heterosexual people by many readers.
   b. Referring to lesbians, gay men, and bisexual persons in situations other than sexual relationships . . .
   c. Omitting discussion of marital status unless legal marital relationships are the subject of the writing . . .
   d. Referring to sexual and intimate emotional partners with both male and female terms (e.g., "the adolescent males were asked about the age at which they first had a male or female sexual partner").

e. Using sexual terminology that is relevant to lesbians and gay men as well as bisexual and heterosexual people (e.g., "when did you first engage in sexual activity" rather than "when did you first have sexual intercourse").

f. Avoiding the assumption that pregnancy may result from sexual activity . . .

2. *Clarity of expression and avoidance of inaccurate stereotypes about lesbians, gay men, and bisexual persons.* . . . An example such as "Psychologists need training in working with special populations such as lesbians, drug abusers, and alcoholics" is stigmatizing in that it lists a status designation (lesbians) with designations of people being treated.

3. *Comparisons of lesbians and gay men with parallel groups.* . . . For example, contrasting lesbians with the "general public" or "normal women" portrays lesbians as marginal to society. More appropriate comparison groups might be "heterosexual women," "heterosexual men and women," or "gay men and heterosexual women and men." (p. 974)

## Ethics and Ethical Issues

The APA 1992 *Ethical Principles of Psychologists and Code of Conduct* (hereafter referred to as the APA *Ethics Code*) contains directives to psychologists regarding their treatment of diverse populations. In particular, Principle D, Respect for people's rights and dignity, states that:

> Psychologists accord appropriate respect to the fundamental rights, dignity, and worth of all people. They respect the rights of individuals to privacy, confidentiality, self-determination, and autonomy. . . . Psychologists are aware of cultural, individual, and role differences, including those due to age, gender, race, ethnicity, national origin, religion, sexual orientation, disability, language, and socioeconomic status. Psychologists try to eliminate the effect on their work of biases based on those factors, and they do not knowingly participate in or condone unfair discriminatory practices. (pp. 1599–1600)

A number of the other standards that make up the APA *Ethics Code* make specific reference to psychologists' behavior regarding diverse populations.

> Standard 1.10 (Nondiscrimination): In their work-related activities, psychologists do not engage in unfair discrimination based on age, gender, race, ethnicity, national origin, religion, sexual orientation, disability, socioeconomic status, or any basis proscribed by law.

> Standard 1.12 (Other Harassment): Psychologists do not knowingly engage in behavior that is harassing or demeaning to persons with whom they interact in their work based on factors such as those person's age, gender, race, ethnicity, national origin, religion, sexual orientation, disability, language, or socioeconomic status.

In addition to the professional/ethical mandates prohibiting discrimination against diverse populations by psychologists, counselors should be aware of the ethical dilemmas they are likely to confront when working with persons with disabilities, elders, women, and gay people. The ethical principles of autonomy, beneficence, nonmaleficence, justice, and fidelity identified by Kitchener (1984) as those "most critical for the evaluation of ethical concerns in psychology" (p. 46) along with the ethical principle of paternity will be used to highlight the nature of these dilemmas. Briefly, and in the context of a counseling relationship, autonomy refers to the client's freedom of action and freedom of choice. The principle of beneficence implies that the counselor should promote the client's welfare while the principle of nonmaleficence mandates that the counselor should do no harm to the client. According to Kitchener (1984), justice in the broadest sense means "fairness" and "suggests that equal persons have the right to be treated equally and nonequal persons have a right to be treated differently if the inequality is relevant to the issue in question" (p. 49). Fidelity has to do with trustworthiness and in counseling requires the counselor to maintain confidentiality and obtain the client's informed consent to treatment. The principle of paternalism requires that counselors care for and safeguard the interests of their clients who cannot do so themselves (Steininger, Newell, & Garcia, 1984).

Ethical dilemmas result when the mandates of ethical principles, codes of ethics, statutory law, common law, and/or the counselor's own moral standards come in conflict with each other. The thorniest of these potential conflicts may be when counselors hold certain religious beliefs that conflict with their professional role. For example, to act ethically, counselors must be accepting and affirming toward gay and lesbian clients. Whether that is possible when a counselor holds strongly to the conviction that homosexuality is a sin is highly questionable (see Nelson, 1985, for a discussion of religious perspectives on homosexuality). There are an infinite number of specific ethical dilemmas that the counselor might confront when working with nonethnic minorities; even a thorough review of the dilemmas that can arise from conflicts between the ethical principles alone is beyond the scope of this text. A few conflicts between ethical principles will be cited as examples of dilemmas that the counselor may face when working with persons with disabilities, elders, women, and gay people.

The ethical principle of justice is particularly relevant to clients who have been singled out for differential and inferior treatment but contains within it the basis for a counseling dilemma. In essence, the principle of justice places counselors in the position of deciding when they should provide unequal treatment because the inequality of the client's status is relevant to the counseling concern, or when they should provide equal treatment because the inequality of the client's status is not relevant to the counseling concern. An example of this dilemma might involve vocational placement of a person with a disability. Is the fact that the client has been released by three previous employers after a very brief tenure on the job evidence of disability discrimination (and thereby warranting of unequal treatment, perhaps in the form of counselor advocacy) or lack of effort (and thereby warranting treatment equal to that of a person without a disability)?

Conflicts between the principles of autonomy and paternalism frequently create dilemmas for counselors working with nonethnic minorities. The principle of autonomy (and treatment issues related to empowerment) dictate that the minority client should be allowed to exercise his/her freedom of choice and action. However, the counselor may feel that due to the client's limited cognitive functioning (as in the cases of some elders and most persons with developmental disabilities), the client is not in a position to exercise his/her autonomy in a beneficial way. This situation frequently arises when an elderly person must make a major life decision that affects not only him/herself, but his/her family. Fitting (1986) has identified four types of clients/problems that frequently involve these types of decisions:

> (a) those who are coping with the developmental issues of aging (e.g., retirement, loss of spouse), (b) those who are coping with chronic illness common in late life (e.g., hearing and visual impairments, dementia), (c) those who have major mental illness (e.g., late onset schizophrenia, major depression), and (d) those who are suffering from terminal illnesses (e.g., cancer, end-stage renal disease). (p. 325)

With respect to the autonomy versus paternalism conflict when working with an elderly client, Fitting (1986) recommends that counselors become familiar with their professional code of ethics, knowledgeable about the health and medical status of their elderly clients, and informed about the decision-making capability and psychological functioning of elderly adults. She recommends that the counselor first assess the decision-making capacity of the client, then assess the family relationships within the client's family, and finally weigh the choices in terms of the ethical principles of fidelity, beneficence, and autonomy.

Cayleff (1986) suggests that the paternalism inherent in the counselor-client relationship reinforces societal values that deny women a full measure of autonomy. "To discern the true autonomy of women, it may be necessary to establish women's own beliefs, as opposed to their socialized, sex-specific propensity to accommodate and attempt to please others" (Cayleff, 1986, p. 346). Counselors who neglect to examine the effects of gender-role socialization on their clients' attitudes and choices often unwittingly serve to reinforce the status quo. Counseling that serves to support limited, sex-specific career and personal goals for women violates the ethical principles of beneficence and nonmaleficence as well as the ethical principle of autonomy.

Paternalism, beneficence, and autonomy also can create ethical dilemmas for the counselor working with a gay or lesbian adolescent. Sobocinski (1990) points out that adolescence is a transitional period during which a young person moves from dependence to independence, a change that has special relevance for counseling clients around issues of emerging sexuality and acknowledging sexual orientation. After analyzing the competing ethical principles, Sobocinski (1990) concluded:

> There does not appear to be, a priori, reason to declare youth incompetent to consent to treatment dealing with issues of sexual orientation. Because of the inevitability of internalized negative stereotypes and stigma surrounding lesbians and gays in society, one cannot hope that the resolution of gay and lesbian adolescents' emerging sexuality will be facilitated in a manner in which their autonomy is respected until and unless these factors are addressed within therapy. Only when adolescents view their sexuality as acceptable and worthy can they be truly autonomous and free of the coercive, controlling influences of family, peers, and society. (p. 246)

## Advocate and Change Agent Roles

A theme throughout this book is that many of the problems experienced by nonethnic minorities are the result of the oppression they experience and that counselors may need to assist their nonethnic minority clients to overcome the effects of oppression. This suggests the need for counselors to function as advocates and/or social change agents.

In the advocacy role, the counselor speaks on the client's behalf. This role is called for when the client is unable to speak for him/her self. This might be the case when the client is a person with a disability that limits their ability to communicate. In the change agent role, the counselor attempts to change the oppressive environment, either by directly or indirectly promoting the empowerment of the oppressed group.

A number of authors have suggested how service providers can serve as advocates for people with disabilities. For example, Bruce and Christiansen (1988) propose that occupational therapists "confront persons using pejorative language in their spoken and written communication by politely drawing attention to the negative effects of such language and suggesting preferred word alternatives" (p. 191). Vargo (1989) proposes that counselors "encourage people who are interested to actively agitate for legislation which will ensure measures such as equal pay for equal work and barrier-free design of public buildings" (p. 283). As a person with a spinal cord injury, Vargo (1989) also encourages counselors to "assist people with disabilities to act as their own ambassadors for public attitude change and thereby stop stigmatizing themselves" (p. 284).

Munro (1991) has described a Step Approach Model to training families of persons with severe developmental, psychiatric, or neurological disabilities to be effective advocates. Eight common-sense rules define this model:

*Rule #1: Never use a cannon where a pea-shooter will do!* (p. 2)
The advocate who is overly negative, aggressive or obnoxious may alienate potential supporters and problem solvers and may do more harm than good.

*Rule #2: "Get the big picture"* (p. 2)

By gathering facts about all the factors influencing the institutional decision-making process, the advocate is in a good position to establish realistic goals and to develop effective strategies.

*Rule #3: Time your advocacy strategies carefully.* (p. 3)

To ensure proper timing, the advocate should do three things: first, make sure his/her own motivation and energy level is at its highest before raising a concern; second, present his/her case when the potential problem solver is most willing and able to listen to the concern; third, identify needs as early as possible and before a crisis develops.

*Rule #4: "Use the cards you've been dealt"* (p. 3)

Assess your skills as an advocate and attempt to maximize those skills in the advocacy process. If you are better as a speaker than a writer, present the case verbally and recruit someone else to present the case in writing.

*Rule #5: Don't "go it alone"* (p. 3)

Recruit other advocates; there is power, strength, and support in group advocacy.

*Rule #6: Be willing to compromise* (p. 3)

Politics are inherent in all social institutions. Negotiating a workable compromise can lay the groundwork for future successes.

*Rule #7: Humanize the concern* (p. 3)

A personal testimony from the client or the client's family can often be much more effective than a mountain of statistics.

*Rule #8: Express appreciation and show support to helpful problem solvers* (p. 3)

Failing to express appreciation to helpful decision makers ultimately may be self-defeating. A pat on the back may help ensure future cooperation.

A study by Balcazar, Seekins, Fawcett, and Hopkins (1990) documented that advocacy skills training for persons with physical disabilities resulted in an increase of disability-related issues they reported at monthly advocacy meetings, an increase of advocacy actions on the part of participants, and an increase in the number of targeted actions (i.e., changes in the environment, policy, budget allocations, and services).

Wolff (1987) has described the advocacy efforts of the Highland Valley Elder Service, Inc., an Area Agency on Aging/home care corporation in Northampton, Massachusetts, that was designed to empower elder citizens. The agency funded seven initiatives to this end:

1. A marketing research survey on elder economic needs and interest in a membership system;

2. Gray Panthers of the Pioneer Valley to strengthen advocacy efforts;

3. Western Massachusetts Cooperatives to develop cooperative buying of food through buying clubs for elders;

4. Development of cooperative purchasing of and budget assistance for home energy needs;

5. Development of a self-supporting membership newsletter offering economic benefit packages (coupons and discounts from member merchants) and advocacy tools (e.g., tear-out postcards);

6. Development of employment opportunities for elders in the child care field;

7. Creative Aging Services to develop projects promoting elder emotional and physical health by training elders to be leaders of such self-help groups in their own communities.

These efforts by the Highland Valley Elder Service provide evidence that a group of advocates can bring about significant changes in community services for the elderly.

Netting and Hinds (1989) point out that the Comprehensive Older Americans Act Amendment of 1978 mandated that each state designate an ombudsman for the elderly at the state level. They describe the East Tennessee Advocates for Elders program as an example of a rural volunteer ombudsman program. The program is designed to meet the needs of elderly persons receiving long term care. It has one paid professional director and a number of certified volunteers and is administratively responsible to the Area Agency on Aging. The volunteers are involved in community development, social planning, and social action.

> Community development emphasizes self-help and citizen participation. Individuals and groups work cooperatively to solve problems. . . . Social planning focuses on rational problem solving, which requires professionals to gather and analyze data to plan for community change. Consumers of service are usually relegated to client and recipient roles. . . . Social action attempts to restructure power relationships and to include consumers of service in the process of confronting difficulties. . . . Social reform as a model mixes social planning and social action. (p. 423)

The community development strategy is implemented by having a volunteer ombudsman visit elderly nursing home residents and assist them with their needs. As an example of the social planning strategy, Netting and Hinds cite the use of volunteers who collect information for publication in a consumer guide to health care facilities in the 16-county area served by the program. As an example of social action efforts, they point to the work by volunteers who over 2½ years researched, studied, and drafted nursing home legislation that was introduced in the Tennessee state assembly in 1986.

Crabtree (1988) described an advocacy role for rehabilitation specialists that could be generalized to any counselors or psychologists who work with elders who live in a nursing home (or who work with the families of nursing home residents). Basically, the role involves educating elders, health care providers, third party payers, nursing home administrators, and nursing home staff as to what constitutes quality rehabilitation services and then following up to ensure that these services are provided.

In making the case for gender aware or feminist approaches to counseling, we have already implicitly suggested a social advocacy approach to counseling women. Because so many of the concerns female clients present to counselors are heavily influenced by their gender, we argue that counselors perform a disservice to their female clients if the counselor is not sensitive to gender influences and gender inequities. However, a wide range of options remain as to the most effective ways of working with gender in counseling.

The earliest forms of feminist counseling were the grass roots consciousness raising (CR) groups of the early 1970s, which emerged out of the feminist movement. These were not originally conceptualized as "therapy" groups, but rather as a political force; participants came together to share their perceptions and discuss their experiences as women, with the common goal of social change (Enns, 1993). However it soon became clear that CR participants often reported improvements akin to those we expect from counseling, for example, enhanced self-esteem, increased autonomy and other personal changes, as well as modifications in interpersonal relationships.

> As the therapeutic benefits of CR groups became apparent to women, they were sometimes recommended as an adjunct to therapy. . . . Women therapists, who became members of CR groups, were changed and radicalized through their interactions with other women and expressed interest in using their skills to combat oppression in their professional work . . . [therapy] groups that were modeled after CR experiences . . . became the preferred modality for a substantial number of feminist therapists. . . . Groups were seen as an effective antidote to negative gender socialization in that women could gain power by practicing skills in a safe environment. (Enns, 1993, pp. 6–7)

Gradually, as the limitations of CR groups as the only form of feminist assistance to women became apparent, other methods of feminist and gender-aware therapy emerged focusing more on the personal issues and concerns of women. Today there are a wide range of feminist approaches, some still intimately tied to political activism, others less overtly activist, but retaining some of the basic principles of the earlier feminist CR groups.

Although feminism simply refers to the advocacy of equality between women and men, several feminist philosophies have been articulated. Each adopts a slightly different stance on the presumed reasons for gender inequality, and therefore the manner in which inequalities and gender influences ought to be addressed. Feminist therapy, therefore, is not a monolithic entity; feminist therapies exist, corresponding to different feminist philosophies, each suggesting somewhat different strategies for effecting social change within and outside of counseling (Enns & Hackett, 1990; Hackett, Enns, & Zetzer, 1992). Some of the major traditions within feminist thought have been the liberal, radical, socialist, Marxist, cultural, and woman of color feminist philosophies. Of these, the liberal and radical feminist philosophies have been drawn from most heavily by feminist therapists:

> Liberal feminist writers emphasize current inequalities in educational opportunities and civil rights, focusing on the elimination of these inequalities, especially through legal and educational reform, as the mechanism for achieving a sex-fair society. . . . Consequently, the liberal feminist counselor focuses on expanding clients' awareness of gender role socialization, social barriers, and discrimination, in the context of exploring personal goals and options. Radical feminist theorists . . . see sexism as the fundamental oppression. Radical feminist theorists all share the assumptions that historically women were the first oppressed group, that women's oppression is the most widespread and pervasive form of oppression, and that women's oppression is the hardest to eradicate and cannot be removed by other social changes such as legal or educational reform. (Enns & Hackett, 1991, p. 34)

One of the fundamental differences between the liberal and radical perspectives in counseling is that the radical feminist counselor will be much more active in assisting clients to identify social barriers and structural inequalities, and will be more likely to encourage (though not coerce) the client to engage in external change efforts and political action. The liberal feminist counselor will be more likely to support, but not necessarily actively encourage, clients' social change efforts. Although these philosophical distinctions are helpful in understanding the varieties of feminist approaches to counseling, we must also caution the readers that, in real life, the distinctions are often blurred.

> What these approaches all have in common is an emphasis on empowering women: The social construction of gender [and feminist therapy] relocates women's problems from individual and internal to societal and external. The feminist construction of gender redefines the nature of women's and men's relationships in terms of the expression and maintenance of power. Emergent client populations were "discovered" where problems were never thought to exist [e.g., sexual abuse, sexual harassment, eating disorders]. The challenge of these new client populations stimulated the development of theories, research, and procedures to address their concerns. The combined efforts of women's groups in both the lay and professional communities have resulted in a new agenda for women's mental health. (Worell & Remer, 1992, p. 4).

In essence, counselors who address and explore gender socialization, gender-related beliefs and constraints, and structural influences on and barriers to women, by default engage in a form of social advocacy for all women.

Social advocacy for lesbian women and gay men is also necessary and encouraged by the major professional associations:

> In 1975, the American Psychological Association (APA) took a strong stance regarding bias toward lesbians and gay men, resolving that "homosexuality per se implies no impairment in judgement, reliability, or general social and vocational

abilities". . . . The APA urged psychologists "to take the lead in removing the stigma of mental illness long associated with homosexual orientations." (Garnets, et al., 1991, p. 964)

Despite this exhortation, issued almost 20 years ago, ongoing discrimination against gay people underscores the necessity of continuing efforts on the part of counselors and psychologists in educating ourselves, our clients, and the public at large. Our professional organizations have been involved in public policy debates on issues of concern to gay men and lesbian women; for example, APA issued a review of the scientific research supporting lifting the ban on gays in the military and has also issued briefs on other civil rights issues of concern to gay people (Melton, 1989). Yet therapists and counselors themselves have not universally surmounted the deeply ingrained negative attitudes toward gay people. Although 99 percent of service providers in a recent study reported having counseled at least one gay client (that they knew of), the majority (58%) were also personally aware of incidents of biased or inappropriate treatment of gay clients "including cases in which practitioners defined lesbians or gay men as 'sick' and in need of change, and instances where a client's sexual orientation distracted a therapist from treating a person's central problem" (Garnets, et al., 1991, p. 970). Clearly, social change advocacy for gay clients must begin with each individual counselor. Our earlier review of language usage is a starting point, and the articles on gay affirmative counseling (Chapters 13 and 14) contain many suggestions useful to the counselor attempting to grapple with antigay bias.

However, social advocacy must eventually extend beyond one's own attitudes and can take many forms. For example, Garnets et al. (1991), in their discussion of exemplary practice with gay clients, state that "a therapist is familiar with the needs and treatment issues of gay male and lesbian clients, and uses relevant mental health, educational, and gay male and lesbian community resources" (p. 970). This type of behavior with individual clients alone constitutes a form of advocacy: "A gay man, a client of mine, age 20, told me he particularly appreciated my willingness to gather information about coming out, including meeting with campus representatives, which he was not yet ready to do, having just concluded in therapy he was gay" (Garnets, et al., 1991, p. 970). At some point, however, counselors must begin to engage in more visible advocacy efforts. Recommendations for exemplary practice with gay clients also include public advocacy:

> A therapist recognizes the importance of educating professionals, students, supervisees, and others about gay male and lesbian issues and actively counters misinformation or bias about lesbians and gay men: [for example] A colleague told me of how they changed the intake forms at the agency to include gay/lesbian and space for "significant other" identification instead of spouse. [And] I observed a colleague, at a case conference, ask the presenter if he had asked his single male patient about homosexual experience. The presenter had assumed that because he had never had a girlfriend or been married, he was asexual." (Garnets, et al., 1991, p. 970)

# Counselor Training

The justification for training counselors to work with both ethnic and nonethnic minority groups can be found in their representation among users of counseling and psychological services. As suggested in Chapter 1, women alone make up the majority of clients being seen by counselors and psychologists. Elders also represent a significant (and growing) proportion of the population, as do persons with disabilities. Lesbian women and gay men seek counseling services at a rate 2 to 4 times higher than nongays (Rudolph, 1989). It is imperative that future counselors receive training that prepares them to work with these populations.

Justification for training counselors and psychologists to work with special populations is also provided by the professional and ethical standards of the major professional counseling and psychology associations. For example, the APA *Ethics Code* makes it clear that psychologists are to seek training in order to ensure that they can work with diverse populations. Standard 1.08 states:

> Where differences of age, gender, race, ethnicity, national origin, religion, sexual orientation, disability, language, or socioeconomic status significantly affect psychologists' work concerning particular individuals or groups, psychologists obtain the training, experience, consultation, or supervision necessary to ensure the competence of their services, or they make appropriate referrals.

Also, Criterion II (Cultural and Individual Differences) of the *APA Accreditation Handbook* (1986) states that:

> As a science and profession, psychology deals with the full range of human variability. It follows that social responsibility and respect for cultural and individual differences are attitudes which must be imparted to students and trainees and be reflected in all phases of the program's operation: faculty recruitment and promotion, student recruitment and evaluation, curriculum, and field training. Social and personal diversity of faculty and students is an essential goal if the trainees are to function optimally within our pluralistic society. Programs must develop knowledge and skills in their students relevant to human diversity such as people with handicapping conditions; of differing ages, genders, ethnic and racial backgrounds, religions, and life-styles; and from differing social and individual backgrounds. (Appendix B, p. 4)

Criterion II has been criticized for lacking specificity (Rickard & Clements, 1993), but there is general agreement that the Criterion II guidelines send "a clear signal that it [APA] is committed to work toward the goal of promoting the welfare of all humans" (Payton, 1993). Furthermore, the *APA Accreditation Handbook* (1986) also mandates that programs not discriminate against diverse populations in their student selection process:

> A culturally diverse student body contributes to the professional development and interpersonal sensitivity of students. Students of academic excellence and professional promise will not be systematically excluded on the basis of race, ethnic origin, sex, age, religion, or physical handicap. (Appendix B, p. 14)

Similar statements can be found in the Ethical Standards of the American Association for Counseling and Development and the accreditation requirements of the Council for Accreditation of Counseling and Related Educational Programs (CACREP). It is clear from these statements that training counselors to work with nonethnic minorities is not only desirable for counselor training programs, it is also mandated.

We believe that in order to train counselors to work with nonethnic minorities, three components are needed: (1) a faculty sensitive to diversity issues; (2) a curriculum that is designed to train counselors to work with special populations; and (3) students who are receptive to training in the area of nonethnic minorities. All three are essential ingredients; the absence of any one of these components will seriously jeopardize the effectiveness of the training program.

## Faculty Sensitivity to Diversity Issues

Although the major professional organizations require that counselors and psychologists recognize differences among people and that accredited training programs provide training in client diversity, they have not addressed the issue of faculty development and renewal in this area. Unfortunately, most professors in counselor and psychologist training programs were themselves trained before current professional and accreditation standards were in place mandating training for counseling of special populations. This places the responsibility for designing curricula related to client diversity in the hands of individuals who have no systematic training on the topic. It seems clear that faculty must actively seek out development and renewal activities in order to acquire both the attitudes and knowledge needed to train counselors and psychologists to work with diverse populations. Further, it is unreasonable to assume that graduate students will acquire the necessary sensitivity to and competency with client differences if the counselor training faculty cannot model these attributes.

A recent survey of psychologists on the practice and ethics of teaching exposes the failure of some of the teaching faculty to keep current in areas of diversity. Only 71 percent of the respondents regarded sexual involvement with a student as absolutely unethical; 30 percent of teaching faculty felt that telling a student "I'm sexually attracted to you" was either ethical, or ethical under certain circumstances (Tabachnik, Keith-Spiegel, & Pope, 1991). Sixty-four percent of psychologists branded as unethical the teaching that homosexuality per se was pathological (10% said it was ethical, 16% were unsure, and 8% said it was unethical under rare circumstances), while only 17 percent regarded teaching in buildings that did not accommodate physically challenged students as unethical (Tabachnik, et al., 1991).

Although it is important for counseling professors trained over the past 50 years to develop sensitivity to minority issues through their own professional development and renewal, it is imperative that future faculty appointments include sensitivity to diversity issues as a selection criterion. Since faculty serve as professional models for the students with whom they work, we believe that sensitivity to diversity issues should be one of the top priorities in selecting a counselor educator. Faculty and administrators responsible for selecting new faculty should examine each candidate's background to determine familiarity with diversity issues and should include questions related to sensitivity in this area in any interviewing that is done.

In addition to selecting faculty who are sensitive to diversity issues, every effort should be made to ensure that persons with disabilities, women, and openly gay people are represented among the faculty proportionate to their representation in the general population (most counselor training programs already include a diversity of ages). A mandate to this effect is provided in the *APA Accreditation Handbook* (1986):

> Because individual differences reflected in lifestyle, age, handicapping conditions, gender, ethnic and racial background, and religion are important for both intellectual and professional training purposes, it is essential that the faculty be composed of individuals who are sensitive and constructively responsive to these individual differences. In addition, the department or school housing the program must not systematically exclude candidates from consideration for hiring, promotion, retention, and granting of tenure on the basis of age, gender, ethnic or racial background, lifestyle, religion, or physical handicap. (Appendix B, p. 11)

Although concrete data on faculty with disabilities and gay faculty are generally not available, in a recent survey 62 percent of female graduate students reported that there were no gay faculty in their counseling psychology programs (at least to their knowledge) (Buhrke, 1989a). The data on female representation among counselor education faculties is likewise not encouraging.

Anderson and Rawlins (1985) report that although slightly over 50 percent of the new Ph.D.s and Ed.D.s in counselor education in 1983 were women, only 22.5 percent of the faculty in counselor education programs are women and most of these are in the lower ranks. They suggest a concentrated effort is needed to recruit, select, and advance women in counselor education; we believe this recommendation applies to faculty members with disabilities and gay or lesbian faculty as well. In the area of recruitment for faculty positions they suggest networking to identify qualified women applicants and including women on selection committees. In the area of selection they suggest that screening committees be made familiar with discriminatory questions that are prohibited by law and that faculty discuss the "invisible discrimination of perceptual bias." In order to support the professional development of women faculty these authors suggest research support groups, academic mentors, and selective committee involvement for female faculty. Each of these suggestions can be generalized to the recruitment, selection, and support of faculty with disabilities and gay or lesbian faculty as well.

Those university counseling centers, Veterans Administration centers, and mental health hospitals that participate in training counselors and psychologists through pre- and post-doctoral internships should also take steps to ensure that their training staff is sensitive to and knowledgeable about client diversity. Efforts should be made to expose all interns to the full range of client diversity seen at each agency.

## *Counselor Training Curriculum*

Before examining suggestions for course content that addresses special populations, we will review the current status of counselor and psychologist training for work with persons with disabilities, elders, women, and gay people and the training models that have been proposed for providing this training.

### Training Currently Provided

In order to ensure that counselors are trained to effectively counsel clients from nonethnic minorites, counselor training programs need to focus attention on these groups as part of their curricula. To date, however, it appears that most counselor training programs do not require (or even offer) courses in counseling nonethnic minorities. In a survey of 285 counselor education programs, Scott and McMillian (1980) found that only 4 percent required counselor trainees to take a sex-fair counseling course and only 33 percent offered a sex-fair counseling course as an elective.

With respect to coursework related to gerontological counseling, there is evidence that a trend toward offering such courses may have peaked and leveled off. Salisbury (1975) surveyed 304 counselor education programs and found that not one of them required their students to take a course in geriatric counseling and only 6 percent offered an elective on the topic. Only eight years later, Myers (1983) determined that 37 percent of 306 responding counselor education programs offered courses to train counselors to work with the elderly, a substantial increase but still a clear minority of the programs surveyed. Hollis and Wantz (1986) concluded from their survey of counselor education programs that new courses in gerontological counseling were among the fastest growing courses in counselor education. In a recent survey, however, Myers, Loesch, and Sweeney (1991) found that only 31 percent of the 237 programs responding to their survey offered courses to train counselors to work with older persons. Assuming that programs offering such courses were over-represented among respondents (responses were received from 52% of the counselor education programs in the U.S.), it seems reasonable to conclude that the actual percentage of programs offering coursework in gerontological counseling is something less than 31 percent. Furthermore, 75 percent of the respondents to the Myers et al. (1991) survey indicated that they had no plans to offer additional coursework on gerontological counseling. Similar results were found in a study of psychology providers; Gatz, Karel, and Wolkenstein (1991) surveyed 74 psychologists who designated "aged" as a population they served and found that only 27 percent had any formal training in gerontological psychology. Gatz et al. (1991) concluded that "potential consumers might well be concerned about whether practitioners are adequately familiar with special problems of their age group" (p. 415). To help address the need for more psychologists who specialize in working with the elderly, a conference co-sponsored by the APA Practice Directorate, the National Institute of Mental Health, and the Retirement Research Foundation recommended the development of standards for a specialization in clinical geropsychology (Moses, 1992).

Although rehabilitation counseling programs are specifically designed to train counselors to work with persons with disabilities, counselor training programs in general provide little training related to this population. Several studies have documented that school counselors receive little or no training to work with special education students (Lebsock & Deblassie, 1975; Lombana, 1980). Lebsock and Deblassie (1975) surveyed 359 school counselors in five states and found that nearly half of them (43%) had taken no special education courses. These authors also surveyed 65 counselor education programs and found that only 13 percent required their students to take one or more special education courses. In a survey of 195 school counselors in Florida (Lombana, 1980), 57 percent reported having received no coursework in special education. Furthermore, 35 percent reported having received no in-service training in handicapped student education. Crespi (1988), addressing the lack of counselors trained to work with persons who have visual impairments, points out that as the population ages, the numbers of persons with a visual disability will increase. A similar observation applies to most other types of disabilities and suggests an urgent need for all counselors and psychologists to receive training to work with persons with disabilities.

There has been no research and, until recently, very little attention devoted to the coverage of gay issues in counselor preparation programs (Iasenza, 1989). However, Graham, Rawlings, Halpern, and Hermes (1984), in a study of practicing therapists' attitudes, knowledge, concerns, and counseling approaches with lesbian women and gay men, reported a strong need for additional training in this area. Therapists were generally uninformed about the literature on gay life-styles, many held inaccurate beliefs about gay people, and a significant minority (37%) stated that they would work with clients on the goal of changing sexual orientation (Graham, et al., 1984). McDonald (1982) found misleading information and misrepresentation of data on gay people in a survey of introductory psychology textbooks, a finding that does not bode well for the undergraduate preparation of students entering graduate programs in mental health. Buhrke (1989a) found that almost one-third of female counseling psychology students reported no exposure to gay or lesbian issues during their graduate experience; 70 percent were in programs where no faculty were engaged in research on gay issues; and almost one-half of the respondents had not seen any gay or lesbian clients.

Although inclusion of training for competence with diverse populations is beginning to have an impact on counselor training programs, it seems clear that actual training of counselors in nonethnic minority issues still lags behind professional and accreditation standards that mandate such training.

## Training Models

While there is general agreement that training must be provided, there is disagreement about the kind of training model that is most effective as a means of sensitizing counselors to work with special populations. Some authors have argued for specialized training related to specific groups, and others have argued for changes in the basic curriculum. Copeland (1982) identified four models for training counselors to work with special populations: the separate course model, area of concentration model, interdisciplinary model, and integrated model.

In the *separate* course approach, information about nonethnic minorities is provided in one course. Usually this course would have as its goals the development of sensitivity to the experience of being a minority person, knowledge about each group discussed, and competency in adapting counseling strategies to the groups studied. The separate course can focus on only one minority, in which case a number of separate courses must be offered. Or the course can focus on the effects of discrimination, with an attempt to generalize the content to all minority groups (a human rights approach). In response to the need to increase student awareness, knowledge, and skills for counseling special populations, many counselor education programs have started to offer separate courses for each group. Margolis and Rungta (1986), addressing the issue of separate courses for ethnic groups, offer the following criticisms of this approach:

1. "Adding more and more special courses to an existing program may not be feasible because of budget constraints, the total number of courses that can be imposed on students, and availability of expert faculty" (p. 643).

2. A proliferation of separate courses for special groups may accent differences among them and lead to a separate set of standards and strategies for each group that in turn may lead to unequal treatment.

3. By focusing on one characteristic we may fail to recognize the total person. If we focus on a person's ethnicity, sex, age, socioeconomic class, sexual orientation, or disability, we may fail to recognize important other characteristics or the unique combination of characteristics.

4. Another consequence of providing separate courses for each group is that it may limit the ability of counselor trainees to transfer their learning from one population to another. Margolis and Rungta argue that the common experiences of discrimination among minority groups suggests that some course content should be generalized across groups.

In the *area of concentration* model, students are offered several courses and perhaps a practicum that focus on special populations. These courses are either part of an elective concentration within a larger program, or the entire program is identified as having a focus on a special population. In the former case, it is only helpful for some of the students; in the latter case, the benefits accrue only to those students enrolled in programs that make the resource commitment to the model. Also, those programs that focus on one client population, say older clients, may fail to provide proper training in other types of diversity.

In the *interdisciplinary* model the program makes use of courses that are taught in other departments in order to provide an area of concentration. The interdisciplinary model appears to be inherent in the criteria for certification as a National Certified Gerontological Counselor. The National Board for Certified Counselors requires three graduate courses in gerontology (along with an internship in a gerontological setting and two years of professional gerontological counseling experience) for certification as a gerontological counselor (Myers, 1992). The interdisciplinary approach assumes, of course, that such courses are available through other departments on the same campus. It also assumes the cooperation of other units on campus.

As applied to nonethnic minorities, the *integrated* model provides for integrating information about the elderly, people with disabilities, women, and gay people into all counselor training courses. For example, a counseling theories course would incorporate attention to sexism and heterosexism within traditional counseling theories, as well as address the limitations of extant theory for counseling with people with disabilities and the elderly. A human development course would address the sociopsychological development of the elderly and people with disabilities, gender role issues in women's development, and the process of gay identity development; the unique life-span experiences and the issues of aging for people with disabilities, women, lesbian women, and gay men could likewise be addressed. Similarly, a course in career development would cover the special vocational and avocational needs of women, gay people, and people with disabilities, and the employment problems experienced by all four groups. The integrated model was selected by the Council for Accreditation of Counseling and Related Educational Programs in developing recently adopted standards for training in gerontological counseling (Meyers, 1992). This approach requires that all the faculty be familiar with diversity issues that are related to their courses and be willing to incorporate this content in their courses.

## Curriculum Content

Earlier authors have identified curriculum content needed to train counselors who will work with one of the four nonethnic minority groups discussed in this book. Most of these authors have recommended either an integrated or separate course approach. Some identify specific content that should be included in the curriculum; others focus on process more than content.

As we suggested earlier, counselors and psychologists can take a major step toward becoming more credible and effective helpers by eliminating imprecise and stereotypic language with respect to minorities from their vocabulary. However, can a course designed to teach the use of appropriate terminology have an impact? In order to determine if a course on language used in reference to persons with disabilities could affect the language used by undergraduates in a special education class, Byrd et al. (1991) randomly assigned 107 students to hear either a lecture on appropriate language usage when referring to person with disabilities, or to a lecture on cultural divergence. Based on the results of a test administered one week after the examination, the authors concluded that "students do change their writing behavior, when making reference to persons with disabilities, if they receive a short training module on appropriate use of language" (Byrd et al., 1991, p. 41). Although it can be hypothesized that appropriate use of written language will generalize to oral language, the authors suggest that oral language may require consistent reinforcement in order to produce consistency in language usage.

Myers and Blake (1986) describe how course content related to counseling the elderly can be integrated into all counselor training courses, employing a model that could be generalized to other special populations as well. They suggest that the eight core areas of study and supervised experience included in the *Accreditation Manual* of the Council for the Accreditation of Counseling and Related Educational Program (CACREP) "provide an adequate and appropriate framework for the incorporation of specialized course work on counseling older persons into a counselor education curriculum" (p. 139). Myers and Blake (1986) provide a number of examples of aging-related content that could be included in the core areas of human growth and development, social and cultural foundations, the helping relationship, group dynamics, career development, appraisal of individuals, research, and professional orientation. Table 16.1 summarizes the course content these authors suggest for these eight CACREP core areas. They propose that an integrated model is the best means of ensuring that all students learn about aging and is most adaptable for a program training counselors for a variety of settings. For programs specializing in gerontological counseling they recommend specialized courses taught on an interdisciplinary basis as the best approach to training counselors to work with other clients. Sinik (1979) also suggests that counselor training curricula intended to prepare counselors for work with older clients needs to integrate knowledge and attitude development into all the required courses. In terms of knowledge he specifies life-span development, career changes, retirement, and death and dying as important topics to be integrated into training courses. To address counselor attitudes he suggests formal coursework and direct experience with elders.

# Table 16.1

**Course Content on Counseling Older People by Core Areas
of Study from CACREP\* Accreditation Standards[1]**

| Core | Course Content |
|---|---|
| Human Growth and Development | Life-span development |
| | Theories of aging |
| Social and Cultural Foundations | Older persons as a minority group |
| | Older women |
| | Changing population demography and increased numbers of older people |
| | Leisure and life-style of older people |
| The Helping Relationship | Impact of counselor and client age on interactions |
| | Ageist attitudes and beliefs |
| | Theories of personality and aging |
| | Techniques for use with older persons (such as life review therapy) |
| Group Dynamics, Processes, and Counseling | Pros and cons of groups for older people |
| | Structural versus unstructured groups |
| | Life review therapy groups |
| | Educational and guidance groups |
| | Support groups |
| Life-style and Career Development | Sources of occupational and educational information for older people |
| | Retirement adjustments |
| | Use of leisure time |
| Appraisal of Individuals | Validity of tests with older people |
| | Special techniques for testing older people |
| | Instruments for use with older people |
| | Renorming instruments for use with older people |
| Research and Evaluation | Obtaining access to older subjects |
| | Grant funding in aging |
| | Accommodating needs of older persons as research subjects |
| Professional Orientation | Professional associations in gerontology |
| | Gerontology certificate programs |
| | Roles of gerontological counselors |
| | Legal and ethical issues in gerontological counseling |
| Supervised Experiences | Aging network agencies |
| | Geriatric mental health hospitals and agencies |
| | Settings where older persons comprise a large segment of the clientele |

[1]Adapted from Myers & Blake (1986, pp. 139–140).
\*CACREP = Council for the Accreditation of Counseling and Related Educational Programs

Thomas and Martin (1992) cite efficiency and effectiveness as reasons why counselors should be trained to run groups for their elderly clients. They point out that to train counselors to run reality orientation, remotivation, psychotherapy, reminiscing, and other types of groups for elderly clients, counselor educators need to "bridge the training gaps by combining and connecting . . . three separate professional standards" (p. 57). The three training standards to which they refer are the standards for specialists in group work (Association for Specialists in Group Work, 1991), the standards for gerontological counselors (Myers & Sweeney, 1990), and the standards for counselors in general (CACREP, 1990). Agresti (1992) has provided a rationale for the inclusion of specialized training in ethics for gerontological counselors. He cites the variability among states concerning the reporting of elderly abuse, older adult ability to participate in decisions regarding his or her care, and the complex questions surrounding long-term care as examples of how counseling with older adults may present unique ethical issues.

Similarly, several authors (Buhrke, 1989b; Buhrke & Douce, 1991; Norton, 1982) have offered suggestions for integrating current information on gay people into the core counselor training curriculum. Beginning with the introductory course, counselor educators should ensure that all courses contain current, nonhomophobic information. According to Norton (1982):

> There is not a course in counselor education in which gay issues are not appropriate. It is better that the topic appear as but a minor part of all courses, so that students get a feel for the pervasiveness of the gay group, but also a feel for the fact that this special population is really an integral part of the entire population. (p. 211)

Graham, et al. (1984) offered a useful overview of the content on gay people that ought to be included in counselor preparation programs. Therapists and counselors need information about: (1) lesbian/gay life-styles and social networks; (2) homophobia and heterosexism; (3) self-esteem in lesbian and gay male clients, especially low self-esteem as a function of internalized homophobia; and (4) appropriate and inappropriate therapeutic goals, that is, gay-affirmative approaches. The recent book published by the American Counseling Association (Dworkin & Gutierrez, 1992) and the two special issues of major counseling journals devoted to counseling gay men and lesbians (*Journal of Counseling and Development,* September/October, 1989; *The Counseling Psychologist,* April, 1991) are also rich resources.

In terms of specific courses, introductory courses often include an overview of client concerns and populations; this is a good place to begin to introduce discussions of lesbian women and gay men, for example, through case examples (Norton, 1982). Glenn and Russell (1986) suggest that training experiences that include ambiguous-sex clients can be used in existing courses to assess and confront subtle forms of heterosexual bias. Counseling theories must also be examined for heterosexist bias, e.g., Freud's views on heterosexual development (Buhrke, 1989b); heterosexual bias in assessment and diagnosis should also be an important aspect of any testing or measurement course. In group counseling courses gay issues may be introduced in discussions of screening for group participation (e.g., a struggling gay adolescent in high school would probably not be a good candidate for a general counseling group), and gay support groups should be addressed (Buhrke & Douce, 1991). Gay men and lesbian women experience unique career concerns that warrant coverage in career development course, e.g., occupational stereotypes, employment discrimination, dual career issues, and the work-nonwork interface (Buhrke, 1989b; Betz & Fitzgerald, 1993).

Gay issues should be incorporated into multicultural courses in two ways: (a) counselors must be sensitive to the unique experiences and special needs of gay people of color, for example, the triple oppression experienced by lesbian African-Americans; and (b) counselors need to develop an understanding of gay men and lesbian women as minorities in this society (Buhrke, 1989b). And, of course, gay issues should be well integrated into the practicum sequence. In prepracticum, students should be exposed to the range of issues experienced by gay and lesbian clients via roleplays (Buhrke & Douce, 1991). In practicum attention to the effects of heterosexism on the counseling process and building gay affirmative counseling skills is vital (Buhrke & Douce, 1991). Buhrke and Douce (1991) also provide recommendations for incorporating gay issues into predoctoral internship training, through training seminars and supervision.

The promotion of gender equity in counselor training, and creating a program that will equip counselors with the skills to engage in gender aware counseling, requires an in-depth knowledge of the literature on gender along with an examination of some fundamental beliefs about women (Good, Gilbert, & Scher, 1990). It may also require changes in almost all aspects of most training programs. The Division 17 guidelines for counseling/psychotherapy for women provide the basis for the content that must be integrated into counseling education programs (see Chapter 10, Fitzgerald & Nutt, 1986). In addition, Worell and Remer (1992) offer a detailed overview of the literature on counseling women and provide recommendations for revamping training programs.

Introductory counseling courses might contain information about gender and gender role issues in counseling; students can be introduced to the clinical concerns of special importance to women, for example, depression, eating disorders, sexual abuse, and sexual assault (Worell & Remer, 1992). Theory courses ought to include attention to feminist critiques of counseling theories, new developments in the psychology of women, and the current literature on counseling women (e.g., Brown & Gilligan, 1992; Kaschak, 1992; Laidlaw, Malmo, & Associates, 1990). Assessment courses should include an analysis of the sex bias literature; standardized tests should be critically examined for sex bias; and gender bias in clinical assessment and diagnosis can be introduced. Feminist alternatives to traditional assessment, for example, gender role analysis, might be included (Hackett & Lonborg, 1993). Courses in career development ought to encompass sex bias in career development theories, gender role stereotyping, the changing roles of men and women, and the special career counseling needs of women (e.g., dual career and multiple role counseling) (Walsh & Osipow, 1993). Practicum supervisors themselves must be conversant with the literature to be able to assist counselor trainees in addressing gender issues in the counseling process, and to provide training in gender aware and feminist approaches to counseling (Cook, 1993; Worell & Remer, 1992).

Lofaro (1982) suggests that although counselor education curricula may need to be modified in order to prepare counselors to work with disability-related concerns, new coursework may not be the most desirable alternative. Rather, exercises and course content may be integrated into the existing curriculum. Lofaro (1982) goes on to describe a number of activities that could be included in basic counseling courses to generate sensitivity to disability-related issues and to develop competence in working with clients who have disabilities. Filer (1982) also describes a number of activities that could be integrated into existing counselor education courses to better prepare high school counselors for working with students with disabilities. These activities are designed to (1) motivate counselor trainees to work with children with disabilities, (2) teach counselor trainees the skills and resources needed to work with children with disabilities, (3) teach counselor trainees how to promote social interaction between students with disabilities and nonhandicapped students, and (4) teach counselor trainees how to help students with disabilities optimize their mainstreaming experience.

Other authors feel that specialized training following the separate course model is needed in order to prepare counselors to work with unique populations. For example, Humes (1978), in an article that focuses on inservice training needs, encourages counselor education programs to require one or more courses specifically related to the education of children with disabilities. He recommends that these courses should focus on the following topics: (a) Individual Educational Programs, (b) least-restrictive environment, (c) due process procedures, (d) vocational counseling, (e) and confidentiality of information.

A few authors have recommended the area of concentration model for training counselors to work with special populations. Nickerson, Espin, and Gawelek (1982) describe a master's degree specialization for training counselors to work with women that includes: (1) internships in placement sites that deal with women's developmental issues, (2) supervision of interns by female professionals experienced in counseling women, and (3) course content emphasizing women's developmental issues and acquisition of skills developed for working with women. Russell (1986) describes a 5-week feminist skill-training concentration around four core skills: social analysis, androgyny encouragement, self-disclosure, and behavior feedback. A comparison between counselor trainees who received the feminist training and those who did not indicated that subjects who received the training displayed higher social analysis and self-disclosure skills as well as greater increments in scores on the attitudes-toward-women scale.

## Our Views on Training Models and Course Content

We believe a combination of the integrated and separate course models is the most effective model for training counselors to work with nonethnic minorities. Ideally, issues related to persons with disabilities, elders, women, and gay people should be integrated into all counselor training courses. As suggested earlier, however, this requires that each faculty member is sensitive to and knowledgeable about these special populations. Since most professors in counselor training programs were educated before training in diversity was mandated, we feel that a separate course is needed to supplement attempts to integrate diversity issues into all counselor training courses.

We also recognize that the resources available to a particular program will probably dictate which model is followed. Some programs, due to a unique mix of faculty, may find their faculty resources best suit an area of concentration model. It is important that the faculty of each program assess their resources and adopt an appropriate model for training counselors to work with nonethnic minorities. However, it is also important that the model adopted provide for training across the spectrum of client diversity.

We believe a counselor training program designed to prepare counselors to work with nonethnic minority clients will include three components:
(1) experiences designed to confront students with their own biases and to sensitize them to the discrimination experienced by minority populations;
(2) course content designed to familiarize students with the life-style and mental health needs of diverse populations; and (3) training in counseling strategies that are most effective with minority groups. As suggested earlier, we believe these components should be included in a separate class on nonethnic minorities as well as integrated into all the courses in the counselor training program.

We suggest that each counselor training program develop a master plan for ensuring that content relevant to each nonethnic minority group is included in all required courses. This plan could be based on accreditation requirements as Myers and Blake (1986) suggest or it could be based on the program's own unique curriculum. In developing a plan, it is important to have direct input from representatives of the four groups discussed in this book. To the extent they are not represented on the faculty, the programs should seek out a consultant from nonrepresented groups who can help identify needed appropriate curriculum content and experiences.

The first step in developing a plan is to identify the knowledge and experiences counselors need vis a vis each minority group. The second step is to match knowledge and experiences with appropriate courses. We offer the following outline as an example of the kind of knowledge and experiences that should be integrated into the core counselor training program.

A. Persons with disabilities
  1. Counselor attitudes, values, biases
     a. Discussion of negative attitudes toward disability
     b. Methods of uncovering and addressing negative attitudes toward disabilities
     c. Promotion of positive attitudes toward persons with disabilities
  2. Summary of knowledge competencies
     a. Minimal medical information for counselors working with persons with disabilities
     b. Knowledge of psychological aspects of physical disability
     c. Knowledge of psychological aspects and adjustment to nonphysical disabilities
        (1) Learning disabilities
        (2) Mental retardation
        (3) Knowledge of social conditions
        (4) Discrimination
        (5) Employment
        (6) Health care
        (7) Social services
        (8) Laws
  3. Counseling techniques
     a. Couples and family counseling
     b. Vocational counseling/rehabilitation
     c. Social change advocacy
     d. Environmental change focus
B. The elderly
  1. Counselor attitudes, values, biases
     a. Negative attitudes toward aging
     b. Geriophobia
     c. Positive perspectives on aging
  2. Summary of knowledge competencies
     a. Definitions of aging
     b. Life-span development and life transitions in old age
     c. Counseling needs
     d. Physical disabilities associated with aging
     e. Social conditions
        (1) Discrimination
        (2) Economics
        (3) Health care
        (4) Social services
        (5) Victimization
        (6) Laws

3. Counseling techniques
    a. Consciousness raising
    b. Group work
    c. Social change advocacy
C. Women
    1. Counselor attitudes, values, biases
        a. Sexism
        b. Gender-role stereotyping
        c. Feminism
    2. Summary of knowledge competencies
        a. Gender-fair models of mental health
        b. Biological sex differences
        c. Sex bias in psychological theories
        d. Psychology of women
        e. Psychology of women of color
        f. Knowledge of social conditions
            (1) Discrimination
            (2) Sexual harassment
            (3) Women and work
            (4) Multiple role conflicts and issues
            (5) Health care
            (6) Social services
            (7) Laws
            (8) Violence
    3. Counseling techniques
        a. Gender aware and feminist approaches to counseling
        b. Use of nonsexist psychological tests and interest inventories
        c. Feminist alternatives to traditional assessment (e.g., gender role analysis)
        d. Career counseling for women
        e. Social change advocacy
D. Gay men and lesbian women
    1. Counselor attitudes, values, and biases
        a. Homophobia
        b. Heterosexist bias
        c. Appreciation vs. tolerance of gays
        d. Counselors' awareness of their own sexuality
    2. Summary of knowledge competencies
        a. Past and current research on gay people
        b. Awareness of differences between being gay and nongay
        c. Awareness of differences between lesbian women and gay men
        d. Awareness of issues of gay men and women of color
        e. Theories of gay identity development
        f. The stages of the "coming out" process
        g. Internalized homophobia

    h. Gay relationships, life-styles, and families
    i. Sources of societal oppression
      (1) Discrimination
      (2) Employment
      (3) Health care
      (4) Laws
      (5) Violence
3. Counseling techniques
    a. Gay affirmative counseling
    b. Gay support groups
    c. Gay life-style resources/referrals
    d. HIV/AIDS counseling
    e. Addictions counseling
    f. Social change advocacy

Until such time as knowledge and experiences related to client diversity are integrated into all counseling classes, we feel there is a need to focus on diversity issues in a separate class. A separate class should examine the societal conditions that create oppression and discrimination. It would examine the mental health implications of oppression. It would also include a discussion of human rights counseling, with a focus on changing the environmental and social conditions that create client problems, rather than focusing on changing client attitudes and behaviors per se. A separate course of this type would teach skills that can be generalized to any minority group, ethnic or nonethnic.

## Selection of Counselor Trainees

Assuming a faculty and curriculum sensitive to client diversity, a key component of preparing counselors to work with diverse clients is the raw material the program starts with, i.e., student receptiveness to client diversity. Because nonethnic minorities are discriminated against and because discriminatory attitudes are difficult to change, it is important for counselor training programs to include assessment of discriminatory attitudes in their student selection process. We believe a personal interview with questions that address ethnic and nonethnic minority issues is the best way to detect discriminatory attitudes. A background questionnaire also may be useful in the selection process; the purpose of the background questionnaire is to identify activities in which the applicant has been engaged that suggest discrimination against nonethnic minorites, or conversely, demonstrate interest and experience in working with special populations.

With respect to persons with disabilities, women, and gay people, efforts should be made to ensure proportional representation. Selection of underrepresented populations for counselor training involves three phases: recruitment, admission, and support. A survey of counselor education programs indicated that only limited efforts are being made to recruit, admit, and support female students, students with disabilities, and gay students

(Atkinson & Wampold, 1981). Since the possibility of bias in the selection process may exist for any one of these groups, every effort must be made to ensure they are given fair consideration. This should begin with a careful analysis of the selection process to determine if any built-in biases are operating. Another hedge against bias in the selection process is to have representatives of the minority group involved in all aspects of the selection process. A blind review of application materials, whenever appropriate, is another safeguard. And finally, counselor training programs must cultivate an environment of support for and affirmation of nonethnic diversity to enhance the success and satisfaction of all students.

## Counseling Research

It is evident from psychology's treatment of nonethnic minorities as reviewed in Chapters 2 and 3 that past research has often been biased, usually based on a deficit model of the group being studied. This biased research, and the theories on which it has been based, has had a tragic impact on individuals and society alike. For example, disengagement theory and research have lead many elderly and elderly-care providers to believe that after age 65 an individual's interest in social interaction should be expected to decline. We now know that elders will remain engaged in meaningful, productive interactions as long as social structures exist for their involvement and as long as their health allows for their involvement. Similarly, the variability hypothesis of sex differences was used as an argument in the early part of the twentieth century to deny women admittance to institutions of higher learning. Sex bias has been apparent in almost every area of psychological research and is still with us today (Enns, 1993). Psychological research has often denied the very existence of gay people; and when gays are studied, they are often stigmatized (Herek, et al., 1991). Even in gay affirmative research, generalizations are problematic because of problems with the representativeness of the sample (Herek, et al., 1991). Morin (1977), in a discussion of heterosexual bias in psychological research, pointed out that

> . . . there is no such thing as a representative sample of lesbians or gay men. Researchers are sampling what is essentially a hidden or invisible population. Therefore, when homosexual samples are used, expanded subject descriptions that permit adequate replication are needed. (p. 636)

McHugh, Koeske, and Frieze (1986) described three major types of barriers to sex-fair research that we believe can be expanded to research with any nonethnic minority group. The three barriers are: (1) excessive confidence in traditional methods of research; (2) bias in explanatory systems; and (3) inappropriate conceptualization and operationalization.

Widely shared beliefs and biases may creep into the research process even though efforts are made to follow established research procedures (Denmark, Russo, Frieze, & Sechzer, 1988; McHugh, Koeske, & Frieze, 1986). Excessive confidence in traditional methods of control is not warranted if these methods produce situations that are not reflective of "real-life" situations. "Context stripping" has been an ongoing problem in the study of gender issues (Gilbert, 1992). That is, many gender-related phenomena are manifest in specific social contexts; research that studies gender out of its social context may be seriously misleading. Further, excessive confidence in established (published) findings may cause them to be "cited repeatedly as evidence for a generalization when they are consistent with prevailing paradigms about human behavior, whereas important counter evidence may go unpublished or uncited" (McHugh et al., p. 881). In other words, studies may be (unintentionally) designed to confirm stereotypes of the elderly, people with disabilities, women, and gay people; studies with results that support existing stereotypes are most likely to get published, and once published, most likely to get cited.

Bias in explanatory systems refers to a model that is used to explain behavior for all members of the group, when in fact the model applies to only a few members, if any at all. Biases that can affect explanatory systems include multiple and imprecise use of terminology (as when the term *handicapped* is applied to persons of differing ability regardless of situational factors), imprecision of explanatory model (as when simple biological, psychological, or sociocultural models are proposed to explain homosexual behavior), and "difference models" based on stereotypic assumptions (as when sex differences are proposed to explain differing performance levels between the sexes).

Inappropriate conceptualization and operationalization can occur when cultural ideologies about differences between groups of people influence psychological research and theory. For example, religious values play a prominent role in the deviance view of homosexuality that still underlies the thinking of many psychology researchers and practitioners. Any research that examines human behavior from the standpoint that behavior displayed by one group is inferior to or less desired than behavior displayed by another group may be conceptualizing differences in culturally biased terms rather than descriptive terms.

Other problems with research on nonethnic minority groups that can be generalized from the McHugh, Koeske, and Frieze (1986) concerns with sexist research include the fact that research topics are usually selected by researchers outside the group, minority group samples are often selected without concern for how representative they are of the entire group, tasks employed in an experimental setting may be familiar or salient for one group but not another, and identification of the experimenter as an outsider may affect how minorities respond to the study.

Although more recent studies have begun to dispel some of the myths generated by past research, caution needs to be exercised to ensure that potential biases are reduced in future research. While it is probably impossible to eliminate all bias in psychological research, we feel the most effective way to reduce research bias against any nonethnic group is to include members of the group in the research initiating and reviewing processes. Following are suggested procedures for involving nonethnic minorities in the research initiating and reviewing processes.

1. All members of research teams conducting studies on nonethnic minority groups should be informed about the special issues of these groups and be committed to examining their own stereotypes and attitudes that might bias their research. Research questions should reflect the experiences and needs of the group, rather than be imposed from the outside.

2. Research that includes a nonethnic minority group (elderly, persons with disabilities, women, gay men, lesbian women) as a subject population should include a member of that population on the research team. The nonethnic group representative should be involved in all phases of the research project, including the design, implementation, data collection, data analysis, and reported phases of the project. Publication credit should be assigned on the basis of the representative's contribution to the final product.

3. All research, whether funded by the federal government or not, should be reviewed by an independent human subjects' committee. Whenever a research project that includes a nonethnic minority group as a subject population is under review, the human subjects' committee should ensure that a member of the group is included in the reviewing process. In the case where the group to be studied is not represented by a standing member of the human subjects committee, a representative should be added as a voting member for the purposes of reviewing the relevant proposal.

4. Similarly, research funding agencies should include a representative of any nonethnic minority group that is included as a subject population as part of their review team.

5. Editorial boards of professional journals should include representatives of nonethnic minorities at a parity with their representation in society. Every manuscript considered for publication should be reviewed by at least one board member who represents the nonethnic minority group included as a subject population.

## Summary

Until counselor training and counseling research practices are brought in line with professional ethical and accreditation standards, direct services to nonethnic minority clients are likely to fall far short of ideal practice. The suggestions offered here for changes in counselor training and counseling research should be viewed as a beginning point; at this point in the development of counseling as a profession, we have yet to determine the most effective ways of teaching and researching client diversity.

# References

Agresti, A. A. (1992). Counselor training and ethical issues with older clients. *Counselor Education and Supervision, 32,* 43–50.

American Psychological Association. (1983). *Publication manual of the American Psychological Association* (3rd edition). Washington, DC: Author.

American Psychological Association. (1992). Ethical principles of psychologists and code of conduct. *American Psychologist, 47,* 1597–1611.

American Psychological Association, Committee on Gay and Lesbian Concerns. (1991). Avoiding heterosexual bias in language. *American Psychologist, 46,* 973–974.

Anderson, J. A., & Rawlins, M. E. (1985). Availability and representation of women in counselor education with strategies for recruitment, selection, and advancement. *Counselor Education and Supervision, 25,* 56–65.

Association for Specialists in Group Work. (1991). Professional standards for the training of group workers. *Together, 20*(1), 9–24

Atkinson, D. R., & Wampold, B. (1981). Affirmative action efforts of counselor education programs. *Counselor Education and Supervision, 20,* 262–272.

Balcazar, F. E., Seekins, T., Fawcett, S. B., & Hopkins, B. L. (1990). Empowering people with physical disabilities through advocacy skills training. *American Journal of Community Psychology, 18,* 281–296.

Betz, N. E., & Fitzgerald, L. F. (1993). Individuality and diversity: Theory and research in counseling psychology. *Annual Review of Psychology, 44,* 343–381.

Brown, L. M., & Gilligan, C. (1992). *Meeting at the crossroads: Women's psychology and girls' development.* Cambridge, MA: Harvard University Press.

Bruce, M. A., & Christiansen, C. H. (1988). Advocacy in word as well as deed. *The American Journal of Occupational Therapy, 42,* 189–191.

Buhrke, R. A. (1989a). Female student perspectives on training in lesbian and gay issues. *The Counseling Psychologist, 17,* 629–636.

Buhrke, R. A. (1989b). Incorporating lesbian and gay issues into counselor training: A resource guide. *Journal of Counseling and Development, 68,* 77–80.

Buhrke, R. A., & Douce, L. A. (1991). Training issues for counseling psychologists in working with lesbian women and gay men. *The Counseling Psychologist, 19,* 216–234.

Byrd, K., Crews, B., & Ebener, D. (1991). A study of appropriate use of language when making reference to persons with disabilities. *Journal of Applied Rehabilitation Counseling, 22,* 40–41.

Cayleff, S. E. (1986). Ethical issues in counseling gender, race, and culturally distinct groups. *Journal of Counseling and Development, 64,* 345–347.

Cohen, E. S. (1990). The elderly mystique: Impediment to advocacy and empowerment. Generations: *The Journal of the Western Gerontological Society, 14* (Suppl), 13–16.

Cook, E. P. (Ed). (1993). *Women, relationships, and power: Implications for counseling.* Alexandria, VA: American Counseling Association.

Copeland, E. J. (1982). Minority populations and traditional counseling programs: Some alternatives. *Counselor Education and Supervision, 21,* 187–193.

Council for Accreditation of Counseling and Related Educational Programs. (1990). *Standards for accreditation for graduate programs in counseling and student affairs practice.* Alexandria, VA: American Association for Counseling and Development.

Crabtree, J. L. (1988). Rehabilitation advocacy: A new role for therapists working with the elderly. *Physical and Occupational Therapy in Geriatrics, 6*(2), 3–12.

Crespi, T. D. (1988). Coping in the dark: Counseling adults with visual impairments. *Counselor Education and Supervision, 28,* 146–152.

Criteria for Accreditation of Doctoral Training Programs and Internships in Professional Psychology. (1986). *Accreditation Handbook.* Washington, D.C.: American Psychological Association.

Denmark, F., Russo, N. F., Frieze, I. H., & Sechzer, J. A. (1988). Guidelines for avoiding sexism in psychological research. *American Psychologist, 43,* 582–585.

Dworkin, S. H., & Gutierrez, F. J. (Eds.). (1992). *Counseling gay men and lesbians: Journey to the end of the rainbow.* Alexandria, VA: American Association for Counseling and Development.

Eichler, M. (1988). *Nonsexist research methods: A practical guide.* Winchester, MA: Allen & Unwin.

Enns, C. Z. (1993). Twenty years of feminist counseling and therapy: From naming biases to implementing multifaceted practice. *The Counseling Psychologist, 21,* 3–87.

Enns, C. Z., & Hackett, G. (1990). Comparisons of feminist and nonfeminist women's reactions to variants of nonsexist and feminist counseling. *Journal of Counseling Psychology, 37,* 33–40.

Filer, P. S. (1982). Counselor trainees: Attitudes toward mainstreaming the handicapped. *Counselor Education and Supervision, 22,* 61–69.

Fitting, M. (1986). Ethical dilemmas in counseling elderly adults. *Journal of Counseling & Development, 64,* 325–327.

Fitzgerald, L. F., & Nutt, R. (1986). The Division 17 principles concerning the counseling/psychotherapy of women: Rationale and implementation. *The Counseling Psychologist, 14,* 180–216.

Garnets, L., Hancock, K. A., Cochran, S. D., Goodchilds, J., & Peplau, L. A. (1991). Issues in psychotherapy with lesbians and gay men. *American Psychologist, 46,* 964–972.

Gatz, M., Karel, M. J., & Wolkenstein, B. (1991). Survey of providers of psychological services to older adults. *Professional Psychology: Research and Practice, 22,* 413–415.

Glenn, A. A., & Russell, R. K. (1986). Heterosexual bias among counselor trainees. *Counseling Education and Supervision, 25,* 222–229.

Good, G. E., Gilbert, L. A., & Scher, M. (1990). Gender aware therapy: A synthesis of feminist therapy and knowledge about gender. *Journal of Counseling and Development, 68,* 376–380.

Graham, D. L. R., Rawlings, E. I., Halpern, H. S., & Hermes, J. (1984). Therapists' needs for training in counseling lesbians and gay men. *Professional Psychology, 15,* 482–496.

Hackett, G., Enns, C. Z., & Zetzer, H. A. (1992). Reactions of women to nonsexist and feminist counseling: Effects of counselor orientation and mode of information delivery. *Journal of Counseling Psychology, 39,* 321–330.

Hackett, G., & Lonborg, S. D. (1993). Career assessment and counseling for women. In W. B. Walsh, & S. H. Osipow (Eds). (1993). *Career counseling for women* (pp. 43–85). Hillsdale, NJ: Erlbaum.

Hadley, R. G., & Brodwin, M. G. (1988). Language about people with disabilities. *Journal of Counseling and Development, 67,* 147–149.

Herek, G. M., Kimmel, D. C., Amaro, H., & Melton, G. B. (1991). Avoiding heterosexual bias in psychological research. *American Psychologist, 46,* 957–963.

Hollis, J., & Wantz, R. (1986). *Counselor preparation 1986–89: Programs, personnel, trends.* Muncie, IN: Accelerated Development.

Humes, C. W. (1978). Implications of PL 94-142 for training and supervision. *Counselor Education and Supervision, 18,* 126–129.

Iasenza, S. (1989). Some challenges of integrating sexual orientations into counselor training and research. *Journal of Counseling and Development, 68,* 73–76.

Kaschak, E. (1992) *Engendered lives: A new psychology of women's experience.* New York: Basic.

Kitchener, K. S. (1984). Intuition, critical evaluation and ethical principles: The foundation for ethical decisions in counseling psychology. *The Counseling Psychologist, 12*(3), 43–55.

Laidlaw, T. A., Malmo, C., and Associates. (1990). *Healing voices: Feminist approaches to therapy with women.* San Francisco: Jossey-Bass.

Lebsock, M. S., & Deblassie, R. R. (1975). The school counselor's role in special education. *Counselor Education and Supervision, 15,* 128–134.

Lofaro, G. A. (1982). Disability and counselor education. *Counselor Education and Supervision, 21,* 200–207.

Lombana, J. (1980). Guidance of handicapped students: Counselor in-service needs. *Counselor Education and Supervision, 19,* 269–275.

Margolis, R. L., & Rungta, S. A. (1986). Training counselors for work with special populations. *Journal of Counseling and Development, 64,* 642–644.

McDonald, G. (1982). Misrepresentation, liberalism, and heterosexual bias in introductory psychology texts. *Journal of Homosexuality, 6,* 45–60.

McHugh, M. C., Koeske, R. D., & Frieze, I. H. (1986). Issues to consider in conducting nonsexist psychological research. *American Psychologist, 41,* 879–890.

Melton, G. B. (1989). Public policy and private prejudice: Psychology and the law on gay rights. *American Psychologist, 44,* 933–940.

Morin, S. F. (1977). Heterosexual bias in psychological research on lesbianism and male homosexuality. *American Psychologist, 32,* 629–637.

Moses, S. (1992). More clinicians needed to help a graying America. *APA Monitor, 23*(8), 34.

Munro, J. D. (1991). Training families in the "step approach model" for effective advocacy. *Canada's Mental Health, 39* (1), 1–6.

Myers, J. E. (1983). Gerontological counseling training: The state of the art. *Personnel and Guidance Journal, 61,* 398–401.

Myers, J. E. (1992). Competencies, credentialing, and standards for gerontological counselors: Implications for counselor education. *Counselor Education and Supervision, 32,* 34–42.

Myers, J. E., & Blake, R. H. (1986). Preparing counselors for work with older people. *Counselor Education and Supervision, 26,* 137–145.

Myers, J. E., Loesch, L. D., & Sweeney, T. J. (1991). Trends in gerontological counselor preparation. *Counselor Education and Supervision, 30,* 194–204.

Myers, J. E., & Sweeney, T. J. (1990). *Gerontological competencies for counselors and human development specialists.* Alexandria, VA: American Association for Counseling and Development.

Nelson, J. B. (1985). Religious and moral issues in working with homosexual clients. In J. C. Gonsiorek (Ed.), *A guide to psychotherapy with gay and lesbian clients* (pp. 163–175). New York: Harrington Park Press.

Netting, F. E., & Hinds, H. N. (1989). Rural volunteer ombudsman programs. *The Journal of Applied Gerontology, 8,* 419–431.

Nickerson, E. T., Espin, O., & Gawelek, M. A. (1982). Counseling women: A graduate Master's degree specialization for training mental health professionals to work with women. *Counselor Education and Supervision, 21,* 194–199.

Norton, L. (1982). Integrating gay issues into counselor education. *Counselor Education and Supervision, 21,* 208–212.

Payton, C. R. (1993). Review of APA Accreditation Criterion II. *Professional Psychology: Research and Practice, 24,* 130–132.

Rickard, H. C., & Clements, C. B. (1993). Critique of APA Accreditation Criterion II: Cultural and individual differences. *Professional Psychology: Research and Practice, 14,* 123–126.

Rudolph, J. (1989). Effects of a workshop on mental health practitioners' attitudes toward homosexuality and counseling effectiveness. *Journal of Counseling and Development, 68,* 81–85.

Russell, M. (1986). Teaching feminist counseling skills: An evaluation. *Counselor Education and Supervision, 25,* 320–330.

Salisbury, H. (1975). Counseling the elderly: A neglected area in counselor education. *Counselor Education and Supervision, 14,* 237–238.

Schaie, K. W. (1993). Ageist language in psychological research. *American Psychologist, 48,* 49–51.

Scott, N. A., & McMillian, J. L. (1980). An investigation of training for sex-fair counseling. *Counselor Education and Supervision, 20,* 84–91.

Sinik, D. (1979). Professional development in counseling older persons. *Counselor Education and Supervision, 19,* 4–12.

Sobocinski, M. R. (1990). Ethical principles in the counseling of gay and lesbian adolescents: Issues of autonomy, competence, and confidentiality. *Professional Psychology: Research and Practice, 21,* 240–247.

Steininger, M., Newell, J. D., & Garcia, L. T. (1984). *Ethical issues in psychology.* Homewood, IL: The Dorsey Press.

Tabachnik, B. G., Keith-Spiegel, P., & Pope, K. S. (1991). Ethics of teaching. *American Psychologist, 46,* 506–515.

Thomas, M. C., & Martin, V. (1992). Training counselors to facilitate the transitions of aging through group work. *Counselor Education and Supervision, 32,* 51–60.

Vargo, J. W. (1989). "In the house of my friend": Dealing with disability. *International Journal for the Advancement of Counselling, 12,* 281–287.

Walsh, W. B., & Osipow, S. H. (Eds.). (1993). *Career counseling for women.* Hillsdale, NJ: Erlbaum.

Wolff, T. (1987). Community psychology and empowerment: An activist's insights. *American Journal of Community Psychology, 15,* 151–166.

Worell, J., & Remer, P. (1992). *Feminist perspectives in therapy: An empowerment model for women.* New York: Wiley.

# AUTHOR INDEX

# SUBJECT INDEX